# American Aviation
## An Illustrated History
### 2nd Edition

Joe Christy

Revised and updated
by LeRoy Cook

With contributions
by Alexander T. Wells, Ed.D.

TAB **AERO**

Division of McGraw-Hill, Inc.
Blue Ridge Summit, PA 17294-0850

**Library of Congress Cataloging-in-Publication Data**

pbk 2 3 4 5 6 7 8 9 10 11 DOH/DOH 9 9 8 7 6 5 4

Christy, Joe.
American aviation : an illustrated history / by Joe Christy, LeRoy
Cook. — 2nd ed.
p.    cm.
Includes index.
ISBN 0-8306-4480-6 (pbk.)
1.  Aeronautics—United States—History.  I.  Cook, LeRoy.
II.  Title.
TL521.C546  1993
629.13'00973—dc20                                              93-32097
                                                                CIP

Acquisitions Editor: Jeff Worsinger
Editorial team: Joanne Slike, Executive Editor
            Susan Wahlman Kagey, Managing Editor
            Charles Spence, Editor
            Stacey R. Spurlock, Indexer
Production team: Katherine G. Brown, Director
            Ollie Harmon, Typesetting
            Tina Sourbier, Typesetting
            Lorie L. White, Proofreading
            Joan Wieland, Proofreading
            Rose McFarland, Layout
Design team: Jaclyn J. Boone, Designer
            Brian Allison, Associate Designer                    AV1
Cover design: Holberg Design, York, Pa.                          4442

# Contents

## 21 General aviation—What went wrong?          411

## Appendix A: Objective questions          428

## Appendix B: Answers to objective questions   491

## Index          496

# Foreword to the second edition

Six years have elapsed since the first edition of *American Aviation: An Illustrated History* was published. Timely revisions have been made to bring the book up to date, reflecting the many changes that have occurred in aviation during the 1980s and early 1990s.

An important change has been the addition of LeRoy Cook, who replaces the late Joe Christy as primary author of the revisions in the second edition. A noted aviation historian in his own right, LeRoy continues the tradition set by Joe in providing an informative yet lively and interesting discussion of the subject matter. As a result, the book continues to offer students a well-balanced, thorough coverage of aviation history, including significant events, personalities, and aircraft that have influenced the development of civil and military aviation.

Three new chapters have been added: "Military aviation heads into the '90s," "The airlines soldier on," and "General aviation—what went wrong?" Chapter 19 discusses the changing role of military aviation in light of the breakup of the former Soviet Union. Military aircraft flown during Operation Desert Storm are discussed in detail. The next chapter covers the airline industry during the turbulent decade of the 1980s and the impact of the carriers' financial stress on aircraft manufacturers. Chapter 21 brings the discussion of the general aviation industry up to date by identifying the reasons for its decline in new aircraft sales since 1978. The growing interest in kitplanes and specialty aircraft manufacturers is also thoroughly explored.

All pedagogical features of the text have been reviewed and updated where appropriate. The number of objective questions has almost doubled in this edition, bringing the total close to 800. Combined with review questions at the end of each chapter, students are provided with an excellent source of questions to prepare for tests and quizzes.

Student evaluations of the first edition have been very favorable, and as an instructor, I continue to find the book to offer a solid treatment of the history of aviation for a semester course.

*Alexander T. Wells, Ed.D.*
*Senior Professor—Aviation*
*Broward Community College*
*Fort Lauderdale, Florida*

# Foreword to the first edition

*American Aviation: An Illustrated History* was written in response to the growing need for a comprehensive aviation history textbook to be used in collegiate aviation programs. A history course is required in many flight and non-flight related programs because it is felt that students should have a perspective of the historical factors that have influenced the growth and development of the discipline.

While there are many books covering *some* phase of aviation history—aircraft, personalities, events, periods of time including wars—there are very few that cover the entire *history*—and fewer still that do it adequately. This book is the only one I have found in more than 15 years of teaching an aviation history course at the post-secondary level that is designed for the college market. The book offers a well-balanced, thorough coverage of the history of aviation including significant events, personalities, and aircraft that have influenced the development of civil and military aviation. The extremely important periods covering the World Wars and the growth of commercial aviation in the United States during the 1930s are very well done.

This volume, however, is not written just as an outline of aviation history. The subject is far too fascinating to be displayed only in skeletal form. The book tells the stories that make up the drama of aviation history: the struggles between the Wrights and Glenn Curtiss; the emergence of the military airplanes with their fliers—20th century "Knights of the Air" during the Great War; barnstorming and aerial hijinks during the 1920s; the birth of the air mail and the U.S. Postal Service's role in shaping development of the airline industry; the court-martial of Billy Mitchell; the glamour and innocence of the 1930s, the era of Howard Hughes's great aerial achievements, when pioneers like Charles Lindbergh, Jimmy Doolittle, Roscoe Turner, Walter Beech, and Wiley Post flew farther and faster and higher than ever before; the air war in the Pacific, from the early defeats to the turning point at Midway and the island-hopping campaign leading to the dropping of the first atomic bomb; the war in Europe and North Africa with insight into the personalities, aircraft and events that shaped the world in the 20th century; the Berlin Airlift and the Korean War; the breaking of the sound barrier and the era of commercial jet aviation; and, finally, America's leap into outer space.

Entertaining yet extremely informative, the book represents years of research and writing by one of this country's most noted aviation historians. Complete with fascinating details and behind-the-scenes views, Joe Christy's book captures the vitality of aviation history and makes it come alive to the reader. Profusely illustrated with hundreds of rare photographs, there is no need to refer to numerous other sources for pictures.

Each chapter begins with an outline of the major sections to be covered. This is followed by learning objectives that the student should be able to accomplish upon completing the chapter. Review questions at the end of each chapter cover all of the important points. Finally, there is an appendix which includes a test bank of objective questions to further reinforce learning.

In reviewing *American Aviation: An Illustrated History*, I was guided by several criteria. The book should be interesting to read, cover the main topics that a student needs to know, flow logically from chapter to chapter, factually describe historical findings rather than hearsay, and adopt a professional orientation. Joe Christy's book has exceeded my expectations in every regard and I look forward to using it in my aviation history classes.

*Alexander T. Wells, Ed.D.*
*Fort Lauderdale, Florida*

# Introduction

## Objectives

At the end of the introduction you should be able to:

- Identify the contributions to aviation made by the Montgolfier brothers and von Zeppelin.

- Describe the major accomplishments made by Cayley, Lilienthal, Pilcher and Mozhaisky.

- Explain how Professor Langley almost beat the Wright brothers in developing a successful heavier-than-air flying machine.

- Describe the approach taken by the Wright brothers in developing their gliders during the period from 1899 to 1902.

- Describe the successes experienced by the Wright brothers during the period from 1902 to 1908.

- Summarize the accomplishments of Glenn Curtiss and describe the source of conflict between him and the Wright brothers.

Man's first successful aerial vehicle was a hot air balloon launched at Annonay, France, by Joseph and Etienne Montgolfier on 5 June 1783. Having observed that smoke rises, the Montgolfier brothers decided that smoke contained a mysterious gas that was lighter than air. They constructed a 35-foot balloon (*balon*) of linen-reinforced paper under which they built a fire fueled by damp straw and sheep's wool. Their balloon filled with the dense smoke and rose majestically into the sky.

The brothers followed their triumph with another ascent on 19 September 1783, sending aloft as passengers a duck, a sheep, and a rooster to establish that the upper atmosphere was safe to breathe. Then, the following month, French scientist Pilatre de Rozier and the Marquis d'Arlandes made a flight over Paris in a Montgolfier balloon. Man's conquest of the air had begun.

During the next 100 years, lighter-than-air vehicles—employing either heated air or hydrogen as a lifting agent—became as commonplace as their limited usefulness would allow. They evolved at last into Count Ferdinand von Zeppelin's giant rigid airships. The first of these flew in Germany on 2 July 1900, more than three years before the Wright brothers took to the air in the world's first successful *heavier-than-air*, *self-propelled* flying machine.

The invention of the airplane was preceded by a great deal more wishful thinking than scientific inquiry. A host of experimenters and dreamers proposed—and even built—a number of flying machines during the nineteenth century. None was successful, although several made small contributions to the quest. Britain's Sir George Cayley and Germany's Otto Lilienthal were the most significant of the serious experimenters who preceded the Wright brothers. America's Octave Chanute, a retired structural engineer, built several multi-wing hang gliders in 1896 and 1897 that sailed up to 350 feet along the south shore of Lake Michigan. Chanute's best machine was essentially a refinement of an earlier Lilienthal design, and Chanute's only direct contribution to manned flight was the Pratt truss system for bracing biplane wings.

Lilienthal flew his first monoplane hang glider in 1891, later switching to biplane configurations. Flying from an artificial hill near Berlin and the Stollner Hills near Rhinow, he achieved glides up to 750 feet in length before he was killed in one of his machines on 9 August 1896.

Lilienthal was a long way from achieving controlled powered flight when he died, and his calculations of lift produced by a cambered wing surface were in error, but photos of him in flight were published around the world and his work inspired many others, including the Wrights.

The extent to which Lilienthal was influenced by the work of Sir George Cayley is a matter of conjecture, but Cayley's paper *On Aerial Navigation*, published in 1810, and the successful flights of his model gliders establish that this remarkable Englishman was the first to propose the proper configuration for a fixed-wing, heavier-than-air flying machine. Cayley suggested a curved upper wing surface for increased lift, wing dihedral for lateral stability, and his models featured cruciform tails. In the early nineteenth century he was so far ahead of everyone else in this field that it may be said that nothing more of significance was added to man's meager store of knowledge on this subject until Lilienthal began his experiments 80 years later.

Lilienthal's flights in his hang gliders actually produced almost no new scientific data; his carefully recorded figures on the lifting properties of cambered wing surfaces were found to be in error by the Wrights after they began their experiments. But Lilienthal's influence was great, at least partly because the halftone process for reproducing photographs in newspapers came into use just in time to picture Lilienthal's accomplishments and prove to the world that man *could* sail through the air on artificial wings.

Another Englishman, Percy Pilcher, built an improved monoplane glider following Lilienthal's death, but Pilcher worked in isolation and died in the crash of his machine in 1899 without influencing the invention of the airplane. Also in Russia in 1884 (sometimes mistakenly reported as 1882), a steam-powered airplane built by Alexander Mozhaisky and piloted by I.N. Golubev was thrust into the air from a ski-jump type ramp for a few seconds, but proved incapable of supporting itself in flight.

The most controversial of the early experimenters was Professor Samuel P. Langley, a respected astronomer and secretary of the Smithsonian Institution. Langley became seriously interested in mechanical flight about 1886, and ten years later built a 25-pound steam-powered model of hickory and silk that flew three-quarters of a mile—an event witnessed by Dr. Alexander Graham Bell, who also believed that man-carrying flying machines were possible, and who reported Langley's success to President McKinley.

Langley's model achieved lateral stability in flight by means of dihedral in each of its two wings, which were positioned in tandem—an arrangement used by British experimenters Thomas Walker in 1831 and D.S. Brown in 1874, the latter having tested model gliders so configured. Langley's model also possessed cambered upper wing surfaces (first used by Sir George Cayley in 1809), although Langley's airfoil shape was very inefficient, with its deepest point much too far from the wing's leading edge.

# Government gets involved

Apparently influenced by Dr. Bell's enthusiastic account of Langley's work, President McKinley obtained an army appropriation in the amount of $50,000 to finance construction of a full-size, man-carrying version of the Aerodrome, as Langley called his model.

Langley hired 23-year-old Charles Manley, an engineering student at Cornell University, and designed a quarter-scale model of a full-sized *Aerodrome*. This flew in 1901 with a small gasoline engine.

The full-sized *Aerodrome* was completed in July 1903, and taken to its launch track atop a houseboat in the Potomac River. Manley had built it according to the 63-year-old Langley's instructions, and also designed and built its engine after it became clear that the Balzar engine contracted by Langley was much too heavy and produced only a fraction of the power expected. (Some historians have referred to the *Aerodrome's* powerplant as the "Manley-Balzar" engine, apparently in the belief that Manley merely modified Balzar's creation. Manley did expend considerable effort attempting to get more power from it, but finally gave up and designed a truly remarkable five-cylinder radial that was water-cooled and produced 52.4 hp at 950 rpm; it weighed 207.5 pounds including coolant. This engine proved its reliability in three separate ten-hour test runs, and its weight-to-horsepower ratio was not equalled until the appearance of the *Liberty* engine in 1917.)

On 7 October 1903, the *Aerodrome* was ready for test. Manley climbed aboard, gave the signal for release of the catapult spring, swooshed down the launching rail—and fell into the Potomac. Only slightly injured, he swam to safety. A photo taken just as the machine left its launching device showed its forward wing twisted grotesquely out of shape.

On 8 December 1903 Manley had the repaired *Aerodrome* back atop the houseboat for another try. But this time the machine's rear wing failed as it left its launching track, and

The Langley *Aerodrome* on its catapult in the Potomac River. It failed to fly in two attempts, suffering structural failure each time.

The Langley machine plunges into the Potomac just nine days before the Wright brothers made the world's first successful airplane flight.

to what a flying machine should look like. They produced "eyeball" designs, and few bothered with any serious investigation of the dynamics of flight, while none gave any real thought as to how a flying machine would be controlled if it *should* succeed in getting off the ground and achieve sustained flight. Most appeared to believe that an airplane could be steered like a boat, and that wing dihedral would provide the necessary lateral stability.

The Wrights, however, were concerned with *controlled* flight from the outset, and they approached their task suspicious of every "discovery" and each bit of data that had been passed along by experimenters before them. Thus, Wilbur discovered very early that the best information available on the lifting properties of wings with various upper surface curves—painstakingly recorded by Lilienthal—was in error. The Wrights did adopt the Pratt truss system for wing bracing, but their

Manley narrowly escaped drowning when he became entangled in the wreckage. Nine days later the Wrights flew at Kitty Hawk, and Langley abandoned his project. He died in 1906, a thoroughly honorable man, but the *Aerodrome*—or a reasonable facsimile thereof—would be revived eight years later and used by others to perpetrate a shameful hoax designed to discredit the Wright brothers—about which, more momentarily.

## Seeking controlled flight

Orville and Wilbur Wright possessed a significant advantage over most of those who had preceded them in the quest of manned, mechanical flight: *They approached the question as airmen.* Except for Lilienthal, all the others had mostly proceeded with preconceived ideas as

Wilbur Wright

ultimate success was exclusively theirs. They constructed a small wind tunnel that allowed them to witness the shift in the center of pressure above the wing as its angle of attack was changed, and which aided in the selection of a reasonably efficient airfoil shape for their wings. Eventually the brothers would put a similar, deliberate effort into propeller research, and their marvelously reasoned solution to the problem of roll control and turning flight—wing warping—was the answer to a major aerodynamic question that others had not yet asked. The addition of a hinged rudder, interconnected to the wing-warp controls, solved the problem of adverse yaw in turning flight.

The Wrights built their first aircraft in August 1899. It was a biplane kite with a wingspan of five feet, and was flown tethered to a stake, its primary purpose being to test the wing-warping system. This system warped downward the outer trailing edges of the wings on one side while simultaneously warping upward the trailing edges on the opposite

Orville Wright

The 1902 Wright glider; flight control theories proven, the Wrights needed only to add a proper propulsion system—which required that they design and build their own engine and propellers.

side. Hinged ailerons (first used by the French experimenter Esnault-Pelterie in 1904) would soon supplant the Wrights' wing-warping system, but the principle was the same.

Following tests with their kite, the Wrights built three biplane gliders, one each year 1900 through 1902, and accomplished more than a thousand glides from the sand hills at Kitty Hawk, North Carolina.

At the conclusion of the 1902 tests the brothers were confident that they were ready to build a powered machine, and the Wright *Flyer I* (*Flyers II* and *III* would follow in 1904 and 1905), fitted with a 12-hp gasoline engine designed by the Wrights, was ready to fly late in 1903.

Wilbur won the coin toss for the privilege of making the first flight in the new machine on 14 December, but scarcely got off the ground before overcontrolling with the forward-mounted elevator and nosed into the sand. Damage was slight, and at 10:35 A.M. on Thursday, 17 December, Orville took his turn. He flew 120 feet in 12 seconds into a 20–22-mph wind. During the next hour and a half, three more flights were made with the brothers alternating at the con-

trols. On the final flight Wilbur flew 852 feet while remaining aloft for 59 seconds. Those flights, witnessed by five local people, were the first in the history of the world in which a powered heavier-than-air vehicle had taken off under its own power, achieved sustained, controlled flight, and then landed at a point as high as that from which it had taken off.

During the next two years the brothers regularly flew from Huffman Prairie, about eight miles east of their home in Dayton, Ohio. They made some 40 flights in 1905, the longest for a distance of 34 miles. The Wrights avoided publicity awaiting patent protection and the expected sale of their invention to the U.S. and British governments. Satisfied that their *Flyer III* was a practical aircraft, the brothers did not fly again until the summer of 1908. Orville demonstrated a two-place Flyer at Ft. Myer (near Washington, D.C.) in September that year, the U.S. Army at last having been forced to take the Wrights seriously as reports persisted of successful flights by experimenters in France. (Accurate sketches of the *Flyer III* had been published in France in 1906, and although no one there understood the Wrights'

The age of manned flight begins, 17 December 1903. On his first attempt that day, Orville flew 120 feet in 12 seconds. Three more flights were made, with the brothers alternating at the controls. The fourth flight, at noon, with Wilbur piloting, lasted 59 seconds and was measured at 852 feet.

system of lateral control, Henri Farman had, in 1907, remained aloft for a minute and 14 seconds and completed a wide, skidded circle. The Farman machine had no means of lateral control except for the yaw effect of its rudder.)

At Ft. Myer, one of Orville's propellers failed in flight, damaged the airframe, and sent his machine crashing to the ground out of control. Lt. Thomas Selfridge, riding as a passenger, was killed, Orville seriously injured. But a month earlier, Wilbur had begun a series of demonstrations in France that captivated all Europe, and despite Orville's accident, the world had suddenly become aware that *man could fly.*

Meanwhile, Alexander Graham Bell had brought together and financed a small group of men who were interested, as was Dr. Bell, in manned flight. That was the *"Aerial Experiment Association,"* led by motorcycle racer/builder Glenn Hammond Curtiss. This group produced four flying machines based upon what could be learned about the *Wright Flyers*. These machines appeared between March and December 1908. The first barely flew and crashed on its second test. The next one managed to remain airborne for slightly more than 1000 feet during the best of its five attempts before crashing. The third aircraft built by the AEA members, the *"June Bug,"* made a number of flights, the longest of which was two miles.

The *June Bug* was said to be Curtiss' design; it was fitted with a 30-hp water-cooled V-8 engine that was designed by Curtiss and

Wilbur with passenger near Auvours, France, in 1908. After witnessing one of Wilbur's many flights in France, Maj. B.F.S. Baden-Powell, Secretary of Britain's (hopeful) Aeronautical Society, said, "That Wilbur Wright is in possession of a power which controls the fate of nations is beyond dispute."

Glenn Curtiss (left) is pictured with Chance Vought (third from right) in 1911. Vought would also build airplanes and help found the company that is today known as United Technologies.

engine builder Charles Kirkham, and featured wingtip ailerons. Its best flight did not compare with the flights made there years earlier by the Wrights in their *Flyer III*, but the *June Bug* led Glenn Curtiss into the aircraft manufacturing business, and within two years Curtiss would be the Wrights' principal competitor—as well as their primary target in a series of bitter court confrontations resulting from Curtiss' alleged infringement on Wright patents.

## Shadow on a career

The courts held in favor of the Wrights in every case that went to trial, but Curtiss managed to grow and prosper—primarily from profits generated by the Curtiss exhibition teams—and held the Wrights at bay with appeals and other legal maneuvers until, at last facing a showdown in 1914, Curtiss resorted to a consciousless ploy that will forever shadow his very real contributions to aviation.

It occurred to Curtiss that if the *Langley Aerodrome* could be flown, then he could argue in court that the Wright patents were not based on an original invention.

Curtiss was sympathetically received by the man who had succeeded Langley as secretary of the Smithsonian, Dr. Charles D. Walcott, and Walcott not only lent the Langley machine to Curtiss, but also sent along Dr. Albert P. Zahm of the Smithsonian to document Curtiss' effort. It should be noted that Dr. Zahm had earlier been a Curtiss witness in court.

There were, however, other interested parties—particularly Griffith Brewer of Britain's

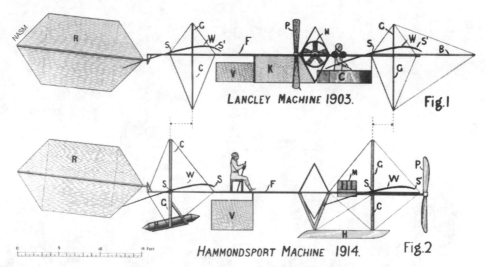

Comparison of the original Langley *Aerodrome* and the Curtiss-modified machine of 11 years later reveals the differences.

*Royal Aeronautical Society*, to whom history is indebted for the facts concerning the Curtiss caper.

Curtiss made no effort to fly the original *Aerodrome*. By 1914 a lot of progress had been made in airplane design. Curtiss was building flying boats by then, and had at least one experienced and able airframe designer on his staff (Douglas Thomas, designer of the famed WWI Curtiss JN-4 Jenny), and it was obvious to Curtiss that the *Aerodrome* was incapable of flight without significant modification.

Curtiss constructed new wings for the *Aerodrome*. They were of different planform, different camber, and differently braced. The Penaud-type tail (fixed surfaces with limited and very slow movement as a unit, and similar to that which Cayley had employed on his models 100 years earlier) was modified to operate with a Curtiss control system; the pro-pellers were changed, the pilot's seat repositioned, and the machine was mounted on floats. There was still no means of lateral control except the stability provided by the dihedral angle at which the four wing panels were attached.

This hybrid could not sustain itself in flight; its longest hop was five seconds. Therefore, Curtiss removed the Manley engine and

its twin pusher propellers and installed a 90-hp Curtiss V-8 with a single tractor propeller in the nose of the machine. Then, on 1 October 1914, he accomplished six takeoffs that resulted in flights of 20 to 65 seconds duration. It was then up to the Smithsonian's Dr. Zahm to legitimize the hoax.

Zahm's affidavit read in part: "The machine was the same machine in construction and operation as the original structure. The frame was the same; the engine was the same; the horizontal and vertical rudder located at the rear was the same; the vertical rudder under the machine was substantially the same; the propellers were the same and the wings were identical in construction with the original machine, except, as I have heretofore stated, they were perhaps a little more roughly built and a little heavier."

Actually, Zahm wrote this affidavit before Curtiss made the engine change. It therefore did contain *one* truth when it was written. We should note that the original *Aerodrome* had a total weight of 830 pounds. The machine flown by Curtiss weighed 1520 pounds.

It is not clear who returned the *Aerodrome* to its original configuration, but it was placed on display in the Smithsonian Institution just

Curtiss making one of several short hops 17 December 1914 in an effort to prove that the Langley *Aerodrome* was capable of flight, and therefore that the Wright patents were not based on an original invention. Curtiss' ploy fooled no one.

as Charles Manley had built it in 1903 along with a plaque that read: "The First Man-Carrying Aeroplane in the History of the World Capable of Sustained Free Flight . . ."

That is why the Wright brothers' *Flyer* remained in Great Britain's Science Museum until 1948. By that time, pressure from many individuals (as well as the possibility of a congressional investigation) brought a formal apology to the Wrights from the Smithsonian, and the *Wright Flyer* claimed its rightful place there on 17 December 1948, the 45th anniversary of its historic first flights. Unfortunately, Orville had died the previous January at age 77. Wilbur had been spared the hurt of the whole shameful mess, having died of typhoid fever in 1912 at age 45.

The Wrights' lawsuits against Curtiss were never settled in court. The WWI patent pool effectively placed them on "hold" until 1919, and by that time neither Orville nor Glenn Curtiss controlled the corporations that bore their names, and neither board of directors was willing to pursue the matter. Both men lived to see the merger of those companies in 1929, which formed the (then) giant Curtiss-Wright Aeronautical Corporation, but Orville had long since retired to his mansion in Dayton, and Curtiss was a Florida real estate developer. Curtiss died a year later of complications following an appendectomy.

We will encounter Curtiss-Wright in chapters to follow.

## Review questions

1. What was the major contribution to the advancement of flight made by the Montgolfier brothers? What distinction is held by Pilatre de Rozier?

2. Briefly describe some of the important contributions to the science of aeronautics made by Sir George Cayley. Identify some of the significant contributions to flying made by Otto Lilienthal; by Percy Pilcher.

3. What was the reason for Professor Langley's failure to successfully launch his *Aerodrome* in October and December 1903? How did two obscure bicycle mechanics from Dayton, Ohio, with little formal education and no government support, succeed where

some of the world's most prestigious engineers and scientists had failed? Why was the period from 1903 to 1908 such a disappointing one for the Wright brothers? Why was 1908 a turning point?

4. Explain how the Aerial Experimental Association got started. Describe some of the aircraft developed by this association. How did AEA develop a conflict with the Wright brothers?

# 1

# Those magnificent men and women!

## Objectives

At the end of this chapter you should be able to:

- Identify several of the early air meets and recognize some of the participants, including their accomplishments.
- Discuss some of the daring showmen of the pre-World War I era.
- Describe the epic flight of Calbraith P. Rodgers.
- Identify several of the early women pilots.

The first commercial use of the airplane was exhibition flying. Prior to World War I there was no other way to make money with this exciting new vehicle. Engines were too unreliable; payloads too small. Man could fly, but just barely.

That was enough, however, to justify promotion of several great aerial expositions to celebrate the achievement of this age-old dream. The first was a week-long event held on the Betheny Plain near Rheims, France, in August 1909. By that time France was already beginning to lead the world in development of the airplane. Except for advances made by

Glenn Curtiss (which included off-water flying), almost every innovation, every improvement to the flying machine between 1908 and 1914 originated in France. The French were ready and eager for the air age; the rest of the world had to be dragged into it.

## French pioneers

The roseate aeronautical climate in France was apparently due to several factors. Ballooning had been born there more than a century earlier, but a more direct influence was the work of several Frenchmen who had been experimenting with flying machines since 1903, spurred by published accounts in France of the Wrights' successful gliders. These accounts included detailed drawings and photos of the Wrights' 1902 glider in flight.

Among these French aviation pioneers were Ernest Archdeacon, Robert Esnault-Pelterie, Gabriel and Henri Voisin, Leon Levavasseur, and Louis Bleriot. Englishman Henri Farman and Brazilian Alberto Santos-Dumont added their achievements to the French aviation scene.

The diminutive Santos-Dumont, heir to a coffee fortune, began with a small, cylindrical gas bag fitted with a tiny gasoline engine; in this device he flitted among the rooftops of Paris, much to the delight of Parisians. He turned to heavier-than-air machines in 1906 and, after several failures, produced a 200-pound monoplane of 24 hp, the *Demoiselle*, in 1909. The *Demoiselle's* best flight was about 12 minutes long. Other machines in both America and France were more advanced by then, but Santos-Dumont's contribution was significant because he was a colorful figure and his was such a class act that he provided much impetus to aircraft development in Europe at just the proper time.

## International air meets

The 1909 Rheims Meet attracted all of the top aviators and the best aircraft designs produced up to that time. A French aviator, Maurice Tissandier, flew a copy of the latest Wright machine. The Wrights did not attend. Glenn Curtiss was there, however, with his specially designed Rheims Racer.*

Curtiss won the Gordon Bennett cup race with a speed of 47 mph, the *Prix de la Vitesse* at 46⅝ mph, and placed second in the *Tour de Piste*. There were protests over his misrepresentation of his engine's power, but his reputation as an airplane builder was markedly enhanced.

The success of the Rheims Meet prompted a number of similar events, the next one an air spectacular promoted by actor Dick Ferris and held at Dominguez Field near Los Angeles in mid-January 1910. The ubiquitous Glenn Cur-

tiss established a speed record with a passenger at 55 mph, and leaped into the air with a takeoff run of 98 feet in 6.4 seconds. But France's Louis Paulhan, flying a Farman biplane, took home top honors and most of the money for his 75-mile round trip to Santa Anita with an elapsed time of 1 hour and 58 minutes. Paulhan also established a new altitude record of 4165 feet. It was indicative of the progress being made in aircraft development. The previous altitude mark of 508 feet had been made at Rheims only five months earlier.

The next great aerial meet was at Boston Harbor during the first two weeks of September 1910. Prizes totalled $100,000, the principal one for a race around Boston Light. It was won by England's Claude Graham-White in a Farman, barely nosing out Glenn Curtiss. Graham-White flew the 5½ miles in 6 minutes.

The Boston Harbor Meet was the largest to date, but it was surpassed by the greatest aerial tournament prior to WWI, which was held at New York's Belmont Park, October 22 through 31, 1910. Described as the top society sporting event of the decade, the Belmont meet attracted not only the best pilots from both sides of the Atlantic, but what passed as the "jet set" of that era as well.

The Bennett Cup race at Belmont generated great excitement as Graham-White was hard pressed to beat out such aeronauts as America's John Moisant, flying a Bleriot; England's Hubert Latham, piloting an Antoinette; Alec Oligvie in a Wright Model C; and Walter Brookins in a Baby Wright. Graham-White averaged 61 mph for the 62-mile course. Brookins crashed the Baby Wright when he turned to fly to the aid of Alfred Leblanc, who had wrecked his machine after averaging 66.2 mph in the speed dash. John Moisant won the race around the Statue of Liberty from Belmont Park, but was disqualified on a technicality, and the $10,000 prize went to France's Count Jaques de Lesseps (tenth son of the Suez Canal's builder). Ralph Johnstone claimed an

---

* Curtiss himself referred to this machine as the "Rheims Racer" or the "Rheims Machine." It was also called the "Golden Flyer," and there is evidence that it was the same airplane, fitted with a 50-hp engine, that some researchers have called the "Gold Bug," and which Curtiss sold to the Aeronautic Society of New York in the spring of 1909, powered with a 30-hp air-cooled V-8. It was loaned back to Curtiss in July 1909, and Curtiss appears to have built new wings for it. He registered his machine at Rheims at 30-hp, but it was found to have a new 50-hp engine.

important record for America when he established a new altitude mark of 9714 feet.

At Belmont women first appeared as pilots. Tiny Mlle. Helene Dutrieux was enthusiastically applauded by spectators for her flights, although she was not allowed to compete with the men. Other early "aviatrixes," as they were called, were Americans Blanche Scott, Ruth Law, John Moisant's sister Mathilde, and a petite West Coast drama critic, Harriet Quimby. Katherine Stinson would follow in 1912, and her younger sister Marjorie in 1914.

## Daring birdmen

The success of the first great air meets, with their attendant publicity, correctly suggested that ready-made audiences awaited throughout the United States for living proof that man could actually fly. Therefore, the Wrights, Curtiss, and Moisant organized exhibition teams and toured the country for the edification of the public and the enrichment of themselves. These teams appeared in all the large cities, while free-lancers performed individually at county fairs and in smaller towns. The best of the freelancers were represented by booking agent Bill Pickins as the "Lincoln Beachey Flyers," Beachey being perhaps the most daring and soon the most popular of this nomadic fraternity.

Beachey had begun as a dirigible pilot at age 19 in 1905. He flew a sausage-shaped gas bag from which a light framework containing engine and aeronaut was suspended. But when the spectators at the Dominguez meet showed far more interest in winged aircraft than in Beachey's and Roy Knabenshue's "rubber cows," Beachey went to Curtiss, learned to fly, and by 1911 began giving airplane exhibitions booked by Pickins. His craft was a Curtiss pusher fitted with a water-cooled V-8 engine—an engine that would evolve into the famed OX-5 of WWI.

The Curtiss airplanes of this period had at least two advantages: good engines and pilot's controls that were more natural to use than the Wrights' control systems. (Almost every manufacturer of flying machines employed a dif-

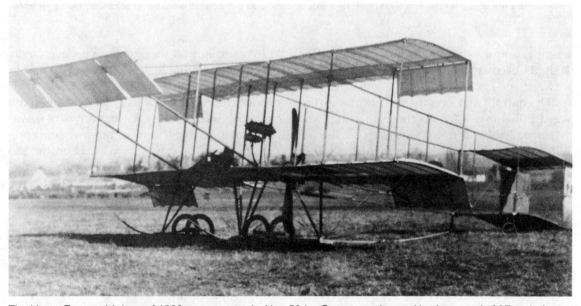

The Henry Farman biplane of 1909 was powered with a 50-hp Gnome engine and had a speed of 37 mph. It was much in evidence at the Rheims meet.

One of the earliest aerial photos shows a spare wheel lashed to the aircraft's skid and was taken over Rheims, France, 1909.

ferent control system through 1911.) The Wrights used two control sticks—one moving forward and backward to activate the elevators (pitch control), and one that when moved forward put down-warp on the right wings and when pulled back put down-warp on the left wings for banking (roll control). At the top of this latter stick was a lever that controlled the rudder for yaw control. Earlier, the Wrights had used a shoulder yoke that produced wing-warp when the pilot leaned in the direction of the desired bank.

The early Curtiss machines used a wheel atop a vertical column that raised and lowered the elevators when pulled back or pushed forward (pitch) and controlled the rudder when turned right or left. Ailerons were activated by a shoulder yoke as in the earlier Wright machines.

Again, it was the French who eventually produced the more logical system in use today, which incorporated foot-operated pedals for rudder control and a wheel that activated both elevators and ailerons. For many years it was referred to as the "Dep" control system, presumably because it was introduced on the Deperdussion machines in 1912. The designer of Deperdussions was Louis Becherau. Most historians have passed Becherau by, but he designed exceptionally clean mid-wing monoplanes, one of which was the first airplane to exceed 100 mph (in 1912), and raised the mark to 126.59 on 29 September 1913. Later, Becherau would design the SPAD of WWI ("SPAD" for the company that built it, *Societe Pour Aviation et Derives*).

Although the Wrights had unlocked the

MIle. Helene Dutrieux flew at Belmont, L.I., but was not allowed to compete with the men.

Marjorie Stinson learned to fly at the Wright brothers' school in Dayton in 1914 and flew exhibitions in a Model B Wright pusher.

secrets of controlled manned flight, it remained for others to build upon those discoveries. By 1912, the pupils could teach the teachers a few things.

However, some of the most famous of the early birdmen preferred the Wright machines, perhaps at least partly because they had learned to fly with the Wright control system. Calbraith P. Rodgers was one of them.

Rodgers may or may not have been a truly competent pilot, but one thing is certain: He had more than his share of determination. He was the first to fly coast-to-coast across the United States. Sponsored by the makers of Vin Fizz, a popular grape drink of the day, and in pursuit of a $50,000 prize offered by William Randolph Hearst to the first aviator to complete such a journey within 30 days, Rodgers left New York on 17 September 1911. He crashed 19 times and required 49 days for the trip, but refused to give up. He finally arrived in Pasadena on 5 November with one leg in a cast and only a rudder and a single wing strut remaining of his original Wright pusher. He had made 69 stops—many unscheduled because of weather and mechanical trouble—and actually spent 82 hours and four minutes in the air, covering 3220 miles. His average speed in the air was slightly over 39 mph.

In mid-1912 (by which time Rodgers had died in a crash), one of America's pioneer women pilots took to the air. Katherine Stinson was not yet 17 years old when she soloed a Wright Model B at Max Lillie's flying school on Chicago's Cicero Field. She required 3½ hours of dual instruction. (At $90 per hour, one tended to learn fast.) Katherine's indulgent mother, Emma, found money for a down payment on a used Model B Wright, and little Katy was soon booked for as many exhibition flights as she cared to make. Represented by Bill Pickins, she received $500 for each appearance—an impressive sum indeed in 1912 dollars. Not that she did anything spectacular by today's standards; at that time it was enough for most people to see a flying machine rise off

Lincoln Beachey began his career as an exhibition pilot in 1905 at age 19. He flew Baldwin dirigibles with Roy Knabenshue's troupe before turning to airplanes in 1910 to become, because of his daring, the best-known of the early birdmen. Beachey died when his monoplane shed its wings during a performance at the San Francisco World's Fair, 14 March 1915.

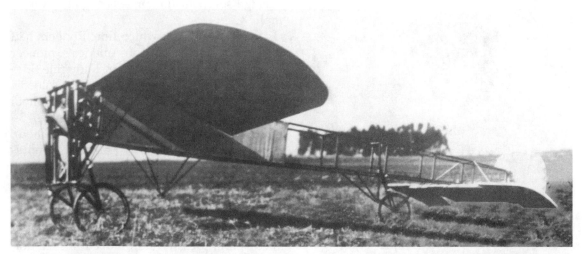

The Bleriot XI of 1909 had a speed of 36 mph, was powered with a 25-hp, three-cylinder Anzani engine, and was commercially available for about $2000. In such a machine, France's Louis Bleriot flew the English Channel 25 July 1909. Many Bleriots were sold or copied in America. Clyde Cessna built his first airplane after inspecting a Bleriot in Oklahoma City.

Calbraith Rodgers (right) made the first transcontinental flight 17 September to 10 December 1911. He crashed 19 times and arrived in California from New York with only a wing strut and rudder of his original aircraft, a Wright Model B. His sponsor was the manufacturer of "Vin Fizz," a popular soft drink.

Crashes during the birdman era often required the services of friends armed with baseball bats to discourage souvenir hunters.

A. L. Longren of Topeka, Kansas, built this copy of a Curtiss pusher and toured the county fairs on the southern plains in 1912-1913.

Matty Laird's first airplane, built in 1913 when Laird was 17 years old, was "a loose formation of discarded material arranged in airplane form." A friend wrecked it.

the ground and sail overhead; and to witness such a feat performed by an unassuming young woman was indeed a memorable sight.

In 1914, sister Marjorie followed in Katherine's propwash, attending the Wright school at Dayton, Ohio. Another Model B Wright was purchased for Marjorie's use; then she too began touring the county fair circuit. Brother Eddie attended the Wright school a year later, after hav-

ing spent most of 1914 living in a hangar at Cicero Field with the Laird brothers, Matty and Charles, and Buck Weaver. These four would all significantly affect American aviation in years to come.

In 1915, Lincoln Beachey was killed while performing at San Francisco's Panama Pacific Exposition. Katherine bought the wreckage of his airplane to obtain its 80-hp Gnome rotary

Katherine Stinson with her 1916 airplane, which was built for her by "Pop" Keller and Elmer Partridge. Engine was the 80-hp Gnome rotary salvaged from Lincoln Beachey's airplane.

engine for a new biplane being built for her by Elmer Partridge and "Pop" Keller. She performed a loop in this machine, becoming the fourth American pilot to master this maneuver, and then included a "loop-the-loop" in her subsequent appearances. (The first inside loop in history was performed by France's Adolphe Pegoud in 1913. Beachey was the first American to do it, followed by DeLloyd Thompson, Art Smith, Katherine, and, in 1916, Matty Laird. Jimmy Doolittle performed the first outside loop in 1927.) Matty Laird appears to be the first pilot to perform a loop with a passenger, that passenger being Marjorie Stinson.

Laird exhibition flight at St. Paul, Minnesota, 7 November 1916, by that time including a loop, crowded Presidential election news to a secondary position on front page of the Dispatch.

*Daring birdmen*  **9**

Poster announcing Laird visit to La Grange, Indiana, 6 October 1916 reveals the hype designed to attract crowds to see the "death-cheating aviator". Promoter Bill Pickens had also booked Beachey, the Stinson sisters, and other top exhibition pilots of the time.

## Matty Laird

The mid-wing monoplane was constructed of old barrel hoops and redwood latticing. Its spruce wings, muslin-covered, were treated with hide glue and formaldehyde. It was powered with a four-cylinder engine built up from automobile and motorcycle parts. It had no ailerons, no instruments, and no good reason to fly. But it did—and at the same time provided its creator with his first flying lesson.

This unlikely craft, which took to the air on 15 September 1913, was the handiwork of 17-year-old Emil Matthew "Matty" Laird, a $4.50-per-week office boy who had left school after the eighth grade to help support his family. Matty had decided to become a flier three years before, after witnessing a flight by a Wright brother's exhibition pilot, Walter Brookins, at Chicago's Grant Park.

Walter Brookins was one of several early "birdmen" (a term common at the time) hired and trained by the Wrights as exhibition pilots. Prior to WWI there was no big market for airplanes in the United States, either civil or military, but there was money to be made—a great deal of it—simply demonstrating to the public that man could fly. The Wrights' gadfly, Glenn Curtiss, also formed an exhibition team, and both were highly successful. And a number of freelance exhibition pilots flew aircraft purchased from the Wrights or Curtiss homebuilt copies, and a few—such as Clyde Cessna and Matty Laird—defied the laws of gravity and reason in airplanes of their own design.

In light of what was then known about the art and science of manned flight, it seems remarkable that so many such creations actually flew. Less surprising is the fact that so many crashed. In 1910 alone 37 pilots were killed, and it was axiomatic that a crash always followed a stall. No one knew how to recover from a spin until Eddie Stinson reasoned it out and demonstrated spin recovery in 1916. The pioneers who led us out of the aeronautical wilderness were possessed of both great courage and unusual perception. The merely brave seldom survived.

Young Matty Laird acquired aeronautical knowledge from the building and flying of model airplanes and many hours spent at Chicago's Cicero Field, where Wright-trained Max Lillie taught flying. By 1912, Cicero Field had become one of the most active aviation centers in America, largely due to the interest and financial help of Harold McCormick of the International Harvester Company and seed magnate Charles Dickinson.

Among the habitués of Cicero Field, in addition to Laird, were Buck Weaver, later a co-founder of WACO; Bill Brock, who would one day make a record flight to Tokyo; Elmer Par-

Glenn Curtiss pioneered flying boat designs beginning with his "F" Boat of 1912.

Flying was truly a dangerous business in the beginning. In 1910 alone, 37 pilots were killed, perhaps one in seven then flying in the United States, although, due to the low airspeeds, most accidents were not fatal.

tridge and Les Bishop, who would become pioneer air mail pilots; and "Shorty" (he was 6'5") Schroeder, who would investigate high altitude flight for the army, among other things. Max Lillie's students included Katherine Stinson and Chance Vought, who were destined to leave indelible marks on the pages of aviation history. Thus, the Windy City's Ci-

Marjorie C. Stinson

E.M. "Matty" Laird at Chicago's Cicero Field, 1916.

cero Field—replaced in 1915 by Ashburn Field, on the site of today's Midway Airport—nurtured a significant bit of our air heritage.

Dual instruction in Lillie's Wright Model B was $90 per hour or $1.50 per minute, and one could rent the airplane for solo flight at the rate of $50 per hour, although a cash deposit of $1000 was required in case the student broke something expensive. Considering the value of the 1912 dollar, it is easy to see why so many early birdmen were forced to act as their own flight instructors.

Laird began his flight test/flight instruction program by hooking his machine to an ice scale attached to a fence post, then operating his engine at maximum rpm to determine the "pounds of thrust" thus obtained. He didn't know how much he needed, so the figure obtained was of no value to him, but the practice was common at Cicero Field and Laird felt that it served to make him appear a bit more "professional."

Matty's first surprise was the torque effect created by his propeller. After he managed to control that and taxi in a reasonably straight line, he found himself airborne, a circumstance he had not planned to confront so abruptly.

"I had thought that I would know exactly what to do," Laird said later, "but there I was, twenty feet in the air, trees rushing at me from the field boundary, and I wasn't so sure anymore. I had an overpowering urge to get back on the ground as quickly as possible."

In his haste to return to earth and give himself some time to think things out, Matty shoved forward on his control wheel, struck the ground, wiped out his landing gear, splintered his propeller, and flipped upside down in a cloud of dust.

Matty's cuts and bruises had healed by the time his machine was repaired, and he continued—cautiously—to teach himself to fly, beginning with a long series of very short hops. At first, he would reduce power as soon as his wheels left the ground. Gradually he increased both the height and distance of each hop. By late fall he had climbed to an altitude of 200 feet and had mastered a complete 360-degree turn. After that, his progress was rapid.

During the winter of 1913–14, Matty built a small biplane and flew it evenings and weekends throughout 1914. A raise in pay at the bank where he worked allowed him to recover the "Baby Biplane," as he called it, with Irish linen and finish it with a new French product, cellulose-nitrate dope.

By mid-1915 it could be said that Laird had become a pilot, as skillful as most others of that day. He had rigged a small auxiliary oil tank for upper cylinder and valve lubrication of his homemade engine, and that extended the length of time it could be operated to as much as 30 minutes. Without quite realizing it, Matty had positioned himself for a career in this exciting new industry.

His first opportunity manifested itself in the form of the country's foremost booking agent for exhibition pilots, Bill Pickins, who

Edward A. Stinson, Jr., was the first to demonstrate spin recovery (1916); he was later a famed pilot and plane builder.

saw Matty fly and promptly offered to arrange professional appearances for him.

At first, Matty was booked at small county fairs and lesser events, while the more famous pilots received the most lucrative contracts. But the $350 Matty was paid to take off, circle the field a few times, and land at Sebring, Ohio, represented 4½ months' pay in his regular job, so he gave notice at the bank and joined the ranks of Lincoln Beachey, Art Mix, and the Stinson sisters as a "Daring Birdman" who travelled about the country introducing the miracle of flight to the (often skeptical) citizenry.

## The Stinson sisters

During the winter of 1915–16, Katherine and Marjorie Stinson established a flying school near San Antonio, Texas, and Katherine commissioned Elmer Partridge and Pop Keller to build a new, "modern" biplane for her, fitted with an 80-hp Gnome rotary engine salvaged from the wreck of the airplane in which famed exhibition pilot Lincoln Beachey had died a few months earlier. At the end of the 1916 season, Katy took this machine, along with Matty Laird's new Anzani-powered biplane, and left for a triumphal tour of Japan. Brother Eddie, having learned to fly at the Wright school, opened a flying school in Houston, Texas, while Marjorie was busy in San Antonio instructing a group of Canadians who would help form the nucleus of a future Royal Canadian Air Force.

Early in 1917, Laird visited Marjorie in San Antonio and, while waiting for the exhibition season to begin, installed a new tail on a biplane Bill Brock had built for Katherine. Test-flying this machine, Matty crashed and was seriously injured.

That incident deserves more than passing comment because it illustrates the difficulty today's serious researcher sometimes encounters in attempting to accurately record the activities of our aviation pioneers. Matty told me that this airplane entered a flat spin at an altitude of approximately 2000 feet as he investigated control response at low airspeeds. He described in great detail his futile efforts at recovery. However, Marjorie, who was on the scene, disputed Laird's account, telling me in no uncertain terms that Matty simply stalled the airplane on takeoff.

Such disputes are not exactly rare. Over the years I have interviewed many great names in aviation, and while I can honestly say that every one, without exception, was courteous, modest, and really a class act, I learned quite early that some will rewrite history for you if given the chance. The writer is forced to do a lot of cross-checking. Sometimes it is not possible to firmly document the truth. All I can say in regard to this incident is that, cross-checking where possible, I uncovered no other questionable statements by Matty Laird in eight hours of taped conversation. When I

The Stinson sisters with Katherine's Wright Model B. Marjorie is on left. Katherine was the fourth U.S. pilot to master the inside loop.

went back to him with Marjorie's statement, he smiled and replied, "Well, that's Marjorie for you." He refused to say anything against her, and nowhere in his account did he offer anything but praise for the Stinsons.

It was obvious to me that Marjorie—still attractive, elegant, intense, and very sharp indeed late in life—held an extraordinary amount of personal dislike for Laird, which the years had not softened. It's one of those little footnotes to history—an intriguing if minor mystery, and all that it really means, I suppose, is that those legendary figures of our industry were, after all, only human.

Matty spent many months in the hospital as a result of his crash at San Antonio and was left with a permanent limp and an improperly knitted arm, which precluded any possibility of military service in WWI, but his most important contributions to civil aviation were yet to come.

## Glenn Martin

Meanwhile, other early birds were placing a few stones in the foundation of this infant industry. Glenn Luther Martin operated a small garage in Santa Ana, California, when, in 1909, at the age of 20, he built his first airplane. Known as the "Flying Dude" for his immaculate dress, he became one of the first motion picture pilots in 1915, appearing in the Mary Pickford film *The Girl From Yesterday*. Martin flew exhibitions, built 17 training planes for the U.S. Signal Corps, and moved to Cleveland in 1918 to produce bombers for the army. Among early Martin employees were Lawrence Bell, James "Dutch" Kindelberger, and Donald W. Douglas.

When Martin moved to Cleveland from the West Coast, it was to form a new company. All of the fledgling planemakers of the bird-

E.M. Laird

Ralph McMillan and his homebuilt copy of a Curtiss pusher shared the billing with Laird at the Harrison County Fair, Missouri Valley, Iowa, 17 September 1915.

E.M. Laird

Matty Laird with his Anzani-powered exhibition airplane. Buck Weaver is at extreme left.

man era, needing capital, were gobbled up by combines of investment bankers soon allied with automobile interests. The Wrights put up their U.S. and Canadian rights late in 1909 to form Wright Aeronautical Corporation with J.P. Morgan, Cornelius Vanderbilt, George Gould, and several other multimillionaires. Orville and Wilbur received $100,000 in cash, 40 percent of the stock, and a 10 percent royalty on each airplane sold (they also sold manufacturing rights in France, Germany, and England between 1908 and 1913).

## Curtiss reorganized

All this was paced by aircraft engine development at Curtiss. The first Curtiss airplane engine had been an air-cooled V-8 of 30 hp that was fitted, in turn, to the first three machines produced by Bell's Aerial Experiment Association in 1908. It was followed by improved versions of up to 60 hp, and it seems clear that Charles Kirkham, who machined and assembled these engines, was also the designer. Curtiss had no engine facility at his Hammond sport factory.

By 1912, Kirkham was building the Curtiss Model O water-cooled V-8 of 75 hp, and an improved valve-actuating system on this engine—the work of Henry Keckler and John H. McNamara—resulting in the Model OX in 1913, which, with additional detailed improvements, became the famed 90-hp OX-5 in 1916. Shortly after the introduction of the Model OX, Charles Kirkham was appointed chief engineer at Curtiss; McNamara had the title of "engine superintendent."

At this point, Curtiss faced the need for significant expansion capital. He could offer a good military trainer and a good engine. Orders were coming in from Britain and Canada, while the U.S. Congress was certain to approve a pending bill that would authorize a large air training program for the army and navy. Therefore, Curtiss went to investment banker Clement M. Keys, who consolidated

Curtiss' holdings, formed Curtiss Aeroplane and Motor Company, and marketed its stock.

Automobile mogul John North Willys emerged as the chief minority stockholder in Curtiss Aeroplane and Motor, and during WWI the Willys-Overland and Willys-Morrow plants accounted for more than 7000 of the 12,600 OX-5 engines built, while new Curtiss factories at Buffalo and Garden City, New York, produced JN-4 and JN-6 (the latter, Hisso-powered Jennies) trainers for the army, and JN-9 (essentially, the JN-6 on floats) trainers for the navy. About 6750 Jennies were produced by war's end.

After the war, surplus Jennies and Canucks (the latter being the Canadian-built Jenny) became the primary mount of barnstormers, and surplus OX-5 engines could still be found in privately owned biplanes on the eve of WWII.

## Keys controls Curtiss

With the cessation of hostilities on 11 November 1918, existing wartime contracts were, of course, cancelled. But the government had financed construction of expanded manufacturing facilities for Curtiss and others, and Curtiss directors decided to maintain their factories, with greatly reduced payrolls, and attempt to serve whatever markets—both civilian and military—could be developed. Although fewer than 1000 American pilots were in combat units overseas when the war ended, almost 10,000 were in training in the United States at hastily constructed airfields about the country, and therefore many people in the aircraft industry expected a boom in civil aviation, predicting a strong market for "flivver" planes (small and cheap single-placers), as well as larger commercial craft.

When the boom did not develop, Willys sold his stock in Curtiss Aeroplane and Motor Company to Clement Keys, who had organized the corporation back in 1916. The Willys stock, plus the shares already held by Keys, put Keys in control of the company, and wheeler-dealer Keys would dominate Curtiss—and build an aviation empire from it—when the boom did materialize in the late 1920s.

## Review questions

1. Where was the first international air meet held? Who were some of the participants? Where was the first meet held in the United States? Describe some of the records which were established at both meets. What was the outcome of the Bennett Cup race at Belmont Park in 1910?

2. Who were Lincoln Beachey and Calbraith Rodgers? Describe the control system developed by the French which was a considerable improvement over the ones used in the Curtiss and Wright machines.

3. Who were some of the early women pilots? What significance was the development of aircraft by Matty Laird, Clyde Cessna, and Buck Weaver?

# 2

# The first air war

## Objectives

At the end of this chapter you should be able to:

- Discuss the role of the U.S. First Aero Squadron.
- Recognize the importance of WWI in accelerating aircraft development.
- Describe the evolution of fighter aircraft which took place during the war years.
- Discuss some of the problems faced by U.S. aircraft manufacturers in gearing up production for the war.
- Understand the role played by Billy Mitchell in shaping the U.S. Air Service.
- Describe the role of the U.S. Naval Air Service during World War I.
- Identify some of the leading aces on both sides of the conflict and the aircraft which they flew.

At the outbreak of WWI, in August 1914, there were no military aircraft in the world. True, France, Germany, Britain, and the United States military forces all possessed airplanes by that time, but none were designed for any specific military mission. The airplane had been under development in Europe for less than six years, and most of that effort had been directed toward improving performance. The Wright

Model A, or Military Flyer, of 1909 cruised at slightly more than 40 mph. By 1914 a speed of 130 mph had been achieved in the British single-place SE-4, but since the army generals could envision only one possible use for airplanes—the scouting of enemy troop movements—speed was not regarded as an asset.

Actually, three years earlier in the United States, artillerymen had foreseen the possibility of employing airplanes to direct artillery fire. A 1911 newspaper report is to be found in the files of the Field Artillery Museum at Fort Sill, Oklahoma:

"Junction City, Kansas—A successful aeroplane artillery test was conducted during the War Department's aeroplane maneuvers here. Battery E, Sixth Field Artillery, Lieutenant Palmer commanding, was stationed on the side of a hill. An imaginary enemy was placed on the other side. Lieutenant Milling, Aviator, with Lieutenant Sands as observer, flew over the hill obtaining the enemy's position. The messages giving the information secured were dropped to the artillerymen. No wireless tests were made."

## The 1st aero squadron

At the time of the above mentioned experiment, the U.S. Signal Corps had a total of six airplanes in service or on order. Except for pilot training at San Antonio, Texas, and College

Park, Maryland, this appears to be the first field test of a U.S. Army airplane. In any case, whatever flying was done by the army through 1912 was that of true pioneers feeling their way. Then, in January 1913, Lt. Harold E. Geiger inaugurated the Signal Corps Flying School at North Island, off San Diego, California, and in December of that year War Department General Order No. 75 authorized the First Aero Squadron, although this unit was not actually formed until 15 July 1915 from students trained at North Island.

On 26 July the squadron was sent to Fort Sill, Oklahoma, for duty with the Field Artillery School. The squadron consisted of 15 officers, 85 enlisted men and eight Curtiss JN-2 aircraft, Capt. Benjamin Foulois commanding.

USAF

The Army's Capt. C. DeF. Chandler (left) and Lt. Roy Kirtland in the Wright "B" airplane were first to fire a machine gun from an airplane, 7 June 1912.

According to official reports, the 1st Aero Squadron "carried out various exercises" at Fort Sill, including artillery spotting and some aerial photography. One pilot, Capt. G.H.

Knox, and two aircraft were lost, which led to the squadron being re-equipped with Curtiss JN-3s (extended upper wings and improved engines). Then, in November 1915, the squadron was ordered to fly its eight aircraft to Fort Sam Houston, near San Antonio. This was done without serious mishap although it was undoubtedly the longest cross-country mass flight attempted up to that time.

An uneventful winter was spent at Fort Sam Houston erecting living quarters. Then, on 13 March 1916, the 1st Aero Squadron received orders to report to Gen. John J. "Blackjack" Pershing at Columbus, New Mexico, to serve with an American punitive expedition charged with the task of capturing the Mexican rebel leader Francisco "Pancho" Villa. Early in the morning of 9 March, Villa, with 400 men, had raided the border town of Columbus, killing nine civilians and seven United States troopers. More U.S. citizens certainly would have died had not Col. H.J. Slocum charged into town with the 13th Cavalry and chased the raiders back into Mexico.

## Chasing Villa in Mexico

General Pershing entered Mexico with 5000 men on the 15th of March, and the 1st Aero Squadron, with 10 officers and 80 enlisted men, began operations from Columbus on the 19th. The squadron's duties consisted mainly of reconnaissance, courier, and communications assignments. Pershing was an old horse soldier and clearly felt that the airplanes were more bother than help. Considering the state of aircraft development at that time, Pershing wasn't completely wrong.

Two of the eight airplanes were lost almost at once. Lt. T.S. Bowen escaped with only a broken nose when, in a high wind, his craft "dipped and plummeted in almost a straight 50-ft fall to the ground," according to a Fourth Army press release. And a news flash reported "Flight Lieutenants Edgar S. Gorrell and Robert H. Willis, Jr. overdue and apparently down somewhere in the Chihuahua desert." Fears for the downed fliers' safety deepened when it was pointed out that, in the great waste over which they were flying, men on foot could wander for days without reaching help. Each carried only three days' rations and two canteens of water. An additional danger was the possibility of capture by Villa's forces.

However, both survived with little ill effect. Willis walked 32 miles to the pueblo of Casas Grandes. Later, when a crew returned to his airplane, they found that the seats and instruments had been removed and the wings slashed. Only the engine was salvagable. Gorrell was found plodding along the road three miles from another village. He had gone down with a fuel leak two days earlier. A bit of solder and a can of gasoline were all that were needed to allow him to fly his airplane back to Columbus.

Another pilot, Lieutenant Dargue, and his observer, Captain Willis, crashed on the side of a mountain while on a mission to reconnoiter the roads leading into Chihuahua City. Neither was seriously injured, but their walk back to the Mexican village of San Antonio covered about 60 miles of very rough terrain.

The actual campaign into Mexico was short, and the squadron had but two serviceable airplanes left when it returned to Columbus after 33 days in the field. Still, a lot of lessons had been learned in that short time. Operating their primitive craft under harsh conditions over inhospitable desert and mountains (the Sierra Madres were often higher than the absolute ceiling of the JN-3), the men of the 1st Aero Squadron proved more durable than their machines.

Pancho Villa was never captured. He and his men remained under arms in the Sierra Madres until, in 1920, the Mexican Government coaxed him into retirement with the gift of a large estate. Three years later, he was assassinated.

Meanwhile, shortly before the 1st Aero Squadron was recalled from Mexico, President Wilson had sent an ultimatum to Germany demanding the U-boat (submarine) attacks on U.S. shipping be stopped. It would be another year before America would be forced into the

In November 1910, civilian pilot Eugene Ely made the first aircraft takeoff from a ship when he flew a 50-hp Curtiss from a platform on the bow of the light cruiser Birmingham.

"Fly by wire" was method of launching the U.S. Navy's first airplane in 1912. The float-equipped Curtiss Triad took off from greased wires. Liaison aircraft were similarly flown from navy LSTs during WWII.

war in Europe, and meanwhile the 1st Aero Squadron would remain at Columbus, New Mexico. After the United States entered the war, the squadron would go overseas in August 1917, and, following a six-month wait for airplanes, would enter combat in April 1918, flying French-built Salmson observation planes.

## The United States in WWI

Debate still continues among historians as to just how much the United States contributed to Allied victory in WWI, especially in the air. Starting with an army of 200,000 in April 1917, the United States had 2.8 million men under arms when the war ended, with 43 divisions overseas. True, they were sketchily trained and much of their armament came from France and Britain, but this was a typical American Army of "civilians in soldiers' suits," and they performed as Americans have always performed in battle. They griped and they joked and they fought superbly.

When Americans entered the battle zones in the spring of 1918, the war had been stalemated for more than three and a half years while 8 million men died in the mud. But the Bolshevik revolution took Russia out of the war and freed the Germans on the Eastern Front for a series of spring offensives in France that may well have at last defeated the exhausted British and French but for the arrival of the Americans, commanded by Gen. "Blackjack" Pershing. In fact, long before the Americans arrived in force, the mere promise of their coming gave new resolve to the tottering Allies, and the popular cry "The Yanks are coming!" was alone probably worth a couple of new divisions on the Western Front.

The Americans did, of course, make all the difference in the key battles fought during the spring and summer of 1918. They stopped a major German offensive that had broken through Allied lines east of the Aisne River and which had advanced to within 40 miles of Paris. In July, eight U.S. divisions—two of them spearheading—led the Allies to victory in the Aisne-Mame Offensive which left the Allies with the initiative. Two months later, Pershing had 27 American divisions (11 of which he used) for the St. Mihiel offensive in a successful, totally American operation. That in turn allowed the joint American-French (630,000 Americans, 138,000 French) Meuse-Argonne Drive on 26 September 1918 which would end the war seven weeks later on 11 November.

Those are the essential facts, unclouded by detail, but the fact that all of it was accomplished in less than seven months and at what the Allies regarded as a small sacrifice (53,403 Americans killed, 202,261 wounded), and after they had suffered four years of unbelievable carnage fighting over that same ground, led some to downgrade America's role in the Allied victory when in truth it was American troops, American food, and the U.S. Navy guaranteeing the delivery of both, that ended the bloody stalemate in Flanders and allowed the Allies to dictate the terms of peace.

Those peace terms, spelled out in the Treaty of Versailles in 1919 and primarily drafted by France, were so harsh and unrealistic that they made the appearance of Hitler all but inevitable—about which, more later.

The 1914-1918 war in the air greatly accelerated aircraft development, but the airplane did not significantly influence the outcome of that conflict, and WWI in the air was not a dress rehearsal for future air warfare. Neither side had airplanes in sufficient numbers or of sufficient performance to make airpower a decisive factor. Important concepts in strategy and tactics emerged, but their implementation in each case was on a scale too small to establish their validity.

At the beginning of the war, airplanes on both sides were unarmed, and opposing machines often passed one another, sometimes exchanging pistol fire, on missions to scout one another's positions and troop movements. Of course, both sides recognized the desirability of denying the enemy access to their skies while

Glenn H. Curtiss began building successful flying machines in 1908 and was repeatedly sued for patent infringement by the Wrights. Curtiss pioneered flying boat designs.

remaining free to invade enemy air, and that prompted the appearance of the first fighter planes. The Germans presaged the doctrine of strategic airpower with their dirigible raids on England as early as 1915; close air support of advancing ground troops was convincingly demonstrated by Col. Billy Mitchell's fliers during the Battle of St. Mihiel.

## The first fighter airplane

The world's first fighter plane was the Morane-Saulnier Bullet, a single-place mid-wing monoplane operated by the French early in WWI. It became a fighter when an 1885 Hotchkiss infantry machine gun was mounted on its cowling, and a wedge-shaped steel deflector was attached to the back of each propeller blade to protect the prop from the estimated one bullet

An early Curtiss triplane design, the Model L, crashed in test for the army.

The 42nd airplane purchased by the U.S. Army was this Curtiss JN-2, forerunner of the famed JN-4 "Jenny." Engine of this 1915 aircraft was the Curtiss OX-5, evolved from a series of water-cooled V-8s designed by Curtiss dating back to 1908.

in seven that did not pass between the blades. French aviator Roland Garros is said to have shot down several German airplanes with this machine before going down behind enemy lines in April 1915.

The Germans inspected Garros' crude gun installation and soon had forward-firing, line-of-sight guns on their airplanes. Theirs uti-lized an interrupter gear activated by an en-gine-driven cam, allowing the gun to fire only between the prop blades. The British and French followed with similar systems.

The air war steadily intensified as aircraft on both sides improved. Throughout 1916, and for much of 1917, the Germans were gen-erally better equipped. The Pfalz DIII, Alba-

Curtiss R-4 of 1916 had red star on rudder, the first although unofficial attempt toward adoption of a national insignia for U.S. Army airplanes.

World's first fighter airplane was the French Morane-Saulnier Bullet of 1914, which mounted an 1885 Hotchkiss machine gun for line-of-sight aiming by the pilot. Wedge-shaped steel deflectors on rear of propeller blades protected the blades from the estimated one-in-seven rounds that did not pass between.

tros DIII, and Fokker DRI Triplane (the Red Baron's favorite mount) were excellent fighters for their time. Their most serious challenger was the French *Spad* VII, which entered combat in the fall of 1916. The British FE-5a and Sopwith *Camel* were in service by mid-1917 and were, perhaps, the equal of any German fighters with the possible exception of the Fokker DVII, which entered combat at about the same time. So the Germans were never, for any significant length of time, confronted with Allied aircraft of superior performance.

Had WWI continued into 1919, the Allies would certainly have controlled the air. By that time, aircraft production in the United States would have, despite much wasted effort, become a major factor, as would the 10,000 American pilots in training when the war ended. Given time, America really would have "darkened the skies over Germany" with her warplanes.

While the United States could have produced a lot of airplanes through 1919, no notable American designs would have been

The British BE2 of 1914 served the Royal Flying Corps as an observation plane and light bomber early in WWI. Skids beneath nose were to prevent nose-over during landings.

German Fokker E-1 Eindecker (monoplane) of 1915 was fitted with an 80-hp Oberursel rotary engine. Speed was 80 mph and the machine gun was synchronized by an interrupter gear to fire between the rotating propeller blades.

The L-30, a typical German military zeppelin, appeared in 1916 and raided London and other cities in England as well as targets on the Eastern Front. L-30 was 649 ft in length, 178 ft in diameter, 90 ft high. She could carry 5 tons of bombs, had 10 machine guns for defense, and cruised at 60 mph.

among them. Most would have been deHavilland DH-4 observation planes. Perhaps some would have been the American-designed Orenco D and Thomas Morse MB-3 pursuits (fighters), had the 300-hp Hispano-Suiza engines been available for them. Both of these 150-mph craft appear to be copies of the French Spad (of which the United States ordered 6000 on three contracts, later cancelled).

## U.S. aircraft and engine production

The U.S. aircraft production effort during WWI is epitomized in the story of the Liberty engine. Within days of America's entry into the war, a joint British-French commission arrived in the United States to aid manufacturers in selecting the most useful airframe and engine designs. This commission was directed to Detroit, where it was met by Jesse Vincent, the Packard Motor Car Company's vice president for engineering. As early as 1916, automobile interests had purchased the Wright patents and gained control of the Curtiss company. Therefore, aircraft and aircraft engine production would be in the hands of the car makers.

The commission recommended that U.S. factories build two-place fighter-bombers and engines of 200 to 400 horsepower. To save time, they suggested that those planes and engines be British and French designs already

battle-proven. That was a realistic suggestion because, by 1917, the United States was years behind the combatant nations in aircraft development, and no U.S. manufacturer had any real experience in the volume production of airplanes, a product that had to be largely hand-built.

But the automobile people were in control, and whatever the problems they would solve them, *profitably*.

Vincent went to Washington and conferred with the automobile executives who had been appointed by President Wilson to the key aircraft procurement posts, Edward Deeds and Howard Coffin, top men of the hastily-created Aircraft Production Board. Deeds was an associate of Charles Kettering at Delco; Coffin was a Hudson Motor Company official.

This group determined that Packard should design and build the 400-hp engine needed. It would be known as the "U.S. Standard Aircraft Engine." This engine would power the deHavilland DH-4, the airplane selected by the board for mass production. The British Bristol Fighter was a newer, superior two-place fighter-bomber, but it would not accept the V-12 engine that Vincent planned. Vincent would later say that he and E.J. Hall designed the Standard Aircraft Engine, which became known as the Liberty, over a single weekend following his meeting with Deeds and Coffin, but the truth was that Vincent had

The Germans lost a number of the world's first strategic bombers to Allied fighters, although most dirigible raids were made at night when few defensive airplanes were able to fly.

been working on such a design for more than a year, and had actually built two test versions.

The Liberty was no better or no worse than most aircraft engines of its day. It was billed as a triumph of engineering, but it required hundreds of modifications during its first few years of service, and its official time-between-major-overhauls was 120 hours, although few Liberties ever ran that long without repair. (When the army flew Liberty-powered planes around the world in 1924, engines were changed every 50 hours, but even that didn't prevent several engine failures on the four airplanes.)

The Liberty was a water-cooled engine, but it cylinders were not cast in a single block. What Vincent and Hall actually designed was a single cylinder which could be stuck into different crankcases to make engines of four, six, eight or twelve cylinders. It sounded good when stated that way, but there was nothing new about it, and the V-8 version could hardly have been taken seriously when the superior Hispano-Suiza, built under license by the Wright Corporation, had already proven itself. (Later the six-cylinder version of the Liberty—a six in-line, not a V-6—did enjoy minor success in the post-war civilian market.)

A French Maurice Farman observation plane proceeding toward the front in 1915. Engine was a 110-hp Le Rhone rotary.

British F.E.2d fighter-bomber was often used to escort the vulnerable observation planes. Engine was a 250-hp Rolls-Royce. Forward gunner had a good field of fire.

But the most interesting feature of the V-12 Liberty was its automobile-type Delco ignition system, a major component that was, of course, dear to Mr. Deed's heart. All other aircraft engines, then as today, used magnetos for a hotter spark and greater reliability.

Meanwhile, the car manufacturers and their financial backers divvied-up the market in an interesting way. Wright Aeronautical, controlled by a syndicate that owned the Simplex Automobile Company (the principals being Richard Hoyt of Hayden, Stone; Thomas Chadbourne and Harvey Gibson of Manufacturers Trust, and Albert Wiggen of Chase National Bank) bought out the Glenn L. Martin Company (the third most important airplane builder behind Wright and Curtiss) and formed the Wright-Martin Company. With that kind of muscle, the Wright-Martin Company could put a hammerlock on the production of the 150 to 300-hp aircraft engine market.

Many American pilots trained in France in the Caudron C-3, which employed wing-warping for lateral control.

Another "Wright" company was formed by wheeler-dealers Deeds, Coffin, Vincent, and Kettering. It was called Dayton-Wright (Orville Wright was listed as one of the original organizers, though he was not active in the company). Dayton-Wright was the prime contractor for the deHavilland DH-4.

At the Curtiss Aeroplane and Motor Company, John North Willys, who was something of a maverick among automobile biggies, seems to have had little or no influence with the "in" bunch comprising the Aircraft Production Board, but he didn't need it. Curtiss was well established as a purveyor of flying machines to the Signal Corps, already had substantial orders for its JN-4 trainer by the time the Aircraft Production Board was formed, and could hardly be denied additional orders for the "Jenny," the standard army training plane. On floats, it was the N-9 navy trainer.

A total of 4846 DH-4s was produced: 3106 by Dayton-Wright, 1600 by Fisher Body (a General Motors subsidiary), and 140 by the Standard Aeroplane Company. About 1500 DH-4s were shipped overseas. However, Gen. Halsey Dunwoody, director of the Air Service's supply system, later said, "We never had a single plane that was fit for use." Those that reached the front had to be rebuilt by the A.E.F. aircraft production center at Romorantin, France.

Altogether, 13,574 Liberty engines were built before the war ended, by Packard, Ford, GM, and Marmon, but the first one did not fly over the fighting front in France until 7 August 1918.

For a reason never explained, Liberty engine production continued into 1920, by which time more than 22,000 had been built. The army was stuck with these engines throughout the '20s, and army observation planes designed ten years after WWI were forced to use them. The last Liberty was retired from service at Kelly Field, Texas, in 1935.

For all the money and effort invested, less than 200 American-built airplanes—Liberty-powered DH-4s—were in the battle zone and fit for service when WWI ended. The remain-

Crash of French Farman, 1917

Charles W. Meyers

ing 550 aircraft in American hands at the front were purchased from France and Britain. When the fighting stopped, there were 45 U.S. combat squadrons in action with a strength of 800 pilots and 500 aerial gunners and observers.

In seven months of combat, American losses were 289 planes and 48 observation balloons. U.S. pilots and gunners were credited with 781 enemy planes and 73 balloons shot down.

Eventually, in mid-1918, President Woodrow Wilson became aware of the Aircraft Production Board's blatant boondoggle and cleaned house. But the combines formed by Deeds and his cronies continued to possess their contracts, probably because there were no alternate sources at that late date. And because both public memory and political retribution are notably short-lived, both Deeds and Coffin would soon resurface in other positions of authority.

## Airpower prophet

The man who planned the highly successful U.S. Air Service tactics in WWI was Col. William "Billy" Mitchell. (The Aviation Section of the Signal Corps became the "Airplane Division" on 2 June 1917, although it was generally called the "Air Service." Separation from the Signal Corps came on 20 May 1918. On 4 June 1920 Congress approved the Army Reorganization Bill that officially recognized the "U.S. Air Service" as a "separate and coordinate branch of the army." Then, on 2 July 1926 the Air Corps Act changed the Air Service to the "U.S. Army Air Corps," and it remained as such until 20 June 1941 when, with a new autonomy under Maj. Gen. Henry H. "Hap" Arnold, it became the "United States Army Air Forces" (USAAF). Today's independent United States Air Force (USAF) was created by the National Security Act of 1947, which became law on 18 September that year. We will try to use the appropriate term for each period discussed here.)

Mitchell had learned to fly at a civilian school and at his own expense while stationed in Washington, D.C. An excellent military record spanning 18 years service in the Signal Corps had resulted in assignment to the Signal Corps Headquarters staff and promotion to major. Mitchell had enlisted as a private in 1898 at the outbreak of the Spanish-American War, and had shown himself to be an innovative officer. Early in 1917, he convinced his superiors that he should be sent to Europe to study Allied air tactics. He was there when the U.S. declared war on Germany.

He flew as an observer with the French and went to England to talk with pilots and Royal Flying Corps brass. He was greatly impressed with Britain's Maj. Gen. Sir Hugh Trenchard, and Mitchell later wrote (Memoirs of WWI, *Liberty* magazine, 1928; Random House, 1960) that most of his philosophy on the proper use of airpower was based upon that of "Boom" Trenchard. Each clearly saw that a nation's air force should be an independent service, that a strategic air arm should be committed to the destruction of an enemy's critical industries, that tactical aircraft should be sent against the enemy's lines of supply and communication, and that close air support of an advancing ground force must include control of the air above that force.

Mitchell's immediate boss was Maj. Gen. Mason Patrick, Commander of the Army Air Services and an old classmate of Pershing's at West Point. Patrick never made public statements about Mitchell, but there is evidence that he supported Mitchell whenever possible, not only in France, but years later, when Mitchell was publicly kicking a lot of sacred military cows, to the delight of the press and to the consternation of the War and Navy Departments. General Patrick was almost certainly responsible for Mitchell's appointment to the post of Chief of Air Service, First Army, with a promotion in rank to colonel, because Pershing wasn't big on placing flying officers in command positions. Most flying officers

Albatros D-IIIs of Richthofen's Jagdstaffel 11, spring, 1917. A 160-hp Mercedes engine gave these fighters a speed of 120 mph.

were not "regular army," and Pershing held the professional soldier's prejudices against reservists.

Mitchell was regular army, and by stretching friendship (with Patrick) only a little, that made him acceptable to Pershing. However, Mitchell was not a West Pointer, and that definitely left him forever outside the council of the army's General Staff. The highest permanent rank he could ever realistically expect was that of "bird" colonel. His later, temporary rank of brigadier general went with his job as the number two man in the Air Service. It also left when he was relieved of that position.

The army's policy of placing veteran regular army officers in command of flying units generally worked very well. There's no substitute for experience, especially command experi-ence. But it produced a few unusual situations. At one flying school, when the new CO was informed that the students disliked their ancient Cuadron training planes because they employed the old wing-warping principle for lateral control rather than hinged ailerons, he ordered the planes kept indoors and out of the sun when not in use to prevent such warping. An ex-cavalry major in charge of a squadron had a hitching post installed outside the Operations office and went about the aerodrome on horseback. (There were so many ex-cavalry officers in the Air Service that spurs were part of the Air Service regulation uniform for several years.)

The most embarrassing example, perhaps, was the case of the major in charge of the 96th Bombardment Squadron who led a six-plane

Nieuport 17 fighters of the Lafayette Escadrille at Cachy, Somme, 1916. The Lafayette was made up of American volunteers flying for France prior to America's entry into WWI.

formation over Germany in marginal weather and eventually landed on a German aerodrome, believing it to be an Allied field. The Germans captured the whole outfit intact. The next day they dropped a note on the 96th's base which read; "We thank you for the fine airplanes and equipment you have sent us; but what shall we do with the major?" (When later reminded of the incident, Mitchell replied, "Needless to say, we did not reply about the major, as he was better off in Germany at that time than be would have been with us.")

Mitchell's chance to demonstrate some of his theories of aerial warfare finally came on 1 September 1918 when U.S. troops under Pershing began the great St. Mihiel Drive. From his headquarters at Ligny-en-Barrios, Mitchell commanded a force of 1476 aircraft, most of them placed at his disposal by the French, British and Italians. It constituted the greatest concentration of airpower the world had seen up to that time, and would appear to indicate that the French and Italian air commanders agreed with the Trenchard/Mitchell doctrine.

The St. Mihiel salient held by the Germans was shaped like a huge horseshoe, its foremost part on the Meuse River, its ends anchored on the German Border. Mitchell sent 400 planes to each end of the horseshoe to sever enemy lines at those points and split the enemy's air defenses. Meanwhile, U.S. fighter-bombers (DH-4s, Breguets, Salmsons), along with elements of the U.S. 1st Pursuit Group, blasted in at treetop level across the horseshoe's center. While the American fliers were giving close support to the advancing infantry, the French and Italians far to the rear concentrated on the destruction of trains and trucks to immobilize all movement, effectively blocking both the possibilities of reinforcement and retreat. This was the employment of massed airpower as a tactical striking force as Mitchell envisioned it.

The operation was highly successful. The drive ended in quick victory for the American forces and the taking of thousands of prisoners who had been denied both help and an avenue of escape. General Pershing was impressed; Mitchell was soon promoted to the temporary rank of Brigadier General.

A few weeks later, Mitchell proposed to Pershing, via Patrick, that the U.S. Army form a paratroop division, but Pershing apparently did not take that suggestion seriously. Other Mitchell ideas (that the Air Service be a separate and equal department of the U.S. military, for example) *were* taken seriously—in fact, viewed with alarm. Just the hint that the upstart Air Service should someday independently take a share of the responsibility—and appropriations—for the nation's defense was enough to corrode a lot of brass. And well it might, for they were to hear a lot more from Billy Mitchell.

# U.S. naval air in WWI

Some natural rivalry has always existed between the branches of the U.S. military, but seldom has it been more pronounced than in 1917-18 when the army and navy fought each other over aircraft procurement at home and the deployment of airplanes overseas. That may seem strange when one considers that *neither* service professed much faith in the effectiveness of aerial vehicles in their respective operations. The generals and admirals, however, whatever their private or public positions concerning the value of military air machines, obviously believed that, since there *were* such things, *their* branch of the service should have the authority—preferably the *exclusive* authority—to operate them.

In mid-1918, long before the U.S. Navy possessed a rigid dirigible (or could fathom any use for one), the navy managed to obtain from the Secretary of War exclusive authority to operate rigid dirigibles. Upon America's entry into the war, the navy had rushed to sign contracts with all the major U.S. plane builders to tie up their entire production. The army retaliated by taking charge of all sources of spruce (from which airframes were made). It was this bitter interservice squabble that hastened formation of the Aircraft Production Board.

Both services gave primary flight training to as many of its aviation enlistees as their limited facilities would permit, then shipped them overseas for advanced training (in some cases, all flight training). Therefore, many American pilots, in American uniforms, both army and navy, initially entered combat in French and British squadrons, because the U.S. had neither the airplanes nor the organized personnel and supporting equipment to establish its own air units until mid-March 1918. The navy's first fighter ace, Lt. (jg) David S. Ingalls, scored all his air victories while flying with RAF Squadron 213.

The first aerial victory credited to a navy airman went to Ens. Stephan Potter on 19 March 1918, when he shot down an enemy seaplane, one of several that attacked Potter's formation of flying boats attempting a reconnaissance mission along Germany's north coast.

The navy air units were chiefly concerned with coastal patrol, but began offensive operations in August 1918, when Air Squadron One, Northern Bombing Group, made a single-plane night raid on enemy submarine docks at Ostend. The first raid in force by the navy's Northern Bombing Group was made by eight aircraft of Marine Day Squadron Nine, which dropped 17 bombs, totalling 2218 pounds, on the German-held railroad junction at Thielt Rivy, Belgium, 14 October.

USAF

The British Handley Page V/1500 of 1918 was designed to carry 1000 pounds of bombs to Berlin. Wingspan was 126 feet.

USAF

The Fokker DR-1 Dreidecker (triplane) was Richthofen's favorite mount. Highly maneuverable, it was powered with the 110-hp Oberusel rotary engine and had a speed of 115 mph.

USAF

The body of Max Immelmann in the wreckage of his Fokker Eindecker. The originator of the "Immelmann Turn" fell to the guns of Lt. George McCubbin, RFC, 18 June 1916. McCubbin was flying an F.E.2b.

these numbers, 18,000 officers and men and 570 aircraft were overseas, serving at 20 shore stations in France, England, Ireland, Gibraltar, Italy, and in the Azore Islands. The navy's claims for its air units were modest: 27 enemy submarines sighted, 25 attacked, and 12 damaged. Naval aviators dropped 63 tons of bombs. The navy's commander in chief, Adm. H.T. Mayo, refused to commend the war effort of naval aviation, complaining that it had failed to work with his battleships.

## Combat

Although the Americans made the difference in WWI, breaking the stalemate and spearheading Allied victory, we are allowed another perspective of the U.S. air contribution when we compare the number of aces (pilots officially credited with five or more enemy aircraft destroyed in aerial combat) produced by each country. Britain's RFC/RAF (the Royal Flying Corps became the Royal Air Force in mid-1918) could count 533 aces, their highest scorer being Maj. E. Mannock with 73 victo-

More than two years of trench warfare took the lives of millions and left the war stalemated and the combatants exhausted, prior to U.S. entry into the war in April 1917.

When the armistice was signed ending the hostilities of WWI, the strength of naval aviation had grown to a force of 6716 officers and 30,693 men in navy units, and 282 officers, 2180 men in Marine Corps units, with 2107 airplanes and 230 lighter-than-air vehicles. Of

The Curtiss H-12L flying boat used by the U.S. Navy during WWI as a patrol craft. Engines were 350-hp versions of the army's Liberty.

DeHavilland DH-4 at Fort Sill, Oklahoma, 1918.

Joe R. Reed collection

ries. There were 158 French aces, Capt. Rene Fonck being the greatest with 75. Of the 44 Italian aces, Maj. Francesco Baracca was tops with 34. Among the 360 German aces, Rttm. Manfred Frhr von Richthofen headed the list with 80 victories, and of the 83 American aces, Capt. Eddie Rickenbacker was the top scorer with 26 official victories.

These figures seem to suggest that U.S. Air Service pilots would have at least equalled the British record had the Americans been in combat a comparable length of time. It is a fair assumption. General Trenchard remarked on the "aggressiveness of the Americans," and a look at the service records of a few American aces underscores this observation. All were individualists, a trait not uncommon in a free society.

Take, for example, Elliot White Springs. His 12 air victories were topped by a half-dozen other U.S. pilots, but Springs typifies the attitudes, experiences, and the kind of young Americans who volunteered for the Air Service. Springs was a student at Princeton when the United States was forced into the war, a bright young man of small responsibility and large appetite for pleasure.

Thousands like Springs, in the best universities, were attracted to the Air Service because of newspaper accounts that had, throughout the previous year, lionized the aces and offered glowing accounts of chivalrous air duels in the skies of France. The air war was a romantic war, fought between fleet-winged machines in the crisp, unspoiled blue. The air war was a gentlemen's war.

Springs attended aviation ground school at Princeton, and in the fall of 1917 was sent to England with 209 others for flight training. Then, in May 1918, he was posted to RFC No. 85 Squadron, which was commanded by famed Canadian ace Maj. Billy Bishop (72 victories) and equipped with SE-5a fighters. The squadron was stationed near Petite Synthe, France, and Bishop allowed his rookies a few short patrols but forbade them to fly near the front lines. That, however, was asking too much of the impatient Springs. He took off alone and flew into Germany looking for enemy aircraft.

Springs didn't find the enemy; the enemy—a flight of six Pfalzes—found him. Somehow he managed to escape and returned to his field in a badly damaged airplane. At-

The Curtiss N-9H was the navy's version of the JN-4 Jenny trainer.

tempting to land his crippled machine, he careened into Major Bishop's SE-5 and destroyed that one as well.

The next day, Bishop led six of his pilots, including Springs, on patrol in the Courtrai area where, with the advantage of altitude, they attacked a formation of 12 black Pfalz fighters. Springs, determined to vindicate himself, shot down one of the enemy as two others fell before the guns of his squadron mates. Then, returning to 85 Squadron's field, Springs, in high spirits, hot-dogged over a

train for a dramatic landing—and wrecked his airplane.

Bishop determined that his eager rookie was unhurt, then sternly confronted him: "Well, Springs, pile up just two more SE-5s and you'll be a German ace. Whose side you on, anyway?"

The veteran Bishop knew, of course, that a fighter pilot's natural instincts should not be curbed, but directed. Springs would do well once a bit of responsibility was thrust upon him.

French-built Nieuport 17 fighters at the U.S. Air Service training school, Issoudun, France, 1917. These aircraft were flown by all the leading Allied aces.

There followed a period of several weeks during which 85 Squadron escorted DH-9s of RFC 311 Squadron to bomb the U-boat pens on Germany's north coast (311 also contained Americans). Then, in June, 85 Squadron was transferred to St. Omer to help repulse what was to be the last great German offensive of the war.

While at St. Omer, Bishop was sent home to Canada to organize a Canadian air force (Canadians and other Commonwealth airmen had been fighting in the RFC), and Lieutenant Springs was promoted to flight commander.

Springs scored two more victories before he took a burst of fire in his engine during a battle with a Hannoveraner (an armored two-seater designed for trench strafing) and went down just behind British lines. His face smashed into his gun butts as his plane flipped end-over-end. He was pulled from the wreckage in shock. Four days later, he slipped out of the hospital in his pajamas and hitched a ride back to his squadron.

Meanwhile, as planes and equipment became available, Patrick and Mitchell were reclaiming American airmen from the British and French and forming U.S. combat squadrons. The first of these, the 12th and the 94th, had begun operations in April 1918, but Springs and a number of other Americans with the RFC did not make the transition until July, when they were, at last, able to fight under their own flag as the 148th Aero Squadron of the U.S. Air Service.

The 148th was equipped with Sopwith Camels, fighter planes the British were replacing with the superior SE-5, as Gen. Trenchard reorganized the Royal Flying Corps and the aircraft of the Royal Navy into the independent Royal Air Force (RAF).

The *Camel* had its good qualities. "It could turn so fast it could bite its own tail," according to Charlie Meyers, an instructor at the U.S. Air Service training base, Issoudun, France. It had a fast rate-of-roll and was a good machine in a dogfight—if one had mastered the manipulation of its rotary engine.

The rotary radial engines, used by both sides in WWI, seem a bit incredible today. Their crankshafts were bolted solidly to the airframe, while the cylinders and propeller rotated together around the crankshaft. A rotary always ran at full throttle, and power was controlled by a button on the pilot's control stick which cut out the ignition. A great deal of blipping with the cut-out button was required on every flight, along with adjustments to a two-lever fuel/air mixture control. Castor oil was used for lubrication, and the average time-between-overhaul on the rotaries was about 20 flying hours.

On 22 August, 148th Squadron was ordered to destroy a troublesome German observation balloon, a highly dangerous assignment because the *drachens* were tethered by steel cable to winch trucks that were surrounded by anti-aircraft machine guns and fearsome devices known as "flaming onions" that formed a curtain of fire around the balloons. These hydrogen-filled "rubber elephants" could be hauled down very quickly as they were seldom raised above 1500 feet. The observer, suspended in a wicker basket, often took to his parachute when attacked, fearing a hydrogen explosion. (Balloon observers were the only airmen on either side equipped with parachutes until shortly before the war's end when some German pilots received them.)

Springs was unwilling to order any of his men to make the attack, so he took the mission himself, and assigned to his flight the job of keeping enemy fighters off of him while he was vulnerable at low altitude.

Springs planned the attack carefully, and dove on the *drachen* from out of the sun. He banked steeply away as it flamed and, continuing at low altitude through the hail of lead from the balloon's defenders, sped for home.

A few days later, while flying alone, Springs dove into a formation of five Fokkers, downing two of them before his guns jammed and he was forced to dive from the fray and make a run for his home field. He was on the ground just long enough to refuel and have his guns cleared, and then took off to aid an RAF observation plane under attack by three Fokkers over Bapaume.

Attacking out of the sun, Springs shot down one of the enemy fighters over Bapaume and, in a running fight that carried well into Germany, eventually downed the other two.

We single out Springs for this report not because of an unusual combat record, but rather because his actions were not unusual. The traits and abilities he displayed were fairly representative of all the young Americans who participated in that war. There were many others like him, in the trenches, at sea, and in the air. They were products of their time—naive, bold, idealistic. They were patriots, and they truly believed that they were fighting to "make the world safe for democracy."

The 148th Aero Squadron could count 66 enemy aircraft destroyed during its four months of combat. Rickenbacker's much-publicized 94th, in action three months longer, had 69 air victories.

America's second-ranking ace of WWI was less typical. In fact, he was one of those rare people who defy understanding. He obviously believed in the same things that most of the rest of us claim as our standards, but he was so uncompromising in these beliefs—even when death was the only alternative to compromise—that we can only look at him with uncomprehending awe. Lt. Frank Luke, Jr scored 21 victories in a 17-day period—and nine of those days he did not fly. It is doubtful that any U.S. airman before or since has equaled that record. Luke's primary targets were as dangerous as any he could have chosen: German observation balloons. And if that is not enough to mark him as one-of-a kind, consider this: Luke is the only man in the annals of flight to be awarded the Congressional Medal of Honor for a deed done while under military arrest.

Francis H. Dean collection

The Curtiss Jenny was the standard primary training plane of the U.S. Air Service during WWI. Powered with the 90-hp OX-5 engine, it had a top speed of about 75 mph. Approximately 6750 were built by Curtiss and several war-born firms, and surplus Jennies were the barnstormers' airplanes of the 1920s.

The Liberty engine was tested in eight-cylinder configuration atop Pike's Peak. Almost all Liberties were built as V-12s.

Lieutenant Frank Luke's story would make an absorbing book in itself, but not enough is really known about him to ensure that such a work would be accurate. Much of it would have to be speculation. We *do* know that he tended to be a loner, but on the other hand, former schoolmates characterized him as a pleasant fellow who made friends easily despite the fact that he wasn't much of a talker. A for-real John Wayne? Perhaps. As a native of Arizona, he spent much of his time as a teenager in the saddle. With a .30/30 carbine tucked in its scabbard close to his reins, he'd ride out of town trailing a pack animal and disappear for days. Some need within himself lured him into the heat-soaked desert and the silent mountains beyond. Perhaps it was a simple appreciation for raw nature—the

desert is beautiful to those who truly know it—perhaps a subtler siren beckoned.

Luke learned of America's declaration of war one day in April 1917, when he rode into a small mining town after days in the trackless wasteland. He returned home and told his parents that he had to enlist because it was his duty. He was 20 years old.

Luke chose the Air Service, and after primary flight training at North Island, was sent overseas for advanced training at Issoudun, France. He served as a ferry pilot for a time and was at last posted to combat duty with the 27th Aero Squadron late in July 1918. The 27th Aero Squadron was commanded by Maj. Harold Hartney and equipped with the French-built Spad.

Maj. Raoul Lufberry scored 17 victories as a member of the Lafayette Escadrille. He was killed soon after transferring to the U.S. Air Service.

Luke's first combat patrol came on 15 August, but no enemy aircraft were encountered. Several days later, after more "milk runs," Luke deserted his formation and dove down to destroy a German observation balloon. His airplane was so badly damaged in the encounter that it had to be junked. Hartney chewed him out for leaving the formation without permission, but when Billy Mitchell saw the report of the incident, he phoned Hartney and said that if Lieutenant Luke really wanted to "bust balloons," allow him to do so. Other pilots dreaded the assignment,

and since the enemy "sausages" directed a lot of artillery fire against the U.S. positions, their destruction was always gratefully acknowledged by ground commanders.

Luke accepted the mission, although Major Hartney warned that only one man could be spared to accompany Luke as top cover. Lt. Joseph Fritz Wehner immediately volunteered for that duty. He and Luke had become close friends during their brief acquaintance, perhaps because Wehner, too, had been cast from a different mold. Wehner had twice been arrested and questioned by army intelligence people, apparently because of his German background, because he had worked for the YMCA in German prison camps before the U.S. entered the war, and possibly because he spoke fluent German.

The Salmson observation plane was a superior French design operated by some U.S. units. The pilot had two forward-firing guns, and the observer had two flex-mounted Lewis guns.

While a new *Spad*—fitted with special .45-caliber machine guns, one of which would be armed with incendiary ammunition—was being made ready for Luke, the squadron moved up to Rembercourt, about 12 miles behind the front lines, to prepare for the great St. Mihiel offensive. Along with the move, the 27th Aero Squadron received a new commanding officer, Captain Grant, as Hartney was promoted to Group Commander.

The St. Mihiel offensive began on 12 September, but Luke remained on the ground because his new machine wasn't ready. Then, on the 14th, he took Wehner with him and shot down two balloons. Wehner attacked a formation of eight Fokkers to keep them off of Luke, and the two of them made it safely back to base with no serious damage to their aircraft.

The next day, Luke got two more balloons. Wehner shot down two enemy fighters that were intent on attacking Luke, then peeled off and flamed a balloon that Frank had not seen. On the ground again, the two of them laughed uproariously over that one.

By this time, the enemy had come to know this pair of *Spads* very well. On the morning of the 16th, when they appeared over the lines, every German balloon in the sector was quickly hauled down.

Frank and Joe returned to Rembercourt and waited for sunset. They decided to take off just before dark, stay low, and catch the *drachens* by surprise just before they were hauled down for the night. "We'll get three of them," Luke casually informed the squadron adjutant. "The first at 7:10, the second at 7:20, and the third at 7:30." They did. However, they were a few minutes late flaming the last one because they took time out to strafe an enemy truck convoy.

They remained on the ground the next day while the many bullet holes in their airplanes were patched, then returned to action on the 18th. Near Labeuville, they found a pair of balloons and Luke attacked while Wehner circled above.

It was an enemy trap. The sky was full of Fokkers before Luke completed his first pass. The enemy fighters had apparently managed to track Wehner and Luke directly up-sun where they could not be seen. Stubbornly, Luke held his dive, and as the first balloon began to burn from a short burst from his guns, he levelled off very low and came upon the second balloon from underneath. It exploded behind him as he made a steep climbing turn in a bid for altitude. A glance behind revealed

A German Hannoveraner CL-II observation craft forced down intact 2 October 1918 by U.S. pilots Reed Chambers and Eddie Rickenbacker after observer was killed and pilot wounded.

two enemy fighters dropping on his tail. Wehner was right behind them, guns aflame, but the remaining Fokkers were closing in behind Wehner.

Luke nosed down again to gain speed, reversed direction with an Immelmann turn, rolled inverted, and split-essed to bring his guns to bear on the closest of Wehner's attackers. A short burst directly into the enemy's cockpit sent that one down. Rolling to his right, Luke got the next one as well before he was forced to level off only a few feet above the ground. It was frustrating trying to fight with so little space between him and the ground in which to maneuver. As his airspeed built up once again, he looked around to evaluate the situation. The remaining enemy fighters were breaking off the engagement. Wehner was nowhere in sight.

Low on fuel and countless bullet holes in his machine, Luke turned for home. On the way, he stumbled onto a German observation plane and shot it down with a short burst into the pilot's cockpit. It was his fifth victory within ten minutes, but he did not know then that he would drink no toast with Joe Wehner that evening. The Fokkers had shot down Wehner over Labeuville.

Luke's official report of that mission is very brief and closes with: "Confirmations requested, two balloons, three planes . . . Lieu-

tenant Wehner is entitled to share in the victories . . . " (Wehner had eight confirmed victories when he died.)

That evening, Major Hartney (an ace in his own right, and aware of the close bond between Luke and Wehner) came down from headquarters and ordered Luke to take a week's leave in Paris. Luke went, but was back at the end of three days, asking to be returned to duty. Hartney stalled for several days, believing that Luke needed rest, but by 26 September Luke was back in the air. Lt. Ivan Roberts volunteered to fly with him.

As they crossed the lines into enemy territory, they were joined by another *Spad* from a neighboring squadron. Then, in the vicinity of Consonvoye and Sivry, Luke spotted a large formation of Albatros fighters and led his three-plane element to the attack. Luke downed one of the enemy almost at once, but was forced to dive away from the fight when his guns jammed. Lieutenant Roberts did not return.

Luke seemed to brood over the loss of Roberts, apparently blaming himself. He took a motorcycle and left the field without permission, and when that drew a reprimand from Captain Grant, Luke simply went to his plane and took off, also without permission.

He found a German balloon over Bantheville, but was unable to reach it before it was pulled down. He turned away as if disinterested, but then, a few minutes later, roared in on the deck and exploded the drachen in its nest.

He did not return to the 27th's field, but spent the night with the *Cigognes* ("Storks"), a famed French fighter squadron, flying back to his own base the next day. Captain Grant immediately grounded him. Luke responded by taking off again, telling his mechanic that he would have his plane serviced at a temporary forward aerodrome commanded by Captain Vasconcelles. Grant's reaction to that was a phone call to Vasconcelles ordering Luke's arrest.

Vasconcelles apologetically relayed this order to Luke. But, when Major Hartney landed there a few minutes later, Vasconcelles re-

Crew of U.S. observation balloon prepare to launch.

U.S. sausage balloon explodes on ground, 1918.

Captain Eddie Rickenbacker (left) was America's leading ace in WWI, with 26 victories. Captain Douglas Campbell (center) scored six victories. Major Kenneth Marr at right.

Lieutenant Frank Luke, Jr. and his Spad fighter

Recently discovered rare photo is believed to be of Luke just as he flamed a German drachen.

mained silent when Luke casually asked for—and received—Hartney's permission to attack three *drachens* hanging in the sky near Dun along the east bank of the Meuse River. Hartney was unaware of the arrest order.

Lieutenant Joseph F. Wehner flew top cover for Luke.

Luke took off just at sunset. He stayed low and caught the first balloon crew by surprise, but left a flaming beacon in the air that quickly brought a flight of eight Fokkers that had apparently been waiting for the lone Spad and its sundown attacks.

Luke destroyed the second balloon before he was forced to turn on the Fokkers and attempt to deal with them. He shot down two of them (many believed that Luke was the best aerial marksman on the Western Front), then broke away to get the third balloon which was hastily being hauled down near Milly. As the third *drachen*, exploded, Luke swung over the village of Murvaux and strafed a column of German infantry, then landed in a field beyond with a dead engine.

He jumped from his cripped plane, Colt .45 automatic in hand, and tried to escape toward the river, but enemy soldiers cut him off. From the gathering darkness, they called upon him to surrender. He replied with his Colt.

It was futile, of course, but Luke never wavered. He fell from chest wounds, with an empty pistol in his hand.

On the Allied side of the lines, Luke was listed as "missing in action" until two months after war's end. Observers at the front had seen the three balloons go down, but that was all that was known about Luke's last flight until U.S. Graves Registration Officers reached the village of Murvaux in January 1919. Their first report read:

From: Graves Registration Officer, Neufchateau Area No. 1.
To: Chief of Air Service, APO 717.
Subject: Grave, unknown American aviator.

1. Units of this service have located the grave of an unknown aviator killed on Sunday, 29 September 1918 in the village of Murvaux.
2. From inspection of the grave and interviews held with inhabitants of this town, the following information was learned in regard to this aviator and his heroism. He is reported as having light hair, young, of medium height, and of heavy stature.
3. Reported by the inhabitants that previous to being killed this man had brought down three German balloons, two German airplanes, and dropped hand bombs killing German soldiers and wounding others.
4. He was wounded himself in the shoulder and evidently had to make a forced landing. Upon landing he opened fire with his automatic pistol and fought until he was killed.
5. It is also reported that the Germans took his shoes, leggings, and money, leaving his grave unmarked.

(Chester E. Staten, Captain of Infantry, G.R.S. Officer)

Upon receipt of this report, General Mitchell ordered further investigation that turned up Luke's wrist watch, which was under the sleeve of his flying suit and which the Germans had missed. An affidavit signed by the mayor and 14 inhabitants of Murvaux provided the eyewitness account upon which the Graves Registration officer's report was based. Later, this affidavit was verified by Lt. B. Mangels of Monster, Germany, who com-

manded German balloons numbers 35 and 64 of the 5th German Army, the last two destroyed by Luke that fateful Sunday. (*Note:* Previously published accounts of Luke's last flight do not agree with this presentation. However, it appears that those versions were written without benefit of the official records, particularly, the report of Captain Staten, and the much more detailed affidavit sworn to by the villagers of Murvaux. One such story mentions the affidavit, but then misquotes it. There is no need to tamper with the facts. The villagers' impression that Luke dropped "hand bombs" on the enemy infantry is the kind of natural mistake one expects when the witnesses are unfamiliar with airplanes. Luke's twin .45-caliber machine guns could create a lot of havoc in the narrow, dusty street of Murvaux. The villagers also believed that Luke landed in order to get a drink of water from the river, but in all other details their account agrees with that of Lieutenant Mangels, the German balloon commander.)

Luke's body was removed to the American cemetery at Romagne and buried with full military honors. He was posthumously awarded the Distinguished Service cross, France's Croix-de-Guerre, and America's highest military award, the Congressional Medal of Honor.

## Review questions

1. When was the First Aero Squadron established? Describe its makeup—aircraft and personnel. What was its first duty assignment? Why did the United States fall so far behind the Europeans in aircraft development?

2. What was the role of aircraft at the beginning of the war? How did this change? Identify some of the fighter aircraft used by both sides during the war.

3. Why did the U.S. aircraft manufacturers choose to build training aircraft and the

British de Havilland DH-4 instead of our own fighter aircraft? What were some of the problems encountered? How did President Wilson correct the production problem?

4. How was Billy Mitchell's philosophy of air power influenced by General Hugh Trenchard? Give an example of how Mitchell implemented some of his ideas during the latter part of the war.

5. What was the role of the U.S. Naval Air Service during the war? Why did the navy's commander in chief, Admiral Mayo, refuse to commend the war effort of Naval aviation?

6. Who were some of the leading aces on both sides of the conflict? Describe several of the combat episodes involving such American aces as Elliot White Springs and Frank Luke.

7. Why do you think that the news media romanticized the role of the fliers, dubbing them "Knights of the Air" and reporting, in great detail, their adventures in aerial combat?

# 3

# The wings grow stronger

## Objectives

At the end of this chapter you should be able to:

- Understand the prevailing attitude of the U.S. military in the immediate post WWI period.

- Recognize the burdens placed on Germany as a result of the Treaty of Versailles which led to political and economic instability.

- Describe the first successful flights across the Atlantic by Lieutenant Commander Read, Alcock and Brown, and Maj. G. H. Scott.

- Explain why General Mitchell had his army pilots attempt a number of head-line flights.

- Describe the first flight around the world by the U.S. Army Air Service.

U.S. military aircraft were improved during the two decades between WWI and WWII, but little credit for those advances can be given to America's leaders, either civilian or military. Military planning, at the highest levels, reverted to pre-WWI concepts. The Atlantic and Pacific Oceans were viewed as America's great natural barriers to foreign aggression, and the U.S. Navy was regarded as the primary defender of American shores—indeed, the entire Western Hemisphere. The Monroe Doctrine, which served notice to the world that the United States would tolerate no "outside" intervention into the affairs of any North, Central, or South American nation, was an unambiguous cornerstone of U.S. foreign policy.

Because every American knew that the United States was not going to start a war anywhere, there was really no need to maintain a large, well-equipped army. American arms were for defense only. Such a posture seemed perfectly reasonable at the time. (If man were half as civilized as he should be, it would be reasonable today.) Unfortunately, the bitter seeds that would blossom into WWII were planted at the conclusion of WWI, and America's determination to avoid future involvement in Europe's squabbles would fade when it appeared that the Nazis could well become the rulers of all Europe, including Great Britain.

It was the terms of the peace treaty signed with Germany at the close of WWI—in a railway coach at Versailles, France, 28 June 1919—that led to the Nazi takeover of Germany. Had it not been the Nazis, a similar movement almost certainly would have evolved, because the Treaty of Versailles doomed Germany to economic servitude and the status of a second-class nation.

Military budgets of the early '20s forced the Air Service to fly the WWI DH-4s. A DH-4 training flight at Fort Sill ended against a barbed wire fence.

Germany was stripped of all her overseas territories, along with 25,000 square miles of Germany itself, and the Allies demanded that Germany pay billions in "reparations." There was no way that a bankrupt Germany could pay, in either money or goods, but the French, especially, were adamant and repeatedly sent troops into a prostrate Germany in attempts to force the Germans to pay. Many other sanctions were imposed, including the provision that Germany be allowed no military aircraft of any kind. In short, the Treaty of Versailles, which the United States refused to sign, made it impossible for Germany to regain political and economic stability. By 1923, German money was worthless and there were food riots in the streets of Berlin.

Nevertheless, the Allies did not relent, and in 1930 the final amount that Germany must pay in damages was set at 121 billion Reichmarks. Two years later, German unemploy-ment passed the six million mark, and the following January Adolf Hitler was elected chancellor of Germany, brought to power by eleven years of political and economic turmoil. True, the Nazis received only 33 percent of the vote in the election and Hitler, was, in effect, a compromise candidate. But all Germany, after years of deprivation and humiliation, was ready to follow a leader who could quicken its national pulse with visions of a new pride, prosperity, and Germany's return to its rightful place in the world.

During this period the American people, their representatives in Congress, and their presidents believed that the United States could avoid future wars with other major powers, especially if no entangling commitments were made overseas. The U.S. Army shrunk to 137,000 officers and men during the 20's as military appropriations dwindled. The Air Service stood at the end of the line for its share. The Air Service/Air Corps' average yearly expenditure from authorized appropriations was $25 million for the years 1921 through 1938 inclusive, while average personnel strength for those years was less than 14,000 officers and men.

For the first ten years after WWI General Pershing dominated War Department policy. Although he had, during the closing weeks of the late war, been given a glimpse of the airplane's potential as a military weapon, he did not project that lesson into planning for the future defense of the nation. He removed General Patrick from his post as Chief of Air Service and replaced him with Gen. Charles Menoher, an infantry commander with no background in aviation. General Billy Mitchell was appointed Menoher's deputy, and that epitomized the War Department's attitude toward the Air Service: Mitchell was able; Menoher was army. That priority of command would continue until the eve of WWII.

The navy, meanwhile, actually had several top officers who recognized the airplane's potential value to the fleet, among them Admirals Fiske, Fullam and Sims. Primarily due to their influence, the navy kept its aviation program alive after the war ended and, in 1919, decided to test the efficacy of large flying boats as long-range patrol craft by attempting to fly the Atlantic. That decision may have been given a little boost by the fact that Glenn Curtiss had built a flying boat early in 1914 expressly for that purpose, although war came before the flight could be attempted. Then, the navy contracted with Curtiss to build four large flying boats that could be flown to Europe for submarine patrol. However, only the first of those, the NC-1, was completed by war's end.

## First Atlantic flight

Rear Adm. Douglas Taylor, apparently abetted by Comdr. John Tower (one of the navy's first pilots) seems to have been the one who initially pushed for the Atlantic flight and who obtained permission from the Secretary of the Navy Josephus Daniels to complete the NC-2 through NC-4 sister craft for that ambitious project. The NC-2 was cannibalized to provide components for aircraft numbers one and four which were damaged in a hangar fire. On 8 May 1919, planes NC-1, NC-3 and NC-4 left Rockaway Beach, Long Island bound for Plymouth, England, by way of Newfoundland, the Azores, Portugal, and France.

The NCs (for "Navy-Curtiss;" inevitably called the "Nancies") were large for their time.

USAF

The Orenco D fighter was a 1918 U.S. design fitted with a 300-hp Hispano engine that had a speed of 139 mph. Curtiss built 50 for the Air Service in 1920.

The Douglas C-1 was the standard army transport of the '20s. It was Liberty-powered.

Wingspan was 126 ft, hull length was 45 ft, and each was powered with four 400-hp Liberty engines mounted in nacelles between the wings, a tractor and a pusher mounted back-to-back in the center nacelle with a tractor on either side. All-up weight was 28,000 lbs and cruising speed was 77 mph.

Delayed by engine trouble and weather, the three planes at last left Newfoundland on 16 May headed for the Azores, 1200 miles away.

Approximately half of the flight was made in darkness and much of the rest through recurring patches of fog. The NC-1 landed on the ocean in dense fog about 300 miles short of its destination, and the NC-3 did the same 100 miles away. The crew of the NC-1 was picked up by a passing ship, although their airplane sank in heavy seas. Commander Towers taxied the damaged NC-3 on the surface, arriving in the harbor at Horta, in the Azores, 60 hours later, his airplane a wave-battered wreck.

Meanwhile, Lt. Comdr. Albert C. Read and his five-man crew aboard the NC-4 had flown nonstop from Newfoundland to Horta in 15 hours and 18 minutes. They left Horta on

the 20th, after a two-day rest, and flew on to Lisbon by way of Ponta Delgada, and ended their epic flight at Plymouth, England, on 31 May. The U.S. Navy was first to fly the Atlantic—but just barely.

Two weeks later, on 14 June 1919, RAF Capt. John Alcock and Lt. Arthur Whitten-Brown took off from Newfoundland in a British bomber, the twin-engined Vickers Vimy and, after 16 hours and 28 minutes (1890 miles) at an average speed of 118.5 mph, landed at Clifden, Ireland, to claim a cash price of $50,000 offered by a British newspaper publisher for the first transatlantic nonstop flight.

Two weeks after *that*, on 2 July 1919, the British rigid airship R.34 left Scotland bound for New York. The R.34, commanded by RAF Maj. G.H. Scott and carrying a crew of 30, landed in New York on 6 July after covering a distance of 3600 miles in 108 hours. On 9 July, Scott turned his airship around and flew back to the British Isles, thus completing the first aerial round trip across the Atlantic.

Eight years later, Charles A. Lindbergh would fly alone nonstop from New York to

Paris in a single-engine monoplane, and that would be the aerial crossing of the Atlantic that would capture the fancy of the world and convince people everywhere that the airplane had become a reliable and useful machine to serve mankind.

In the meantime, several other Atlantic flights were attempted. Most ended in disaster, although the German rigid airship, Zeppelin ZR-3, was flown to America in mid-October 1924, by a German aircrew comanded by Dr. Hugo Eckener, and presented to the U.S. Navy as part payment on war damages claimed by the United States. (The United States did ask for some reparations, although the amount was comparatively small and no serious effort to collect was made. The United States and Germany signed a separate peace treaty in 1921.)

The NC-4's successful Atlantic crossing had a predictable effect on Gen. Billy Mitchell. In the fall of 1919, he sent 60 of the army's DH-4s across the United States in a "reliability" test. Thirty flew westward from New York as 30 others left San Francisco. Several were lost,

and nothing much was proved, although it could be said that the Air Service had blazed a trail which the air mail (begun on a limited basis by Air Service planes in 1918) would later follow.

The following June (1920), four DHs, commanded by Capt. St. Clair Street, flew from New York to Nome, Alaska. They returned in October, having covered 4345 miles (much of it over unchartered wilderness) in 112 flying hours.

## Army and navy racers

Because Air Service budgets—about five percent of the army's total budgets—did not allow the acquisition of new airplanes in significant number, Mitchell convinced his boss, General Patrick (who replaced Menoher in 1921), that what money they had should be spent on headline-grabbing flights that would impress the public in general and the Congress in particular, especially as such activities could be justified as useful research and development. Accordingly, the Air Service (quickly followed by the navy, of course), fostered the

USN

The four Curtiss-built NC flying boats were designed at the Naval Aircraft Factory. Powered with four Liberties (one pusher and three tractors), three of these craft attempted the first Atlantic flight in 1919.

The navy's NC-4, commanded by Lt. Comdr. A.C. Read, proudly taxies into the harbor at Lisbon, Portugal, 27 May 1919, after completing the first transatlantic flight from Trepassey, Newfoundland.

design and construction of a series of racing planes to compete in several popular international air races during the early twenties. The army and navy Curtiss racers dominated these events. The publicity returned no discernible benefits, and the U.S. Congress remained as stingy with appropriations as ever. However, the races did prove the new Curtiss D-12 engine of 435 hp—a vast improvement over the wartime Liberty—and the D-12 would power army fighter planes throughout the '20s and lead to the development of far more powerful engines of the same type.

The Curtiss D-12, a V-12 water-cooled engine, was developed by Finlay Porter from a design initiated by a long-time Curtiss engineman Charles Kirkham. It featured cast cylinder blocks, which, up to that time, had not been successful in aircraft engines of that power. The British were so impressed with the D-12 that the Air Ministry purchased one and gave it to Rolls-Royce, along with an appropriate government subsidy, to copy or improve. The result was the 1295 cubic-inch Kestrel of 480 hp which went into production in May 1928. By 1937 the Kestrel XVI was rated at 750 hp as installed in the RAF's Hawker Fury

fighters, and it was this engine, with its displacement raised to 1650, that became the famed Merlin of WWII.

Ironically, Curtiss, after developing the D-12 into the 600-hp *Conqueror* (which powered the last of America's biplane fighters) decided, in 1931, to discontinue development of liquid-cooled aircraft engines, and in America that role went by default to the (then) tiny Allison Division of General Motors. Allison was given a navy contract at that time to build five such engines for possible use on its big rigid dirigibles. That engine, the Allison V-1710, was never installed in a dirigible. By the time it was ready for delivery, the navy's *Akron* and *Macon* had both crashed, but it was concurrently developed during the mid-30s with the British Merlin to become a principal WWII fighter airplane powerplant. But all this takes us ahead of our story.

## First world flight

Because the navy gained as much from the well-publicized air races of the early '20s as did the army, Billy Mitchell came up with another idea. Although his bombers had, at least to his own satisfaction, demonstrated in 1921, and again in 1923, that the most impregnable battleship was vulnerable to air attack (about which, more later), the Air Service needed to demonstrate its potential versatility in an even more dramatic fashion. Mitchell took his idea to General Patrick who officially announced it late in 1923: The U.S. Army Air Service would fly around the world!

That was, indeed, a bold undertaking, viewed against the background of air progress up to that time. There would be a few landing fields, no navigational aids, no radio, and no weather reports. The art of instrument flying was still far in the future, and the fliers themselves would have to perform all maintenance on their machines—a truly herculean task since it would include half a dozen complete engine changes in each of the four planes. They dared not trust the Liberty engine beyond 50 hours of flight, and it was the only engine of sufficient power available. (The new Curtiss D-12 was still in test and had been operated for only short periods in the military racers.)

A small California airframe builder, Donald Douglas, was awarded a contract to build five World Cruisers, four of which would attempt the journey with the fifth held in reserve. Douglas was 28 years old in 1920 when he opened for business in the rear of a barber shop with $600 in capital. But he had a degree from M.I.T., which he had earned in two years, and a year's experience working for Glenn Martin, during which time he designed the prototype of the Martin bombers in army service during the 20's. Douglas had sold some torpedo planes to the navy and, when he began design and construction of the World Cruisers, had a payroll of 112 and occupied an abandoned movie studio just off Wilshire Boulevard in eastern Santa Monica.

The World Cruisers, which were identical, had a wingspan of 50 ft, maximum weight of 8200 lbs, service ceiling of 8000 ft, and a normal cruise near 90 mph. These were hefty, two-place, open-cockpit biplanes with fittings for either floats or wheels because both would be needed in different parts of the world. Their

The navy's Curtiss CR-2 racer, fitted with a Curtiss D-12 engine, attained an average speed of 193.2 mph around a closed course in the 1922 Pulitzer race.

crews were selected by General Patrick from among hundreds of volunteers.

The crews and their planes were: Maj. F.L. Martin and Sgt. Alva Harvey in World Cruiser #1, the *Seattle*; Lts. Lowell Smith and Leslie Arnold in #2, the *Chicago*; Lt. Leigh Wade and Sgt. Henry Ogden in #3, the *Boston*, and Lts. Erik Nelson and John Harding in #4, the *New Orleans*.

Equipped with floats, the four planes left Seattle shortly after sunrise on 6 April 1924 and followed the Inside Passage to Alaska through spring blizzards—one of which claimed the *Seattle* when Major Martin, blinded by snow, literally flew into the ground. Neither he nor Harvey was seriously injured; they walked out to civilization on their own, while the remaining three cruisers continued across the North Pacific with Lt. Lowell Smith in command.

The adventures of the three remaining crews would (and did) fill a book in itself. Weather forced them down in Russian waters off the Komandorski Islands, but as the ceiling lifted, Smith led the flight into Paramushiru, navigating, as he did the entire trip, by dead reckoning. The Air Service had accomplished the first aerial crossing of the Pacific.

The cruisers flew southward over Japan's 4000 home islands to Tokyo where, for the second time, the crews installed new engines, and then fought heavy rains down the South China Coast to Saigon in what was then French Indochina. The *Chicago's* engine blew up over the Gulf of Tonkin, but Smith hired a native to tow the plane with a fleet of sampans to a village dock where a new *Liberty* delivered by a navy destroyer, was quickly installed. The *Chicago* joined the other two planes in Saigon from where the flight turned northwestward for Bangkok, Rangoon, and Calcutta.

Switching from floats to wheels, the three cruisers left Calcutta on 1 July and made good time across India despite a newspaperman stowaway in the *Boston's* tool compartment, sandstorms, and the oppressive heat until, a few miles short of Karachi, the *New Orleans'* engine began to disintegrate. With oil bathing the entire nose of the airplane, Lieutenant Nelson managed to reach Karachi.

Another engine change for the three aircraft required two days, then the fliers were off for Bagdad on 7 July. Later, they were beset by sandstorms over the Arabian Desert and

USAF

The army Curtiss R3C-1 was first in the 1925 Pulitzer race with an average speed of 249 mph; engine was the new Curtiss Conqueror, a 600-hp, glycol-cooled V-12.

The Curtiss D-12 (V-1150) engine of 400 to 460 hp

The *New Orleans*, flown by Lts. Erik Nelson and Jack Harding, was one of the two Douglas World Cruisers to complete the first around-the-world flight, 6 April to 28 September 1924.

Uncovered forward fuselage reveals fuel tanks beneath seats of the Liberty-powered World Cruisers.

threaded their way through passes in the Taurus Mountains. The Cruiser's 8000-ft service ceiling did not permit them to climb over the mountains. They reached Constantinople on 11 July, and five days later were in London.

By then, the six airmen were international heroes. This caused a problem because crowds awaited their arrival at every stop and officials in each city along their route planned ceremonies and dinners in their honor. The fliers understood that they were representing the United States and therefore had to smile through a lot of speeches and try to remain awake through a lot of formal dinners they would have much preferred to have skipped. It all took time, and they badly needed that time to rest and to work on their airplanes.

In England, the planes received new engines and had wheels replaced by floats once again, while the U.S. Navy positioned ships in the North Atlantic along the Cruisers' course and rushed fuel to planned stops in Iceland and Greenland. No airplane had ever been to either place.

The North Atlantic, however, would exact its price. The *Boston* was forced down at sea with a dead engine. Although the navy ship *Billingsby* rescued Wade and Ogden, their airplane sank in heavy seas.

The *Chicago* and *New Orleans* continued the flight and, after a navy-assisted engine change in each plane on the Greenland Coast, and a link-up with Wade and Ogden in Nova Scotia on 3 September (where General Patrick had sent the reserve Cruiser, christened *Boston II*), the world fliers reached Boston on 6 September, and were back at their starting point at Seattle on 28 September 1924, having

The *Boston* goes down in the North Atlantic after rescue of her crew, Lts. Leigh Wade and Henry Ogden

been mobbed and laden with gifts at every stop across the United States.

The total distance flown was 26,345 miles, and the *Chicago* and *New Orleans* had been in the air 363 hours and seven minutes at an average speed of 72.5 mph. The fact that the journey required 177 days elapsed time primarily reflected the inadequacies of the Cruisers' engines. Each plane used nine engines averaging slightly more than 40 hours on each, yet the fliers still suffered four engine failures. When it is realized that the fliers themselves performed seven of those changes, usually under primitive conditions (the Liberty engine weighed more than 700 lbs) and attended to all other servicing of their aircraft, their feat appears all the more remarkable.

There wasn't much navy fliers could do to top the army's world flight, which undeniably added to America's prestige abroad, and except for General Patrick and the crews of the World Cruisers, all of whom sent warm notes

of thanks to the navy, few others stopped to consider that the flight would not have been completed without the navy's help, particularly over the North Atlantic.

Meanwhile, Gen. Billy Mitchell, looking to the future, had just completed an extensive tour of the Far East. On 24 October 1924, he submitted a 325-page secret report to the War Department in which he warned of a coming war with Japan:

". . . the Japanese have specialized on their air force since 1918 . . . it now appears that the Japanese are probably the second air power in the world with between 600 and 800 airplanes . . . Japan estimates that, if war comes, America will begin the war with the methods and systems of the last war . . . She knows that war is coming someday with the United States . . . Air operations for the destruction of Pearl Harbor will be undertaken . . . the attack to be made on Ford's Island at 7:30 A.M. . . . nothing can stop it except air power . . . the Philippines will be

Left to right: Lt. Lowell H. Smith, Secretary of War John Weeks, Maj. Gen. Mason Patrick, Brig. Gen. William Mitchell, Lts. Erik Nelson and Leigh Wade

attacked in a similar manner . . . The initial success, as things stand now, will probably be with the Japanese."

Mitchell's sadly prophetic 1924 secret report was ignored by the War Department (now the "Department of Defense"), and Mitchell became ever more public in his crusade for a strong and independent Air Force.

# Review questions

1. What was the prevailing attitude of the U.S. military in the immediate post WWI period? Why was so little thought given to the potential of air power? Why can it be said that "the terms of the peace treaty signed with Germany . . . led to the Nazi takeover of Germany"?

2. Who was the first pilot to successfully fly across the Atlantic in a specially built Curtiss seaplane? Who were the first airmen to fly nonstop from Newfoundland to Ireland? What was the significance of the flight of the R-34?

3. What was the reason for General Mitchell to stage so many spectacular and record-breaking flights during the early 1920s? What was the reaction of Congress and the public?

4. Describe the first flight around the world by pilots of the U.S. Army Air Service. Who built the aircraft for this flight? How did the War Department respond to General Mitchell's secret report regarding Japanese military air power?

# 4

# Naval air and Billy Mitchell

## Objectives

At the end of this chapter you should be able to:

- Identify some of the early proponents of naval air power.
- Discuss the significance of the sinking of the German battleship *Ostfriesland* by Mitchell's bombers.
- Summarize the development of the Wright Whirlwind and Pratt and Whitney Wasp engines.
- Identify several navy dirigibles and briefly describe their primary function.
- Describe the events leading up to the court-martial of Billy Mitchell.
- Highlight the purpose and findings of the Morrow Board.

Rear Adm. William Adger Moffett demonstrated that a man may prevail against the errors of his friends if only his enemies will help a little. Admiral Moffett greatly advanced U.S. Naval aviation during the '20s. He did so despite anti-airplane prejudices held by the old sea dogs who were his superiors, because he was aided—unintentionally, of course—by a man he detested. That man was the army's Brig. Gen. William Mitchell, who consistently made the issue of U.S. Airpower front-page news and thereby kept the blood pressures of the "battleship admirals" at dangerously high levels.

William Moffett had risen to the rank of captain in the battleship navy when in March 1921 he was appointed "Director of Naval Aviation," an office tucked into the navy's planning division, and which was not expected to do much directing. The office was useful primarily as the authority responsible for whatever went *wrong* in naval air operations, while direct control of the air units was spread among the several commands to which the units were attached.

This piecemeal administration meant that no single voice possessing real authority could speak for naval air, and that's just the way most of the ranking officers wanted it. The Chief of Naval Operations, Adm. William S. Benson, had spoken for the saltiest of them when he declared, "The navy doesn't need airplanes. Aviation is just a lot of noise."

There were, however, a few top naval officers who had a different view and the courage to say so. These included Adms. Bradley Fiske, William S. Sims, and W.F. Fullam. None was radical in his thinking, and none suggested that airplanes could supplant warships in the nation's defense. They were simply agreed that the navy needed airplanes, and recommended to the Secretary of the Navy in 1919 a development program that would establish a naval air service "capable of accompanying and operating with the fleet in all waters of the globe."

This recommendation, the last of a series forwarded by the Navy's General Board, was endorsed in its essentials by Navy Secretary Josephus Daniels. Daniels added an earlier request for funds to build a rigid dirigible, along with Admiral Sims's strong plea for an aircraft carrier, and then sought congressional approval. That followed on 11 July 1919, with passage of the Naval Appropriations Act for fiscal 1920.

Congressional approval, while necessary, was not a guarantee. Money for naval air was buried within the total navy appropriation, and naval aviation would stand at the end of the line for its share when the navy's budget bureau divvied-up the cash. Thus, the aircraft carrier that Admiral Sims had hoped for turned out to be a coal barge, the collier *Jupiter* that was to be converted by addition of a flight deck, and the request for 108 fighter aircraft to equip America's first aircraft carrier was first cut to 75, and finally to ten.

Even that was too much to suit Admiral Benson. In the fall of 1920, he countermanded the order to convert the *Jupiter*. But Capt. Thomas T. Craven, who was then Director of Naval Aviation, managed to get a direct order from Secretary Daniels and work on the *Jupiter* was resumed.* That cost Craven his job. Shortly after the crews returned to work on the *Jupiter*, he was replaced by Captain Moffett.

Moffett took over Craven's desk at a propitious time. Throughout the previous year, newspapers around the country had given a lot of space to Gen. Billy Mitchell's crusade for

Major. General Patrick (left), and Billy Mitchell. Patrick, as Chief of Air Service, was Mitchell's boss and quiet supporter from 1921 until Mitchell was forced to leave the service four years later.

an independent air force, and his claim, made before several Senate committees, that the airplane had rendered the navy's surface ships obsolete. Because 1920 was an election year, the issues Mitchell raised probably received more national attention than would have otherwise been the case. His seemingly far-out pronouncements on political/military matters were custom-made to fit charges of waste, outdated policies, and maladministration at high government levels.

A few days before President Harding took office in March 1921, the War Department announced that several German warships, taken as prizes under terms of the Treaty of Versailles, would be destroyed in naval ordnance tests. General Mitchell reacted predictably, and the nation's press enthusiastically took up his challenge to the navy that the Air Service be allowed to prove that airplanes could sink battleships.

This at last prodded the navy into covering its own aviation bets. Clearly, if Mitchell's

---

\* The office of Chief of Naval Operations was established 2 March 1915, and the scope of CNO's authority was challenged for years thereafter by the navy bureau chiefs. Not until President Truman issued Executive Order 9635 on 29 September 1945 were CNO's authority and duties clearly defined.

Martin GMB (above) and Martin MB-2 were the bombers sent by Mitchell to prove that airplanes could sink battleships in 1921. Left to right: Donald Douglas, test pilot Eric Springer, and Lawrence Bell.

USAF

preachments should gain significant support in Congress, then it was at least possible that an independent air force, of (God forbid!) co-equal status, could emerge, and the effect of *that* on naval appropriations was too frightening to consider. Therefore, prudence dictated that the navy quickly establish a substantial legal equity in its own air service.

Congress obliged on 1 July 1921 with an act that created a Naval Bureau of Aeronautics (BuAer), "possessing such responsibilities and authority pertaining to naval air as the Secretary shall prescribe." When this office began to function on the first of September, Moffett, as its director, was elevated to the rank of rear admiral.

Meanwhile, on 21 July, an 11-plane formation of Mitchell's bombers had, indeed, sent the German battleship *Ostfriesland* to the bottom with two direct hits and four near-misses employing 2000-pound bombs. At the time, that seemed to prove everything or nothing, depending upon one's prejudices. Ultimate proof would wait upon another day—a Sunday morning in Hawaii, to be described as a day that would "live in infamy."

It should be noted that Congresses of this period reflected little polarization of opinion over "Mitchellism." Mitchell's opinions occasioned no great debates on Capitol Hill, probably because most lawmakers saw no urgent need for major changes in the defense alignment in the absence of a definite threat. In any case, military spending was certain to remain at a minimal level for the foreseeable future.

62 *Naval air and Billy Mitchell*

Developed at navy insistence, the Wright J-5 Whirlwind was America's first truly reliable and efficient air-cooled radial aircraft engine.

The nation was recovering from the effects of WWI, and Harding had won the Presidency with the slogan, "Back to Normalcy."

But whatever one's views on Mitchellism, it must be credited with aiding (however unintentionally) at a critical time the cause of that small band of visionaries within the navy that recognized the developing need for a strong naval air arm. With establishment of the Bureau of Aeronautics, headed by an officer of flag rank, naval aviation had its *Magna Carta*—albeit a poorly funded one—and a secure anchorage to attract gifted, airminded personnel.

## Navy aircraft engine development

Among such personnel was Lt. Comdr. Bruce G. Leighton, Naval Aviator No. 40, a pleasant, outgoing type chosen by Moffett to head up the bureau's Aircraft Engine Section. Leighton and his engine program typified the kind of officer and the kind of action that gave BuAer its special character under Moffett. The soft-spoken Moffett believed in encouraging initiative. He told his subordinates what he wanted, but seldom how to accomplish it. That sometimes resulted in methods he may not have chosen, but which he always stood ready to support. He knew that loyalty begets loyalty, and future commanders must learn to command. It was an approach that paid great returns in Leighton's case, not only for the navy, but for the army and civil aviation as well, because Lieutenant Commander Leighton jawboned private industry into the development of the most successful aircraft piston engines ever built, the Wright *Whirlwinds* and the Pratt & Whitney *Wasps*.

Leighton was pointed in the right direction at the outset, because the officer previously responsible for the navy's aircraft engines, Lt. Comdr. S.M. Kraus in the Bureau of Steam Engineering, had determined that the air-cooled static radial engine ("static" as opposed to the rotary-type radial engines of WWI), was best suited to the navy's needs if it could be made reliable. It promised more horsepower for less weight, and would be easier and cheaper to maintain than the water-cooled engines then available. Therefore, Kraus had obtained some navy money to foster development of the Lawrance Model J, a radial design of 200 hp with which Kraus hoped to power the small fighters that would be needed if and when Admiral Sims got his aircraft carrier.

The Lawrance J was the product of tiny Lawrance Aero Engines Company, operated by Charles Lanier Lawrance, who had switched from automobile to airplane engine design after working for Allesandro Anzani in Paris prior to WWI. Returning to the United States in 1914, Lawrance set up shop in a New York City loft where he produced, during the next four years, some two and three-cylinder air-cooled engines. In 1919, he designed an experimental nine-cylinder static radial engine for the U.S. Army Air Service. Early in 1920, after Admiral Sims (who had commanded U.S. Naval Forces in the Atlantic during WWI) gave his support to the air advocates within the navy and called for construction of U.S. aircraft carriers, Lawrance designed and built the Model J engine with navy funds supplied by Lieutenant Commander Kraus.

This prototype engine was running in test when Lieutenant Commander Leighton was introduced to the program in March 1921. This was actually four months before creation of BuAer, but Moffett had begun collecting his key people in anticipation of his new job. Leighton studied the Model J and concluded that Kraus had bet on the right horse (power). Then, at the end of June 1921, Moffett backed Leighton's decision and approved purchase of 50 Lawrance J-1s, a deal apparently made possible because the navy had some unspent monies in the fiscal 1921 budget that were about to be returned to the Treasury.

The first production J-1 passed a 50-hour test, producing its rated 200 hp, in February 1922, a month before metamorphosis of the *Jupiter* into the *USS Langley* was completed. In the meantime, Comdr. Jerome C. Hunsaker, Moffett's chief of aircraft design at the Naval Aircraft Factory in Philadelphia, was constructing the first TS-1 fighters (43 were eventually built, 11 by Curtiss) to equip the *Langley*, so Lawrance was given a contract for an additional 200 J-1s, along with a lecture from Leighton on the need for increasing the engine's reliability factor.

By this time, however, it had become clear to Leighton that Lawrance was either unwilling or unable to find enough expansion capital to properly develop and efficiently produce engines in such quantities. In time of national emergency such a supplier would be of small value. Therefore, Leighton, knowing that both Curtiss and Packard were adamant in their stand against development of air-cooled aircraft engines, decided to pressure Wright Aeronautical Corporation into taking over the Lawrance design.

Wright Aeronautical's boss was Frederick Brant Rentschler, a sharp young man of sound family and an Ivy League education. Rentschler had served as an airplane engine inspector for the Air Service during the war and, in 1919, had formed Wright Aeronautical Corporation from the liquidated remains of the Wright-Martin Corp. Rentschler's principal products were Hispano-Suiza aircraft engines, excellent (for that time) water-cooled V-8s built under a license agreement with a French manufacturer. Both the Army Air Service and the navy bought Wright "Hissos" in some numbers. Navy planes fitted with Hissos included the Curtiss N-9 trainer, Thomas Morse MB-3 fighter, and Vought VE-7 all-purpose aircraft, but by 1923 the army, although stuck with thousands of war-surplus Liberties that it would have to use in its bombers and observation planes, was looking to the new Curtiss D-12 of 400 hp for its new fighters. As there was no civil market for new airplane engines worth mentioning, that gave Leighton some muscle at Wright Aeronautical.

Leighton was just the man to use it. He told Rentschler that the navy would buy no more Hissos or Hisso parts. Then he suggested that Wright buy out Lawrance and develop the engine the navy wanted.

Rentschler had little trouble recognizing Dame Opportunity, especially when she stood by with a club in her hand. With his board of directors concurring, he acquired Lawrance Aero Engines for half a million dollars (and a Wright vice-presidency for Charles Lawrance). Then, Rentschler directed that his ablest engineers, George J. Mead and Andrew V.D. Willgoos, take over the J-1 engine project and crank in a large dose of reliability.

Mead and Willgoos had already learned a lot about air-cooled engine reliability—or rather, the lack of it—with their markedly deficient Wright R-1 of 1920, a nine-cylinder radial built for the Air Service. But engine men, a stubborn and secretive lot who hear things in engine exhausts that are denied to the rest of us, have always worked empirically, aided only by the metallurgist, the petroleum chemist, and a good deal of intuition. This process

allowed Mead and Willgoos to announce, in September 1923, the evolution of Lawrance's J-1 into the Wright J-3. Following additional slight improvements the next year, it became the Wright J-4, the first Whirlwind. That was the penultimate step in development of an engine destined to touch off a transportation revolution and provide the basic design for all naval aircraft engines and a majority of Air Corps engines for two critical decades. (The Air Service would become the Army Air Corps in 1926.)

Meanwhile, nervously glancing over its shoulder at Billy Mitchell, the navy decided to install turntable airplane catapults on some of its capital ships. Originally powered by compressed air, and later by gunpowder, the first of these devices was fitted to the stern of the *USS Maryland* in May 1922. After Lt. Andrew C. McFall's Vought VE-7 floatplane was successfully flung into the air by this mechanism, such launchings slowly became routine.

Recovery of these scout planes was tricky, however, because the aircraft had to land on the sea, taxi close to the ship, and be returned to the deck by crane. This could prove interesting in a rough sea.

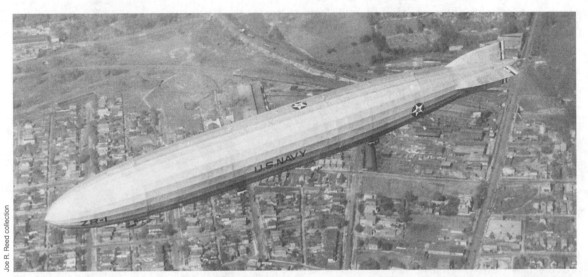

Joe R. Reed collection

The ZR-1 *Shenandoah* was completed in September 1923; it was lost two years later in a storm over Ohio.

During the next four years, 22 ships in the fleet were equipped with catapults (12 battleships and 10 light cruisers), and most of their captains grudgingly came to appreciate the far-ranging reports of their "slingshot" aviators. The fleet had extended its vision. It could, with its take-along scout planes, establish picket lines up to 200 miles in radius about the fleet. That constituted a security blanket of no small dimensions.

Patrol of the seas to greater distances by big, multiengined flying boats evolved more slowly. That was due partly to the lack of reliable engines of sufficient power, and partly to Admiral Moffett's great faith in large, rigid dirigibles for such duty. It was Moffett's most serious hangup. His dirigible programs ended in disaster, and he died in one.

## The first navy dirigibles

The navy had established its right to operate U.S. military dirigibles at the end of WWI, and two such machines were included in the 1920 navy budget. But that didn't necessarily mean that the top brass believed all that much in the usefulness of the big airships. There is a good bit of evidence that the navy's primary concern was to prevent General Mitchell from claiming such craft for the Air Service. Obviously, a lot of money could be spent for the air giants, and it would be much better to have those funds added to, rather than subtracted from, naval appropriations. Besides, knowing Mitchell, one must expect that he would, if in possession of such craft, employ them in an attempt to usurp at least some of the navy's rightful areas of responsibility.

The ZR-1 *Shenandoah* was completed in September 1923, and made its first flight from Lakehurst Naval Air Station in New Jersey with Capt. F.R. McCrary in command. It was a copy of a WWI German rigid dirigible. ("Rigid" airships have a structural framework, fabric-covered, within which a number of individual "ballonets" contain a lifting gas. The "non-

rigids" such as modern blimps have a single fabric envelope without internal framework.)

The ZR-2, purchased from Britain and called the "R-38" by the British, had been completed two years earlier, but during a trial flight broke in half and fell into the Humber River at Hull, England, carrying 28 Britons and 16 Americans to their deaths.

The navy's ZR-3 *Los Angeles* was ordered from the Zeppelin works at Friedrichshafen, Germany, in June 1922, after the Allied Reparations Commission levied a $33 billion "war damage" claim against Germany. As partial payment on this assessment, Germany built the ZR-3 for the United States, along with similar craft for France and Italy. The *Los Angeles* was delivered in mid-October 1924, and served with the fleet for eight years until, during a fit of economizing, it was scrapped. It

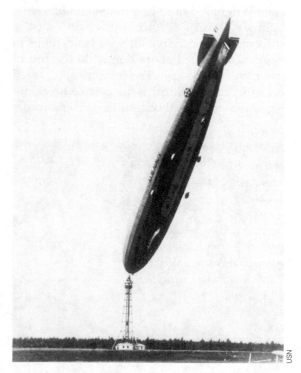

The ZR-3 Los Angeles was German-built and entered navy service in 1924; retired in the early '30s. Improper handling resulted in this nosestand while anchored to mast in 1927.

was the only dirigible to be successfully operated by the navy.

Perhaps contributing to the *Los Angeles'* relatively long service was the fact that it was designed and built by those most experienced with such craft (Count von Zeppelin built his first dirigible before the Wright brothers flew), and because of the caution attending operation of the *Los Angeles* after the *Shenandoah* was lost. Caught in a line squall over Byesville, Ohio, during the early morning hours of 3 September 1925, the *Shenandoah* was torn apart and its wreckage scattered. There were 29 survivors, but 14 persons were killed, including Lt. Comdr. Zachary Lansdowne, the airship's commander.

This disaster stalled the navy's airship programs for a time. It would be another three years before Admiral Moffett could get money for more, and bigger, dirigibles. But the *Shenandoah* tragedy served the navy in an unexpected way: it provided the vehicle that carried Billy Mitchell to oblivion.

## Mitchell court-martialed

After the sinking of the *Ostfriesland* in 1921, Mitchell was quietly supported in his abrasive crusade for a strong independent air force by his new boss, Maj. Gen. Mason Patrick, who replaced the more conservative General Menoher as Chief of Air Service late that year.

Patrick also agreed with Mitchell on how best to get the most from tiny Air Service appropriations. Lacking funds to buy new airplanes in meaningful numbers, General Patrick spent as much as possible on research and development. At some future date, the need to defend America in the air must become evident; when that time came superior planes must be ready. Therefore, Patrick okayed Air Service participation in national and international air racing, and daring long-distance flights as a means of developing high-horsepower aircraft engines and advanced airframe designs.

Such activity gathered favorable news coverage for the Air Service. This was important, because from the time that Mitchell began to kick up a fuss over the proper role and status of U.S. airpower, there was a federal investigation of some kind—20 in all, between 1919 and 1925—looking into the "aviation question." The most thorough of these was that of the Lampert-Perkins Committee in the House of Representatives (68th Congress) which, in 1924, made recommendations largely favorable to the Mitchell-Patrick position. But the Lampert-Perkins Committee report was soon submerged in another controversy when the army's General Staff decided that Mitchell should not be reappointed as Assistant Chief of the Air Service. Indeed, as his tour of duty ended he was "allowed" to revert to his permanent rank of colonel and transferred to Fort Sam Houston, Texas.

Mitchell probably expected as much. The Army General Staffs of that era were made up of old horse soldiers, dominated by Gen. John J. "Blackjack" Pershing, and to a man all were schooled in strategy and tactics that had not changed since the Civil War. Mitchell had become as bothersome to them as he was to the navy.

Many newspapers cried "Shame!" and the public generally agreed that Mitchell was being punished for daring to disagree with his superiors. Columnist Mark Sullivan may have summed it up best when he observed: "The American people admire a man who has the courage to sass his bosses." There is small evidence that the people were actually much concerned with the issues raised by Mitchell. His public support was simply rooted in that basic human trait which compels us to cheer for the underdog.

Whether or not Mitchell understood that, he did know that the public constituted his only court of appeal. He recognized that his career was finished; the most he could do was to inform the people of the facts and let history be his judge. He therefore continued to make strong statements to the press, alleging gross mismanagement of America's military establishments, and he ignored orders to obtain prior approval from his superiors for these public utterances.

The inevitable showdown came two days after the *Shenandoah* went down and while a navy flying boat was missing over the Pacific, when Mitchell handed reporters a lengthy prepared statement in which he charged that these losses were due to the "incompetency, criminal negligence, and almost treasonable administration of the national defense by the War and Navy Departments."

Mitchell went on to accuse the army and navy of forcing officers to falsely testify before various Congressional committees, condemned the War Department for retaining the Air Service's obsolete "flying coffins", and concluded by saying: "I can no longer stand by and see these disgusting performances by the Navy and War Departments, at the expense of the lives of our people, and the delusion of the American public."

That, of course, resulted in headlines of arresting proportions, and before the stunned War and Navy Departments could regroup for a common defense, Mitchell followed up with a demand that the President appoint a panel of representative Americans to investigate these departments.

President Calvin Coolidge, a humorless, unimaginative man thrust into the White House by President Harding's sudden death in mid-1923, first directed that Mitchell be court-martialed under the 96th Article of War. Then Coolidge appointed a nine-member President's Aircraft Board "to make a study of the best means of developing and applying aircraft in national defense."

No one ever accused this board of being representative of the American people. It was headed by Coolidge's school chum, Dwight Morrow, a partner in the J.P. Morgan banking firm, and contained Senator Hiram Bingham, already on record as opposed to Mitchellism; Maj. Gen. (ret) James Harbord, who had sought Mitchell's resignation earlier; and Howard Coffin who was, it will be recalled, chairman of the bungling Aircraft Production Board of WWI.

This hip-pocket assembly, popularly called the "Morrow Board," sat for about three weeks, and Coolidge timed release of its report to immediately precede the verdict in the Mitchell trial. This report summed up its rejection of Mitchell's proposals with the statement: "The next war may well start in the air, but in all probability it will wind up, as the last one did, in the mud." Then it dangled an aerial carrot, recommending acquisition of new and modern airplanes for navy and Air Service.

As for the verdict in the Mitchell trial, there was never any doubt about that once the court ruled, shortly after the proceedings began on 28 October 1925, that *truth was not a defense*. Whether or not Mitchell's statements were true had no bearing on the case, the six generals sitting in judgment decided. Mitchell was *not* charged with lying, but with "conduct prejudicial to good order and military discipline." It was a catch-all canon applicable to everything from kicking a horse to making an improper advance to another officer's wife. And although Mitchell pleaded not guilty to each of eight counts, he knew that the whole procedure was mere formality. The proceedings were in the best judge Roy Bean tradition: Give'em a fair trial and then hang 'em.

Mitchell was eloquent, and managed to turn the whole affair into an indictment of his accusers—at least, for the record. Then he directed his legal counsel to withdraw from the case and make no closing argument.

The court's guilty verdict was announced on 17 December 1925. The only dissenting vote was cast by Gen. Douglas MacArthur. The court decreed that Colonel Mitchell be suspended from rank, pay, and allowances for five years. Mitchell responded by resigning from the army.

But nothing is so hard to destroy as the truth, and the principles that Mitchell championed were firmly held by others in both the army and the navy. The time would come when their counsel would be sorely needed.

Billy Mitchell, however, would not live to see that day. He would die five years before the Japanese attacked Pearl Harbor—exactly as he predicted they would, early on a Sunday morning.

## Review questions

1. Describe the predominant attitude in the early 1920s by the "battleship admirals" and "horse-soldier generals" towards aviation. Who were some of the leading military men who opposed this attitude? How was the Naval Bureau of Aeronautics created?

2. What was the purpose of the sinking of the *Ostfriesland*? Did the event achieve its purpose? Why?

3. Why was the development of the Wright Whirlwind and Pratt and Whitney Wasp engines such a breakthrough in engine design? Who was Charles L. Lawrance? Frederick B. Rentschler?

4. Identify some of the navy's early dirigibles. How were they used? What was their fate?

5. Why was Billy Mitchell court-martialed? Why did Gen. Mason Patrick allow army pilots to participate in air racing and daring long-distance flights?

6. Did the public support General Mitchell's changes? Do you think Mitchell was surprised at the outcome of the trial? What is meant by the statement "truth was not a defense"? What was the purpose of the Morrow Board?

# 5

# Birth of the air mail

## Objectives

At the end of this chapter you should be able to:

- Describe the first attempt at air mail service in the United States.
- Discuss some of the problems encountered by the Post Office Department in inaugurating air mail service.
- Identify the type of aircraft flown on the early air mail routes.
- Discuss the significance of Jack Knight's epic flight.

The nation's airline system grew from the airmail routes of the early 1920s. A relative handful of civilian pilots, employed by the U.S. Post Office Department, flying WWI surplus biplanes, pioneered the transcontinental airways. They flew their schedules with remarkable constancy, without radio aids, with few instruments and sketchy weather reports. Their contribution to civil aviation in general and a future airline industry in particular was out of proportion to their number.

## Well, anyway, it's a start

The morning of 15 May 1918 dawned bright and crisp in the nation's capitol. It was a proper morning for the historic event jointly planned by the Post Office Department and the U.S. Air Service, the inauguration of the world's first scheduled aerial mail service. But despite nature's invigorating promise, it was a morning that Lt. George Leroy Boyle should have, as the saying goes, "stood in bed." As things turned out for Boyle that day, his contribution to the momentous event was an embarrassing one.

Actually, it wasn't Boyle's fault. He should not have been given the honor of flying that first load of mail. He was a new pilot; he had never flown beyond sight of his training airfield.

A regularly scheduled aerial mail system in the United States had been the dream of U.S. Senator Sam Sheppard of Texas since 1910, and he had argued for it, first in the House of Representatives later in the Senate, until, with the support of Postmaster General Albert Burleson, Sheppard managed to obtain Congressional approval for an experimental route between New York City and Washington, D.C. in 1916. The necessary funding was included in the steamboat mail appropriation for fiscal 1918. Therefore, President Woodrow Wilson, who viewed such a service as good training for army pilots as well as possibly being of some value to businessmen after the war, directed Secretary of War Baker to provide planes and pilots to fly the route, with

Major Reuben Fleet briefs Lt. George Boyle as Boyle prepares to take off with the nation's first load of scheduled air mail on 15 May 1918.

a stop in Philadelphia, each way every day except Sunday. The Post Office Department would administer the program.

The President and Mrs. Wilson, along with a number of other dignitaries including Assistant Secretary of the Navy Franklin D. Roosevelt, were gathered at the polo field on the banks of the Potomac by 10:30 A.M. on that pleasant spring morning to give the aerial mail an appropriate sendoff. The airplane, a Hisso-powered Jenny, had arrived an hour earlier, flown in from Philadelphia by Maj. Reuben Fleet, who had been placed in charge of the Air Service's part in the joint effort. (Reuben H. Fleet was a National Guard officer who learned to fly at the army's school on North Island, San Diego, in 1917. He came from a pioneering lumber family in the State of Washington. His army rank and position in Washington, D.C., reflected both family political influence and Fleet's early enlistment. In 1923, Fleet would form Consolidated Aircraft Corporation from the remains of Dayton-Wright and tiny Gallaudet Aircraft Corporation, and Consolidated would merge with Vultee Aircraft in 1943 to form Convair. We will take note of the Consolidated flying boats and Convair airliners in subsequent chapters. Mostly, Consolidated/Convair produced military aircraft.)

Major Fleet produced a map that depicted the railroad tracks in the area and huddled with Lieutenant Boyle to point out the location of prominent checkpoints along Boyle's route to Philadelphia.

Boyle climbed into the cockpit, the shutters of press cameras clicked, and Sgt. E.F. Waters grasped the Jenny's eight-foot propeller. "Switch off!" he called.

"Switch off," Boyle responded.

Waters pulled the prop through a few turns to prime the engine, then yelled, "Contact!"

"Contact!" Boyle echoed, flipping the ignition switch.

Waters swung the prop. The engine fired on one or two cylinders, blue smoke belched from the exhaust, and the prop stopped stiffly.

Two more attempts were made to start the engine. The "sparking plugs" were checked; then someone peered into the fuel tank and discovered the problem.

At last properly fueled, Lieutenant Boyle took off with 140 pounds of mail bound for Philadelphia. He circled the field, gaining altitude, and flew away—in the wrong direction.

The first scheduled air mail out of the nation's capitol was quietly put aboard a train at Waldorf, Maryland, approximately 24 miles from its point of origin when Lieutenant Boyle landed in a plowed field, hopelessly lost.

The other pilots completed their flights successfully. Lt. Torrey Webb took off from the infield at Belmont Park, Long Island, at 11:30 A.M. and arrived at Philadelphia's Bustleton Field at 12:40 P.M., where Lt. James C. Edgerton was waiting to take the 150 pounds of New York mail on to Washington. Edgerton touched down at the polo grounds at 2:30 P.M. Meanwhile, Lt. H. Paul Culver, after a long and fruitless wait for the northbound mail, left Philadelphia for New York carrying about 200 letters.

But it was a beginning, and in the days that followed, the army pilots (without Boyle) managed to maintain the service with commendable constancy under the direction of Capt. Benjamin B. Lipsner. Lipsner was not a

The army flew the mail in Jennies fitted with 150-hp Hispano-Suiza water-cooled V-8 engines; these craft were designated JN-6H.

pilot, but he was a hard worker and able administrator.

During the first year of operation, 1208 air mail flights were completed. There were 90 forced landings, 53 due to weather and 37 chargeable to engine failure. In anticipation of increased mail loads, a couple of Curtiss R-4Ls were placed in service on the New York-Philadelphia segment during the first month of operations. The R-4L was larger than the Jenny, and powered with the 400-hp *Liberty* engine. The Jennies were JN-6H versions, fitted with the 150-hp Hispano-Suiza produced by Wright-Martin and known as the Wright Model A engine.

## The Post Office takes over

The army pilots had the service well established by the middle of July 1918 and the Post Office Department was ready to operate the system. At that time, the price of an air mail stamp was reduced from 24 cents to 16 cents; Captain Lipsner was separated from the army to become the first superintendent of the air mail; six new airplanes were ordered, and half a dozen civilian pilots were recruited. The first civilian air mail pilots were Max Miller, Ed Gardner, Maurice Newton, Ed Langley, and Robert Shank, plus a reserve pilot by the name of Boldenweck. Newton came from the Sperry Gyroscope company; the others had been instructors for the Air Service.

The new airplanes, built by the Standard Aircraft Company of Elizabeth, New Jersey, (a small company owned by Mitsui in Japan) were designated Standard JR-1Bs and, equipped with 150-hp Hisso engines, were superior to the Jennies in that they were a little faster and had significantly longer ranges.

On 12 August 1918 the civilian pilots began flying the mail between New York and

Washington, D.C., employing the same shuttle system used by their predecessors and with equal reliability. At the end of a year, including the period flown by the army pilots, the service had generated postal revenues totalling $162,000. Total cost of the operation was given by Superintendent Lipsner as $143,000 for an average of $64.80 per hour of flying time. Up to 300 pounds of mail could be carried in the Standards when flown with half of their normal 60-gallon fuel supply.

The Post Office Department would continue to operate an ever-expanding system until, in 1925, the Congress decided that the pioneering had been done and that the time had come to turn the air mail over to private contractors. The Congress was substantially influenced by the railroad lobby. As the air mail sacks had steadily grown fatter, the rail-roads had increasingly complained that it wasn't fair for them to compete with the government in transporting the mails.

On 2 February 1925 Congress passed HR 7064, the Air Mail Act, sponsored by Representative Clyde Kelly of Pennsylvania, known as "the voice of the railway mail clerks." The railroaders undoubtedly felt comfortable with the Kelly Bill. Except for the air mail's first year of service, it had never made a profit. As the routes grew to span the nation coast-to-coast, costs had outstripped revenues by a margin of three-to-one. If the Post Office Department was so far from making money on the air mail, how could private operators expect to make it pay?

The Post Office Department had not expected profits. From 18 July 1919 until 1 July 1924 the special air mail rate was abandoned

Mail is put aboard the DH-4B of mail pilot E. Hamilton Lee. Lee would eventually retire from United Air Lines in 1949.

and the planes loaded with as much first class mail as they could carry. The important thing was to establish the system.

In May 1919, the Chicago-Cleveland segment began operation, and six weeks later scheduled air mail service between Cleveland and New York over the Alleghenies was inaugurated. By the time the air mail was two years old it had reached Omaha, and on 8 September 1920 the Post Office offered regular transcontinental service between San Francisco and New York. The trouble was, it wasn't air mail all the way. The planes flew only during daylight hours, and the mail was transferred to trains overnight. Not much time was saved, but airfields were built coast-to-coast, and the pilots gained experience (especially in dealing with the weather), while the longer and more difficult routes provided useful lessons in the operation and maintenance of their airplanes.

There were 98 air mail planes in service by the end of 1921, about half of them war surplus deHavilland DH-4s. As time passed, the DH-4 became the standard air mail machine. These craft were obtained at no cost from the army and rebuilt by the Post Office mechanics for about $2000 each. The Liberty engines, also free from large government stocks, required a number of modifications to pistons, gears, and oil systems and were made reasonably dependable. The resulting aircraft were not exactly ideal for the job, but were relatively cheap, and since there was at the time little incentive for the few airplane companies to develop new commercial airplanes, the Post Office Department had small choice.

Advances in a number of technological disciplines had to come together to produce significantly better airplanes. Better engines depended on the work of metallurgists and petroleum chemists as well as engine designers. More efficient airframes awaited development of improved airfoils and more suitable materials, allowing designs that would provide structures of greater strength-to-weight ratios, along with minimum maintenance and maximum durability.

American Air Lines

The wartime DH-4s were completely rebuilt for service with the Post Office Department's air mail routes. Fuselages were plywood-covered.

All of that cost money and could be justified only by the promise of a reasonably profitable market. But during the early '20s, there existed almost no market for new civil aircraft, and the military budgets were reduced to levels that allowed no funds for the acquisition of new airplanes in meaningful numbers.

Nevertheless, during this time, the country was blessed with a series of postmasters general (and a generally favorable Congress) that supported America's air mail effort and, by 1926, when the Post Office Department began letting contracts to private operators to fly the mail, the airway was lighted coast-to-coast for 24-hour operation, and 17 weather reporting stations, linked by radio, were positioned along the route.

A total of 289 flashing beacons marked the airway, including those at emergency fields and in between. There were no radio aids to navigation, but on clear nights a pilot could always see several beacons ahead on his course. The lighted emergency fields averaged about 30 miles apart.

That was as safe as the Post Office Department could make it. Instrument flying as we know it today was still years in the future. A few veteran mail pilots learned to maintain control under instrument conditions for short periods of time once the gyro-activated turn needle became available to them in 1924. Keeping the turn needle centered, or average-center in rough air, kept the wings level, while the altimeter's tendencies indicated a climbing or descending attitude. If a pilot lost control or found himself in or above clouds with fuel near exhaustion, he deliberately stalled the airplane and applied full rudder to enter a spin. A spin was a known condition, and a safe way to lose altitude without gaining excessive airspeed. Then the pilot's only concern was that he would break into clear air beneath the clouds with sufficient altitude remaining to recover from the spin.

The pilots did have an alternative to such a procedure. Seat-type parachutes were issued in 1919, although most were slow to wear them.

Jack Knight in the cockpit of his DH-4. Knight would retire from United Air Lines in 1937 as a DC-3 captain.

Mail pilots received a maximum base pay of $3600 per year, plus 5 cents to 7 cents per mile flown. Normally, each pilot flew five to six hours per day, two to three days per week.

But Homer Berry, one of the pilots flying between Cheyenne and Rock Springs, Wyoming, supplemented his income by operating his personal airline, carrying passengers between Laramie and Rawlins for $50 each. However, Berry's free enterprise venture cost him his job when one of his customers attempted to make a reservation at the Post Office in Cheyenne.

Resourcefulness was the mark of the early mail pilot. When Frank Yeager encountered dense fog flying his run from Omaha to Cheyenne, he landed on the prairie and taxied more than thirty miles to his destination. He turned around at each fence, circled back for a run to gain flying speed, hopped to the other side, and continued on his way.

Today, every non-instrument pilot knows that "pushing the weather" is an invitation to disaster (although some do it, accounting for

Charles Lindbergh flew DH-4s over the St. Louis-Chicago mail route before making his historic flight to Paris in 1927.

almost 40 percent of all fatal accidents in civil aviation), but the pioneering mail pilots had small choice. There was no other way to establish the air mail service. If humanly possible, the mail had to go through. And it did so at high cost. Once coast-to-coast service was established, an average of 40 pilots was employed by the Post Office Department. During the time the Post Office operated the system, 43 pilots were killed and 23 seriously injured.

Why did they do it? Dean C. Smith, a seven-year veteran of the service, put it this way: "I knew that I could fly and fly well . . . I certainly had no wish to get killed, but I was not afraid of it. I would have been frightened if I had thought I would get maimed or crippled for life . . . then, too, sometimes I was called a hero, and I liked that . . . But what I could never tell of was the beauty and exultation of flying itself . . ."*

* By the Seat of My Pants, Dean C. Smith, Little, Brown and Company, 1961.

## Jack Knight's epic flight

There was also pride. That was demonstrated one winter night before the airway was lighted. Senator Warren Harding, who had taken the position that the air mail was a waste of money, was elected President in November 1920 and would be inaugurated the following March. Foreseeing the likelihood that Harding would shoot down the service once in office, Postmaster General Burleson and his Assistant Postmaster General Otto Praeger (actually, the active boss of the air mail system), decided that if the mail could be flown all the way across the United States, without transferring it to trains during the hours of darkness, such a demonstration should have a dramatic effect on the public and influence the faint of heart in the Congress.

Therefore, at 6 A.M. on Washington's Birthday, 1921, two mail planes took off from Hazelhurst Field, Long Island, New York, headed west, and two left Marina Field, San Francisco, at 4 A.M. (Pacific Time) flying east.

Pairs of relay planes awaited at all the regularly scheduled stops in between.

Flying eastward, pilot W.F. Lewis crashed to his death shortly after takeoff from Elko, Nevada, but J.L. Eaton continued eastbound, arriving in Salt Lake City shortly before noon. Jim Murray then took Eaton's load on to Cheyenne, touching down there just before dark. Frank Yeager, waiting in Cheyenne with his Liberty engine warmed, was airborne within five minutes, his big deHavilland biplane established on course for North Platte, Nebraska in gathering darkness. It was clear and cold over the high plains and Yeager was able to follow the "iron beam" (Union Pacific railroad tracks) into North Platte, landing in the snow at 7:50 P.M. where James H. "Jack" Knight was waiting to take the eastbound mail into Omaha.

Meanwhile, the westbound flights had gotten only as far as Chicago, where they were grounded by a blinding snowstorm. Even as Knight prepared to leave North Platte, the westbound air mail was being put aboard a train in Chicago. Knight did not know it, but there would also be no airplane waiting in Omaha to take his mail sacks eastward. That pilot, too, was sitting out the storm in Chicago.

A last-minute check of Knight's DH-4 revealed a badly cracked tailskid, and repairs delayed his departure until 10:44 P.M., but the winter night remained reasonably clear over Nebraska, and people in the towns of Lexington, Kearney, and Central City lit huge bonfires as they heard the sound of Knight's approaching engine. Jack Knight was grateful. He didn't really need the fires because he had sufficient visibility to see the railroad tracks and other prominent checkpoints, but the peoples' cold vigil below reached out to him from the darkness and he was touched by their concern and support.

Knight reached Omaha at 1:10 A.M. in the early morning of the 23rd and, as he warmed himself by the big pot-bellied stove in the operations office, was told of the huge winter storm over the Midwest that had apparently doomed the air mail service's trail-blazing effort. The backside of the storm was somewhere between Omaha and Chicago. Knight had never flown the route east of Omaha.

He filled his coffee cup and backed up to the stove again. Perhaps he thought about the bonfires. He stuffed folded newspapers across his chest inside his fur-lined flying suit, filled his coffee thermos, and announced to the surprised station manager that he would take the mail to Chicago.

Knight left Omaha at 2 A.M. He intended to land at Des Moines for fuel. Gradually a thin haze turned into broken clouds and he dropped low, following the Rock Island tracks into Des Moines. The city was asleep and the airfield appeared deserted. Knight buzzed the field and, unable to gauge the depth of the snow cover, decided to try for Iowa City, 120 miles to the east. Whatever the conditions, it would be necessary to land there for fuel. Steadily the clouds thickened, and halfway to Iowa City his prop began whipping a blizzard of snowflakes about the cockpit. He flew as low as he dared and was allowed intermittent glimpses of the ground. He guessed the crosswind at about 25 mph. It was a good guess. He was forced to climb a few hundred feet as Iowa City loomed out of the swirling snow. He was unable to locate the darkened airfield, but a night watchman heard him circling, rushed to the center of the field, and lit a flare.

The two then refueled the airplane, then Knight sat in the office close to the stove. It was 200 miles to Chicago.

Knight took off into the darkness at 6:30 A.M. The snow had stopped falling, but the sky was murky, with large areas covered by ground fog over the Mississippi Valley. He held to his course and concentrated on keeping his wings level. He was cold, and very tired. Slowly, the sky grew lighter and the sun appeared. The ground below remained shrouded in mist, but smoke spreading from the Windy City's industries marked his destination and the big wheels of Knight's DH-4 were rolling in the snow covering Checkerboard Field at 8:40 A.M.

The mail had come by air all the way from San Francisco, and Jack Knight had flown 830 miles through the winter night to make it possible.

Pilot J.D. Webster departed Chicago for Cleveland at 9 A.M. and Ernest Allison took the mail from there to New York, arriving at 4:30 P.M. to complete the bold demonstration. Seven pilots had spanned the 2660 air miles between San Francisco and New York in 33 hours and 20 minutes with the United States mail (slightly less than 26 hours flying time). The fastest transcontinental trains required 108 hours for the same journey.

The feat was headlined in newspapers throughout the country, and President-elect Harding, who knew a good bandwagon when he saw one, praised the air mail service and later supported the Post Office Department's request for money to light the airway. It was one of those times in history—and there are many more of them than one might think—that the determined act of one individual made all the difference.

The airway was lighted from coast-to-coast by 1 July 1924 and, following a 30-day test, the air mail began scheduled day and night operation. The transcontinental route was divided into three zones—New York-Chicago, Chicago-Rock Springs, and Rock Springs-San Francisco—and postage was fixed at 8 cents per ounce for transit of each zone.

It was a beginning. The Post Office pilots, in their war-surplus machines, had pointed the way.

## Review questions

1. The first air mail route was established between which cities? Describe Lieutenant Boyle's ill-fated flight. How long did the Post Office Department continue to fly the mail?

2. What was the reaction of the railroad lobby to the Kelly Act? Discuss some of the advances in aviation that took place during the early 1920s which aided in the development of air mail service. What were some of the problems encountered by the Post Office pilots flying at night or under poor weather conditions?

3. What was the purpose of the Post Office Department staging a cross-country flight in February 1921? What was the significance of Jack Knight's flight? When was the airway system lighted from coast to coast?

# 6

# The barnstorming era

## Objectives

At the end of this chapter you should be able to:

- Identify some of the barnstormers of the early 1920s and recognize their contribution to the growth and development of aviation.
- Describe the purpose and significance of the Air Commerce Act of 1926.
- Explain why Jake Moellendick is recognized as the father of Wichita's aviation industry.
- Describe how Clyde Cessna, Walter Beech, and Lloyd Stearman formed Travel Air Manufacturing Company and their own individual companies.

Production of the first private and commercial airplanes in the United States began in 1919. Few were sold because there were few practical uses for those open-cockpit machines powered by unreliable and inefficient engines. The barnstormers and air mail pilots were almost the only visible evidence of civil aviation into the mid-1920s, but the essential ingredients for a boom were coming together.

## Charlie Meyers

Charles W. Meyers was not a tall man. He was, in fact, rather short. One comes to realize this only in retrospect, because you would never notice it in his presence. There was something about Charlie—an indefinable something that caused the world to stand aside while he passed. He was a man of courage and talent; he was a man of the sky.

Charlie grew up on Long Island and made his first flights in 1913, at age 17, in gliders of his own design. Prior to WWI, he found a job with Aeromarine Plane & Motor Corporation in Keyport, New Jersey, one of about a dozen very small plane builders (including Sloan, Standard, LWF, Burgess-Dunn, etc.) that were at the time hoping to share the miniscule airplane market dominated by the Wrights, Curtiss, and Martin.

Meyers learned aircraft construction at Aeromarine, and by mid-1916 had managed to obtain about 12 hours' flying time with company test pilot Allen Adams as his instructor. Thus equipped, Charlie offered his services to the U.S. Army Signal Corps' 40-plane air arm. Rejected, he went to Canada, where his limited flying experience was more appreciated. Britain and her dominions had been at war in Europe for nearly two years. After an hour and 45 minutes additional air time with a Canadian officer, Charlie was commissioned in the Royal Flying Corps and made an instructor. Later he was sent to England, where he spent the remainder of the war training British and American pilots in Avro 504s.

Briefly airborne in a glider of his own design, 17-year-old Charles Meyers begins a lifetime as a pilot in 1913.

Back in the United States after the war, Charlie bought a surplus Canuck (Canadian Jenny), joined forces with E.P. Lott and George "Buck" Weaver, who were similarly equipped, and went barnstorming. Weaver, it should be noted, had worked as an assistant to Matty Laird on the county fair circuit before the war, and had become an Air Service instructor at Rich Field, Waco, Texas, during the war. Also at Rich Field was Master Signal Electrician (sergeant-mechanic) Walter Beech.

Meyers was unhurt in the crash of his glider, but hammed it up for his father's camera.

Meyers, Lott, and Weaver were joined in mid-summer by Elwood "Sam" Junkin and Clayton Bruckner, and their five-plane aerial circuit fared very well, selling three-minute rides from Mid-western pastures for $20.

## WACO is born

The group decided to spend the winter in Lorain, Ohio, and, having convinced themselves (as had others, including Matty Laird and the Lockheed brothers) that a profitable market awaited the appearance of a small and inexpensive personal airplane, pooled their resources to design and build a tiny single-place parasol monoplane fitted with a two-cylinder Lawrance engine. They called it a "WACO," since Buck Weaver was the prime mover behind the project and they worked under the name of Weaver Aircraft Company, and because Buck had fond memories of his service at the army training field near Waco, Texas. (While Texans pronounce it "Way-ko," the personnel at Rich Field called it "Wah-ko," and all WACO airplanes were so called.)

Buck narrowly escaped serious injury in the crash of the first WACO after its engine failed on a test flight, and he left the company soon afterwards, but Bruckner and Junkin were determined to build airplanes and eventually produced the successful WACO 9 in 1925. WACO's success during the late '20s would be largely owed to Charlie Meyers, but no one at Weaver Aircraft Company suspected

Meyers, on wing, and Clayton Bruckner load a Jenny with newspapers, which they delivered to Ohio farm families by air in 1919. It was a way to make a dollar with a war-surplus airplane.

First WACO was this anemic single-place monoplane fitted with a 26-hp Lawrance air-cooled two-cylinder engine. This 1919 craft was destroyed in test.

it then, and Charlie left the group early in 1920 to barnstorm in the Carolinas.

Meyers was typical of the gypsy barnstormers of the early '20s, and among them were many whose names are familiar today: Walter Beech, Clyde Pangborn, Wiley Post, Charles Lindbergh, Roscoe Turner, and Clyde Cessna, to name a few. They took chances because it was necessary, but few were irresponsible daredevils; a busted airplane earned no money. They operated from the nation's cow pastures because there were no civilian airports except for the sod fields used by the air mail pilots.

Buck Weaver hopping passengers in 1920 in his Canuck (Canadian Jenny). The barnstormers could charge $20 for a three-minute ride during the early '20s. By 1925, competition lowered the price to $2 or $3 per passenger.

In the Carolinas in 1921, Meyers (center) converted a war-surplus Thomas Morse Scout to two-place and substituted an OX-5 engine for the plane's original rotary. At right is fellow barnstormer Harry Herman.

If they spliced a broken wing spar with a piece of yellow pine from an orange crate, that was an economic necessity. If they replaced a worn rocker arm brushing in an OX-5 engine with the steel barrel from an Eversharp pocket pen, that was because it fit and it worked. In any case, there were no aviation regulations, no pilot licenses required, and no airworthiness certificates needed for their machines. The sky was free, and anyone with a few hundred dollars to pay for a surplus jenny or Standard could do whatever he pleased, or was able to do, with it. Barnstorming was a matter of survival of the fittest and the only way most could both fly and eat with some regularity. No one ever got rich at it. Indeed, it was commonly said within this hardy clan that "The greatest danger in flying is starving to death."

Nor was all of it pure fun. As barnstormer Earl C. Reed put it, "There were more pleasurable things than overhauling an engine somewhere on the plains when the temperature stood at 105 degrees. No one ever looked forward to hand-propping a Hisso engine after a cold night in the open, or washing the cow dung from the underside of the wings, or sitting miserably under a wing during a thunderstorm, your raincoat draped over the wooden propeller to keep it from soaking up moisture which could cost rpms. But we were fliers, and that whole vast sky out there belonged to us alone, and that was enough."

But the times were changing. By 1925 the ever-increasing number of barnstormers was finding customers ever more scarce and the price of a ride around the patch had dropped to

Earl C. Reed

The "TLR Flying Circus" consisted of a surplus Standard, pictured, and a Jenny. Owner Reed in center; pilot is Beeler Blevins, with paying passengers in front cockpit.

$2 or $3 per passenger. A few innovative entrepreneurs would continue to barnstorm right up to the eve of World War II, offering night flights in Ford and Stinson TriMotor airliners, along with spectacular airshows. At $1 per head, even with a full load of 15 passengers, that was hardly an airlift to affluence.

## Air Commerce Act

So the barnstormer faded from the scene because he could no longer survive economically. But he would have gone anyway. The Kelly Bill promised profits to civilian air mail contractors, and if there was money to be made in aviation, the investment bankers were interested, and bankers like things tidy and well-regulated. The U.S. Congress obliged with the Air Commerce Act of 1926, which provided for the first aviation regulations, and required federal licenses for all civil pilots and aircraft.

## Morrow Board

The Air Commerce Act of 1926 also drew upon recommendations of the Morrow Board, a commission appointed by President Calvin Collidge in response to sensational public charges by the Air Service's Gen. Billy Mitchell accusing the army and navy of gross incompetence and near treason in their refusal to recognize the importance of airpower to the nation's defense. The Morrow Board (officially, the President's Aircraft Board) was chaired by the President's old college chum, Dwight Morrow, a partner in the J.P. Morgan banking firm; among eight members was Howard E. Coffin of the discredited WWI Aircraft Production Board.

It seems incredible today, in view of the testimony given before this assembly during its three weeks of hearings, that Dwight Morrow and his cohorts could have decided that Mitchell was wrong. But they dutifully rejected "Mitchellism" (which called for a strong, independent air force, and accurately predicted a surprise attack on Pearl Harbor by the Jap-

anese, among other things) and, having accomplished their primary purpose—the denigration of Mitchell—Morrow, Coffin, and friends offered some suggestions for the federal regulation of civil aviation.

The Morrow Board's recommendations for civil aviation were modified by Secretary of Commerce Herbert Hoover, with some input from the National Advisory Committee for Aeronautics, (forerunner of NASA) and Senator James W. Wadsworth of New York, an advocate of federal air regulations for several years. The result was the Air Commerce Act (also known as the Bingham-Parker-Merritt Bill, for its sponsors), which has often been characterized as U.S. civil aviation's Magna Carta. It was hardly that. True, sensible regulation was due and desirable. However, it was but one leg of the required triad. Of equal importance were more efficient airplanes and an infusion of risk capital. If civil aviation had a Magna Carta, it was the Kelly Bill, which offered a dependable source of revenue to private operators. That, in turn, attracted investors. More efficient airplanes were certain to follow.

More efficient commercial airplanes evolved slowly during the early '20s because of the very limited and ill-defined market, and the fact that designers had little choice in the selection of a proper engine. Nevertheless, some progress was made because of those who saw the future potential of commercial aviation.

In Chicago, Matty Laird envisioned that potential and presumptuously painted a sign on his Ashburn Field hangar that read "E.M. Laird Company" after agreeing to build an airplane for barnstormer Billy Burke early in 1919. But the immediate market, Matty believed, was for an inexpensive personal or sport plane, a market generated by the thousands of pilots so recently trained by the military.

Matty was wrong, of course. That same euphoric expectation was shared by others then, and again 25 years later after WWII, and materialized neither time.

Reed's Standard is damaged in a cow pasture landing incident, not an uncommon sight. Military insignia was painted out with green barn paint.

The civilian fliers of the post-WWI years were forever seeking ways to make a dollar with an airplane. Vic Carlstrom (right) established inter-city records in 1919 with a Curtiss Model R powered with a Curtiss VX engine of 180 hp. Curtiss's chief motor engineer, Charles Kirkham, is second from left; early exhibition pilot Art Smith, center, and with back to camera at left is Matty Laird, then using a crutch as a result of a crash in Katherine Stinson's Brock-built machine two years before. Photo taken at Chicago's old Ashburn Field.

Matty sold but the one Laird Model S—a two-place biplane powered with an 80-hp rotary engine—and although Burke was pleased with the craft, no other customers appeared. Matty then began planning a larger, three-place "Commercial" biplane, and had three-view sketches of it on hand when Burke returned late that fall.

## Jake's airplane works

Burke was a successful Buick-Franklin automobile dealer in Okmulgee, Oklahoma, but his passion was airplanes. He had instructed at Rich Field during the war, and when offered the chance to manage a newly organized and apparently well-financed flying service in Wichita, Kansas, Burke took it and soon was off to Chicago to look for airplanes that were more efficient than the pair of tired Canucks possessed by the Wichita Aircraft Company.

The three ex-Army pilots who had organized the Wichita Aircraft Company as a barnstorming and air taxi service had the financial backing of several Wichita businessmen, including hotelman George Siedhoff, contractor J.H. Turner, and Jacob Melvin Moellendick. Jake Moellendick must be recognized as the father of Wichita's aviation industry—although, as things turned out, he was a lousy parent.

Jake had earlier followed the oil-drilling rigs from Okmulgee's well sites to the booming Wichita discovery, arriving with little more than the shirt on his back. But Jake was a true high-roller. As far as he was concerned, if a man couldn't be rich he may as well be broke. He was a driller, and a good one (the top job on a drilling rig), but working for wages, however high, just wasn't Jake's idea of living. Therefore, he often offered his services in exchange for a "piece of the hole," and the nature of oil wildcatting being what it is, his offer was sometimes accepted. One day Jake's bit twisted into pay dirt, and his bank account suddenly began growing faster than Jake could deplete it—which is saying a lot, because he had a large

Meyers' barnstorming airplane of 1923 was a craft of his own design and construction. Built in a barn, it was powered with a surplus OX-5 engine of 90 hp.

The barnstorming era produced another phenomenon, the "wing walker," who performed gymnastics on the outside of airplanes in flight as a means of attracting crowds from which paying passengers could be solicited.

W.A. "Billy" Burke, one of the three original founders of Wichita's first airplane factory. Billy is shown while an instructor at Rich Field, Waco, Texas, during WWI. Also at Rich Field were Buck Weaver and Walter Beech.

appetite for personal pleasure. Jake Moellendick was soon an important man around Wichita. He was also loud, abrasive, and usually drunk.

So Moellendick was a natural target for the partners in the Wichita Aircraft Company when they went looking for additional capital. Theirs was the kind of long-shot proposition that was made to order for Jake. He not only bought in, but became the majority stockholder.

Aware that this made him the boss, Jake immediately started bossing. He didn't know anything about airplanes, but he knew a man who did—his old friend Billy Burke down in Okmulgee. Jake sent for Burke, and that is what led to Burke's appearance at Matty Laird's "airplane factory" late in 1919.

Burke was so impressed with the sketches of the proposed Laird *Commercial* that he thrust aside all thought of the Wichita Aircraft Company and immediately suggested that they move the Laird operation to Wichita, where the economic climate was much better, and manufacture the Commercial in quantity. Inevitably, perhaps, that led back to Jake Moellendick and formation of the E.M. Laird Company of Wichita, which was a three-way partnership with Laird contributing his equipment and know-how, and Burke and Jake each putting up $15,000 in cash.

The first product of Wichita's first airplane manufacturing plant was test-flown in mid-April 1920, by which time the Laird company had absorbed Jake's original air taxi operation and acquired its airfield at 29th and Hillside. Among the spectators as Matty completed the test flight was hotelman Bill Lassen, who remarked that the plane flew "just like a swallow," whereupon Moellendick announced that Lassen had just named it.

## The Laird Swallow

The Laird *Swallow* was an immediate success by the standards of that time. The first company advertisement, appearing in the June 1920 issue of Aviation, described it as the "First commercial airplane; capable of carrying a pilot and two passengers with fuel enough for 225 miles at full speed." This announcement was greeted by orders for 11 airplanes, and freewheeling Jake Moellendick opened the company throttle, calling for production of 20 Swallows for the rest of the year.

That also called for additional employees, among whom was Lloyd Carlton Stearman, a 20-year-old architectural student who had learned to fly in the navy during WWI. A few months later, Walter Beech and Buck Weaver were hired as pilot-salesmen as Jake pumped more cash into the company, began construction of a new factory building, and asked Matty to design a twin-engine transport plane. Jake had visions of starting his own airline.

Buck Weaver test-flew the twin-engine Laird in July 1921. However, the big seven-place biplane was underpowered (with a pair of OX-5s) and spent most of its time in the

The first Laird Swallow under construction in Wichita. Built of wood and fabric, the early Swallows were, essentially, Jenny replacements that carried two in the front cockpits, and were advertised as the country's first commercial airplanes.

E.M. Laird

Brand new Laird Swallows on the field at Wichita, 1921

hangar until Laird reworked it around a single 300-hp Packard engine, after which Beech wrecked it following engine failure.

That loss, coupled with the crashes of two Swallow demonstrators, the cost of the new building, and the general business recession of 1921, required more transfusions of cash from Jake, while Jake seemed to become more difficult to get along with in direct proportion to his investment in the company. Both Burke and Weaver left the company early in 1922 after fights with Jake, and Laird quit in September 1923. Forty-three *Swallows* had been built.

Jake reorganized the company, changing its name to Swallow Airplane Manufacturing Company. Walter Beech became the chief pilot, and Lloyd Stearman moved up to the position of chief design engineer.

But scarcely had Jake got things moving again before his two top hands raised another issue: Stearman and Beech were convinced that the Swallow's wood-framed fuselage should be redesigned and constructed of tubular steel.

Jake refused to listen, and the argument ended when Beech and Stearman resigned on the spot. Jake continued with Matty's brother, Charles Laird, as chief of design, and with Red Jackson as chief pilot.

Laird returned to Chicago and Ashburn Field, where he soon introduced the Laird Commercial, the first of a long line of quality-built single-bay biplanes with steel tube fuselage frames—including some famous racers—that would be advertised throughout the '20s and early '30s as the "Thoroughbreds of the Airways." Laird would never again accept a partner.

Swallow, meanwhile, had a head start in the civilian airplane market. Its products, well crafted, had established a good reputation for the company, and with almost no competition (the Curtiss Oriole was priced higher and was a poor performer), was in position to dominate its market for the foreseeable future if properly managed. Lloyd Stearman, during his brief tenure as chief engineer, had redesigned the

Standing before the twin-engine Laird Transport in 1921 are employees of Jake's airplane works. Buck Weaver is second from left; Jessie Chacon, later with Travel Air and Beech, second from right; Jake Moellendick in straw hat third from right; Charles Laird fourth from right; Lloyd Stearman in cap, center.

Businessmen-pilots of the '20s used their airplanes more for advertising than for business travel. Walter Beech sold this Laird Swallow to a Wichita businessman in 1922.

original Laird Swallow, eliminating one set of wing struts on each side to make a trimmer, more efficient single-bay biplane, a configuration that would be the standard for all two and three-place biplanes to follow, and Charles Laird modified that airframe to allow installation of Hisso engines up to 180 hp.

Beech and Stearman quit Swallow in October 1924, and it is just possible that there was more behind it than Jake's refusal to switch to metal framing in the Swallow fuselage. Stearman had drawings of a new biplane that looked very good to Walter, and perhaps Walter may be pardoned if he decided that what Stearman could do for Jake might just as well be done for Beech. In any case, Beech looked up barnstormer Clyde Cessna, whose maturity and judgment Walter respected, and proposed that the two of them open their own airplane manufacturing plant to build Stearman's new design.

## Clyde Cessna

Clyde Vernon Cessna had a solid background in aviation. He had been a 31-year-old farm implement mechanic in Enid, Oklahoma, when, in 1910, a trio of early birdmen staged an exhibition in Oklahoma City. Clyde attended and was smitten. He made sketches of the Bleriot monoplane flown by one of the "aeronauts" and, back in Enid, ordered a bare fuselage from the Queens Aeroplane Company of Bronx Park, New York, which was licensed to make Bleriots in the United States. He designed and built his own wings, depending on the sketches he'd made in Oklahoma City. The tail section and control systems were added from memory, and he converted a 4-cylinder, 60-hp Elbridge marine engine to power his creation. The craft was ready for its first flight in May 1911.

Like so many early birds, Clyde had to teach himself to fly and test his airplane simultaneously. Both projects suffered. But on his 13th attempt, Cessna got off the ground and back down again without doing serious violence to either his machine or himself. He thereupon quit his job and took off on an exhibition tour.

An accident early in his flying career wrecked the plane and put Clyde in the hospital for a few weeks. By then, however, he had flown a couple of successful exhibitions—the first, at Cherokee, Oklahoma, earned him $300—and he had other county fair dates contracted.

During the winter of 1911–12, Cessna took his wife and two children, Eldon and Wanda, to the Cessna family homestead near Rago, Kansas, and built a new plane powered with an Anzani engine. This craft, the *"Silver Wings,"*

Cessna Aircraft Company

Clyde Cessna's 1912 "Silver Wings" was a homebuilt copy of the French Bleriot. Clyde favored monoplanes from the beginning.

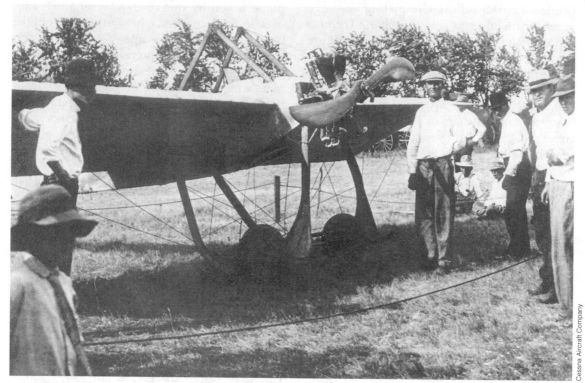

Cessna with his 1914 airplane at Burdette, Kansas

prophetically employed the leaf of a buggy spring in its landing gear.

For the next four years Cessna worked the county fairs in season and built a new and improved airplane each winter. Late in 1916, he built three airplanes in the plant of the Jones Motor Car Company at Wichita when the makers of the Jones Light Six offered free use of their facilities in exchange for the advertising value of this activity. One of these craft, the "Comet," had an enclosed cockpit and was capable of almost 100 mph. Clyde found buyers for the other two.

Cessna was not accepted for military service in WWI (he was 37 years old), so he spent the war years on his farm at Rago growing wheat. He returned to barnstorming in 1919, and in the late summer of 1923 purchased a new Swallow from Walter Beech. Clyde had made money barnstorming, and was the kind of man who saved much of it.

Clyde wasn't especially enthusiastic over the prospect of producing Stearman's biplane; he had favored monoplanes from the beginning, and had recently come to believe that monoplanes with cantilever wings—wings without external bracing, such as Bill Stout was building for Henry Ford—would be the most efficient. But the monoplanes would surely follow if the proposed company was successful.

## Travel Air formed

Cessna put up $6200, Beech got together $5700, and Stearman's minority share was represented by $200 and his drawings of the new airplane. Other investors included Daniel C. Sayre, Walter Innes, Jr., and other Wichita businessmen. The company was incorporated 5 February 1925 as the Travel Air Manufacturing Company with Cessna as president and Beech vice-president.

## Walter Beech

Both Beech and Cessna were reared on farms—Walter being a native of Tennessee—and both were into automobile mechanics before WWI, but there the similarity ended. When they joined together to form Travel Air late in 1924, Clyde was 45 years old and Walter 33. Clyde was a quiet, deliberate type, a solid family man with grown children. Walter was an outgoing, ambitious man, an excellent salesman, and a bachelor who is said to have had a fine appreciation for a "well-turned ankle," to put it in the idiom of that time.

When and how Walter learned to fly is very difficult to determine. The official line at Beech Aircraft Corporation has long been that Walter rebuilt a Curtiss pusher in Milwaukee in 1914, taught himself to fly it, and was a flight instructor at Rich Field during WWI. Walter worked for a truck manufacturer prior to the war and was sent to Europe to represent that firm. He held the rank of sergeant (master signal electrician) at Rich Field, and several who knew him there have confirmed that he was in charge of the engine overhaul shops. However, when Walter showed up in Arkansas City, Kansas, in 1919 at the Williams-Hill Flying Service, he was hired as a pilot (Pete Hill had known Walter at Rich Field). Apparently, Walter learned to fly while serving in the army as a mechanic, a not uncommon practice at the time. In any case, Walter barnstormed for Pete Hill and Errett Williams until Moellendick hired him early in 1921.

## Lloyd Stearman

Lloyd Stearman was 26 years old when he joined with Walter and Clyde to form Travel Air. Lloyd, from Harper, Kansas, was an intellectual who played the violin and relaxed with classical music, and who had learned to fly in the navy at San Diego in 1918. He was working as an architect for the S.S. Voigt firm in Wichita when his continuing interest in aviation took him to the Swallow company, at reduced pay, in the summer of 1920.

Travel Air produced 19 of their OX-5 Model 2000 biplanes during 1925 and production more than doubled to 43 units the following year, aided by Beech's showing in the Ford Reliability Tour both years. By the end of 1926 Travel Air had moved onto Wichita's new mu-

Beech Aircraft Corporation

The first Travel Air, fitted with a fully-cowled OX-5 engine. A total of 19 was sold in 1925.

Walter Beech and Travel Air powered with a Curtiss C-6 engine of 160 hp. Walter flew this airplane to first place in the 1928 Ford Reliability Tour.

nicipal airport on East Central Avenue, and both Stearman and Cessna had left the company to build airplanes on their own.

Stearman left in September 1926 and, with backing from West Coast Travel Air dealer Fred Hoyt, produced the Stearman C-1 and C-2 in Venice, California. Several of the latter craft went to Walter Varney, one of the first contract air mail operators. Then Lloyd was lured back to Wichita in November 1927, when several local businessmen, led by Walter Innes, raised $60,000 to put the Stearman Aircraft Company solidly to business, where it would remain until absorbed by the Boeing Division of United Aircraft Corporation two years later. Stearman and Varney would join with others in 1932 to purchase and revitalize the bankrupt Lockheed company in Burbank, California.

Cessna left Travel Air in April 1927 to organize his own company. Although Travel Air was producing a cabin monoplane by that time, the Model 5000, it was not the kind of monoplane that Clyde wanted. In any event, it was inevitable that he would leave. Cessna,

Olive Ann Mellor (right) was Travel Air office manager and girl Friday; she sold tickets while Walter hopped passengers on Travel Air paydays. She and Walter were married in 1930.

Stearman, and Beech could not long remain under a single roof. They differed greatly in character, and the traits they had in common sharply conflicted. Each had strong convictions and the courage to pursue them. Travel Air suffered from an overabundance of talent possessed by men who were poor compromisers.

Earlier, late in 1926, Clyde had built, in his spare time and at his own expense, a trim cabin monoplane fitted with a 120-hp Anzani engine. But in order to offer it to an air mail contractor, Walter decreed that Clyde's design be substantially modified with a new, deeper fuselage, Travel Air tail, and powered with the new 225-hp Wright Whirlwind engine. The resulting airplane was successfully marketed as the Model 5000, but it was no longer Clyde's airplane.

## Cessna Aircraft formed

Clyde organized the Cessna Aircraft Corporation, moved into a modest plant at 200 East Douglas in Wichita, and began work on his Model A cabin monoplane, a design that was to be the basis for Cessna airplanes for the next 25 years.

The Model A Cessna, originally called "Type 3-120," was powered with a 120-hp Anzani engine, was four-place, had a top speed of 120 mph, and sold for $3575. The French-designed Anzani engines were generally considered cantankerous beasts with excessive vibration, but Clyde had flown them extensively and had worked out modifications that made the Anzani-Cessnas reasonably reliable.

Nevertheless, aware of the Anzani's reputation, Clyde also offered his new ship with a choice of engines. The Warner-powered Cessna AW, and the Whirlwind-Cessna certified in 1928 as the Model BW, became the most popular. The BW, with 225 hp, had a top speed of 150 mph, landed at 45, and its initial climb rate was 1400 fpm. It was widely flown as a racer in the air meets that were popular during those years.

In August 1927 the company name was changed to "Cessna-Roos Aircraft Corporation" when Victor Roos came in as a stockholder. Roos had been associated with Guiseppe Bellanca in the short-lived Bellanca-Roos company of Omaha (which made Anzani-powered monoplanes very similar to the Cessna Model A). But Roos' tenure with Cessna was also brief, for he sold

The 1927 Cessna Model A was Clyde's first project after leaving Travel Air and forming his own company.

The 1929 four-place Cessna DC-6A was powered with a Wright Whirlwind J6-9 engine of 300 hp, and maximum speed exceeded 160 mph. Price at factory was $11,000.

out to Clyde before the end of the year and took a job as general manager at Swallow.

Swallow badly needed some managing. Moellendick's latest caper had bankrupted the company and Jake was in a sanitarium for treatment of alcoholism.

## Moellendick bankrupt

The first six months of 1927 had been profitable ones at Jake's airplane works. Then, in June, Capt. William Erwin, a WWI ace and barnstormer, appeared in Wichita and asked Moellendick for an airplane capable of flying nonstop to Hawaii. Erwin said that he had some backing from a Dallas newspaper, and if Jake would sell him an airplane on credit, Erwin was confident that he could win the $25,000

offered by Hawaiian pineapple king James Dole to the first civilian pilot to reach Hawaii after August 12th. There was also a $10,000 second prize.

It was the kind of proposition that Jake could not resist. Charles Lindbergh had flown to Paris just two weeks before, and the world was enchanted with the evidence that men could span the oceans in a matter of hours. People of far lands who could not name the president of the United States knew all about Lindbergh, the "Lone Eagle," and his Ryan monoplane, the *Spirit of St. Louis*.

Jake blew the whistle on the Swallow production line. Ignoring the protests of Swallow dealers and minor stockholders, Moellendick ordered all hands to work on a new long range monoplane for Erwin.

Typical biplanes of the middle '20s were, right to left: Standard (WWI surplus); Alexander Eaglerock, commonly called the "Eaglebrick," built in Denver, designed by Al Mooney; New Swallow, and WACO 10. All above are powered with OX-5 engines except the Standard, which was usually refitted with a Hispano-Suiza engine of 150 or 180 hp.

Winners of the 1927 "Pineapple Derby" were Art Goebel and Lt. Bill Davis flying this Travel Air 5000.

The plane was completed early in August; Bill Erwin christened it in the *Dallas Spirit*, then ferried it to Oakland to prepare to earn the money to pay for it. It had already cost Jake plenty, both directly and in lost sales of the Swallow production aircraft.

By that time, two airplanes, a Fokker Tri-Motor piloted by army fliers Les Maitland and Al Hegenberger, and the prototype Travel Air 5000 crewed by Ernie Smith and Emory Bronte, had made the flight to Hawaii and, although too early to collect the Dole prize, had dimmed the glory for the nine entrants that were ready for takeoff on 16 August.

Of the nine, only two made it to Hawaii. Art Goebel and Navy Lt. Bill Davis in a Travel Air 5000 got there first. Martin Jensen and his navigator, Paul Schluter, in a monoplane built by Vance Breese, arrived two hours later. (When Jensen landed, his wife, Marguerite, a nervous wreck from her anxious, 26-hour vigil, marched to his plane and, hands on hips, demanded, "Martin Jensen, where the hell have you been?") One plane was disqualified and not allowed to take off. Two cracked up during takeoff runs. Two turned back during the first hour. And two disappeared over the silent Pacific.

Five people died in the two machines that disappeared: Jack Frost and Gordon Scott, flying the first Lockheed Vega to be built, and Augy Pedlar flying a Buhl Airsedan carrying Cy Knope and a pretty 22-year-old sixth grade school teacher, Mildred Doran.

The big silver and green Swallow monoplane, *Dallas Spirit*, was one of the two that turned back. Six feet of fabric had stripped from its fuselage aft of the navigator's station. But Erwin patched the Swallow, and the next day calmly announced that he and his navigator, Alvin Eichwaldt, were taking off for Hong Kong by way of Hawaii and Manila, and would search for the downed planes enroute. That seemed so preposterous that few believed Erwin. However, there were prizes offered for the first flights to Manila and to Hong Kong, however improbable such feats might have been at the time.

Apparently, Erwin and Eichwaldt were serious. They flew a straight and unwavering course for Hawaii, tapping out frequent Morse Code messages to inform the world of their progress. Then, seven hours out and in darkness, Eichwaldt sent the following:

"9:02 P.M. This is the *Dallas Spirit*. We went into a tailspin—SOS—belay that. We came out of it, but were sure scared. It was a close call. The lights on the instrument panel went out and it was so dark that Bill couldn't see the— we are in a spin—SOS . . ."

Nothing further was ever heard from the *Dallas Spirit*.

That broke the Swallow company, and Jake had no money with which to rescue it. His oil-drilling partnership with Charles Landers had sunk a series of dry holes to drain his cash reserves and he had exhausted his credit. A short time later the Swallow company was forced into receivership and Jake, beset by the Erwin-Eichwaldt tragedy and financial ruin, was taken to a sanitarium.

Months later, Moellendick went back to the oil fields and started over. But times, and Jake's luck, had changed. He returned to Wichita in 1929 and, as the Wichita Eagle put it, "joined the Sullivan Aircraft Corporation." Sullivan built but one airplane before closing its doors, a fate suffered by a dozen or so other would-be plane makers in Wichita during the late '20s.

Jake died 23 March 1940. He was penniless. Anonymous aviation people paid for his burial in Wichita Park Cemetery, just across the street from the old Swallow Field.

Today not many people in Wichita can tell you who Jake Moellendick was, not even among the thousands employed at Beech, Cessna, Boeing, Learjet, and their suppliers. And although it is unlikely that any of them would be there had it not been for Jake, he has no monuments in Wichita, no streets or schools named for him. Sure, he was ornery and over-bearing and maybe some other things, but he had guts, and faith, a vision of the future, and he left behind something of value. What else should we ask of a man?

The Swallow Airplane Company, following Jake's departure, was efficiently operated by Vic Roos, W.M. Moore, and C.A. Noll under a "purchase partnership" agreement, and was

Real life "Jonathan Livingston Seagull," Johnny Livingston (left), takes delivery of a WACO 10 from Clayton Bruckner.

Berry Brothers aircraft paints flew a WACO 10. Photo is dated 16 September 1929.

soon solvent again. They added a two-place sport-trainer to the production lines and had reason for some optimism until overtaken by such competitors as Travel Air, WACO, and Eaglerock. The last Swallow biplane was the Sport HC model of 1931, which was fitted with a 70-hp Continental radial engine. It found few buyers until Swallow, along with many other aircraft manufacturers, succumbed to the Great Depression.

## WACO prospers

WACO was one that survived the depression. After Buck Weaver's departure, Sam Junkin and Clayton Bruckner ended up in Troy, Ohio, in 1923, after brief tries in Alliance and Medina. They called their airplanes "WACOs," but worked under the name Advance Aircraft Company (Advance would at last become WACO Aircraft Company in June 1929).

The first WACO built at Troy was the Model 6, similar in configuration to the early Laird Swallow, although lacking the Swallow's modest success. A Model 7 followed, essentially a cleaned-up 6, then the Model 8, which was a four-place cabin biplane powered with a 6-cylinder Hall-Scott engine. Advance produced fewer than 10 airplanes through the Model 8.

Advance Aircraft's lean days came to an end with the appearance of the Model 9. Thirty of this model were sold during its first four months of production late in 1924 and early in 1925, and 275 were built by the time the improved WACO 10 was introduced in April 1927.

The WACO 10 was designed and tested by Charles W. Meyers. Meyers, you will recall, had worked with Bruckner and Junkin during the winter of 1919-20. In the intervening years he had barnstormed and built a couple of airplanes of his own, one being the Meyers Midget, a tiny biplane that attracted national attention at the 1926 National Air Races, and which Charlie hoped to market in kit form. That plan was abandoned when he crashed it in a Philadelphia railroad yard in the fall of 1926. And that was when he went to Troy, Ohio, in response to a telegram from Clayton Bruckner.

"After the crash of my Midget, I went to WACO," Charlie recalled. "Designer Sam Junkin had just died, and when I arrived there

Aerobatic pilot "Fearless Freddie" Lund rolls a Whirlwind-powered WACO Taperwing in the early morning sun over Ohio.

John Wood, winner of the 1928 Ford Reliability Tour, with his WACO Taperwing and new Chrysler roadster.

Clay Bruckner didn't know what he was going to do. He could make anything, and he knew shop procedure, but without Sam he was thinking of folding up. But he had enough material on hand for some twenty-odd Nines, so I suggested we put them together. In the meantime, I got busy thinking and designed a follow-up airplane . . . the WACO 10. We got up to a five-a-day production on those, and even so were sending people to Travel Air because we couldn't supply them."

WACO sold 435 of the 1000 new civil aircraft built in the U.S. in 1927, and late that year the WACO 10 airframe was given a J-5 Whirlwind engine as an option, which made it the WACO Sport ASO model. Then, when Charlie Meyers designed a set of tapered wings for this airplane, using a slightly modified version of Max Munk's new M-6 airfoil, the resulting WACO Taperwing ensured that Walter Beech's increasingly-popular Travel Airs would have all the competition they needed.

## Great Lakes formed

By the late fall of 1928, the Advance Airplane Company was indeed prospering, as was the entire aircraft industry in the U.S. Many new plane builders had come into existence during the preceding two years to ride the boom, and WACO's sales manager, Charles Van Sicklen, had discovered an opportunity to get into airplane manufacturing with a minimum of risk. He had learned that Glenn Martin wanted to move from Cleveland to Baltimore, and would leave behind a contract with the navy for some torpedo bombers then in production at the Cleveland plant. Van Sicklen found financing and formed the Great Lakes Aircraft Corporation, taking Charlie Meyers with him.

In Cleveland, Meyers teamed up with young Cliff Leisy in the old Martin factory to design a two-place sport-trainer that would make use of the 4-cylinder air-cooled Cirrus engine of 90 hp. The Cirrus was the American version of the British deHavilland Gipsy engine, and was built under license in the U.S. by the American Cirrus Motor Company; its use was dictated by the fact that Cirrus Motor Company money was invested in the original Great Lakes Corporation.

The Great Lakes Sport-Trainer, Model 2T-1, initially appeared with straight wings and was found to be tail-heavy in flight, so Meyers and Leisy solved that the quickest and cheapest way possible: They gave the little biplane nine degrees of sweep-back in its top wing panels, and the happy result of that was a distinctive craft with excellent performance that was popular then, as well as a generation later, when it was revived and put back into production with a modern engine. The original Great Lakes company, however, disappeared forever into the maw of the Great Depression after some 500 Sport-Trainers were built with Cirrus and Menasco engine installations.

Charlie Meyers left Great Lakes in 1931, about a year before its demise, to fly the Goodrich Rubber Company's Lockheed Vega, *Miss Silvertown*, testing the new wing deicer boots. Charlie eventually "Busted hell out of Miss Silvertown" (his phrasing) following engine failure with a load of ice. The early P&W Wasp engines had inadequate carburetor heat available. If one picked up carb ice, the standard procedure was to lean out the fuel/air mixture until the engine backfired, then, according to Charlie. "That either got rid of the ice or blew the damn carburetor off."

## Meyers goes to Eastern

After months of seeking out bad weather for the deicer tests, Charlie was hired by Eastern Air Transport to fly the mail in one of their Pitcairn biplanes. He remained with them after they became Eastern Air Lines, and flew everything from Curtiss Kingbirds to Douglas airliners. He retired from Eastern in 1956 as a senior captain flying DC-7s.

Meyers Midget, with M-6 airfoils, flew 106 mph in closed-course race with 32 unreliable horsepower.

Charlie maintained his pilot's certificate and flew his Cessna *Skyhawk* for another dozen years, during which time he taught a grandson to fly. Charlie died of natural causes in 1972, leaving behind a part of our air heritage, along with his wife Jessie, whom he married during barnstorming days, and two daughters, both married to airline captains.

## Review questions

1. Identify some of the barnstormers of the early 1920s. What did they do? Why can it be said that they contributed to the growth and development of aviation? Why did the Air Commerce Act of 1926 mark the beginning of the end of the barnstorming era?

2. What were some of the Morrow Board's recommendations for civil aviation? Who was Jake Moellendick? Why is he known as the father of Wichita's aviation industry? How was the Swallow Airplane Manufacturing Company formed? What happened to Matty Laird?

3. How did Clyde Cessna get started in aviation? What characteristic of the original Bleriot Monoplane did Cessna adhere to in all of his aircraft? How was Travel Air Manufacturing Company formed? Why did the company break up?

Charles Meyers, codesigner of the Great Lakes 2T-1 Sport Trainer, was also company test pilot and raced modified versions of the Great Lakes.

The Great Lakes biplane was a favorite of aerobatic pilots into the '60s. This one was flown by three-time national champion Harold Krier.

A popular sportplane of the late '20s was the Model 113 Monocoupe, a two-place craft with a 65-hp air-cooled Velie engine, which sold for $2865 in 1929. Stinson Detroiter in the foreground. Both aircraft were returned to flying condition in the mid '60s.

Ryan B-5 of 1929 was produced by the Ryan Aircraft Corp., St. Louis, which purchased the Mahoney-Ryan company of San Diego that built Lindbergh's *Spirit of St. Louis*. The Ryan Broughams were all advertised as "sister ships" to Lindbergh's famous airplane.

Another, and highly successful, St. Louis-built airplane was the Curtiss-Robertson Robin. The prototype, and many production Robins, were powered with OX-5 engines or an OX-5 modification known as the "Tank." Others were fitted with the Curtiss Challenger radial. The Robin was three-place.

Captain Meyers shortly before his retirement from Eastern in 1956. Meyers maintained his pilot's certificate for another dozen years, flying a Cessna Skyhawk for pleasure.

Eastern Air Lines

# 7

# The first airlines

## Objectives

At the end of this chapter you should be able to:

- Explain the significance of Charles Lindbergh's epic flight to the growth of aviation.

- Discuss the importance of the Kelly Bill to the development of airlines in the U.S.

- Identify the successful bidders on the first Contract Air Mail (CAM) routes.

- Understand how the Ford Motor Company got started in aviation and developed the famous TriMotor.

- Describe the formation of the following three aviation empires which monopolized the industry: United Aircraft and Transport Corporation, North American Aviation, and Aviation Corporation (AVCO).

The late 1920s witnessed the formation of important aviation empires. The airplane's great potential as a commercial vehicle was at the threshold of realization, and significant risk capital appeared as investors poured money into a small and fragmented industry unaccustomed to such munificence. It was a turbulent, exciting time. It was a time for wheeler-dealers.

## The Lindbergh boom

Charles Augustus Lindbergh was not solely responsible for the boom in private and commercial flying that followed his solo flight from New York to Paris in May 1927. Civil aviation was ready to dramatically expand in America by 1927, and the boom was simmering on a back burner when Lindbergh lifted the lid.

The trend was discernible as early as 1925, when more than 300 new civilian planes found buyers, compared to a total of 60 the year before. In 1926, new plane deliveries topped 650, aided by orders from private contractors to the air mail service. So the airplane's potential as a commercial vehicle was at the threshold of realization when Lindbergh made his historic flight and turned the world's eyes skyward.

This is not to denigrate Lindbergh. He planned and executed his trailblazing flight with skill and courage, and afterwards he could have accepted any of dozens of motion picture or other offers that would have made him very rich indeed, but he refused to exploit his fame. This hero was for real.

It has been said that Lindbergh "sold" 10,000 airplanes overnight, and whether or not that is true, heavy money did flow into aviation enterprises in the wake of his exploit, and some of it, at least, did some lasting good be-

Lindbergh's specially-built Ryan monoplane was powered by a 220-hp Wright Whirlwind J-5C. Lindbergh paid Ryan $10,580 for the *Spirit of St. Louis*.

cause another man, one Walter Folger Brown, was determined that the United States should have the finest domestic airline system in the world.

Brown was in position to make it happen. He was President Herbert Hoover's postmaster general, and as such he administered the provisions of the 1925 Kelly Bill. When Brown saw that the Kelly Bill did not give him all the muscle he needed, he wrote a new law that did. It would be known as the McNary-Watres Act of 1930.

## The Kelly Bill

The Kelly Bill (HR 7064) provided for payment to operators of up to four-fifths of the postal revenues carried, but that proved cumbersome and the bill was amended on 3 June 1926 to allow payment of up to $3 per pound for the first 1000 miles, and 30 cents per pound for each additional 100 miles. As a measure against irresponsible bidding or the undercutting of established operators, a 1928 amendment established a 5 cents per ounce minimum for operators that had satisfactorily flown the mail for two years, and allowed them to exchange their contracts for 10-year route certificates.

The Post Office Department lost money under these provisions; in 1929, for example, actual payments to operators totalled $11,618,000, while air mail revenues came to $5,273,000.

The Post Office expected that. From its own experiences in flying the mail it knew that the only profitable routes had been those established at the beginning—short routes of 200 miles and with 24 cents stamps. But it also understood that the air mail would be truly useful only when it reached all parts of the nation, and with postage rates in keeping with the general economy. In 1929, air mail postage was 5 cents per ounce and that appeared realistic for the times.

Meanwhile, the Post Office hoped and expected that the operators would add passenger service to supplement their mail pay and, as passenger revenues increased and larger, more efficient aircraft were put in service, mail pay could be negotiated downward. The Post

Office Department, in the person of Postmaster General Harry S. New in the Coolidge Administration, made all that clear to the first contract operators.

There was, of course, a great deal of opposition to a subsidy for the air mail carriers, notwithstanding the fact that the railroads had been built with generous land subsidies from the federal government, and the steamship lines continued to receive subsidies with no end in sight. Those who favored the Post Office's subsidy to the air operators insisted that some form of government help was essential to the development of a domestic airline system because private capital would never be available in sufficient amounts and could not justify the large short-term losses with the promise of profit perhaps years in the future. But the subsidies would disappear, they insisted, as air travelers brought new profits to the operators.

The problem was that most of the contract air mail operators were not anxious to carry passengers, not as long as they could get up to $3 per pound for carrying mail in open cockpit biplanes.

However, the Kelly Bill did give the postmaster general considerable control over the operators. He could, for example, award routes only to those bidders that he regarded as responsible, and when bids were opened for the first eight routes on 7 October 1925, Postmaster General New awarded but five contracts because he was not satisfied with the equipment, financial status, or operating experience of the remaining bidders.

The five successful bidders were Colonial Air Lines, Contract Air Mail Route 1 (CAM-1), New York-Boston; Robertson Aircraft Corporation, CAM-2, St. Louis-Chicago; National Air Transport, CAM-3, Chicago-Dallas/Ft. Worth; Western Air Express, CAM-4, Los Angeles-Salt

The first contact air mail routes were flown in open-cockpit biplanes. Here, a Curtiss Carrier Pigeon of National Air Transport lands at Kansas City. Barnstormer Ben Gregory's Standard is in foreground; a New Swallow in background.

Lake City; and Varney Speed Lines, CAM-5, Elko, Nevada-Pasco, Washington. Two weeks later, Henry Ford's Ford Air Transport was awarded CAM-6 and CAM-7 for the Detroit-Cleveland and Detroit-Chicago routes. Then CAM-8, Seattle-Los Angeles, went to Pacific Air Transport, and CAM-9, the Chicago-Twin Cities route, was awarded to Charles Dickinson, millionaire Chicago seed merchant.

**CAM-1.** Colonial started in 1923 as the Bee Line, an air taxi service apparently meant to occupy the free time of a group of ivy league types of good family and old money. Its stockholders included William Rockefeller, Cornelius Vanderbilt Whitney, Sherman Fairchild, Juan Trippe, and Harris Wittemore of Connecticut and Bond and Share. After winning CAM-1, it became Colonial Air Transport.

**CAM-2.** The Robertson brothers, Frank and Bill, were WWI pilots who were able to obtain financing from St. Louis businessmen. One of their pilots was Charles Lindbergh.

**CAM-3.** National Air Transport had been organized immediately after passage of the Kelly Bill by Clement Keys of Curtiss Aeroplane and Motor Company, William Rockefeller, Charles Kettering of GM, and the ubiquitous Howard E. Coffin.

**CAM-4.** Western Air Express was put together in July of 1925 by former automobile racing driver Harris "Pop" Hanshue, and was backed by Harry Chandler, publisher of *The Los Angeles Times*, and other West Coast investors.

**CAM-5.** Varney Air Lines (at one time called Varney Speed Lines), was put together by Walter Varney, who had been in aviation since 1916, and his airline grew from a flying school and air taxi service in San Mateo, California. Varney would be in and out of the airline business (selling out at a profit each time), including one operation in Mexico.

**CAM-8.** Pacific Air Transport belonged to Vern C. Gorst, another old timer who had been a pilot since 1912, and who operated a West Coast bus line.

**CAM-9.** Charles Dickinson's operation of CAM-9 pointed up the need for prior experience in maintaining scheduled air mail service.

E.M. Laird

Laird Speedwing (left) and Laird Commercial flew CAM-9 in the beginning. Northwest Orient Air Lines would grow from this route.

Although he was a rich man, Dickinson identified with aviation's little guys, and he bid on CAM-9 only to keep National Air Transport (NAT) from getting it. As Dickinson put it: ". . . to keep Wall Streeters from reaping the profits from an industry nurtured to the point of gain by the risks and sacrifices of men the system was bypassing." Dickinson made sure of the contract by offering to carry the mail between Minneapolis and Chicago for 48 percent of the postal revenues, a very low figure at a time when 80 percent was the maximum.

Dickinson's CAM-9 began operation 7 June 1926 equipped with three new Laird biplanes, plus a cabin biplane built by Elmer Partridge and an open-cockpit craft constructed by H.J. "Pop" Keller. In addition to Partridge, Dickinson's pilots included Matty Laird (temporarily), Billy Brock, and Charles "Speed" Holman. Partridge and Laird were the only two men to fly the mail in airplanes they had designed and built themselves.

CAM-9 was 400 miles in length, possessed no airway beacons, and had been abandoned by the Post Office Department six years earlier because of a series of crashes induced by bad weather. The weather hadn't changed since 1920. Partridge smashed to his death on his initial flight. Laird and Keller, flying OX-5 airplanes, were forced down by weather. Only the two Whirlwind Lairds made the trip successfully. In following weeks, the pair of Lairds kept CAM-9 alive and on a reasonable schedule, but Dickinson was losing money on every trip, and began looking for an honorable way out of the air mail business.

He went to Bill Stout, whom he had known as a member of the Aero Club of Illinois back in 1910. Stout, who would later take over Henry Ford's airlines, required little sales talk. He quickly rounded up H.H. Emmons (a lawyer and a member of the WWI Deeds-Coffin Aircraft Production Board) and banker Frank Blair of Detroit, brought in Col. L.H. Brittin, and incorporated under the name Northwest Airways. Northwest successfully rebid CAM-9, and one of its first pilots, in addition to Speed Holman, was David L. Behncke, who would later found the influential Air Line Pilots Association. Northwest Airways, of course, would one day be known as Northwest Orient Air Lines.

Northwest Airways' first airliners were Hamilton Metalplanes, built in Milwaukee by Tom Hamilton (also responsible for Hamilton Steel Propellers), and designed by Jim McDonnell, who would later form McDonnell Aircraft—today, McDonnell-Douglas. Charles "Speed" Holman was chief pilot at Northwest.

*Maiden Dearborn* was one of a pair of Liberty-powered Stout 2-ATs operated by the Ford Motor Company in scheduled service between Detroit-Chicago and Detroit-Cleveland transporting automobile parts prior to flying the mail.

Bill Stout's first airplane was his 1919 Batwing, planned as a prototype of a navy torpedo bomber.

**CAM-6 and CAM-7.** Henry Ford's CAM-6 and CAM-7 began flying the mail on 15 February 1926, the first private operator to do so, because Ford 2-AT Transports had been flying over these routes, carrying automobile parts and Ford Motor Company personnel on schedule, since the previous April.

Henry Ford had become interested in aviation at least as far back as 1914, when he sent one of his best attorneys to help Glenn Curtiss in Curtiss's court battles with the Wrights. And that interest had been rekindled late in 1923 as the result of an improbable letter written by an improbable man, William Bushnell Stout.

# Stout metal planes

Bill "Jackknife" Stout, a mechanical engineer, interested in aircraft design since leaving school (there were no university degrees offered in aeronautical engineering until 1922), was a flier and an extrovert. He had founded and edited *Aerial Age*, one of the earliest U.S. aviation magazines, worked for Jesse Vincent at Packard, and, in WWI, was in charge of invention studies at the army's McCook Field. Stout's letter, sent to a hundred of the nation's top industrialists, informed each that he needed capital to build a new kind of airplane and suggested that each send Stout $1,000. The letter ended with the unsettling statement that no contributor should expect to see his money again.

Apparently, Bill Stout had a good reputation: 25 people sent checks, among them Edsel and Henry Ford.

The plane Stout wanted to build was a three-place monoplane fitted with an OX-5 engine; it was evolved from his earlier "Bat Wing" and incorporated two advanced features: all-metal construction and a wing braced from within. Both principles were unusual in the United States, although the German Junkers company had built such craft as early as 1915, and Eddie Stinson was flying a Junkers in the United States at that time.

Bill called his airplane the Stout Air Sedan. Only one was built, and it barely flew, but the Fords were convinced of the soundness of Stout's approach to airplane design. Within a few months the Ford Motor Company provided a factory building and an airfield, and put the Stout Metal Plane Company in business.

During 1924 Stout produced two machines, the Model 2-AT ("AT" for Air Transport"). These were eight-passenger versions of the Air Sedan, but powered with 400-hp Liberty engines and with redesigned wings, the latter being the work of George Prudden, Stout's chief engineer who later became noted for his design work at Lockheed after a brief fling at marketing a small trimotor under his own name in 1928.

Stout's pair of 2-ATs were tested and ready for service by the time Congress passed the Kelly Bill and, with two more added to the Ford fleet, began scheduled operation. Eleven were eventually built, seven sold to other lines, and all had perfect safety records. Meanwhile, in July 1925, the Ford Motor Company had bought out the Stout Metal Plane Company.

Ford's entry into aviation at that time gave the industry important psychological as well as practical benefits. He was respected for his business acumen, and his participation encouraged other sources of money. On the tan-

The Stout Air Sedan, which impressed the Fords, reflected Batwing's influence.

Joe Durham

The German Junkers J-1 of 1917 was an all-metal aircraft with full cantilever wings, one of a number of Professor Junkers' "Tin Donkeys." Stout introduced the Junkers concept to America.

Stout Air Pullman was the prototype of the 2-AT model. Pilots did not like the enclosed cockpit, so the 2-ATs that followed, as the first TriMotors, left pilots in the open.

gible side, Ford built the first concrete runways in the U.S., the first control tower, pioneered in air-to-ground radio communications, and spent large sums advertising air travel in leading magazines.

## Ford TriMotor

Early in 1926, at Ford's direction, Stout and his engineers produced the first Ford TriMotor Model 3-AT. Large (for that time) multi-engine airplanes had become more practical with the introduction of the Wright Whirlwind engine. The 3-AT, however, was less than a rousing success and was providently destroyed in a hangar fire. Then Stout's crew went to the other extreme and produced a winner, the prototype of the classic "Tin Goose." The Goose flew on 11 June 1926 with Shorty Schroeder at the controls, and it would become a major tool in the development of the emerging airlines.

Boeing and Fokker also contributed early multiengine planes in significant numbers. In fact, the Ford TriMotor was undoubtedly inspired by the first Fokker TriMotor, which appeared a year earlier and which the Fords had bought for Comdr. Richard Byrd's attempt to fly over the North Pole.

## Fokker TriMotor

Anthony Fokker was a Dutchman who built his first flyable airplane in 1910 and later designed some very good fighter airplanes for Germany during WWI after the British and French refused his services. Following the lead of Professor Junkers, Fokker adopted cantilever wings (no external bracing) and metal-framed fuselages, and, with a factory in Amsterdam after the war, opened an office in New York with Robert B.C. Noorduyn in charge. Noorduyn would later open his own aircraft factory in Montreal. By the time the Ford TriMotor appeared, Fokker was building airplanes as the Atlantic Aircraft Corporation in Teterboro, New Jersey.

## From nowhere to nowhere

As expected, almost none of the new operators showed a profit in the beginning. Average income was approximately 43 cents per mile,

First Ford TriMotor was the 3-AT. Performance matched its looks.

while operating costs began at about 50 cents per mile and went as high as 80 cents per mile. Few were discouraged, however, because they were sure that the government would never allow the service to die. The operators were confident that if they showed good faith and operated as dependably as possible, reasonable adjustments in mail payments would be made after a decent interval. And such adjustments were made by way of amendments to the Kelly Bill, notably in 1926 and again in 1928 as previously mentioned. By the end of 1928, when air mail postage was reduced to 5 cents per ounce, most operators were making money, averaging 90 cents per plane mile. A year later, this was up to $1.10 per mile. The 5 cents air mail stamp increased loads by 95 percent, and because the air carriers were then being paid by the pound to fly the mail, that meant that their incomes almost doubled while their costs increased very little.

The Post Office Department, with the Republican Congress concurring, wanted it that way. Air mail revenues were far below the cost of the service, but many new routes were added during this period, and some operators were buying equipment that accommodated a few passengers because most understood that a change in Washington could modify or even reverse the government's policy of subsidizing the air mail carriers. In any case, it could not be expected to last forever. Most understood that they were expected to develop enough passenger and air freight business to allow reductions in mail pay to levels below that of air mail revenues.

While there was some indication that this would happen at some future date, the lines were evolving slowly, largely because the routes were too fragmented to attract such business. Too many CAM routes were flown "from nowhere to nowhere," and those that flew "somewhere" had no connecting flights to serve potential air passengers. For example, Boeing Air Transport flew Boeing Model 40A biplanes between San Francisco and Chicago that had cabin space for two hardy passengers, but NAT, which took the mail on to New York from Chicago, had no provision for passengers.

Ford 4-AT TriMotor was flown by Shorty Schroeder at the Philadelphia Air Races in September 1926. The 4-AT carried eight passengers and was powered with Wright J-4 Whirlwinds.

Fokker F-10 of Western Air Express was a 12-passenger airliner fitted with three Pratt and Whitney Wasps of 420 hp each.

NAT's Curtiss Carrier Pigeons were hefty biplanes designed for the large mail loads of CAM-3 and the New York-Chicago route that NAT was awarded in September 1927. They were Curtiss-built because C.M. Keys at Curtiss was a principal organizer of NAT. Boeing Air Transport (BAT) flew Boeing airplanes for the same reason, and this would be the case as other major operators appeared. American Airways flew Stinsons because both had a common corporate parent. Thus, the trend to what may be called "semi-cartels" was apparent by the time the Hoover Administration took charge of the White House on 4 March 1929.

## United Aircraft

By then, the aviation empires of the several financial power blocs were identifiable. The first to emerge was United Aircraft and Transport Corporation. It was put together after William E. Boeing of the Boeing Airplane Company in Seattle was awarded CAM-18, the transcontinental route between Chicago and San Francisco, following the second round of air mail bids in January 1927. Boeing had waited be-

cause the transcontinental line was not offered to private contractors until that time, and he was not interested in anything less.

Bill Boeing came from a pioneer lumber family in the Pacific Northwest, and his Boeing Airplane Company could trace its beginning back to the Pacific Aero Products Company, formed by Boeing and Conrad Westervelt in 1915 to build what were, essentially, improved copies of the Martin training plane. Boeing sold 50 of those craft to the navy early in WWI, and had concentrated on military orders ever since.

## Whirlwinds and Wasps

United Aircraft was the creature of Bill Boeing and Frederick Rentschler, with Chance Vought included as a sort of junior partner. You will recall that Rentschler formed Wright Aeronautical from the remains of the WWI Wright-Martin company to manufacture Hispano-Suiza engines. In 1922 the navy convinced Rentschler that Wright Aeronautical should buy out tiny Lawrance Aero Engine Company and develop Charles L. Lawrance's promising 200-hp air-cooled radial engine. It had not been a difficult decision for Rentschler because the navy—his best customer—said it would buy no more Hissos, and that it expected to standardize on air-cooled radials for its shipboard airplanes.

Rentschler's enginemen, George Mead and Andy Willgoos, had brought the Lawrance J-1 engine to a high state of reliability as the J-4 *Whirlwind* by 1924, and Rentschler recognized the opportunity of a lifetime. Aware that Sam Heron and Ed. T. Jones at the army's McCook Field engine research facility had developed a superior air-cooled cylinder and valve system, he resigned from Wright Aeronautical and took Mead and Willgoos with him. Rentschler quickly found financing. He secured it from Niles-Bement-Pond, a company that owned the idle Pratt & Whitney Tool Company factory in Hartford, Connecticut. A principal stockholder and officer in Niles-Bement-Pond was the unsinkable E.A. Deeds. Thus was formed the Pratt & Whitney Aircraft Company. Employing the Heron-Jones air-cooled cylinder, Mead and Willgoos quickly produced the first P&W *Wasp* engine, the R-1340, initially rated at 400 hp.

The Wasps and Hornets that followed in quick succession were fabulously successful, being purchased in great numbers by the navy, army, and civil aviation alike, and when Boeing joined forces with Rentschler to form United Aircraft and Transport Corporation in October 1928, they were looking far down the pike at civil aviation's great potential, determined to profit as much as possible from it.

Beginning with the purchase of Chance Vought's company and Pratt & Whitney, they also acquired—within a year, and mostly by way of stock swaps—Hamilton Propellers, Standard Steel Propeller, Stearman, Northrop, and Sikorsky. They brought Boeing Air Transport into the fold as United Air Lines, and then went after the New York-Chicago air mail route in order to possess the entire transcontinental route coast-to-coast.

## North American

The bug in United's cup of tea was, of course, National Air Transport, which had the air mail

Hudek Collection

The Wright Whirlwind J-6 series of 225 hp.

The R-1340 Pratt and Whitney Wasp of 400 hp. In later years, this engine was rated at 600 hp.

contract for the New York-Chicago route. NAT had the same visions of aeronautical sugar-plums dancing in its corporate head as did United. NAT was controlled by the Curtiss-C.M. Keys group and Keys was also dreaming of an aviation empire.

The battle was an expensive one for United, because it drove NAT stock from $15 per share to $30, and while United was buying up NAT common, Keys formed North American Aviation, a holding company backed by Bankamer-ica-Blair, and proposed an exchange of stock between NAT and North American. That would have given Keys a preponderance of the votes in NAT, which he did not have as things stood. But Boeing and Rentschler obtained a temporary court injunction to delay Keys' ploy, and by the time a hearing was scheduled on the matter, United had enough NAT stock and proxies to take NAT into the United family.

Meanwhile, Boeing and Rentschler had bought out Walter Varney, whose air mail route had been expanded to fly between Seat-tle and Salt Lake City. Shortly afterwards they would purchase Vern Gorst's Pacific Air Trans-port that flew between Seattle and Los Angeles, and Bill Stout's nonmail line that had suc-ceeded Ford's Detroit-Cleveland route. As the emerging airlines faced the era of expansion, United was already fat and sassy.

Clement Key's North American Aviation grew apace, although it eventually took a dif-ferent turn. Formed solely as a holding com-pany, North American was soon backed by General Motors, which gained full control in 1933, and Hayden, Stone & Company, along with Bankamerica-Blair. It had Curtiss Aero-plane and Motor Company as its cornerstone. Other important properties soon acquired in-cluded Eastern Air Transport (New York-At-lanta at that time), Sperry Gyroscope, the Ford Instrument Company, Keystone Aircraft (bom-bers), Moth aircraft, Curtiss-Caproni, and New York Air Terminals, Inc. Robertson Aircraft, in

Francis H. Dean

Clement M. Keys (right), aviation empire builder

St. Louis, and Walter Beech's Travel Air company would be added in mid-1929, but first, North American's airline was born as Transcontinental Air Transport (TAT).

## Transcontinental Air Transport

TAT was unique in that it was a combination air and rail passenger service. Leaving New York at night via Pennsylvania Railroad pullmans, the passengers were transferred to Ford TriMotors that next morning at Columbus, Ohio. They flew to Waynoka, Oklahoma, then boarded a Santa Fe pullman for Clovis, New Mexico, where another Ford airliner waited to

take them on to Los Angeles. The trip was comfortable and safe, but it was also expensive (16 cents per mile), and not much faster than a transcontinental train. TAT lost $2.75 million during its 18 months of operation, but would be rescued by a forced merger with Western Air Express to become TWA—about which, more momentarily.

## AVCO formed

The third large aviation combine to appear at this time gathered its holdings together as the Aviation Corporation (AVCO). AVCO was incorporated in March 1929 with a working capital of $35 million, and its directors included Sherman Fairchild; three investment bankers; D.K.E. Bruce, who was a son-in-law of Andrew Mellon; Robert Dollar, steamship magnate; Harry S. New, former postmaster general; and Gen. Mason Patrick, former chief of the U.S. Air Service. While $35 million may not sound too impressive these days, we should keep in mind that these were 1929 dollars, equal, perhaps, to ten times that amount today.

AVCO began by acquiring Embry-Riddle's operation over CAM-24, Chicago-Cincinnati. T.H. Embry and Paul Riddle had previously run a flying service in Cincinnati and were dealers for the new Fairchild monoplane built in Hagerstown, Maryland. Sherman Fairchild had entered the airplane manufacturing business because there was no airplane on the market that provided a suitable platform for the excellent aerial cameras he had perfected. Fairchild promoted AVCO with the help of the above-named fellow incorporators. Within a short time this new holding company controlled a number of companies, including its own subsidiary holding company, Colonial Airways Corporation, originally organized as Colonial Air Transport, which held CAM-1. AVCO then looked toward the South, where it found Southern Air Transport (SAT) with several of the essential mail contracts.

SAT could trace its roots back to Temple Bowen, a tough old bus operator whose Texas Air Transport flew the mail between Dallas/Ft. Worth and Galveston and San Antonio. Bowen sold out to A.P. Barrett's Southern Air Transport in 1928, and Barrett, a Tennessean who had gone to Texas with nothing and parlayed a charming manner and a politician's instincts into a natural gas supplier serving five states, then purchased Gulf Coast Airways, which flew between Atlanta and Houston by way of New Orleans. It was at that point that AVCO negotiated an exchange of stock with SAT that gave AVCO controlling interest in these important southern routes—and Barrett a vice presidency in AVCO.

AVCO purchased other small operators, such as Interstate Air Lines (Chicago-Atlanta, CAM-30), and successfully bid on an air mail route in Alaska. Then it went after Universal Aviation Corporation.

Universal was backed by a group of St. Louis, Chicago, and Minneapolis bankers and, like the other aviation combines, was started during the halcyon days of the Lindbergh Boom when almost any aviation stock could find eager investors. As an example of the boom, the stock of Seaboard Air Lines experienced a sudden increase in value following the Lindbergh flight to Paris until it was discovered by investors to be an East Coast railroad.

Fokker F-32 had four P&W Hornets of 575 hp each, two tractors and two pushers. The F-32 had a span of 99 feet and seated 32 passengers. Ten were built for Western Air Express and Universal Air Lines.

Stinson SM-1 Detroiter flown by Ruth Elder and George Haldeman attempted Atlantic flight five months after the Lindbergh flight to Paris. Elder and Haldeman were plucked from the ocean near the Azores by a passing ship.

Universal was built from Robertson Aircraft Corporation, which flew the mail between St. Louis and Chicago, a well-managed company that was well known because of Lindbergh's employment there before his epochal flight to Paris.

Universal successfully negotiated with the Post Office Department for the Cleveland-Louisville route, CAM-16, acquired some small flying services, and bought Tom E. Braniff's

Braniff Air Lines, a passenger service at near bus fares flying between Kansas City and Dallas/Ft. Worth. In 1930, Braniff and his elder brother would start another airline.

Late in 1929, Universal directors voted to accept an exchange of stock with AVCO that left AVCO with a 95 percent controlling interest in the Universal properties.

Meanwhile, AVCO was buying into every other aviation firm it could find, including E.L.

Stinson 6000-B was a nine-place airliner flown by American Airways. Engines were 215-hp Lycomings. These craft were in service 1932 through 1936.

Cord's Lycoming Motors and Stinson Aircraft Corporation.

## Stinson Aircraft

Eddie Stinson built the first of his famous Detroiters in a Congress Street loft in Detroit and tested it on 25 January 1926 at Selfridge Field. It was a four-place cabin biplane with wheel brakes and electric starter. Eddie's financial backers, a group of Detroit industrialists, were impressed with the machine. An empty factory was obtained in nearby Northville, Michigan, and the Stinson Aircraft Corporation organized. The first production model of the Stinson biplane Detroiter, completed in August 1926, was sold to Reed Chambers' Florida Airways, CAM-10. The first Stinson monoplane appeared ten months later. By that time Eddie was wearing spats, smoking 25 cents cigars, and had 200 workers on his payroll.

## American Airways formed

At that time, AVCO organized American Airways and brought all of its subsidiary holding companies into American. Eventually, all the subsidiaries were dropped and AVCO ended up as the sole stockholder of American Airways, which would be renamed American Air Lines in 1934. That simplified the corporate structure considerably, but the airline itself was still a collection of disjointed routes, and it would fall to the new postmaster general, Walter F. Brown, acting under the powers given to him by the next amendment to the Kelly Bill, the McNary-Watres Act of 1930, to fill in the blanks that would allow American Airways to become a major airline system.

All of the new aviation combines—indeed, the entire aircraft industry—anticipated continued prosperity as the Republicans maintained control in Washington with the 1928 elections, and although there were disquieting signals from Wall Street early in 1929, few paid heed. Significant money continued to be available to aviation enterprises, and the combines continued to expand.

## Curtiss and Wright merge

In August 1929, C.M. Keys engineered the merger of Curtiss Aeroplane and Motor with Wright Aeronautical Corporation to form Curtiss-Wright Aeronautical Corporation, a $200 million corporate marriage that brought 29 aviation step-children under the same roof, including Travel Air, acquired within days of the Curtiss and Wright vows. Curtiss-Wright, of course, was related by corporate marriage to North American Aviation.

Later, in July 1930, North American founded China Airways Federal Corporation to buy 45 percent Chiang Kai-Shek's China National Aviation Corporation (CNAC). Pan Am would end up with that stock after the Democrats at last returned to the White House in 1933, but that is getting ahead of our story. (If you have concluded that Keys, Boeing, and Rentschler were wheeler-dealers, just wait until we examine the maneuverings of Juan Trippe as he built Pan Am.)

First, however, comes Walter Folger Brown, who was either a dictator who served the money interests in civil aviation or a dedicated public servant. That is a determination you will have to make for yourself.

## Review questions

1. Why can't it be said that Lindbergh's flight was a catalytic event? How did Postmaster Brown exercise so much power? Describe some of the provisions of the Kelly Bill. Why weren't the carriers anxious to carry passengers?

2. Identify some of the early CAM routes and the successful bidders. How did the Ford

Motor Company become involved in aviation? Describe the formation of United Aircraft and Transport Corporation by Boeing and Rentschler. Who was Clement Keys? Name some of the companies under the North American holding company. Who were some of the founding directors of AVCO? Name some of the companies which were acquired and came under its holding company umbrella.

3. How did the Stinson Aircraft Corporation get started? How was American Airways formed? Who engineered the merger of Curtiss Aeroplane and Motor with Wright Aeronautical Corporation?

# 8

# Czar of the airways

## Objectives

At the end of this chapter you should be able to:

- Discuss the importance of the McNary-Watres Act in shaping the early airline route structure.

- Summarize the purpose and results of the "Spoils Conferences."

- Describe how TWA and Delta were formed.

- Describe the fate of many smaller carriers such as Reed Airline and Century Air Lines.

- Explain how the competition between Ludington Line and Eastern Air Transport led to the air mail scandals of 1934.

America's domestic airline system was pieced together during a critical five-year period: 1928 through 1932. Surrounded by controversy and charges of political favoritism, the routes were parceled out behind closed doors, nurtured by government subsidy, and directed by the postmaster general. No single person, before or since, has held such power over the nation's airways. The question is, did Walter Folger Brown wear a white hat or a black one?

## McNary-Watres Act

Walter F. Brown was a Toledo attorney who had toiled faithfully in the Republican orchards for more than two decades when President-elect Herbert Hoover rewarded him with the portfolio of the U.S. Post Office Department. After taking office in March 1929, Postmaster General Brown spent months studying the air mail system and the state of commercial aviation in America. Then, in February 1930, he appeared before the House Committee on Post Office and Post Roads to urge passage of HR 11704, an amendment to the Kelly Bill popularly known as the McNary-Watres Act after its sponsors, Senator Charles McNary of Oregon and Representative Laurence Watres of Pennsylvania. Actually, Brown himself was the author of this significant bit of legislation, with some input from William P. McCracken, a former assistant secretary of commerce who had initially administered the Air Commerce Act of 1926, and who was, by 1929, a lobbyist for airline interests.

Congress approved the McNary-Watres Act 29 April 1930, and the important provisions in the new law were: 1) Operators were to be paid for flying the mail according to space available for mail in their airplanes, which could be as much as $1.25 per mile for a Ford or Fokker TriMotor; 2) The postmaster

Walter Folger Brown, President Hoover's postmaster general, fostered legislation that gave him the power to build America's domestic airline system. He used that power ruthlessly.

general could extend or consolidate routes "when in his judgment the public interest will be promoted thereby;" 3) Routes would be awarded to the lowest responsible bidder who had owned an airline operated on a daily schedule of at least 250 miles over a period of six months.

These provisions gave Brown almost absolute control over the airlines, and practically guaranteed profits to those who cooperated. The act offered the air mail contractors outright subsidies. In that respect the primary intent of Congress and the Post Office Department seemed clear: Give the operators substantial incentive to acquire large multi-engine

airplanes and develop passenger revenues. That, in turn, would promote the development of safer and more efficient machines, and as passenger revenues increased, mail payments could be decreased; eventually, the airlines would be self-supporting and would carry the mail at rates that would be below that of the postage represented.

Brown and the Congress were obviously right. The contracts let in 1929 averaged $1.10 per mile; by 1933 the average was down to 54 cents per mile over a vastly expanded system. Then, on the brink of self-sufficiency, the whole structure would be pulled down by the Roosevelt Administration, as we shall see momentarily.

It is possible that the Republican lawmakers did not fully realize the extent of the power they were giving to the postmaster general with the McNary-Watres Act. The authority to extend or consolidate routes could be (and was!) broadly interpreted, as was the inclusion of "responsible" in the "lowest responsible bidder" provision. The requirement that a bidder have six months experience over a route of at least 250 miles effectively eliminated most small, poorly financed operators. Taken together, what these provisions really meant was that only the fat cats need apply. Postmaster General Brown meant to erect a great airline system, possessing the best available equipment and the most effective management. There wasn't much room in his plan for the little independents with limited resources. Brown had the muscle and he intended to use it.

## Spoils conferences

The power of Brown's muscle became apparent just two weeks after passage of the McNary-Watres Act when he called a series of meetings in Washington to divvy up the new air mail contracts. These meetings would later be called the "spoils conferences" by the Democrats. Brown made it clear to the invited

In 1928, Harris "Pop" Hanshue's Western Air Express flew its profitable Los Angeles-Salt Lake City air mail route with half a dozen Liberty-powered Douglas M-2s.

Pacific Air Transport, later absorbed by United, began flying the mail between Los Angeles and Seattle in September 1926, equipped with six Ryan M-1s. PAT's pilots included Lee Schoenhair, who later flew for Goodrich and would contract with Matty Laird for the famous Laird "Solution" racing plane, and Ralph Virden, who was fated to die while testing the Lockheed P-38.

John K. "Jack" Northrop pioneered all-metal stressed-skin construction after leaving Lockheed (where he designed the wooden Lockheeds, beginning with the Vega), and his Northrop Alpha was purchased by Transcontinental and Western Air (TWA) and National Air Transport (NAT) in 1930. Forward cabin was configured for three to six passengers on most Alphas.

operators (those regarded as "uncooperative" were not invited) that he intended to have three transcontinental routes and that each must be under a single management. United had the northern route and Brown was quite satisfied with it. The middle route would be established by the merger of TAT and Western Air Express, and American Airways would have the southern route, because Brown would extend or consolidate where necessary to take American all the way to the West Coast without the threat of "outside" bidding.

Just in case some troublesome bidder should crop up, Brown had a remedy for that, too. When the contracts were duly advertised for bidding, he inserted the provision that qualified bidders must have flown at night for six months over a route of not less than 250 miles. Since only the big carriers could meet that qualification, it was met with anguished cries of protest. Brown calmly pointed to the original air mail act, the Kelly Bill, which clearly stated that the postmaster general was empowered to "make such rules, regulations, and orders" as were necessary for the carrying out of provisions of that law.

The independents on the outside looking in were understandably angry. Brown's approach was unfair and counter to the basic tenets of free enterprise. But the major operators soon came to resent Brown almost as much as did the little guys who were squeezed out. The postmaster general favored them because they had the means to build the system he envisioned. True, he saw to it that they made money, but along with the federal largess came total federal control, and Ringmaster Brown's fat cats obediently lined up on their designated perches as he cracked his mail-pay whip.

Two contributing factors that worked in Brown's behalf was the airlines' deep distrust for one another, and the fact that the nation was sinking into the Great Depression following the stock market crash in October 1929. But the central fact that none could ignore was that no airline could survive with the airplanes then available with passenger fares alone. The difference between profit and loss was an air mail contract. Therefore, the airline operators did things Brown's way or not at all.

## TWA formed

An early example of doing things Brown's way was the forced merger of Western Air Express (WAE) and TAT. Pop Hanshue's WAE was one of the few lines that had made money from the start. Flying CAM-4 between Los Angeles and Salt Lake City, WAE connected with United, and because so many people in the Los Angeles area had ties in the east, Hansue's mail loads were large. WAE netted about $1 million per year on this route. Then, in 1929, WAE inaugurated a passenger service, sans mail pay, between Los Angeles and Kansas City. Although the passenger line lost money, Hanshue kept it in operation because he believed that it would be the logical west half of the transcontinental middle route that was certain to come, and because he knew that the more direct route to the East Coast from Los Angeles would drain business from CAM-4.

Burrell Tibbs

Oilman Erle Halliburton owned Southwest Air Fast Express (SAFEway), which operated Ford TriMotors in Missouri, Arkansas, Oklahoma, and Texas; was absorbed, after a fight, by American Air Lines, with Postmaster General Brown forcing the merger.

TAT went all the way across the country from New York to Los Angeles, flying in daylight and transferring its passengers to trains at night. It was a big money loser, and Hanshue wanted no part of it. Brown liked TAT because it was well-financed and had good equipment and experienced management, it had an aura of permanency and responsibility about it, and it had a pioneering equity in the route every bit as valid as WAE's. Besides, Brown was unwilling to split a coast-to-coast route between two different managements. The fact that, under Brown's own rule, TAT was not a qualified bidder because it lacked of night flying experience was not a problem, the postmaster general pointed out, because, if the two lines merged, WAE would bring the necessary night flight experience to the new company.

Hanshue and his directors fought the merger, but in the end they had to capitulate. On 13 February 1931 Western Air Express and Transcontinental Air Transport exchanged stock on an equal basis and became Transcontinental & Western Air—TWA.

Hanshue was bitter, especially after TWA lost $1 million during its first year of operation. He blocked the purchase of Curtiss Condor airliners, which former TAT people favored due to their affiliation with Curtiss via North American. TWA bought Fokker TriMotors instead because of TAT's affiliation with North American and because General Motors owned the American Fokker Company and was a major stockholder in North American.

## SAFEway and Delta

The only bidder on the transcontinental southern route was AVCO's American Airways, although American did not get the route without challenge. Two men who thought they should have it were Erle Halliburton, an Oklahoman who operated Southwest Air Fast Express (SAFEway), and C.E. Woolman of Delta Air Service.

Halliburton made his money in oil (Halliburton Oil Well Cementing Process). His passenger airline, which flew Ford TriMotors out of Tulsa into Texas, Kansas, and Missouri, was very close to the break-even point despite fares that were near those of the bus lines.

Woolman's Delta Air Service began as a crop-dusting business in Louisiana in the early '20s, and his airline, started in 1925, flew between Birmingham and Dallas across the Deep South.

Both Delta and SAFEway were excluded from the bidding by Brown's night flying requirement. Woolman sold out to American Airways just as Brown intended, but Halliburton chose to fight and was preparing to go to court when American bought him out for $1.4 million. SAFEway's hard assets totalled less than $800,000. Thereafter, Halliburton continued in his very successful oilfield business, although Woolman would return with another Delta airline after President Franklin Roosevelt's "New Deal" forced the airlines into a 180-degree turn in 1934.

By the spring of 1931, one could travel by air between all major American cities, as well as a great many lesser ones. United, TWA, and American offered daily schedules coast-to-coast. Eastern (affiliated with TWA through their North American parent) flew up and down the East Coast; United served the West Coast over the old Pacific Air Transport route, and also branched south at Chicago to fly into Texas. Northwest, meanwhile, was receiving route extensions from the postmaster general to take it across the northern states toward Seattle as fast as it could digest them. Although the independents should have gotten the word by then, they nevertheless continued to proliferate, most seeking to establish pioneer equities over routes between smaller towns, hoping for a mail contract. Most were sincere if unrealistic, proceeding on faith and belief in fair play, honest effort, and the free enterprise system. Sad to say, most of them fared poorly. Others, who were less constrained by such traditional values and dared buck the system, managed to make something out of nothing.

## Reed Airline

An example of the former, and typical of dozens of other small independents, was Joe Roy Reed. Reed was an honorable man who seemed perpetually in good humor. He had learned to fly during WWI at Ft. Sill's Henry Post Army Airfield, barnstormed in the early '20s, and returned to active duty with the Air Corps Reserve in the late '20s, flying Douglas O-2Hs with the 320th Observation Squadron at Post Field. Reed, like many of his contemporaries, foresaw the ultimate role of the airplane as a commercial vehicle and, at some point while serving as an army aviator, acquired his airline dream. In 1929, he left the Air Corps to pursue his dream.

Reed had already selected his route. His southern terminus would be Wichita Falls, a rich north-Texas city of 50,000; he operated from there to Lawton, Oklahoma, 40 miles northward, which could boast only of some 20,000 people (but was adjacent to Fort Sill and potential military business), then 85 miles to Oklahoma City, where he would connect with United's Chicago-Ft. Worth run and, finally, 95 miles to Ponca City, his northern terminus.

The only weak point in Reed's planned route was the lack of facilities at Lawton. Lawton had no airport, and apparently no suspicion that it needed one. Therefore, Reed began a campaign to convince those worthy citizens that they should move to share the blessings of the air age. He spoke before school assemblies, women's clubs, the chamber of commerce and, eventually, the city council. It took almost a year, but he aroused sufficient interest to provoke a bond issue, approved by the voters in the amount of $35,000, for the construction of a municipal airport.

Reed took a lease on the new Lawton airport and, with savings in hand, plus a frightening note at the bank, bought a Spartan C-3 biplane for charter and instruction and began searching for a secondhand airliner that pos-

Typical of America's small-town airports of the early '30s was the sod field at Lawton, Oklahoma, home base for Reed Airlines. Author Joe Christy's first flying lessons were received in the Spartan C-3 at right. Ryan Brougham at left.

sessed a price tag to match his limited working capital. His first ad in the local paper read: "Learn to Fly! Pilots make big money! Complete flying course $250! Rides $2!"

The new airport was dedicated on Labor Day 1930, and Reed worked through the fall getting his base of operations set up and more or less self-supporting. He was forced to cut the price of his "complete flying course" to $175, but at the beginning of 1931 he had eight students, some charter business, and had hired a mechanic from the local Pontiac garage who apparently encountered no problems in transferring his bolt-busting talents from automobiles to airplanes.

In the meantime, Reed had located his airliner, a six-place Travel Air 6000B monoplane owned by the Wadlow Brothers Flying Service in Wichita, Kansas. It had sold new for $13,500. The Wadlows, feeling the pinch of the depression, were willing to sell it for $7500, the amount they had paid Central Air Lines for it a few months earlier. (That was one of at least three "Centrals." It was established in 1928 and flew between Wichita and Tulsa for a time. Another, established in 1930, flew a Detroit-Washington route and merged with Pennsylvania Airlines in 1936 to form Pennsylvania Central Air Lines; it was renamed Capital Air Lines in April 1948, and absorbed by United 1 June 1961. The third began service in November 1949, flying between Dallas/Ft. Worth and Wichita, and was merged with Frontier Air Lines 1 October 1967.)

Central had christened the Travel Air "Romancer" because, in late February 1929, Charles Lindbergh had borrowed it for a flight to Mexico City and a visit with his fiancee, Anne Morrow, whose father was ambassador to Mexico. This was the same Dwight Morrow whose

The six-passenger Travel Air 6000B *Romancer* and airline owner and chief pilot Joe R. Reed (right) with speed flier Frank Hawks.

1925 Morrow Board repudiated Billy Mitchell's position on U.S. airpower. There, the Travel Air lost a wheel on takeoff with Miss Morrow aboard. The famed flier stacked cushions around her and landed in the thin air of Valbuena Airport, flipping upside down, though leaving Anne uninjured. This incident, coming just a few days after public disclosure of the Lindbergh-Morrow engagement—surely the most extensively reported romance of the roaring '20s—bathed the orange-and-green Travel Air in publicity and pixie dust, making it a symbol of the ideal romance, with adventure in the clouds thrown in for good measure, that an adoring public could vicariously share with the Lone Eagle and his mate.

Therefore, when Lindbergh offered to buy the slightly damaged Travel Air from Central, those officials would not hear of it. The airplane was easily fixed good as new—in fact, somewhat better than new, as any public relations man would testify.

The immediate result was some 50-odd airborne marriages in the Romancer that, added to its regular airline runs between Wichita and Tulsa, must have given it a utilization rate that would warm the heart of any airline president. But Central fell upon evil times with the deepening depression, and the enchanted Travel Air felt a new hand on her control wheel—the hand of a man who appreciated her for herself rather than for her past associations.

"She was a sweetheart to fly," Reed later recalled. "She had an indicated cruise of 95 mph, which was respectable enough then, and a short-field landing and takeoff performance that would be respectable now. She was licensed for a pilot and five passengers, along with 30 pounds of baggage for each, but if six or seven fares showed up, it didn't strain her any to add a couple of kitchen chairs in the aisle in order to accommodate everyone."

In 1931 there was no legal barrier to the formation of an airline. All it took was a little money and a lot of faith. And in the middle of the Great Depression there was little question concerning the fares to be charged. It was merely a matter of competing with the bus lines. Reed's first published rate table listed ticket prices very near those of the bus lines.

When asked about federal regulation, Reed chuckled. "That was before the time of the FAA, or even the CAA, although the Department of Commerce had been issuing pilot licenses since 1926. I recall that they did make a rule requiring airline pilots to pass an instrument flying test, which I did, but nothing was ever said to me about having a blind panel in the airliner, which I did not have."

Reed Airline began operations 1 September 1931 and the Romancer averaged four passengers per flight during the first month. That was not solely due to low fares, but at least in part to Reed's tireless huckstering, and perhaps because he would cheerfully bend a schedule to make a paying customer happy. For example, a lady with two preteen children wanted to go to grandmother's farm for a visit. Grandma lived 25 miles west of Oklahoma City so the Lawton-Oklahoma City flight that morning deviated from its normal route. Reed obligingly put the Romancer down in grandma's south forty, then, with a wide grin to his other paying customers, took off and continued to the capitol city. (That incident is recorded from firsthand knowledge; I was one of the kids.)

Early in 1932, Reed added another Travel Air 6000, hired young Joel Pitts for $65 per month plus expenses to fly it, and began pressing the Post Office Department for an air mail contract.

At the end of his first year, having met 94 percent of his schedules, Reed noted a small but steady increase in boardings and optimistically purchased a third airliner, a sesquiwing Buhl Air Sedan (sesquiwings were of biplane configuration, but the lower wings were far smaller than the upper ones) and hired another pilot. Throughout 1932 and 1933, when the depression imposed its hungri-

Travel Air 6000s under construction at Walter Beech's Travel Air plant in Wichita. Travel Air biplanes in background.

In addition to two Travel Air 6000s, Reed Airlines also operated a 300-hp sesquiwing Buhl Air Sedan. The Buhl was built in Marysville, Michigan. The company's chief pilot, Lou Meister is at right.

est days on the southern plains, Reed Airline met its schedules and almost broke even financially, while Reed made several pilgrimages to Washington pushing for the air mail contract that would, in the end, determine the fate of his bold venture.

In retrospect, it is easy to see that Reed Airline never had a chance. But Reed held on by slashing his rates 20 percent, reducing the price of his solo flying course at his home field to $120, and returning to Washington in March 1934 to make a final attempt at securing a mail contract. He was denied.

Reed Airline met its last schedule on 1 April 1934. Reed sold his airplanes to the Charles A. Babb aircraft brokerage firm in Glendale, California, and the Romancer went to Central America where it faded into oblivion.

Joe Reed traveled a lot late in life, before his death in 1982, but the young captains of Metro Air Lines' Convairs never knew why the white-haired gentleman with the wide smile always waved at them as he boarded the airplane at Lawton.

## Airway Scrooges

E.L. Cord was a different kind of man. And while it is not easy today to characterize him (even *Time* magazine of the '20s and '30s, a usually productive source for research into that lusty era, ignored Cord), it is safe to conclude that Cord was more than a match for the likes of C.M. Keys or even Walter F. Brown.

Cord had risen from car salesman to head of the Auburn Automobile company (which should tell us something) when he detected opportunity in the airline business. In 1931 he started two small passenger lines, Century Air Lines and Century Pacific Lines, each of which paralleled high-density routes flown by American Airways out of Chicago and San Diego.

It is not clear whether Cord, without mail contracts, expected to successfully compete with the big AVCO line, or whether he planned from the beginning to make such a nuisance of himself that American would be forced to buy out his Century lines at an inflated price. The latter seems more likely, be-

Stinson 6000B of E.L. Cord's Century Air Lines. Cord cut fares and suffered a pilot's strike in an unsuccessful bid to obtain an air mail contract, but he ended up in control of American Air Lines.

cause Cord not only undercut American's rates but offered to fly the mail over American's routes for approximately half the amount that American got for it. Cord maintained that American, and most other airlines, were poorly managed and, with proper cost controls, could profitably operate with far less money from the Post Office Department. As if to underscore his position, Cord forced a strike by his own pilots late in 1931 when he decided that the $7200 per year average pay for captains—fostered by Tex Behncke's AFL-sponsored infant Airline Pilot's Association—was ridiculous at a time when plenty of qualified pilots were looking for jobs.

It wasn't Cord's low rates or his fight with the union that set the industry on edge. It was his claim that the airlines were being grossly overpaid for flying the mail that tended to give the operators a nervous twitch—especially American, because it was receiving 70 percent of its revenues from mail contracts, or about one-third of all air mail appropriations for transporting approximately 10 percent of the mail.

Interior of the Stinson 6000 TriMotor airliner

Joseph P. Juptner

The same charges had been made before by other independents, but Cord was a credible threat because, whether or not he was bluffing, he apparently had the resources to back up his low bid and, although the operators were assured by the postmaster general that Cord had no chance at a mail contract, that could change with a new administration in Washington. So American decided the best way to silence Cord was to buy his airlines and make him an AVCO stockholder.

Cord's price was 140,000 shares of American Airways, and that was enough to make him a director of AVCO. Shortly afterwards, when other AVCO directors sought to buy into the Curtiss-Keys combine—which is to say, North American Aviation—Cord saw that such a deal would weaken his position at AVCO and he successfully fought the transaction and emerged in control of AVCO, holding 19 percent of American Airways stock.

Cord would remain a strong and unsettling influence in the industry until after the "air mail scandals" of 1934; then, apparently to avoid answering some embarrassing questions posed by the Securities and Exchange Commission, he fled to England.

Another independent, very much like Cord's Century lines, was Ludington Line, which flew between New York and Washington from September 1930 until February 1933, when it was forced to sell out to Eastern Air Transport. The Ludington brothers got their investment back, and that was all. But Ludington Lines was destined to greatly, if indirectly, influence the future of the entire industry.

Ludington actually showed a small profit flying passengers. Largely financed by the socially prominent Charles and Nicholas Ludington of Philadelphia, and sharply managed by Gene Vidal (formerly with TAT and another Ivy Leaguer), Ludington Lines instituted "Every Hour on the Hour" service over a short, high-density route, offering rates close to those of the railroads. Every economy was utilized: The equipment was Stinson TriMotors

Ludington Lines employed low-cost ($18,000) Stinson Model 6000 TriMotors, and effected every possible economy of operation to fly "every hour, on the hour" between New York and Washington, but the Ludingtons were forced to sell to Eastern when denied a mail contract by Postmaster General Brown.

that, at $18,000 each, cost about half as much as Ford TriMotors. Ludington Captains flew alone, handled baggage, taxied on one engine, and cruised on automobile gasoline in flight.

Ludington operating costs were therefore approximately 35 cents per mile, an amount usually equalled or exceeded by passengers' fares alone. Whatever Ludington could get for flying the mail would have been pure profit.

But Eastern Air Transport was awarded the mail contract between New York and the nation's capitol at 89 cents per mile. When a Ludington official bitterly complained to a Washington newspaper reporter about Eastern's contract, awarded despite Ludington's bid of 25 cents per mile, that enterprising young reporter, Fulton Lewis, Jr., sensed a good story and began digging into Post Office Department records.

The deeper Lewis dug, the more excited he became. He found abundant evidence that Ludington's treatment at the hands of the postmaster general was typical of that ac-corded to the small independents. Lewis learned of the meetings between Brown and the selected airline executives when the important routes were planned soon after passage of the McNary-Watres Act, and he discovered how thousands of miles of the air mail routes had been parceled out to the big combines by way of the "route extension and consolidation" clause, immune from any threat by outside bidders.

It has been suggested that since reporter Lewis was the son-in-law of Postmaster General Brown's chief political rival, Lewis' motives in pursuing the air mail story were less than pure. That is unfair to Lewis and irrelevant to this account. True, he developed but one side of the story, a common fault in news reporting then and now, but the media's never-ending search for misconduct in government is a valuable service to the nation, whatever prompts it.

Oddly, Lewis' boss, publisher William Randolph Hearst, refused to allow publication of Lewis' scoop, and whatever Hearst's motive, his repression of a story so pertinent to the public interest would seem to be at least as immoral as Postmaster General Brown's alleged misdeeds.

Although Lewis was denied the satisfaction of breaking the story of the "air mail scandals," his material was the basis for the inquisition visited upon the industry after the Democrats returned to office in 1933.

## Review questions

1. What was the purpose of the McNary-Watres Act of 1930? List some of its important provisions. Why did Postmaster Brown call a series of meetings with airline executives shortly after passage of the act? Why did it become known as the "Spoils Conferences"?

2. How was TWA formed? Why did Harris Hanshue fight the merger? Why were SAFEway and Delta excluded from bidding on the transcontinental southern route?

3. Describe the plight of such airlines as Reed and Century. How did the bidding for the New York to Washington, D.C., air mail route between Ludington Line and Eastern Air Transport lead to the air mail scandals of 1934.

# 9

# Glass houses

## Objectives

At the end of this chapter you should be able to:

- Describe the purpose and political implications of the Black Committee.
- Summarize Walter F. Brown's testimony and response to the Ludington-Eastern Air Transport affair.
- Explain why the army was ordered to fly the mail and their experience from February to May 1934.
- Define the purpose of the Air Mail Act of 1934 (Black-McKellar Bill) and the Civil Aeronautics Authority Act of 1938.
- Describe how Pan Am was formed and how Juan Trippe was able to obtain the Key West-to-Havana route.
- Discuss some of the problems faced by Pan Am in developing service into Central and South America.
- Describe the postwar competitive environment for international routes.

The day of reckoning came for W.F. Brown and his favored airline operators but was poorly managed by their prosecutors. Nevertheless, the domestic airlines were severely punished.

Meanwhile, a U.S. overseas airline, enjoying an even greater degree of federal favoritism, along with generous subsidies, continued to grow. Justice, if that is what it was, could wait.

## New Deal or raw deal?

The Special Committee on Investigation of the Air Mail and Ocean Mail Contracts, popularly called the "Black Committee" after its chairman and chief inquisitor, Senator Hugo L. Black, was authorized by the Senate a month before President-elect Franklin D. Roosevelt took power with his "New Deal" in March 1933.

Senator Black was an Alabama Democrat with a mail-order law degree. At age 47 he was unprepossessing in appearance, with sandy, thinning hair, a folksy manner, and a dry wit. He was an economic liberal and a social conservative, an ambivalence endemic to southern politics. He was a small man with a large ambition, and he would be appointed to the Supreme Court by FDR in 1937, but when his committee began its hearings in 1933, Black was little known outside Alabama. The air mail scandals, real or manufactured, would make him a national figure.

The Black Committee was made up of two Republicans and three Democrats. The former were White of Maine and Austin of Vermont. The Democrats, in addition to Black, were

William King of Utah and Pat McCarran of Nevada. Later, McCarran's conduct in the Senate as a tireless crusader for Pan Am's monopoly on overseas routes would leave his ethics subject to question. However, when this worthy body began taking testimony in September 1933, in Room 312 of the Old Senate Office Building, it was immediately apparent that Hugo Black was to be the star of the show.

There were, of course, plenty of disgruntled independents in, or formerly in, the airline industry to ensure that the Black Committee became acquainted with the material gathered by reporter Fulton Lewis, Jr.

Black was an accomplished politician and had no intention of allowing other newsworthy events to detract from his performance. The Black Committee pecked at the ocean mail mess, which was an old story and strictly ho-hum stuff to news reporters, in a desultory manner, marking time while the goings-on in the room next door grabbed the headlines.

Next door, the Senate Banking and Currency Committee was, in effect, putting America's private banking institutions on trial for whatever blame could be charged to them for the 1929 market crash and the ensuing worldwide depression. Because the witnesses called to testify before that committee included such famous names as J.P. Morgan and the partners in Morgan's investment/banking empire (among Morgan's partners was Dwight Morrow, Charles Lindbergh's father-in-law), all of the news reporters were at this hearing.

But the Senate's banking probe eventually died of malnutrition and, in October, Black was ready to raise the curtain on his exposé of the former postmaster general and his airline cronies.

Now, in justice to Black (no pun intended), we should concede that the Democrats had been out of office for 12 years, and were understandably anxious to discredit the policies and programs of the Republicans. Black smelled thievery and conspiracy in the air mail program and, in the long tradition of old-fashioned, gallus-snappin' politics, he saw the opportunity to right some grevious wrongs, save some taxpayers' money, and make a great deal of political hay in the process.

Therefore, even today it's not easy to decide whether or not the New Dealers acted in good faith, or at what point the good faith degraded into simple demagoguery or a stubborn determination to save face at whatever cost.

True, there was undoubtedly plenty of thievery and political favoritism to be uncovered in the previous Republican administrations had the Democrats looked for it in the right places, but they seem to have seized upon the air mail question prematurely, and made it into a media event, before it became evident that there was another side to the story. The testimony before the Black Committee did, indeed, confirm the facts gathered by reporter Lewis. However, it soon became clear that the airline operators, big and small alike, had simply followed the rules set down by Walter F. Brown.

Brown denied nothing. His testimony made it equally clear that he was determined to give the American People the greatest air carrier network in the world, and that could not be done by awarding air mail contracts to small independents who merely wanted to fly the mail over hundreds of short routes and, for the most part, were not interested in developing passenger services. Such a policy would indeed be a waste of the taxpayers' money. As for Ludington, it was merely skimming cream from a short, high-density route. If Ludington had to provide service comparable to that of EAT over great distances, its costs would match EAT's 70 cents per mile. EAT was simply the more responsible bidder, and was making a significant contribution to the overall airway network. It required money—lots of money—to build the stable systems that covered the nation, and therefore Brown dealt with the companies that had plenty of capital, although he had often been less than gentle with them. He forced the major lines to accept route extensions when he considered those extensions to be in the public interest.

Yes, he got rid of independents who appeared to intend to speculate with a mail contract. He had been ruthless and his enemies were legion. And he was completely unrepentant. As one aviation reporter put it, "About all that can be said in Brown's favor is that he has given the United States a domestic airways system second to none; and there is not a shred of evidence that Brown himself has made anything from it except a lot of enemies."

So the Black Committee established that Brown had been a dictator. No formal charges were brought against him because he had apparently acted within the law. However, President Roosevelt, acting on the advice of Attorney General Homer Cummings, announced on 9 February 1934 that all air mail contracts would be cancelled on the 19th. He told reporters that the airways system had been mapped out in a series of "spoils conferences" attended by Walter F. Brown and a handful of his favored airline operators, that small operators were denied the chance to bid on air mail routes, and that some airlines had been grossly overpaid for carrying the mail.

## The army flies the mail

Roosevelt then called in Gen. Benjamin Foulois, chief of the impoverished Army Air Corps, and asked if the army could fly the mail. Foulois, of course, had no choice but to reply in the affirmative, but he knew full well that the Air Corps had neither the airplanes nor trained pilots to take over scheduled all-weather flying.

The Air Corps began flying the mail on 19 February. Although Roosevelt's postmaster general, James Farley, agreed that only 9000

The Curtiss T-32 Condor, fitted with a pair of Wright Cyclones, seated 12–15 passengers, and served both American and Eastern from mid-1933 through 1936. Brown favored the well-financed lines that were willing to promote passenger service.

The Curtiss O-39 observation plane was typical of the several types pressed into service to fly the mail when FDR cancelled all air mail contracts in 1934. Lt. Otto Wienecke died in an O-39 approaching Cleveland in a snowstorm.

miles of the 27,000-mile system would be served and no passengers carried, the army faced an impossible task. With only 10 days' preparation, airplanes with few instruments (some even lacked compasses), and non-instrument pilots, the attempt was made during the worst weather of the year. At the end of a week, five pilots were dead and six critically injured. And that was just the beginning.

By the second week in March, the mounting toll of accidents appalled the nation and President Roosevelt began looking for a way out. On 10 March he announced that the air mail would be returned to the airlines as soon as possible.

A total of 12 army fliers died before the mail could be handed back to the airlines. Had the air carriers actually been guilty of collusion, that was the time to get together for their mutual good. But they were so anxious to get back their mail pay, and so great was their distrust of one another, all submitted very low bids for their former routes, confident that fair adjustments could be negotiated later.

Jim Farley piously pointed to these bids as proof that the airlines had been overpaid, as the new administration had said all along.

But no one was listening to Farley at that point. The press and the public's reaction to the deaths of the army fliers, as the result of what many believed to be a political witch hunt, overshadowed any culpability that may have otherwise been borne by Brown and the airlines.

The New Dealers obviously felt that they should not be the subject of such calumny since their intentions were pure. More than ever, they had to insist that the airlines were guilty as charged, and then fix an appropriate punishment.

## The "Rascals" are punished

The extent to which the New Dealers were merely trying to save face with their continuing vendetta against the airlines, or whatever the measure of their belief that Brown and the major operators had conspired to loot the U.S. Treasury, is impossible to determine. It appears

The nation's press blamed President Roosevelt and his postmaster general, James Farley, for the deaths of the army fliers. This example appeared in *Aero Digest* magazine.

Cowboy humorist Will Rogers, who poked fun at Democrats and Republicans alike, was a firm supporter of the airlines and criticized the New Dealers' handling of the "Air Mail Scandals." The Ford TriMotor in background belonged to Maddux Air Lines, a West Coast operation that merged with TAT before the shotgun wedding of TAT and WAE that produced TWA.

that Senator Black never wavered in his hard-nosed position, and was willing to destroy the whole airline system that had been built during the Coolidge and Hoover Administrations. But President Roosevelt, while agreeing that the airline rascals should be made to suffer, was unwilling to see the system completely dismantled. Therefore, Postmaster General Farley's job was to get the system back in operation with a New Deal label on it, and with substantial penalties to the semi-cartels that owned the big airlines.

Farley managed that by decreeing that no airline which had been represented at the 1933 spoils conferences would be given a mail contract, and that the major air mail routes would be awarded only to bidders possessing multi-engine aircraft. That is why American Airways suddenly became "American Air Lines;" Northwest made a similar change; EAT became "Eastern Air Lines," while TWA, a bit bolder, simply added "Inc." to its name, and United Air Lines remained unchanged because its original mail contract had been obtained in the name of Boeing Air Transport. The multi-engine provision kept most of the independents from bidding on the major routes (shades of W.F. Brown!).

Some of the more responsible independents were admitted to the fold. Tom Braniff was back and was awarded United's route from Chicago to Texas; C.E. Woolman squeezed through Farley's door to put Delta back in business in the South.

Meanwhile, new regulations were drawn to punish the industry. These were contained in a bill written by Senator Black and the chairman of the Senate Post Office Committee, Democrat Kenneth McKellar of Tennessee. The Black-McKellar Bill (Air Mail Act of 1934), with the President's endorsement, sailed through Congress 12 June 1934, a month after the mail had been returned to the airlines. This legislation repealed all antecedent laws and left the air carriers subject to control by three federal bodies. Air mail contracts, routes, and schedules would be determined by the Post Office Department; the fixing of rates and air mail payments fell to the Interstate Commerce Commission, while the Bureau of Air Commerce would continue regulation of the airways and the licensing of pilots and aircraft.

The new law extended the temporary—and financially unsound—contracts signed when the mail was returned to the airlines following the cancellations, and limited the system to its existing routes. All airlines were required to separate themselves from manufacturing affiliates, and all routes were to be rebid each year.

All of the major airlines operated at a loss. United's first quarter deficit was $852,000, a crippling sum in 1934 dollars. TWA and Eastern, then owned by North American Aviation, lost $405,000 between them during the same period. American was able to cut its losses by reducing schedules. But all could look to the future with little hope. Long-range planning was impossible as long as the routes went up for grabs each year, while separation from manufacturing affiliates meant not only large auditing and legal fees, but reduced capitalization at a time when airline stocks were down to a fraction of their pre-cancellation values. United Air Lines stock dropped from 35 to 14; North American, listed at 8 just prior to the cancellation, dropped to 2⅝, while AVCO plunged from 10 to 4 during the same period. It was a bad time for the air carriers to be cut off from their solvent parent combines.

There were a few glimmers of hope during the next four years. New airliners appeared—the Douglas DC-2 and DC-3—that were so efficient they promised profits on passenger traffic alone. Another was found in the small print of the Black-McKellar Bill, a clause that empowered the President to appoint a Federal Aviation Commission to recommend future legislation.

A low-cost ($37,500) airliner for the short-haul air carrier of the mid-'30s was the Stinson Model A, powered with three Lycoming R-680 engines of 260 hp each. The Model A carried eight passengers and a crew of one. American and Delta flew Model As, as did Central.

It was this latter hope, transformed into reality, that produced the Civil Aeronautics Act of 1938, which at last brought sanity and stability to civil aviation in the United States.

In 1935, the 23 scheduled airlines that made up the domestic system owned 459 airliners with a total value of $12.5 million. They employed 652 of the 736 pilots holding an Air Transport Rating. Department of Commerce records also reveal that the airlines employed 335 copilots and 212 "hostesses and stewards," which roughly suggests how many of the 459 airliners were multi-engined. This source lists 679,000 passengers carried in 1935, at an average rate of 5.7 cents per mile. Total air carrier employment was 8333.

This tiny industry, less than 10 years in existence, beset by political shenanigans and economic impossibilities, nevertheless would prevail. It would manage to do so for another three years before Senator Pat McCarran, allied with Representative Clarence Lea, gained presidential approval of what was to become known as the Civil Aeronautics Act of 1938—legislation that was pronounced "fair and sound" by the Airline Pilots' Association, and which at last loosened the industry's crippling bonds.

## The CAA Act of 1938

The new law that established the Civil Aeronautics Authority (CAA) authorized the President to pick its administrator with the approval of the Senate. The remaining members would also be presidential appointees, but during their six-year terms could not be dismissed except for cause.

In practice, this worked well, and made for a reasonably autonomous authority be-

Following two record-breaking round-the-world flights in 1931 and 1933, former barnstormer Wiley Post went on to explore the problems of high-altitude flight and the design/test of pressure suits.

cause the Supreme Court had previously held that federal regulatory bodies were beyond the overt control of the President.

This board had plenty of power. It formulated policy and determined rates. Its decisions were law with regard to civil aviation. Left to the postmaster general was his time-honored right to enforce rules and regulations for transporting mail and determining schedules for mail transporters, but the amounts paid to the airlines for carrying the mail were set by the CAA.

The CAA took over the aviation property and personnel of the Post Office Department, the Interstate Commerce Commission, and the Bureau of Air Commerce on 22 August 1938, and established an Air Carrier Economic Regulation Division to control the airlines. This division immediately moved to protect the established air carriers by decreeing that only those lines to which it issued "Certificates of Convenience and Necessity" would be allowed to operate scheduled air services, a rule that would remain in effect until the industry was deregulated 40 years later. Operators could not open new routes or abandon existing ones without CAA approval, and it abolished the contract air mail system in favor of negotiated rates. It was a remarkably good

law, and it served the best interests of the airlines, general aviation, and the public.

In 1940, Roosevelt forced reorganization of the CAA and created the Civil Aeronautics Board (CAB) to regulate the airlines and investigate air accidents. The CAB was essentially independent, but the CAA was returned to the Department of Commerce. No one liked it that way except the President, who never explained why he demanded such action from the Congress (the Congresses of the Roosevelt era normally acted as FDR wished); however in practice, the regulation of civil aviation seemed little affected by the change, and the CAB would survive for more than 40 years under seven subsequent presidents.

Concurrent with development of the U.S. domestic airline system was the extension of American wings to foreign shores, and one airline was destined—indeed, chosen—to fly the oceans: Pan American Airways.

## Pan Am formed

Juan Terry Trippe built Pan Am with influence, money, ruthlessness, and ability. He regarded competition as wasteful, and "robber baron" was just one of the more printable so-

Pan Am's first airliners were three Fokker TriMotors, two F-7s (above) and a C-2. As with the early Fords, pilots remained in open cockpits in the F-7s. Engines were Wright J-5s. Scheduled passenger service between Key West and Havana began in January 1928.

briquets that were used by his contemporaries to describe him.

Trippe was 28 years old when he started Pan Am in 1927. He had the proper requisites for empire-building. Born to wealth, educated in the best schools, and possessing as friends other young men of influential families, Trippe was assured of a hearing before those holding financial and political power. He made the most of it.

Trippe had learned to fly in the navy during WWI, and gained some experience between 1923 and 1925 operating, with a surplus navy airplane, "Long Island Airways," a charter service. That part-time venture expired quickly and Trippe joined Colonial Airways as a minor executive. He left Colonial when it began scheduled service in 1926 as CAM-1, worked briefly for the banking firm of Lee Higginson & Company, and tried to decide whether or not he should accept the security (and, presumably, the boredom) of a position in his family's business, Trippe & Company, Brokers and Investment Bankers.

With aviation in his blood and avarice in his heart, the decision was not difficult. Juan

Trippe inhaled deeply of the roseate atmosphere that bathed all things aeronautic following Lindbergh's flight to Paris and saw opportunity. It was an opportunity reserved for those who could think big, and one must credit Juan with that: He could think big.

He established that when he outmaneuvered two other airlines to obtain a mail contract for a route between Key West, Florida, and Havana, Cuba. That 90-mile stretch held little value in itself, but as one of only two gateways to the Caribbean and Latin America, its potential was tremendous.

Trippe's company, entirely on paper when he submitted his bid to Postmaster General New, was the Aviation Corporation of the Americas (not to be confused with AVCO), and his rivals were Florida Airways and Pan American, Inc.

Florida Airways, organized by John Harding and war aces Eddie Rickenbacker and Reed Chambers, wanted to extend its Atlanta-Jacksonville run, CAM-10, through Miami and thence to Havana.

Pan American, Incorporated, was originally formed by Air Corps Maj. H.H. "Hap"

Sikorsky S-38 amphibians carried eight passengers (as did the Fokkers); entered service with Pan Am late in 1928. Engines were 420-hp Wasps.

Arnold (later, general, and chief of the U.S. Army Air Forces), and John K. Montgomery, a former navy pilot, after Arnold became alarmed at the expansion plans of the German airline, SCADTA, based in Columbia, which proposed service to Panama. Arnold decided to remain in the Air Corps for patriotic reasons after the Billy Mitchell court martial, and Montgomery was joined by G. Grant Mason. Their major backer was Lewis Pierson of the Irving Trust Company.

Pan American, Inc., seemed in a favored position to gain a mail contract for the Florida-Havana route because Mason had obtained exclusive landing rights in Cuba from Dictator Gerado Machado. However, it appears that Trippe may have had his own private spoils conference with the postmaster general, because he went to Cuba and somehow convinced Machado that the dictator should tear up his agreement with Pan American, Inc., and replace it with one granting Trippe's company exclusive landing rights in Cuba.

Thus armed, Trippe won the air mail contract at the maximum rate allowed under the law. He purchased, at bargain prices, both Pan American, Inc., and Florida Airways, renamed his company Pan American Airways, and began scheduled operations 28 October 1927 when Capt. Hugh Wells took off from Key West with a handful of mail in the Fokker Tri-Motor NC-53. Passenger service to Havana began the following January.

## The chosen instrument

From this 90-mile base route, Trippe reached out to the Dominican Republic and, in July 1928, gobbled up West Indian Aerial Express, which had been in operation just seven months, flying between Haiti and Puerto Rico. WIAE investors retrieved some of their money because the postmaster general insisted upon it. The Post Office Department and the State Department agreed with Trippe very early that Pan Am should be the United States' "chosen instrument" to carry the American flag on overseas air routes. Perhaps conscience-stricken, the postmaster general demanded that Pan Am at least purchase the equipment of the operators destroyed along the way.

The 13-passenger Ford 5-AT-B began flying Pan Am's Mexico and Central American routes in March 1929. Pan Am paid $55,000 each for these Wasp-powered craft.

In January 1929, Pan Am acquired control of Compania Mexicana de Aviacion, the Mexican airline that had been in operation since 1924. That gave Trippe a route from Brownsville, at the tip of Texas, along the Gulf of Mexico through Guatemala to Nicaragua. In September, service was extended through the Canal Zone to Barranquilla, Colombia, then continued eastward via Caracas to Port of Spain, Trinidad, where the system turned back northward to complete its circle of the Caribbean at San Juan, Puerto Rico. That locked up for Pan Am the two primary air routes to South America from the United States, with one approach through Texas and Central America, the other by way of Florida and the Antilles. Meanwhile, Miami replaced Key West as the Florida terminus, and America's overseas flag carrier began measuring the distances to Buenos Aires and Santiago, where some very formidable competition was firmly entrenched.

Anticipating continued expansion, Trippe sent Pan Am representatives throughout Latin America to obtain landing and operating rights. This involved State Department people, because a simple, unilateral agreement was seldom enough. Colombia, which already had a pretty good German-operated airline and had not forgotten Teddy Roosevelt's perfidy in wrestling away Colombian territory for the Panama Canal, was particularly difficult. That nation bargained so stubbornly that it ended up with a bilateral agreement that gave Colombia aerial access to the entire U.S. coastline—Atlantic, Pacific, and Gulf of Mexico. That was considered meaningless by American diplomats at the time, because everyone knew that such little countries could not operate an international airline. But years later—after WWII—times had changed, and when Colombia began to eye the lucrative American air travel market with its carte blanche agreement in hand, that occasioned some State Department backpedalling of truly magnificent form.

Trippe's toughest early antagonist was W.R. Grace & Company, a shipping, banking, trading monopoly that had for years been a mighty power on South America's west coast. Pan Am and Grace sparred warily for a time, then each decided that the other was too strong to risk a nose-to-nose showdown. So they formed a holding company in Peru, each

Pan Am acquired 14 Consolidated Commodore flying boats in September 1930, when Trippe absorbed James Rand's New York, Rio, and Buenos Aires Line.

The 40-passenger Sikorsky S-40, first of the famed "Clippers." Four P&W Hornet engines of 575 hp each maintained this 17-ton aerial houseboat in the air at 117 mph.

taking 50 percent of the stock, and the airline that resulted was called Pan American Grace Airways (Panagra), which flew the route from Buenos Aires up the South American west coast to Panama. Not until 1965 did Panagra's name drop from the list of international air carriers as Pan Am took over the route and Pan Am subsidiaries were limited to domestic operations.

Trippe faced another determined opponent on South America's east coast, the New York, Rio & Buenos Aires Line. NYRBA (referred to as "Near Beer" by its crews), was organized in 1929 by Ralph O'Neill, formerly associated with Boeing, and was backed by James Rand of Remington-Rand (later Sperry-Rand and still later Rand Corp.), along with Lewis Pierson of the Irving Trust Company, who, as a backer of Pan American, Inc., had jousted with Trippe before. J.K. Montgomery was also back, as an NYRBA officer.

NYRBA was as rich as Pan Am at the time, and its fleet of 14 Consolidated Commodore flying boats was superior to Pan Am's assort-

ment of Sikorsky S-38s, Ford and Fokker *TriMotors*, and Fairchild 71s. But NYRBA never really had a chance once Trippe was ready to muscle in, because its officials lacked the State Department backing that Grace's steamship lines commanded. The mail contract went to Pan Am (at the maximum rate of $2 per mile), and on 15 September 1930 Trippe acquired NYRBA and added the entire east coast of South America to his routes. That closed the big circle from Miami all the way around the South American Continent and back to Brownsville. In order to facilitate the takeover of NYRBA's Brazilian agreements, Trippe formed Panair do Brasil, and this subsidiary flew the route south of Belem to Buenos Aires. It, too, disappeared as an international carrier in the mid-'60s.

In the meantime, foreseeing the need for future Pacific terminals, Trippe purchased a couple of small Alaskan lines and bought into Chiang Kai-Shek's China National Aviation Corporation. He also obtained a mail contract for a Boston-Halifax route, anticipating Atlantic service.

# Across the Pacific

In the end, Pan Am did not need the Alaska bases for inauguration of transpacific service, because Glenn Martin, by then building airplanes in Baltimore, provided Pan Am with new, long-range flying boats that made possible a route to the Orient from California via Hawaii, Midway, Wake, Guam, and the Philippines. That was a route that very much pleased the U.S. Navy, which lent Pan Am all possible assistance in establishing those bases, for the navy had long been looking for an excuse to get such facilities on the stepping-stone islands of Midway, Wake, and Guam without upsetting the Department of State's delicate relations with Japan. Therefore, with help from the U.S. Navy, Post Office Department, Department of State, and Department of Commerce (and, surely, the Good Lord Himself, all things considered), Pan Am began scheduled flights across the Pacific to Hong Kong 22 November 1935. Capt. Ed Musick was in command of the Martin M-130 China Clipper on her initial flight.

Sikorsky S-42 entered service with Pan Am in August 1934; it carried 42 passengers in unparalleled luxury at 140 mph.

Pan Am began regular service across the Pacific—via Hawaii, Midway, Guam, and the Philippines—on 22 November 1935, with a trio of Martin M-130 flying boats. The M-130, capable of carrying 48 passengers, was powered with four P&W R-1830 Twin Wasps of 800 hp each.

## Across the Atlantic

Regularly scheduled Atlantic flights were delayed for several years when the British stalled negotiations on a reciprocal agreement until they possessed transport airplanes capable of flying the route. Finally, on 8 July 1939, Capt. Arthur LaPorte lifted the Boeing-built Yankee Clipper from the channel at Port Washington, Long Island, and headed northeast on a Great Circle course for Southhampton, England.

By that time, Pan Am faced trouble from another quarter as Hitler's aggressions in Europe at last prodded America into looking with concern at her deficient air defenses, and it became evident that the U.S. would be well-advised to build up its aerial lifeline to Britain in case of war and an attendant submarine menace in the Atlantic.

Of course, the last thing on Earth (or above it) that Juan Trippe wanted was to share one of his oceans with a competitor. He offered to schedule extra flights at little extra cost to the Post Office Department (Pan Am was already being paid nearly six times as much per mile for carrying the mail as any domestic airline). There was no point in wasting taxpayers' money by giving a mail contract to a competitor.

## American Export Lines

But a potential competitor had quietly been preparing to challenge Pan Am's Atlantic monopoly for more than two years. This was American Export Airlines, Inc. (AMEX), which was headed by John E. Slater and James M. Eaton. Slater had earlier rescued the steamship company, American Export Lines, and put it on a paying basis through good management practices. Eaton was a former official of Ludington Lines and Pan Am. Amex was conceived as a subsidiary of the steamship company, but separated itself from its parent during the ensuing battle with Trippe after filing for a route certificate in May 1939.

Trippe bitterly fought the AMEX application with the help of Senator Pat McCarran, who won an advantage for Pan Am even after the AMEX route certificate was approved. McCarran convinced his friends in the House that no money should be included in the Post Office appropriation for an AMEX air mail contract. Normally, that would have meant the end for AMEX, but at the beginning of WWII, AMEX found so much business waiting that it didn't need an air mail contract to survive. Then, when the army and navy took over all

The Boeing B-314 was the last and largest of the commercial flying boats. Boeing built 12 for Pan Am, with deliveries beginning in January 1939.

U.S. airlines upon America's entry into that conflict, the Pan Am-AMEX battle ended.

The precedent was established, however, and Juan Trippe knew that when peace returned he would be confronted with many AMEXs. But neither Trippe nor his future competition intended to wait for peace to do their planning. The State Department, too, was anticipating the problems of postwar global air travel.

## Postwar overseas routes

Assuming Allied victory, it was clear as early as 1942 that the United States alone would be in position to fly international civil air routes at war's end. The British had been forced to abandon transport airplane development in the late '30s in favor of desperately needed military aircraft. The United States, with its own desperate hour two years delayed, meanwhile produced such excellent transport craft as the Lockheed Constellation and Douglas DC-4.

The British had no intention of allowing U.S. airlines to take over postwar international air transportation, and they were not without effective bargaining power in the matter, because Britain controlled within its (then) far-flung empire many of the overseas bases and terminals essential to such operations. Therefore, a conference was called in Chicago, during November 1944, to divvy up the postwar international air routes.

That conference wasn't as presumptuous as it may sound. No other country, except Australia and Canada, could hope to have overseas airlines soon after the war. Germany, Japan, and Italy would be out of the running. Liberated France, its economy and industry ruined, would not be an immediate factor. The Soviets could be dealt with later.

Agreement between the United States and Great Britain did not come easily because, under Roosevelt, the U.S. Government had decided to discontinue the "chosen instrument" policy and encourage the operation of as many U.S. overseas airlines as the traffic would support. The English looked with horror upon that wasteful Yankee concept because their flag carrier, British Overseas Airways Corporation (BOAC), which had temporarily disappeared into war service, was a state-owned enterprise that Parliament

The Douglas DC-6 was a beefed-up, speeded-up, pressurized version of the DC-4. It began airline service in November 1946 with American and United. Engines were P&W R-2800s giving a total of 8400 hp and a speed of 300 mph. Engine improvements raised the speed of the DC-6B to 370 mph.

regarded as a prestigious symbol of Britain's global influence. Really, old boy, one could hardly expect such an instrument of the government to make money, now could one?

However, after much haggling, British-American differences were settled when the airlines themselves organized the International Air Transport Association (IATA), offered membership to all nations possessing or expecting to possess an overseas airline, and proclaimed that IATA would establish international air fares.

That allayed British fear of rate-slashing by the Americans and promoted an optimistic setting for a new conference, at Bermuda, in January and February of 1946, from which delegates from most of the Free World emerged in happy agreement.

The single dissenter was Pan American. From the time of the Chicago conference, Trippe, aided by his old ally Senator McCarran and new recruit Senator Owen Brewster, had been fighting in Congress to re-establish the "chosen instrument" principle. Senator McCarran repeatedly introduced bills (S 1790, S 326, and S 1814) that would, in effect, return America to its air policies of the early '30s. When the McCarran bills failed to win much support, they were slicked up with fresh goodies to attract other interests and tried again. It was an interesting battle (McCarran never explained why a Senator from Nevada should take such an interest in transatlantic air routes), but all it engendered in the end was a lot of resentment for Pan Am, especially in the executive branch of the government. And since Harry S. Truman had become president in April 1945, resentment in the executive branch was certain to find an outlet.

Pan Am

Lockheed Constellation Model L49 also served Pan Am in the immediate postwar years, with a total of 28 registered to the airline. Later versions of the Connie, which began as a 48-passenger airliner, had more powerful turbo-compound engines (Wright R-3350s), and a fuselage 20 feet 11 inches longer to accommodate up to 95 passengers.

There is evidence that President Truman was ready to substantially penalize Pan Am. He ignored the recommendations of his own CAB and arbitrarily awarded to Braniff Air Lines a route from the U.S. via Mexico City and Rio to Buenos Aires. This was right through the heart of Pan Am's hitherto private preserve. The President also announced that Eastern Air Lines would be granted a route from Miami to San Juan, Puerto Rico, although Eastern had not applied for it. It was another raid on exclusive Trippe territory. But then CAB Chairman L. Welch Pogue managed to calm the President, and the CAB was allowed to proceed with its task of parceling out America's portion of the world's air routes to the 18 U.S. airlines that wanted to share Mr. Trippe's air.

On 1 June 1945 the CAB ruled that three U.S. air carriers should fly the Atlantic to European terminals: TWA, Pan Am, and American Air Lines. United, alone among major U.S. domestic carriers, sought no international routes at the time. United's president, William Patterson, believed that not more than two dozen airplanes would be needed to serve the postwar Atlantic traffic.

Late in 1945, American Air Lines bought 60 percent of AMEX and renamed that company American Overseas Airlines. Five years later, the President overruled the CAB and approved the sale of AOA to Pan Am.

The CAB's route decisions on Latin America were handed down in May 1946. In addition to the routes given to Braniff and Eastern by the President, National Air Lines, American Air Lines, and Chicago & Southern were awarded certificates to operate south of the border. Then, 15 months later, the CAB decided that Pan Am's competitor in the Pacific would be Northwest Air Lines (later, Northwest Orient), which would fly the Great Circle route to the Orient where it would connect with TWA to effect round-the-world service. Pan Am, retaining its prewar Pacific run, would be the other round-the-world U.S. airline. United was at last edged into commercial ocean flying with a San Francisco-Hawaii route, duplicating Pan Am service to the islands.

These decisions, all carefully watched over by President Truman, resulted in the basic structure from which present-day international air routes evolved. There have been many additions, including foreign flag carriers that have the right to serve the United States in return for U.S. airline service to and across their countries, and there have been many route extensions and duplications as traffic increased. Introduction of the jets brought most of this increase. Pan Am was first with jet service, when its new Boeing 707 began flying from New York to Paris in October 1958.

Juan Trippe stepped down as Pan Am's board chairman and chief executive officer

The Douglas DC-7C had a total of 13,700 hp and a cruise speed of 355 mph with 104 passengers. Pan Am operated 26, the last prop-driven planes of the Pan Am fleet.

Pan Am began jet operations over the Atlantic with the Boeing 707-121 in October 1958. The 720B (pictured) went into service on Pan Am's Latin American routes in 1963.

Boeing 727-21, added to Pan Am's fleet in December 1965, cruised at 35,000 ft with 128 passengers, averaging 575 mph.

early in 1968, and Pan Am clearly lost much of its elegant arrogance. Under Trippe, Pan Am was the haughty grand dame of the international airways. She set the standards. Fortunately, Trippe was spared her inglorious end late in 1991; he passed away in 1978.

The Second World War greatly influenced the public's perception of air travel. At war's end, far more passengers awaited scheduled air service across the oceans than United's boss had suspected. The domestic airlines also enjoyed large increases in boardings.

During the war, the average citizen was all but excluded from air travel. The military requisitioned a large part of the airline fleet, beginning with the takeover of 11 Pan Am Boeing and Martin Clippers, along with five Boeing Stratoliners belonging to TWA. A priority system gave what seats there were to people flying on defense-related business. But literally millions of young Americans were introduced to air travel by the military air transports that whisked them to and from the far-flung the-

aters of war, and although that was air travel of the most uncomfortable and otherwise undesirable kind, it was, nevertheless, a firsthand demonstration of the transport airplane's ability to compress time and distance—the basic justification for air travel in the first place.

The airlines needed those first dozen years after WWII to find their proper places in the overall system, because another quantum advance waited at the end of the '50s.

As we have seen, three major factors came together in the late '20s to touch off a transportation revolution. First, the U.S. Post Office Department, historically an important force in the development of the nation's transportation systems, offered the promise of profits to scheduled air carriers. Second, at almost the same time, the first truly reliable and reasonably efficient aircraft engines appeared. Third, a significant influx of risk capital, immediately followed as a result of the first two, and was accelerated by Lindbergh's dramatic solo flight to Paris, which was certainly the greatest public rela-

Lockheed California Company

The Lockheed L-1011-500 began service with Pan Am in 1980. This version of the TriStar is 13½ feet shorter than other L-1011s, but carries 230 passengers 6200 miles, a truly long-range wide-body.

tions coup in aviation history, whether or not it was so intended.

The next great advance, the appearance of the jet airliner, would come as a result of the same factors: plenty of risk capital to reap the profits promised by more efficient machines.

## Review questions

1. What were the political implications of Senator Black's Committee? How did Walter Folger Brown respond to the charges against him? How was the Ludington-Eastern Air Transport bidding affair explained?

2. Why did President Roosevelt order the army to fly the mail? What was the army's experience from February to May 1934? How did the airlines get around the decree that no airline which had been represented at the Spoils Conferences would be given a mail contract?

3. What were some of the provisions of the Air Mail Act of 1934 (Black-McKellar Bill)? What was the purpose of the Civil Aeronautics Authority Act of 1938? Describe the consolidation which took place. What were the "Certificates of Convenience and Necessity?"

4. Who was Juan Trippe? How was he able to secure the Key West-to-Havana route? What was the "chosen instrument" policy of the Post Office and State Departments? What were some of the problems encountered by Pan Am in its expansion into Central and South America? How were these overcome? How was Pan Am able to launch service across the Pacific and Atlantic in little over ten years from the founding of the company?

5. Describe the competition faced by Pan Am in the post-WWII period. Why did the U. S. Government choose to discontinue the "chosen instrument" policy? Why didn't postwar transoceanic air travel revert back to the use of large flying boats?

# 10

# The New Deal
# and U.S. airpower

## Objectives

At the end of this chapter you should be able to:

- Give your reasons for the prevailing attitude of neutrality during the 1920s and early 1930s.

- Discuss the significance of the development of the Pratt and Whitney 400-hp air-cooled WASP engine.

- Give your reasons why the U.S. Naval Air Service placed so much emphasis on rigid airships during the 1930s.

- Recognize the position of Congress and the top military leaders regarding air power in the 1920s and 1930s.

- Describe some of the new-generation aircraft that appeared during the late 1930s.

The fact that President Franklin D. Roosevelt never admitted a mistake is insufficient evidence that he never made one. Of course, any President elected to four terms in that office, and whose supreme self-confidence leaves him unencumbered by doubt and provides him with the courage to make tough decisions without equivocation, is going to make mis-

takes. Nobody's perfect. And whether or not Roosevelt's "New Deal," which pointed the nation down the road to socialism, was a great mistake depends upon the politics of those who judge him, and is beyond the scope of this book. We are concerned here only with the effects of the New Deal on U.S. military aviation and the physical defense of our freedoms.

Still, to attain this limited objective we must take note of the atmosphere that gave birth to the New Deal and certain events that preceded it.

First, however, let us plainly state a couple of simple facts that our nation's leaders must heed in the planning of U.S. security: The American people will unite in support of war only when they believe that their very survival is at stake and that God is clearly on their side. It's just that simple. And a great many Americans view the maintenance of superior military forces as an invitation to trouble, rather than a deterrent to foreign aggressors.

These attitudes are not new; they date back to the Revolutionary War, and they were at least as pronounced during the '20s and '30s as they are today.

Nevertheless, the function of a leader is to lead, and a leader with a mandate from the people as great as that enjoyed by Franklin

McCook Field, located on the outskirts of Dayton, Ohio, was the most significant place in American aviation during the early '20s. Almost all new aerial hardware was either developed or tested there prior to 1927.

Roosevelt has little defense for his failures. The threat to the United States was clearly delineated long before he made any move to counter it, and America's tardiness in preparing to defend itself not only cost countless American lives, but encouraged military conquests that bore heavily on America's vital interests and, eventually, tempted attack on America itself. History offers no examples of a peace dictated from weakness.

America's reaction to the aggressions of Japan, Germany, and Italy during the mid-'30s was funding for an army of 165,000 and the Neutrality Acts passed between 1935 and 1937. As late as 1938, the Army Air Corps' appropriation was $58.8 million (compared to $35.1 million in 1921), and total Air Corps personnel numbered 21,089. At that time, our best fighter airplanes were some 70 Curtiss P-36s in service (plus 139 more on order), and our best heavy bombers were 14 service test YB-17s (plus 39 B-17Bs on order). Just one year later, Hitler would march into Poland to start the Second World War.

There is evidence that Roosevelt shared the anti-Air Corps sentiments held by the Navy Department's battleship admirals right up to the time of Pearl Harbor. Roosevelt, born

The Curtiss Hawk series of biplane fighters, 247 in all, were procured 1925 through 1931 inclusive. Above is a P-1F at Kelly Field.

Lieutenant Otto Wienecke, one of 12 army fliers to be killed flying the mail during the 1934 airmail moratorium, died in this Curtiss O-39 observation plane when he crashed near Cleveland in a snowstorm.

This crash, 2 February 1934, claimed the life of Lt. Ed Lowry about 50 miles southwest of Toledo. Mail bags were scattered far from the scene.

to wealth and position, a Harvard graduate and amateur yachtsman (always expected of such young men), served as assistant secretary of the Navy 1913 through 1921, and was obviously much perturbed at Billy Mitchell's claim that the airplane had made the battleship obsolete. "It is highly unlikely that an airplane, or a fleet of them, could ever sink a fleet of navy vessels under battle conditions," he told the press in 1921.

Later, following Mitchell's demonstrations, Roosevelt was asked by a reporter if he'd changed his mind, to which he replied, "I once saw a man kill a lion with a .30/30 rifle . . . but that does not mean that a .30/30 is a lion gun."

Thirteen years later, the Air Corps would provide him an even greater embarrassment: the dismal failure to carry the mail after Roosevelt took that service away from the airlines. (See Chapter 9.)

The whole episode was an embarrassment to Roosevelt, and he was not the kind of man to forget an embarrassment. During the ensuing four or five years he appears to have ignored the Army Air Corps as much as possible, while the navy received authority to build no less than 34 new battleships and battle cruisers (a program that was modified after WWII began and the importance of the aircraft carrier became evident).

The P&W R-1340 Wasp was introduced in May 1926, rated at 400 hp; by 1938 it had evolved into a 600-hp engine. A smaller version, the R-985 Wasp Jr., similarly grew from 300 to 450 hp.

## Engine development paces the industry

You will recall from Chapter 4 that Fred Rentschler and his top enginemen at Wright Aeronautical Corporation had brought the Wright Whirlwind J-4 to the threshold of success by 1924. Although Rentschler never admitted it, it appears most likely that he recognized the opportunity of a lifetime at that point. Rather than enrich Wright Aeronautical with his foresight, he decided to start his own company. It was a decision worth millions.

Rentschler correctly judged that the 200-hp Whirlwind, when fully developed, would have a great impact on aviation and make a powerful deal of money for Wright. However, he also knew about the work of Sam Heron and Edward T. Jones at the Air Corps' McCook Field experimental center, which had resulted in development of the first truly reliable air-

Allison Division, GM

The Allison V-1710 powered the P-40s, P-39s, P-63s, P-38s, A-36s and F-82s. Pictured is the V-1710-39, which was fitted to the P-40D and P-40E as well as the early Kittyhawks.

cooled cylinders in several sizes, and which featured Heron's sodium-filled exhaust valves. Further realizing that here was the key to much bigger aircraft engines that would match the Whirlwind's reliability, Rentschler resigned from Wright in September 1924, taking his best enginemen (Mead, Willgoos, and Brown) with him.

Then, with a truly first-class dream to sell, he was able to secure the backing of the owners of the idle Pratt and Whitney Tool Company factory for production of his new 400-hp Wasp engine, Model R-1340. This engine and others of the same basic construction that followed were so successful that by 1933, the 1375 shares of Pratt & Whitney stock that Rentschler had purchased for $275 in 1925 had grown to more than $21 million—that's correct, $21 million.

It appears also that Rentschler's principal advisor—the man who encouraged him to build the Wasp engine—was none other than Adm. William Moffett, chief of the Navy's Bureau of Aeronautics. Moffett wasn't concerned with the money to be made from the production of such an engine. The navy badly needed an aircraft powerplant of that size, and Moffett had decided that the navy would use air-cooled radials exclusively for the foreseeable future, principally because they were much easier to service than the big liquid-cooled powerplants.

But Rentschler did not need to be told that the Air Corps and the airlines would also come knocking at his door if he had a reliable high-horsepower, air-cooled radial to sell. By 1938, just 13 years after P&W was formed, the R-1340 Wasp had long since become a 600-hp engine; the R-985 Wasp Junior filled the 450-hp needs, and the R-1690 Hornet was in production at 850-hp, while the new R-1830 Twin Wasp and the R-2800 Double Wasp, at 1200- and 2000-hp respectively, had completed their tests and were just entering production.

Meanwhile, at Wright Aeronautical, the two men who had contributed the most to air-cooled aircraft engine development—Sam Heron and Ed T. Jones—had been lured from the Air Corps' experimental and development center at McCook Field (later, Wright Field, and today Wright-Patterson AFB, Ohio) by Charles Lawrance at Wright Aeronautical where they gave the J-4 Whirlwind their new cylinder and valve system to bring forth the famed J-5 Whirlwind. The J-6 series quickly

A Sparrowhawk returns to the trapeze beneath the *Macon*. The *Macon*'s engines were inside her hull. Normal crew was 10 officers and 50 enlisted men, plus four Sparrowhawk pilots.

followed, ranging in power from 165- to 300-hp, along with the 750-hp R-1820 Cyclone.

Wright Aeronautical was merged with the Curtiss Aeroplane and Motor Company in 1929 by wheeler-dealer financier Clement M. Keys, who had controlled Curtiss since the early '20s, to form the Curtiss-Wright Aircraft Corporation. In 1931, when Curtiss-Wright decided to abandon liquid-cooled aircraft engine development (despite the success of its D-12 and Conqueror engines during the '20s) to concentrate on the Wright air-cooled radials, the Air Corps was forced to look elsewhere for the 1000-hp V-12 it was sure it would need within a decade.

The Air Corps favored the in-line V-12s because they presented a much smaller frontal area (and therefore less drag) than the big radials, and because cooling problems were yet to be solved with the high-horsepower radials above 15,000 ft. So the Air Corps went to General Motors' miniscule (less than 30 employees) Allison Division where a new V-12 of 1710 cubic inch displacement and a planned rating

of 750-hp was in its early stages of development under a navy contract to supply engines for the navy's huge airships *Akron* and *Macon*.

The Air Corps was mostly jawboning, because it had almost no money to spend. It bought a dozen Allison V-1710s between 1932 and mid-1934 that were shipped to Wright Field where Air Corps enginemen under the direction of Opie Chenoweth tried to uprate them to 1000 hp with no success. Not until March 1937, after Allison's Ron Hazen, Charles McDowall and Robert Atkinson had almost completely redesigned the V-1710, did it at last pass a type test at 1000 hp. This was, by the way, just a few months after the Rolls-Royce Merlin passed its type test at 990-hp. Both engines were rated for 87 octane fuel. The V-1710 required pure Prestone as a coolant and weighed 1280 pounds. The 1335 pound Merlin was cooled with a water-Prestone mix.

During WWII, Allison would produce almost 70,000 V-1710s, the last ones rated at 1600 hp. Production would continue into 1947, after a final order to equip the P-82 Twin Mustang,

USN

Trio of Curtiss F9C-2 Sparrowhawks. Engine cowlings were red, white and blue. Engines were Wright R-975s of 420 hp, which gave the Sparrowhawks a top speed of 176 mph.

but none ever propelled a navy dirigible. Both the *Akron* and *Macon* were destroyed in crashes before the Allisons meant for them could be delivered.

# Navy airships *Akron* and *Macon*

Admiral William Moffett (he wasn't the kind of man one called "Billy") never lost faith in the great rigid airships as patrol and reconnaissance vehicles for the fleet. The Germans had used Zeppelins as strategic bombers in WWI with limited success, but the record of the huge airships subsequent to that time was not very good. The Italian-built *Roma* had crashed during test flights in the United States in 1922; the navy's ZR-2, built in Britain as the R.38, also crashed on a test flight, and the Goodyear-built ZR-1 *Shenandoah* was lost in a storm in 1925. Only the German-built ZR-3 *Los Angeles*, in U.S. Navy service since 1924, appeared to be headed for a long and useful life, but was inadequate for the sea duty Moffett envisioned since it was actually a WWI design. It was finally decommissioned in 1932 as an economy measure. The Hoover Administration had, in 1928, approved purchase of two

airships, the ZRS-4 and ZRS-5, which were much larger than the *Los Angeles* and which were specifically designed for extended service at sea.

The two new airships, to be christened *Akron* and *Macon*, were nearly identical. The first to be completed was the *Akron*, which was 785 feet in length, 133 feet in diameter, 146 feet in height. It contained 6.5 million cu/ft of helium. Her eight engines furnished a total of 4480 hp, and she could carry a useful load of 160,000 pounds at speeds up to 84 mph. Her engines were placed inside the great hull; her propellers could be turned in different directions for forward, reverse, or even upward thrust and were mounted outside at the end of extended driveshafts. Also inside the hull was hangar and maintenance space for five small scout-fighter planes that could be launched and returned to the airship in flight by means of a retractable trapeze. Six Curtiss F9C-2 Sparrowhawks (plus two prototypes) were built for the *Akron* and *Macon*, with more planes to be ordered as needed.

The *Akron* was placed in service in October, 1931, with Lt. Comdr. C.E. Rosendahl as her captain, and for a year and a half she seemed well on her way to the vindication of

USAF

Army's Keystone LB-7 bomber of the late '20s was powered with two P&W Hornet engines of 525 hp each. A total of 210 Keystones (crews called them "Keystone Comedies") with different engine installations were procured following the Mitchell trial.

Great Lakes G-1 torpedo bomber of 1929 was typical of the heavy biplanes procured by the navy during the '20s for that mission.

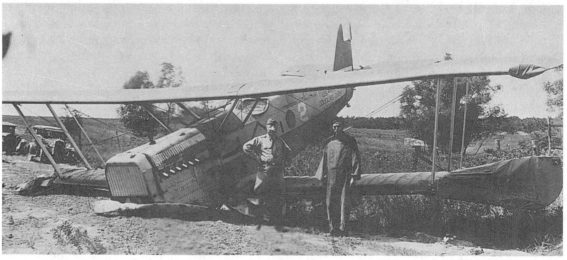

Major Joe R. Reed and his crew chief inspect damage to Douglas O-2H observation plane after the Liberty engine failed at low altitude.

Moffett's support, her 10,000-mile range allowing her to roam the seas for many days without refueling. But then the *Akron* was lost (unnecessarily, most believed) on 4 April 1933, just two months after the *Macon* was christened.

The *Akron* crashed in a storm off the New Jersey Coast while flying at a very low altitude when her helmsman apparently raised her nose too abruptly and allowed the rear of the airship to strike the water. The great aerial machine broke up, and 73 of the 76 men aboard her lost their lives, including Admiral Moffett.

The *Macon* entered service in June 1933, two months after the *Akron*'s loss, and received the *Akron*'s Sparrowhawks, since none of the planes were aboard the *Akron* when it

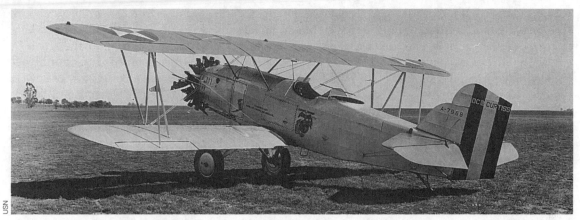

The U.S. Marine Corps' Curtiss OC-2 Falcon of 1930 was Wasp-powered, had a top speed of 155 mph.

went down. At sea, the planes' landing gears were removed and belly tanks added to give the small scout-fighters greater range. The lack of a landing gear didn't matter because the only place the planes could "land" was on the extended trapeze of their mother airship.

This combination an airship of great range, plus four (usually) scouting planes fanning out to patrol all points of the compass— provided the navy with eyes over many thousands of square miles of ocean. If the *Macon* had survived it is quite possible that other, similar airships would have been built, because they easily offered the most effective and economical means of guarding the sea approaches to America's coasts. No nation was in a better position to exploit these aerial behemoths because the United States possessed the world's only known deposits of non-flammable helium prior to WWII. Germany, the master builder of these machines, was forced to use highly-flammable hydrogen in its airships.

The *Macon* was lost to a fatal flaw in her structure. Her vertical tail atop the rear of the airship was improperly attached to the hull, and this critical component failed in flight during marginal weather off the California Coast near Big Sur on 12 February 1935. Miraculously, all but 2 of the 81 aboard survived the ensuing crash. The exact location of the wreck-age remained a mystery until a bit of salvage duralumin initiated a search 55 years later. On 24 June 1990, the U.S. Navy's 3-man submersible *Sea Cliff* located the remains of the *Macon* at a depth of 1450 feet.

Many in the navy believed then (and still do) that the airship program should have continued; but without Admiral Moffett's leadership, the U.S. Navy's lighter-than-air vehicles were henceforth limited to the relatively small, nonrigid "blimps," primarily used during WWII to hunt enemy submarines in U.S. coastal waters.

# Transition:
# The biplane era passes

Despite the impoverished status of the U.S. Army Air Corps during the '20s and much of the '30s, and despite the lack of promotion and the low pay, the Air Corps attracted—and often held—some very able men. It seems remarkable today that any of them should have remained in the service. Following Billy Mitchell's court martial, those officers with any rank who were known to share Mitchell's views were shown by the army's General Staff how foolish that could be. All were exiled to lesser commands: Majs. H.H. "Hap" Arnold, Carl Spaatz, Lewis Brereton and Gerald Brandt; Cols. Hugh Knerr and

Frank Andrews; Lt. Cols. George Kenney and Joe McNamey all suffered career setbacks. Major Arnold, for example, was relieved of his post in Washington, D.C., and sent to Marshall Field where his command consisted of four tired DH-4s and 13 men. Perhaps these blatant punishments merely strengthened the resolve of such men. In any case, they all hung tough—if temporarily silenced—perhaps aware that the time would come when the nation would sorely need their counsel.

During the late '20s and early '30s, significant progress was made in aircraft and aircraft engine development, mostly because of new and expanding markets in civil aviation. The demand for more efficient airliners and a booming market for private airplanes, along with the appearance of truly reliable engines in all power ranges, encouraged airframe builders to push ahead with fresh ideas. By 1931, John K. "Jack" Northrop was building the first of his all-metal, stressed-skin airplanes in which the metal skin carried much of the load, resulting in a lighter internal structure, and the small but talent-ridden National Advisory Committee for Aeronautics developed a wide array of new airfoils and provided much other useful aerodynamic data to industry with its wind tunnel work at Langley Field, Virginia, including engine cowling shapes for the air-cooled radials that not only greatly reduced drag but also improved engine cooling.

These advances produced the first "modern" airliner in 1933, the Boeing 247 for United Air Lines: an all-metal, low-wing, twin-engine craft with retractable landing gear. It was limited only by its small size (10 passengers). Donald Douglas rectified that the following year with the first of his famed DC series airliners, built for TWA. It was the DC-1, which quickly (1936) evolved into the DC-3, known as the C-47 in the Air Corps and the R4D in navy service.

Curtiss F6C-4 Hawk of VF-9M. This craft was plane number two of Fighting Nine.

Boeing P-12C army fighter was powered with P&W R-1340-9 Wasp of 525 hp and had a top speed of 178 mph. Army took delivery of 366 of the P-12 series, 1929–1932 inclusive. Navy version was the F4B series.

Curtiss F11C-2 Goshawk was fitted with the Wright R-1820 Cyclone of 715 hp; had a top speed of 205 mph. The navy bought 27 of this model during the early '30s and later redesignated it the BFC-2 (bomber-fighter).

The Curtiss P-6E Hawk was the last biplane fighter purchased by the Air Corps. Its Curtiss V-1570 Conqueror V-12 engine produced 600 hp and gave the P-6E a top speed of 193 mph. The Air Corps took delivery of 45 P-6Es in early 1932, paying $12,362 each for them, plus an additional $10,000 each for engines, propellers and guns.

The USS *Lexington* as it appeared during the early '30s. The "Lady Lex" and its sister carrier *Saratoga* were commissioned in the late fall of 1927. Both were converted cruisers of 36,000 tons, and both carried 72 aircraft.

Prior to 1936, the military services normally purchased airplanes in batches of 25 or 30 at a time. The army took delivery of only 247 Curtiss *Hawk* biplane fighters ("pursuits") between October 1925 when the first was delivered, and April 1932, when it accepted the last one. During the biplane era, the army favored Curtiss fighters, Douglas observation planes, and Martin or Keystone bombers. The navy favored Boeing fighters and Douglas torpedo planes. The U.S. Marine Corps usually received castoff navy airplanes.

The marines were fortunate to have any airplanes at all, and probably wouldn't have had them were it not for a series of incidents in Haiti and Nicaragua where the marines were sent to restore order and protect what was then seen as America's best interests when rebel guerillas threatened those governments.

Marine Fighting Squadron Nine was also instrumental in saving marine aviation during this period. Aware that a move was afoot to eliminate marine aviation, Fighting Nine organized an aerial exhibition team of seven pilots who flew precision aerobatics in close forma-

tion just as today's Blue Angels do. They called themselves the *Rojas Diablos* ("Red Devils") and, performing at county fairs and other civil celebrations, gained a great deal of favorable publicity and goodwill for the Corps in general and marine air in particular.

Fighting Nine did it all on a shoestring, and with dedicated mechanics who kept their aging biplane fighters in service often by fabricating their own spare parts. On one occasion these crews built an airplane from the salvaged remains of several others and gave it a fictious serial number. That later caused a great flap in marine headquarters where there was no record of the plane's acquisition. Headquarters finally decided that the airplane did not exist and that settled the matter.

# A new generation of aircraft

After the navy received its first aircraft carrier, the *Langley*, in 1922, only two more were added to the fleet during the next dozen years, the *Saratoga* and *Lexington*, converted battle

A BF2C-1 Hawk flown by Lt. Comdr. J.D. Barnwar of VB-5B operating from the USS *Ranger* in 1935. The BF2C-1 had a top speed of 225 mph; power was the 770-hp Wright R-1820-04. Navy bought 27 of this type in 1934.

cruisers that entered service in the fall of 1927. But then four more were commissioned prior to WWII: *Ranger* in 1934, *Yorktown* in 1937, *Enterprise* in 1938, and *Wasp* in 1940. President Roosevelt, always attentive to navy needs, originally funded *Yorktown* and *Enterprise* through a provision of his National Recovery Act (NRA: "recovery" from the Great Depression), and although the Supreme Court later held the NRA to be unconstitutional, Roosevelt had no trouble getting the money from Congress to pay for them, as well as the Wasp. The Congress seldom argued with FDR because of his immense popular support.

The United States should have possessed at least twice that number of aircraft carriers, enough to support a two-ocean navy, but this is a judgment made in hindsight. No one in the Navy Department at that time fully realized the role the aircraft carrier would play in the future defense of the country. The carrier was still a theoretical weapon, actually untried in battle.

The point is, however, that the navy was relatively better funded during the '30s than was the army, and especially the Army Air Corps. Roosevelt did not overtly oppose the Air Corps, he simply ignored it as long as possible.

Unfortunately, the Army General Staff, headed by the temperamental Gen. Malin Craig during the critical late '30s, was overtly opposed to a modern air force and made certain that the Air Corps remained totally subservient to the presumed needs of ground commanders, while admitting no offensive role for army aviation, which was a position shared by most congressmen. The idea of a strategic bombing force was heresy, and any air officer who presumed to disagree with this doctrine was summarily transferred to the boondocks and reduced to his permanent rank.

When Gen. George C. Marshall replaced Craig as Chief of Staff in 1939, Marshall rescued the "Billy Mitchell Crowd" and returned all of them to positions of high responsibility. Hap Arnold was, after a lengthy penance, pro-

Merle C. Olmsted collection

The carriers *Yorktown* and *Enterprise* were christened during 1936 and each received a squadron of Curtiss SBC-3 Helldivers. The SBC series remained in production until 1941.

Douglas O-46A observation plane, 90 of which were delivered to the Air Corps in 1935–1936, was a pretty airplane but already obsolescent when it appeared.

A new era in U.S. fighter airplane design began in 1934 when Don Berlin designed the Curtiss P-36. Pictured is the wooden mock-up.

moted to Brig. Gen. and appointed Chief of the Air Corps in 1938, although that post had been diluted in 1935 with formation of the "General Headquarters Air Force" at Langley Field, which was supposed to be on an equal level with that of the Air Corps Chief. The GHQ Air Force controlled the Air Corps combat arm, while the AC Chief was responsible for training and supply. This confusing arrangement split whatever authority the top air officers possessed under Malin Craig.

Meanwhile, able army air officers did as well as they could under the hostile Malin Craig and, in 1936, as the Congress became mildly alarmed at Hitler's occupation of the Rhineland, Italy's invasion of Ethiopia, civil war in Spain, and Japan's continuing aggressions in China, money was appropriated for 77 new Seversky P-35 fighter planes for the Air Corps.

A year later, Germany, Italy, and Japan signed an anti-Comintern pact, Hitler formally renounced the Versailles Treaty, the Japanese sank a U.S. gunboat on the Yangtze River, and money was found for 210 new Curtiss P-36 fighters for the Air Corps. It was the largest single order for army airplanes since WWI. At the same time, Wright Field issued a specification to the nation's struggling airplane industry asking for proposals for a 2000-hp fighter airplane.

That specification was a bit far out and Wright Field knew it. No 2000-hp aircraft engine existed in 1937, and the Air Corps had no money either in hand or promised to buy such planes. But all concerned knew that the gestation periods for new military aircraft was growing much longer as the planes became more complicated and that engines, especially, required several years to develop. It wasn't simply a matter of increasing the size of existing engines to obtain more power. Better fuels were needed for higher compression ratios, and improved metals had to be formulated to withstand the greater pressures and higher operating temperatures. As aircraft speeds increased, a host of new aerodynamic questions arose. Next to nothing was known about compressibility, a phenomenon that some engineers believed—and others did not—would be encountered as planes approached the speed of sound. (Lockheed was to soon face the problem, which was, indeed, real).

Barely solvent Lockheed, a small company that had produced only 277 airplanes since its organization 11 years before, responded to the Air Corps' specification with exciting plans for a fighter plane fitted with a pair of 1000-hp Allison V-1710 engines (then still in development). Lockheed's proposed airplane would, if built, demand answers to questions which had not yet been asked. On paper it was a 400-mph airplane, at least 100 mph faster than the Curtiss P-36s which would begin entering service a year later, and it would certainly force the state-of-the-art beyond present limits.

But Wright Field (apparently Opie Chenoweth, head of the Air Corps Technical Service Command) liked the Lockheed proposal, which was actually the work of young Clarence "Kelly" Johnson, a recent University of Michigan graduate. Gen. Oscar Westover, who endured for three years under Malin Craig as Chief of Air Corps, approved a contract for one experimental model of the new fighter which was designed the XP-38. It was officially described as a "defensive interceptor" in order to get it past Craig and the Congress.

Prototype P-36 first flew in April 1935 and was penalized by use of the Wright R-1670 engine, a decided failure. Berlin had no choice but to try this engine since he worked for Curtiss-Wright.

Donovan R. Berlin

The Air Corps asked Curtiss to install the new P&W R-1830 Twin Wasp in the P-36 and the happy result was an order for 210 such machines in June 1937, the largest U.S. fighter plane order since WWI.

USAF

In March 1938, P-36 designer Don Berlin suggested to the Air Corps Material Division at Wright Field that the P-36 be fitted with the new Allison V-1710 engine. That resulted in the P-40, and a contract for 524 of those machines in April 1939. Deliveries to the Air Corps began in June 1940, and eventually totalled 13,763, including Tomahawks and Kittyhawks to Britain and the Commonwealth countries.

The navy, too, was looking to the need for faster and better airplanes and let contracts as early as November 1935 for experimental fighters, the Grumman XF4F-1 and the Brewster XF2A-1. At that time, the navy had 867 pilots, the marines 110. Those figures were up to 1068 and 180 respectively when WWII began in Europe.

The navy took delivery of 503 Brewster F2A Buffalo fighters beginning in December 1937, but those were interim craft with a number of weaknesses, and were replaced by the Grumman F4F Wildcat for fleet duty. A total of 1978 Wildcats were built for the Navy (plus 431 for Britain) beginning in 1938. The famed Chance Vought F4U *Corsair* was contracted that same year, designed for the P&W R-2800 2000-hp radial engine that was in its early stages of development at the time. The first Corsair would fly in 1940, and 7829 would eventually be built for the navy and marines.

Actually, all of the American-designed 400-mph fighters appeared as test models at about the same time, with the XP-38 leading the pack in 1939. All the rest followed in 1940, except the XP-51, which was originally built for the British and first flew in 1941. None of these craft was developed and available for combat when Pearl Harbor was attacked. It's true that the P-38 Lightning was thrown into combat in mid-1942, but it was not combat-ready until the P-38J-25 version came off the production lines in 1944. During the early, desperate months of the war for the United States, the navy's F4F Wildcat and the army's P-40 carried the burden.

The P-40 was simply a re-engined P-36. Originally powered with the P&W R-1830 of 1050 hp, the P-36 had a speed of 310 mph and outstanding maneuverability. It was as good as any fighter in the world when it entered squadron service in 1938. By then, however, its designer, Donovan Berlin, chief engineer at Curtiss-Wright, was recommending that it be fitted with the 1090-hp Allison V-1710-19, and that resulted in the 365 mph P-40, which first flew in

Lieutenant Colonel Benjamin S. Kelsey (later General) was the test pilot and Air Corps project officer for the P-38 program. When this photo was taken he was recovering from a broken ankle received when he parachuted from a YP-38 after pulling its tail off in a dive.

October 1938. P-40 deliveries to the army began in mid-1940, and 13,737 were eventually built, many for America's allies during WWII.

The Republic P-47 Thunderbolt, more often referred to as the "*Jug*" by those who flew and serviced her, was a brute of a fighter plane—rugged, powerful and fast. Its prototype also appeared in 1940, and it would be the principal U.S. fighter over Europe when the Luftwaffe offered the most resistance. Therefore, America's top aces in the European Theater of Operations (ETO) were Jug jockeys. The several versions of the P-47 had top speeds ranging from 425 to above 450 mph. Power came from the 2000-hp P&W R-2800 that, with water injection, could produce 2300 hp for short periods.

On the face of it, the P-38 Lightning should have been at least as fast as the P-47, and it probably would have been had it pos-

The Boeing Model 299, a daring project by the Boeing Company, first flew in 1935 and evolved into the famed B-17 series of WWII. A total of 12,726 was built, although only 134 were built or on order early in 1941.

When the U.S. was plunged into WWII, all sorts of civil aircraft were drafted. The famed Beech Staggerwing (Model 17) became the UC-43 in army dress, and was used as a "command transport."

sessed the Thunderbolt's wing. The P-38, however, was a load-carrier that would deliver a bomb load equal to that of a medium bomber and could outclimb just about anything. With a top speed of 405 to 420 mph, depending upon model, it was probably fast enough, and its firepower was truly awesome. Once it received a redesigned intercooler system and automatic controls for its turbosuperchargers, maneuvering flaps, and dive brakes, the P-38 came into its own. All of this finally came together in mid-1944, but not until more than half of the 10,036 Lightnings had been built. The late models were fearsome machines indeed, arguably the best all-around fighter-bomber of the war. The *Lightning's* long range and two engines made it the hands-down favorite of fighter pilots in the Southwest Pacific, that "extra fan" providing a large margin of security for long overwater missions.

The P-38's wing, while a great asset in one way, proved a liability in another, and that was quickly discovered when Maj. Signa Gilkie took one of the first service test YP-38s above 30,000 feet and entered a dive. As the airspeed built above 500 mph the airplane's tail began to buffet severely. As the dive continued the machine became progressively nose-heavy, increasing its dive angle to near vertical, while the control yoke oscillated stiffly and defied Gilkie's utmost efforts to move it. He managed to recover by use of his elevator trim tab after the aircraft entered denser air below 18,000 feet.

Wind tunnel tests at Cal Tech established that the tail flutter was the result of turbulent airflow created by the sharp juncture at wing and fuselage, and that was eliminated by a wing fillet that smoothed out the airflow over the tail.

Not until October 1942, 16 months later, when a scale model of the P-38 was tested in the Ames Laboratory high-speed wind tunnel, was the loss of control in 500 mph dives explained. The P-38's wing was entering compressibility. The airflow around the wing was travelling more than 40 percent faster than the airplane itself, and was reaching Mach 1 (the speed of sound) and creating a shock wave when the aircraft reached an airspeed of slightly more than two-thirds Mach, or Mach .67 to be exact. (Most other WWII advanced fighters could be pushed into aerodynamic compressibility, but not as early. The British Spitfire, for example, encountered compressibility at .82 Mach.)

A new wing was out of the question for the P-38; American fighter planes were desperately needed in every theater of war and production was all-important. There was no time to design and test a thinner wing. Therefore, Lockheed engineers devised a "bolt-on" dive brake that tended to limit the P-38's speed in a dive to just short of compressibility in dives of 60 degrees or less.

Col. Ben Kelsey, the army's fighter airplane project officer, personally tested this modification and approved it in February 1943, but Lockheed was never able to satisfactorily explain why it was not incorporated into the P-38 production lines until mid-1944.

As mentioned, the other high-speed fighters also experienced this phenomenon. At least two P-47s lost their tails to it in test flights, and both Colonels (later general) Kelsey and Lockheed test pilot Ralph Virden pulled the tails off P-38s recovering from high-altitude dives. Virden was killed; Kelsey successfully parachuted. The problem was not solved until after WWII when true transonic airplanes were developed.

Had President Roosevelt and his congressional leaders been properly responsive to the nation's security needs during the '30s, American pilots would not have fought for a year and a half in obsolescent and undeveloped airplanes. (Indeed, they may not have had to fight at all.) Of equal significance is the fact that if the aircraft and other key industries in the United States not had sizable arms orders from France and Britain as early as 1937, we would have been plunged into war with far less.

A $25 million order from the British for medium bombers allowed Lockheed to begin plant expansion in mid-1938 and that in turn would make P-38 production possible. Lockheed was building a handful of small airliners for Japan at the time. In March 1940, the British ordered 667 P-38s, and that got the P-38 production line moving months before the USAAF ordered that airplane in quantity. French orders for 730 Curtiss P-36s in 1939 and 1940 similarly aided Curtiss-Wright. Martin and Douglas also sold airplanes to America's future allies prior to 1940, and all this, including a British order for 1000 P-40s, prompted the U.S. aircraft engine builders along with the airframe makers to expand their production facilities.

True, in 1938 President Roosevelt dramatically called upon the U.S. aircraft industry to produce 10,000 planes per year, and develop a capacity for twice that number, while Britain's

Prime Minister Chamberlain was in Munich to sell out Czechoslovakia to Hitler's insatiable appetite in a bid for time. Less than two years later, in the summer of 1940, Roosevelt would up his appeal to 50,000 planes per year as his Secretary of War, Henry L. Stimson, was noting that "Airpower had decided the fate of nations . . ." By that time Poland was gone; Norway, Denmark, Belgium and the Netherlands had fallen to the Nazi conqueror; France was defeated, and the British stood alone, somehow both pathetic and magnificent in their awful peril.

But while Roosevelt was making these ringing pronouncements, he and his Congress were doing little to actually build U.S. airpower or the aircraft industry in the United States. Whatever expansion the aircraft factories accomplished during this period was done with private capital, which in turn was based upon their orders in hand. Not until the myopic U.S. Congress at last enacted the Lend-Lease Bill (HR 1776) on 11 March 1941—just nine months before the attack on Pearl Harbor—did the U.S. aircraft industry receive federal funds for plant expansion.

USAF

General of the Army George C. Marshall (left) and Army Air Forces Chief Gen. Henry H. Arnold. Insignia on Arnold's jacket pocket is pre-WWI aviator's wings.

Meanwhile, after General Marshall took charge of the army in 1939 (the first non-West Pointer to be Chief of Staff since 1914), the weak and poorly-equipped Air Corps was steadily strengthened with as much speed as could be mustered against congressional opposition. The congressional majority, obviously with Roosevelt's tacit approval, remained adamantly opposed to a U.S. strategic bombing force right up to the minute that they stared disaster in the face. Chief of Air Corps, General Arnold, had employed a deception or two in order to keep Boeing's B-17 program alive and to procure less than 100 B-17s by 7 December 1941.

Under General Arnold, the divided authority of Air Corps command came to an end, and on 20 June 1941, with General Marshall's strong support, the Army Air Corps became the United States Army Air Forces (USAAF), Lt. Gen. Henry H. Arnold commanding. On 9 March 1942 General Marshall completely reorganized the War Department, and the Army Air Forces received virtually complete control of the development of its special weapon—the airplane. Administering its own affairs, it also came to exercise considerable influence over the army's conduct of the war in general.

The hour was late and the enemy was upon us, but somehow, our society has always seemed to produce the kind of people we need the most and, with our survival as a free nation at stake, President Roosevelt seemed to possess the ability to recognize them when they were most needed. He passed over 34 higher ranking officers to select George Marshall as the army's top commander. As events would prove, he never made a better decision.

# Review questions

1. Why was there such a strong feeling of neutrality during the 1920s and early 1930s? Why wasn't Congress or the top military leadership of the time impressed with Billy Mitchell's demonstrations?

2. Why did the U. S. Naval Air Service place so much emphasis on rigid airships? What were the Curtiss F9C-2 Sparrowhawks used for? What happened to the *Akron* and *Macon*?

3. What was the significance of the development of the Boeing 247 and the Douglas DC-3? Name some of the U. S. Navy aircraft carriers that were commissioned during the late 1920s and 1930s. Why was the U.S. Navy better funded during the 1930s? Who was General Malin Craig? What was his attitude toward army air power?

4. Describe some of the aircraft received by the military during the late 1930s. When did the Republic P-47 Thunderbolt first appear? What was the problem with the Lockheed P-38's wing? Why was Congress so slow in responding to the German and Japanese military threat?

# 11

# WWII: The desperate months

## Objectives

At the end of this chapter you should be able to:

- Describe the damage and discuss the political significance of the Japanese attack on Pearl Harbor.
- Describe the U.S. losses in the Philippines during the months that followed the attack on Pearl Harbor.
- Explain why the battle of Coral Sea was a major strategic victory for the United States.
- Give the reasons for and the implications of the U.S. victory in the battle of Midway.
- Discuss the importance of taking Guadalcanal in the southern Solomon Islands.

Sunday, 7 December 1941, dawned clear and beautiful over Hawaii with the mists, as always, scudding low among the peaks of Oahu's Koolau Range. On a lonely hill overlooking Oahu's north coast, Sgt. Joe Lockhard and Pvt. George Elliott were manning a primitive radar set, scanning the empty Pacific. They were bored and eager for their relief crew to arrive.

It was exactly two minutes past 7:00 A.M. when Lockhard called to his companion: "Hey, George. Come look at this." He made a note with his pencil. "I make it 136 miles."

"What is it?"

"I don't know. But it's our job to report it."

Lockhard cranked the field phone and, after some delay, reached the watch officer at Fort Shafter, a young lieutenant. Lockhard made his report, adding that the scope seemed to indicate a large fleet of airplanes, some 130 miles away, approaching Oahu from slightly east of north.

The lieutenant acknowledged the message and hung up. Nothing to get excited about. Twelve B-17s were due about 8:00 or 8:30 from San Francisco.

The lieutenant was right; two flights of AAF B-17s were due from the mainland. He was also wrong; what Lockhard and Elliott had observed on their scope was indeed something to get excited about. It represented the radio echos from 352 Japanese airplanes from six aircraft carriers: 171 Val dive bombers, 102 Kate attack bombers, and 79 Zero fighters. At 7:55 A.M., approximately 45 minutes after Lockhard's alert was logged at Fort Shafter, that deadly aerial armada began raining destruction on Pearl Harbor.

No warning was ever sounded. The attacking force achieved complete surprise, partly because the Japanese ambassador and a special envoy continued to negotiate settlement of U.S.-Japanese differences until, literally, the last minute. This pair of Japanese officials was actually in Secretary of State Cordell Hull's office with a note from their government when Hull was informed of the attack.

The military's primary failure at Pearl Harbor was the failure of reconnaissance, which should have been the navy's responsibility. With a large part of the navy's ships at anchor in Pearl Harbor, the sea approaches to the great base were essentially unguarded. Although the PBY series of long-distance patrol planes had been available since the mid-'30s, the navy had not seen fit to procure them in sufficient number to provide a viable early warning system for vital installations vulnerable to attack by enemy fleets. Also, prior to WWII the U.S. was completely without another form of reconnaissance which might be classified as a "super long-range warning system," a worldwide intelligence gathering organization that could have given the President and his advisors critical data concerning the military and political composition of Japan as well as her probable intentions.

It was, of course, the question of Japan's intentions that figured most prominently in America's vulnerability. Britain's Prime Minister, Winston Churchill, said (*The Second World War*, Houghton Mifflin Co., 1948): "All the great Americans around the President and in his confidence felt as acutely as I did the awful danger that Japan would attack British or Dutch possessions in the Far East and would carefully avoid the United States . . . " And Gen. Hap Arnold said in his memoirs: "Like most officers in the War Department, I was under the impression that, if a Japanese attack occurred, it would be made first against the Philippines and then would be carried down the east coast of Asia to Singapore, to the Islands of Borneo, Java and Sumatra." Obviously, it never occurred to Roosevelt, Churchill, or any of their advisors, that the Japanese could misjudge us as badly as we misjudged them.

With this erroneous position permeating the thinking at the top, there should be small wonder that the army and navy commanders in Hawaii were lulled into similar attitudes. Both were sacked after the debacle at Pearl, however.

Army fighters in Hawaii at the time of the Japanese attack included 99 P-40Bs and Cs, along with 36 P-36As, in the 15th and 18th Pursuit Groups.

The Japanese Kate bombers, most of them armed with torpedos, concentrated on the navy ships at anchor around Ford Island, while the *Vals* struck at navy, marine, and army airfields and other key installations. The Zeros were free to strafe targets of opportunity since they encountered virtually no U.S. fighter opposition. Eight army fighters (six P-36As and two P-40s) managed to take off during the attack, and accounted for 10 enemy bombers between them. Lieutenant George Welch, in a P-40, shot down four. Army and navy anti-aircraft gunners shot down another 18 of the enemy, plus one P-36.

The attack ended at approximately 0945 hours. The departing Japanese left behind 2400 American dead, 1500 wounded, four battleships sunk, 14 ships heavily damaged, and 233 U.S. warplanes destroyed, plus the certainty that they had aroused the sleeping giant.

The surprise attack on Pearl Harbor united the American people in an outraged determination to fight more effectively than anything the President could have said or done. An hour earlier, the U.S. Congress would have rejected war. But after the news reached Washington (about 1325 hours, or 1:25 P.M. due to the time difference), and was flashed to a stunned public, even the isolationists were breaking out their flags and calling for vengeance against this enemy who had so greviously wounded us "without provocation."

President Roosevelt called Sunday, the 7th of December 1941, ". . . a date which will live in infamy," and the U.S. Congress responded with roars of anger. A formal declaration of war against Japan came on 8 December 1941, and when Japan's Axis partners, Germany and Italy, followed with declarations of war against the United States, the nation was embarked upon an all-out, two-front war.

## The Philippines lost

Nine and a half hours after word of the Pearl Harbor attack reached the Philippines, the Japanese treated confused U.S. forces there to a repeat performance. Again, despite those hours of warning, all U.S. aircraft were caught on the ground at Clark Field, near Manila. The navy's Asiatic Fleet under Rear Adm. Thomas C. Hart—if three cruisers, 13 old destroyers, six motor torpedo boats and 29 submarines could be regarded as a "fleet"—was at sea. (Official air force records do not agree as to the time of the attack in the Philippines. Ma-

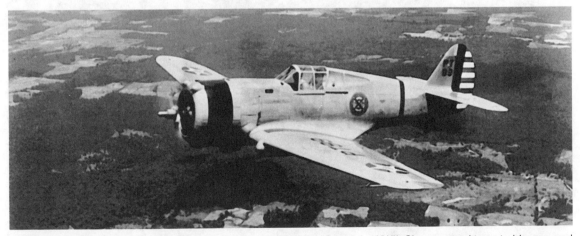

A P-36 may well have scored the first air victory for the United States in WWII. Six managed to get airborne and engage the enemy during the Pearl Harbor attack. Two P-40s also joined the fight. All but 27 P-40s were destroyed on the ground.

A Japanese navy Zero fighter leaves the deck of its carrier early on the morning of 7 December 1941 for the surprise attack on Pearl Harbor and other targets on Oahu.

Japanese Kate torpedo bomber takes off for the strike against U.S. ships anchored in Pearl Harbor.

USN

This captured photo, taken from a Japanese Kate, was snapped at the exact instant the first torpedo struck the battleship *Oklahoma*. The *Oklahoma* is the third from left, with the *West Virginia* anchored alongside.

jor (ret) Al Fernandez, who was on the flight line at Clark when the first bombs fell, told me the time was 1220 hours and, of course, 8 December since the Philippines are east of the International Date Line, though six hours earlier on the clock. Lieutenant General (ret) Joseph Moore, who flew one of the three P-40s that got into the air to engage the enemy, told us it was "about 1130 hours." Official Japanese records give it as 1330 hours Tokyo time, which would have been 1230 hours Manila time.)

In overall command in the Far East was Lt. Gen. Douglas MacArthur, and just what he did with the hours of warning he was given is not easily explained. Admiral Hart's radio man picked up the navy signal from Pearl Harbor 34 minutes after the attack there began, the same signal that was received in

Washington D.C., and Hart ordered that it immediately be repeated to MacArthur's headquarters in Manila, as well as to all British and Dutch forces in the area.

It is clear that MacArthur and his staff were fully functioning no later than 0400 hours, and air force records show that he "alerted" all his air units at 0430 hours. But there is no record of further orders prior to the noontime attacks on Clark and Iba Airfields. There is also no explanation as to why Navy Patrol Wing 10 at Cavite and the 17 B-17s at Clark Field were not dispatched at dawn to reconnoiter, particularly in the direction of Formosa, from which a Japanese air attack must (and did) come. MacArthur certainly knew that the President and the Chiefs of Staff all expected that the Philippines would be an early target if war came.

The *Arizona* explodes, partly hiding the *Oklahoma*, as the *California* burns in the background.

Curtiss P-40s, destroyed on the ground by strafing enemy planes, were bulldozed into pile of scrap during cleanup at Wheeler Field in the days following the attack.

Air Force General Lewis Brereton, who had assumed command of the Far East Air Force (FEAF) only the day before, was at Mac-Arthur's headquarters at 0500 hours seeking permission to send his 17 B-17s against the Japanese airfields on Formosa, but MacArthur was too busy to see his air commander, and MacArthur's Chief of Staff, General Souther-land, told Brereton that "Americans must not fire the first shot in this part of the world." That remarkable order may or may not have been changed before noon. Later statements from those involved do not agree on that question. It should be noted that, although Mac-Arthur had been in Manila since the previous summer, he had no reliable telephone network between his headquarters and his units in the field. The air raid warning system consisted of a radar set at Iba Field, which was out of commission, and a number of designated ground observers along the Luzon coasts. Not one report from a ground observer reached the air units before the enemy arrived. Meanwhile, MacArthur's radioed dispatch to the President late that morning read: "Every possible defense measure is being undertaken. My message is one of serenity and confidence." Mac-Arthur, too, was ready to fight WWI again.

On 8 December 1941, the FEAF consisted of the USAAF 19th Bomb Group, equipped with 34 B-17s (half of which were on the big island of Mindanao, 500 miles to the south of Manila); the 6th Philippine Pursuit Squadron, with 11 obsolete Boeing P-26s, and the four-squadron 24th Pursuit Group (PG), which had 72 Flyable Curtiss P-40s and 35 flyable Seversky P-35s, plus 35 P-40s and 11 P-35s in maintenance or grounded for lack of parts. Some other obsolete aircraft were at Clark Field, but they were of no practical use. The 24th PG's four squadrons, the 3rd, 17th, 29th and 21st, were scattered at Iba, Nichols, Clark, and Del Carmen Fields respectively.

The pilots of the 29th Pursuit Squadron (PS) sat in their P-40 fighters all morning awaiting orders that never came. Then, high in the western sky, someone saw a line of specks, which rapidly resolved into a large number of planes, flying line-abreast, and slanting down toward Clark Field.

Captain (later, General) Joe Moore and Lts. Randy Keator and Eddie Gilmore were the only ones to get off the ground to meet the attacking force. Four P-40s immediately behind them were destroyed while on their takeoff runs, while fourteen others were destroyed or

USAF

The Douglas B-18 Bolo, a DC-2 with bomber fuselage, was the "economy bomber" on hand in Hawaii and the Philippines when war came; it was essentially useless.

Lieutenant Boyd D. Wagner, flying a P-40E, became America's first WWII ace when he shot down six enemy aircraft over the Philippines on 12 and 13 December 1941.

ground at Clark. A few P-35s remained, but they were no match for the Zeros and were not flown in combat. All air combat over the Philippines during the ensuing 90 days was ridiculously one-sided. The invader never appeared with less than 30 *Zeros*, and the Americans never met them with more than six P-40s. Often, the pilots of the 24th PG attacked with two, sometimes four-plane elements.

Spare parts were cannibalized from wrecks, oil was strained through makeshift filters and reused, tailwheel tires were stuffed with rags, and some P-40s seemed to have more bullethole patches than original skin. The ammo problem was never solved; fully a third of it was defective, and aircraft gun oil congealed into a molasses-like varnish in cold air at high altitudes. No mail, no supplies, no help ever reached the Philippines after the war started there. Food, medicine, and eventually ammunition was in extremely short supply, but the American and Filipino forces held out.

The main Japanese invasion, following preliminary landings, began on 22 December 1941. The attack centered on Luzon, the northernmost and largest island of the archipelago, where all but a small fraction of the defending forces were concentrated. The main landings were made on the beaches of Lingayen Gulf in the northwest and Lamon Bay in the southeast, and on 23 December, MacArthur ordered a general withdrawal into the mountainous Bataan Peninsula, across Manila Bay from the capitol city. Manila itself was occupied by the Japanese without resistance. The 15,000 American troops and 45,000 sketchily-trained Filipinos had their food rations cut in half by mid-January, and their air cover had swindled to nine P-40s, while airmen without planes to fly or service took up rifles and joined the infantrymen in foxholes.

This gallant contingent of American men and women (a number of army nurses were with the troops), without hope of relief or rescue, called themselves the "Battling Bastards of Bataan" ("no momma, no poppa, no Uncle

crippled by strafing Zeros before ever reaching the runway. Moore, Keator, and Gilmore shot down five of the enemy before faulty ammunition silenced their guns.

A few minutes after Clark Field was hit, Iba Field, across the mountains, was struck by other enemy raiders, losing 13 of its 15 P-40s. Moore's squadron lost 18 of its 23 P-40s.

After the attack, the fighter squadrons dispersed to small dirt airstrips and pooled their remaining aircraft, and at the end of a week there were but 24 P-40s left. All but one of the B-17 bombers had been destroyed on the

Sam"). With Filipino patriots, they pinned down two divisions of the enemy's best assault troops and greatly upset the Japanese timetable of conquest.

By April, the defenders were subsisting on about 15 ounces of food daily, mostly rice supplemented by lizard meat, and thousands succumbed to dysentery, dengue, malaria and scurvy. The P-40s flew as long as it was possible to get one into the air, and one can guess at the mood of those airmen as revealed in a grimly humorous message relayed by an American submarine: "Dear President Roosevelt. Please send us another P-40. The one we have is full of holes."

Actually, they had two P-40s when the end came. On 8 April, Gen. Jonathan Wainwright, left in command after MacArthur's escape (by order of the president) to Australia a month earlier, retreated to the caves of Corregidor Island in Manila Bay with most of the surviving Americans, and sadly ordered the remaining defenders of Bataan to surrender. Incredibly, the Americans on Corregidor held out another month before they, too, were forced to surrender, their food and ammunition exhausted. More than most Americans, they paid the price for 20 years of what Billy Mitchell described as " . . . incompetency . . . almost trea-sonable administration . . . and the delusion of the American Public."

## Coral Sea and Midway

The chief goal of American deployment to the Pacific during most of 1942, following the initial reinforcement of Hawaii and the Panama Canal, was to build up a base in Australia and secure the chain of islands leading to it. As early as January, a task force of division size was hastily sent to New Caledonia, and for a few weeks an effort, doomed to failure, was made to stem the enemy's invasion of Java. Thereafter, the buildup had as its first object the defense of Australia itself because, at the end of January, the Japanese had occupied Rabaul on New Britain Island, thus posing an immediate threat to Port Moresby, the weakly-held Australian base in southeastern New Guinea at Australia's doorstep. Two U.S. divisions went to Australia in March and April as construction of air bases was rushed to completion on the stepping-stone islands along the ocean routes to Australia and New Zealand. After the western anchor of this chain, New Caledonia, was secured, army and marine garrisons and reinforcements were sent to various

The P-40E was deployed in the Philippines when the Japanese struck, along with some P-40Bs and Seversky P-35s. The P-40E (pictured) had a slightly narrower fuselage than earlier models, shorter landing gear legs, larger radiator scoop, and six wing guns.

other islands along the line, culminating with the arrival of American troops in the Fiji Islands in June 1942.

These moves came none too soon because during the spring, the Japanese, after occupying Rabid, pushed into the southern Solomons, within easy striking distance of the American bases on Espiritu Santo and New Caledonia. They also occupied the northeastern coast of New Guinea, just across the narrow (but mountainous) Papuan peninsula from Port Moresby, where the Americans and Australians were preparing bases and airfields.

The stage was thus set for a major test of strength in the Pacific: American forces thinly spread along an immense arc from Hawaii to Australia; the Japanese securely in possession of the vast areas north and west of that arc, prepared to strike in force at any point.

Nevertheless, as tenuous as this deployment may have appeared, the security of Australia and New Zealand was essential. Later, as American arms grew stronger, this southern semi-circle could be matched with a string of stepping-stone bases across the Central Pacific and, with MacArthur proceeding up the east coast of New Guinea to retake the Philippines, the giant jaws of the pincer would be closed and all enemy forces within cut off from supply, reinforcement, or retreat.

All that would take time, American lives, and a great deal of America's treasure, but during those early, desperate days, it did provide the blueprint for victory. There can be little doubt that the Joint Chiefs planned well in the Pacific war with Japan. Admiral Ernest J. King, Commander-in-Chief of the U.S. Fleet (appointed immediately after Pearl Harbor; another excellent choice made by President Roosevelt), clearly dominated most of those decisions. Admiral King was 62 in 1942, a 1901 Naval Academy graduate—fourth in his class—who spent most of his career at sea until 1927 when he qualified as a naval aviator. He became chief of the Navy's Bureau of Aeronautics in 1933, and was regarded as an "airplane admiral" thereafter.

The first test of the American military posture in the Pacific came in May, when the Japanese made an attempt from the sea to take Port Moresby. That precipitated the great aircraft carrier battle of the Coral Sea. The battle itself was indecisive, but it constituted a strategic victory for the Americans because the enemy was forced to abandon its planned invasion of Port Moresby. Thereupon the Japanese struck eastward, hoping to complete the destruction of the U.S. Pacific Fleet and to seize Midway—a bid for clear naval supremacy in the Pacific.

The *Lexington* was lost in the battle of the Coral Sea. Crew abandons ship as escorts stand by.

We should mark the boldness of the U.S. Navy as it ventured forth to fight in the Southwest Pacific when it was the inferior force and in hostile waters. Early in May 1942, two small task forces, which had earlier made surprise raids against the enemy's troop buildup on New Guinea's northeast coast, joined forces south of the Louisiades and moved northward to intercept the Japanese invasion fleet bound for Port Moresby.

The American units were Task Force 17 under Rear Adm. F.J. Fletcher, who had the carrier *Yorktown* and her escorts, and Task Force 11, consisting of the carrier *Lexington* and her support vessels, commanded by Rear Adm. A.W. Fitch. On 7 May, this combined force, strengthened by the addition of Australian cruisers and destroyers, sent its aircraft against the enemy force and sank the Japanese light carrier *Shoho* during a furious air battle, although some enemy planes were able to sink a U.S. destroyer and tanker. Darkness brought a lull in which both sides lost track of one another, but on the following day Japanese air-

craft set fires aboard the *Lexington*, which destroyed her, and severely damaged *Yorktown*, while U.S. Navy pilots seriously damaged the enemy's fleet carrier *Shokaku* and shot down most of her planes. The Japanese invasion force, with its air cover gone, had no choice but to flee.

The "Lady Lex" was a poor trade for the *Shoho*, but Moresby—and Australia—had been saved from invasion and all that portended.

The Battle of the Coral Sea was unique in another way: For the first time in history, a great sea battle had been fought solely in the air, the opposing ships never within sight or gunrange of one another. There would be many more such battles.

Less than a month later, the still confident enemy was ready to take Midway and deliver a knockout blow to the U.S. Pacific Fleet. In the bargain, the enemy would occupy Attu and Kiska in the Aleutians, and bomb the U.S. Navy base at Dutch Harbor, Alaska. All this should have worked out as planned. It did not because the commander of the U.S. Pacific

Navy F4F Wildcat fighters prepare to take off from the carrier *Enterprise*, 12 May 1942.

Rare photo, dated 4 June 1942, of one of the *Yorktown*'s SBDs just prior to takeoff during the Battle of Midway. A handful of these aircraft were about to become the most significant planes in U.S. naval history.

Fleet, Adm. Chester W. Nimitz, was aware of the enemy's intentions.

Details are unavailable even today, because U.S. intelligence people are loath to talk much about codes, but we do know that U.S. Navy cryptographers in the Office of Naval Intelligence had broken the Japanese diplomatic code prior to Pearl Harbor, and since that code belonged to the same family of codes employed by the Imperial Japanese Navy, Admiral Nimitz was reading portions of the Japanese Navy's radioed messages. That is what allowed Nimitz to plan the ambush of an over-whelmingly powerful enemy force at Midway. Nimitz knew a little of Yamamoto's plan, and correctly guessed the rest of it.

Admiral Yamamoto had reason to feel confident. With the *Lexington* gone, the *Saratoga* and *Yorktown* under repair, and the *Ranger* and *Wasp* in the Atlantic, the Americans should have no more than two carriers, *Enterprise* and *Hornet*, in

the Pacific (the ancient *Langley* had long since been down-graded to tender status), while Yamamoto would have an armada of truly awesome proportions. He would send two aircraft carriers and their phalanx of supporting ships northward to attack the U.S. Naval base at Dutch Harbor, Alaska, and to occupy the Aleutian Islands of Attu and Kiska. Concurrently, far to the south, would be his Midway invasion force, containing one carrier, troop transports, and escorting vessels. Between these two would be his Midway Strike Force One under Adm. Chuichi Nagumo, consisting of four aircraft carriers (*Akagi, Kaga, Hiryu* and *Soryu*), two battleships, three battle cruisers, and 12 destroyers. Finally, Yamamoto himself would loiter about 300 miles behind Nagumo with one carrier, three battleships and a host of escorts, serving as a reserve or mop-up force. Meticulous planner Yamamoto also dispatched submarines to act as pickets in Hawaiian waters; their job was to at-

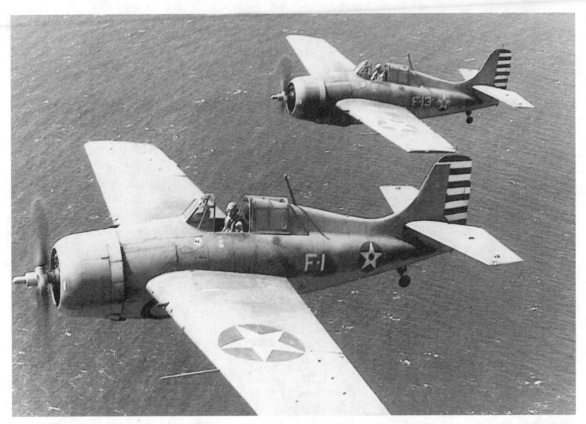

U.S. Navy aces in their F4F-4 Wildcats just after Midway are Lt.Comdr. John Thatch in No. 1 and Lt. Edward "Butch" O'Hare in No. 13.

tack the U.S. fleet as it (presumably) charged out of Pearl Harbor in response to the attack on Alaskan territory.

Meanwhile, Admiral Nimitz was doing some planning of his own. He inspired repair crews at Pearl to complete a two-month repair job on the *Yorktown* in a matter of days, sent three heavy and three light battle cruisers, with ten destroyers, to harass the enemy's Aleutian invasion force, and assembled two task forces with which he hoped to dry-gulch Nagumo. All were gone from Pearl Harbor by 28 May—before the enemy subs arrived to attempt interception.

Task Force 16, commanded by Rear Adm. Raymond A. Spruance, was made up of the carriers *Enterprise* and *Hornet*, six cruisers and nine destroyers. Task Force 17 consisted of the carrier *Yorktown*, two cruisers and five destroyers, commanded by Rear Adm. Frank J. Fletcher, the senior commander over both forces. These two forces sailed to a point—Admiral Nimitz called it "Point Luck"—350 miles northeast of Midway, where they were to figuratively "lie in the bushes" and wait for Nagumo's powerful strike force.

Fletcher and Spruance reached Point Luck on 2 June and settled down to wait, Nimitz having deduced that the enemy intended to strike sometime between the 4th and 6th of June. In the meantime, navy PBY Catalina long-range patrol planes from Midway were searching for the Japanese fleet, although they were limited by a large storm front advancing from the northwest. The U.S. commanders knew that Ya-mamoto would very likely take advantage of the rain and low clouds to make his approach undetected. Radar was a new invention at the time and of limited value.

Early on the morning of 3 June, Yamamoto's Aleutian invasion force made a successful attack on Dutch Harbor, and later landed unopposed on Kiska and Attu in the Aleutians. Weather conditions were so poor that a number of Jap-anese pilots were lost when they failed to find their carriers after the strike—a problem shared by the U.S. task force in the area.

Also on 3 June, at about 0900 hours, Ya-mamoto's Midway invasion force, approaching Midway from slightly south of west, was dis-covered by a Catalina patrol plane some 700 miles from its destination. Army and marine air-craft based on Midway unsuccessfully attacked this force during the late afternoon and evening hours while, out at Point Luck, Admiral Fletcher listened to their radio chatter and decided that was not the prize he sought. He could ask no questions because his command was maintain-ing strict radio silence. As night fell, he and Spruance moved to a point about 200 miles north and slightly east of Midway, with about ten miles separating the two task forces. With the enemy invasion force nearing its objective, his heavy guns were certain to come charging out of the fog and rain by daylight.

Fletcher was right. Under scattered clouds ahead of the weather front, Nagumo began launching bombers and fighters from his four carriers for the attack on Midway at 0430 hours on 4 June. Just an hour later, at 0536 hours, a pair of Catalinas found Nagumo's force and imme-diately radioed its position, course, and speed.

At that moment, the advantage passed to Fletcher and Spruance, because Nagumo was totally unaware of their presence.

Between 0700 and 1000 hours, Midway-based planes struck at Nagumo's force but were driven back with serious losses. Then, 41 TBD Devastator torpedo planes from *Enter-prise, Yorktown,* and *Hornet* went in at wavetop level, but the enemy ships' massed defensive firepower, plus that of their Zero combat air patrols, was impenetrable. The Devastators achieved no meaningful hits and only four re-turned to the *Enterprise,* two to *Yorktown,* and none to *Hornet,* its Torpedo Squadron Eight be-ing completely wiped out.

But those crews had not been sacrificed in vain, because their determined attacks had drawn Nagumo's Zeros down to the surface and left the defending fighters low on fuel and ammunition. As the few surviving torpedo planes left the scene, high above—unmolested at 20,000 feet—*Yorktown*'s 17 SBD Dauntless dive bombers, led by Lt. Comdr. Maxwell F. Leslie, were peeling off and taking dead aim on the Japanese carrier *Kaga.* It was 1022 hours and time had run out for Nagumo.

A minute and a half after Leslie's 17 planes began their dives, Lt. Comdr. Clarence W. McClusky, leading 37 Dauntlesses from the *Enterprise,* arrived to select two more fat tar-gets: Nagumo's own flagship, the carrier *Ak-agi,* and the smaller carrier *Soryu.*

Thus it was that, within the space of a few hundred heartbeats, the Imperial Japanese Navy suffered a blow from which it never re-covered. By 1029 hours, the 51 Dauntlesses from *Yorktown* and *Enterprise* were reforming in a ragged, exuberant formation for the flight back to Point Luck, leaving behind three en-emy aircraft carriers aflame and sinking.

Nagumo's fourth carrier, the *Hiryu,* had a short reprieve because the *Hornet*'s air group failed to immediately locate it after the enemy fleet changed course following the initial at-tacks. They would sink the *Hiryu* later in the day, but not before its planes severely dam-aged the *Yorktown.*

By the time the Japanese realized that they were fighting three U.S. carriers, their strike force had none. Yamamoto ordered a full-speed withdrawal (including, of course, the Midway invasion force far to the south).

The *Yorktown* was listing at too great an an-gle for her flight deck to be used, so her planes returned to *Enterprise* and *Hornet*. Admiral Fletcher transferred his flag to an escorting cruiser, the *Astoria*, and the *Yorktown*'s crew was ordered to abandon ship after it appeared that she would capsize. Fletcher then signaled to Spruance, ordering him to proceed as he saw fit, and that the remaining ships of Task Force 17 would follow.

Spruance pursued the fleeing Japanese for two days, and on the 6th launched two final air strikes against them, sinking the heavy cruiser *Mikuma* and heavily damaging the cruiser *Mogami*. Then, with some of his escort vessels running low on fuel, Spruance reluctantly turned back.

But the enemy managed to strike a final blow. Early the next morning, 7 June 1942, Japanese submarine I-168, commanded by Lt. Comdr. Yahachi Tanabe, put two torpedos into the crewless *Yorktown* and sent her to the bottom as she was being towed toward Pearl Harbor by the minesweeper *Vireo*. Tanabe also sank the escorting destroyer *Hammann*. Thus, alone among Yamamoto's entire sea armada, submarine I-168 could return to Japan claiming victory over an American ship at Midway.

After the Battle of Midway, strategic initiative in the Pacific belonged to the U.S. Navy. In addition to his carriers and battle cruisers, the

This F4F-4 on Henderson Field, Guadalcanal, 9 February 1943, has 19 aerial victory symbols on its fuselage, although several pilots had flown this craft to achieve that total for lucky No. 2.

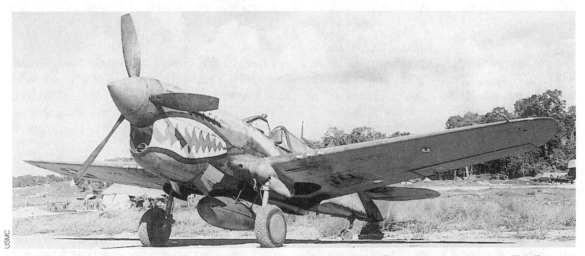

A P-40F of the 44th FS, 18th FG, on the fighter strip at Henderson Field, Guadalcanal, June 1943. The F model P-40 was powered with a Packard-built Rolls-Royce Merlin.

Grumman TBF Avenger comes aboard the escort carrier *Santee* during operations off Guadalcanal, January 1943.

enemy lost 258 airplanes and many of its best pilots. U.S. losses were 40 planes from Midway, and 92 aircraft from three carriers, plus the *Yorktown* and *Hammann*. Few if any Japanese airmen were rescued, although a number of U.S. Navy pilots were plucked from the sea by roving destroyers. After Midway, both the United States and Japan had six aircraft carriers remaining, but America would increasingly add carriers to the U.S. fleet, while Japan, fighting a defensive war following the defeat at Midway, was unable to replace the lost aircraft carriers and highly trained carrier pilots. Japan's far-flung oceanic empire could be maintained only

as long as the Imperial Japanese Navy dominated the Pacific. That dominance was lost at the moment when U.S. Naval Aviator Maxwell Leslie peeled off in his Dauntless and centered his gunsight on the broad deck of the Japanese carrier *Kaga*.

## New Guinea and the Solomons

Neither America's leaders nor the American people knew it at the time—and if they had it would not have mattered after the surprise attack on Pearl Harbor—but Japan entered WWII with limited aims and with the inten-

Lockheed F-5A reconnaissance version of the P-38, with cameras rather than guns in its nose. Bars were added to the star insignia in July 1943.

Fifth Air Force's field-modified medium bombers were so successful skip-bombing and strafing in the Battle of the Bismark Sea that North American was inspired to build the B-25G and H Mitchells armed with 75mm field cannon. Besides its cannon, the B-25H (shown) could also bring 10 forward-firing .50-caliber machine guns to bear on strafing target.

tion of fighting a limited war. Its objective was to secure the natural resources Japan lacked (oil, tin, rubber, etc.) in Southeast Asia and much of China, and to establish what Japan's Premier Tojo described as the "Greater East Asia Co-Prosperity Sphere." In other words, Japan would swiftly grab what it wanted, then stand firm behind a solid defensive position and negotiate a peace that would leave the nation in possession of most of its conquests.

Had Japan followed the course that President Roosevelt and his advisors expected, it might well have gotten away with it. On the eve of Pearl Harbor, there was a lot of senti-ment in the United States against involvement in the war in Europe or a war with Japan. But Japan's decision to "neutralize" the U.S. Navy by a surprise attack unified a divided people, aroused America to wage a total war, and de-nied the Japanese any chance of conducting the war on their own terms.

After Midway, Japan's war planners had to modify their master plan considerably, and with the mobility of their carrier striking forces curtailed, concentrated on strengthen-ing their existing defensive perimeter. They were far from defeat, and were not ready to

negotiate. According to statements made by Japan's military leaders at war's end, they expected the United States to grow weary of attempting to breach those defenses, after which Japan would consider the terms of a negotiated peace.

Meanwhile, the U.S. Joint Chiefs naturally turned to the elimination of the threat to their tenuously held bases in the Southwest Pacific, the lifeline to Australia. On 2 July 1942, they decided to begin a series of operations that would destroy the Japanese stronghold at Rabaul and establish Allied control of the Bis-marck Archipelago.

The Eastern Aircraft Division of General Motors built Wildcats under the designations FM-1 and FM-2. The FM-2 was easy to recognize with its tall rudder. The British received more than a thousand Wildcats.

USAF

Japanese Mitsubishi G4M1 Betty bomber. P-38s of 347th FG bushwhacked a Betty carrying Admiral Yamamoto, costing Japan her best military mind.

The campaign would have three tasks: (1) Forces of the South Pacific Area (under Vice Adm. Robert Ghormley, later commanded by Adm. William "Bull" Halsey) would seize base sites in the southern Solomons; (2) South Pacific forces would advance up the ladder of the Solomons while Southwest Pacific forces (under Gen. Douglas MacArthur) would move up the north coast of New Guinea; (3) The forces of the two theaters would converge on Rabaul and clear the rest of the Bismarck Archipelago. Admiral Nimitz, overall commander of the Pacific Ocean Areas—including the North, Central, and South Pacific—would run the Solomons operations, while General MacArthur would be responsible for the Southwest Pacific. General Marshall and Admiral King would referee the anticipated differences between the hard-bitten Nimitz and the flamboyant MacArthur, although they did not state it quite that way.

MacArthur's air support would be provided by the USAAF Fifth Air Force, born from the ashes of the Far East Air Force in the Philippines, and commanded by Gen. George Kenney. (The former FEAF commander, the fiesty Gen. Lewis Brereton, was in India forming the USAAF 10th AF.)

Air support in the Solomons would be provided by navy and marine fliers, plus a handful of army P-39s and P-40s, until formation of the USAAF 13th AF early in 1943.

The offensive began on 7 August 1942 when the 1st Marine Division landed on Guadalcanal and nearby islands in the southern Solomons. The enemy reacted vigorously, and six times during the next four months challenged the U.S. Navy in a series of sharp battles, while air fighting was almost a daily occurrence.

During the first days of bitter fighting on Guadalcanal, the navy, marine, and USAAF aircraft, commanded by Rear Adm. J.S. McCain, operated from bases on New Caledonia and in the New Hebrides, with some initial assistance from the air groups of *Saratoga, Enterprise,* and *Wasp.* The carriers, operating in confined waters, withdrew from direct support on 9 August. By 20 August, the marines had pushed a stubborn enemy, a few feet at a time, beyond the airstrip and Marine Fighting Squadron 233 and Scout Bombing Squadron 232 moved in. There were plenty of enemy soldiers in the surrounding rain forest, and would be for months, but the fliers took care of their missions and depended upon the "Gyrenes" to protect the airstrip. This was Henderson Field, known to the airmen there by its code name, "Cactus One." A week later, the *Enterprise* brought a deckload of P-40s, and in the weeks to follow other air force and marine air units arrived.

During Christmas Week, marines, strengthened by army troops, took over the area known as "Lunga Beach" on Guadalcanal and it became Fighter One Base, with Marine Fighting Squadron 214 (VME-214, Pappy Boyington's "Black Sheep") at one end of the strip, and the P-40-equipped 44th FS of the 18th FG* at the other. Contrary to Hollywood's portrayal of the Black Sheep, there were no army nurses on Fighter Base One and no liquor. There were Spam, dehydrated potatoes, mosquitos, and dysentery in abundance.

Guadalcanal was not declared secured until 9 February 1943. In the meantime, in addition to the fierce fighting on the island, six major sea battles were fought in the area. *Saratoga's* air groups sank the Japanese light carrier *Ryujo* during the Battle of the Eastern Solomons, 23–25 August; *Enterprise* was damaged by enemy carrier-based bombers during that battle and forced to retire. Then the *Saratoga* took a submarine torpedo on 31 August and went to Australia for repairs, and the *Wasp* was sunk by a submarine on 15 September while escorting a troop convoy to Guadalcanal. During October, the *Hornet*, in Task Force 17, repeatedly sent her planes against enemy targets on Guadalcanal and, with *Enterprise*, fought in the Battle of Santa Cruz (26–27 October) in which she was sunk by Japanese dive bombers. In the final carrier actions of the campaign, *Enterprise*, severely damaged during the Battle of Santa Cruz (the enemy threw four carriers into that battle, two of which were put out of action but not sunk), went to Noumea, New Caledonia for repairs, and was back in action by 15 November.

In the long, proud history of the U.S. Marine Corps, no pages stand out more vividly than those containing the record of the prolonged battle for Guadalcanal. That campaign alone should provide a shining beacon of inspiration for every man and woman who has worn that

---

* In May, 1942, all USAAF Pursuit Groups became "Fighter Groups," and Pursuit Squadrons became "Fighter Squadrons." Normally, a Fighter Group consisted of three squadrons of 35 aircraft per squadron— on paper, at least. In combat areas, groups were often under-strength.

uniform since. On the ground and in the air, the marines spearheaded the bloodiest fighting, and the marine air groups alone accounted for 427 enemy planes destroyed in combat.

The advance from Guadalcanal began 21 February 1943, in the Russells, sixty miles to the northeast. Although there were no noteworthy naval engagements for a time, aerial fighting continued unabated. Enemy air attacks on Guadalcanal, particularly on Henderson Field, did not let up until June, and on 16 April the island was subjected to one of the most devastating air strikes of the campaign. The Japanese sent 160 bombers and fighters that were intercepted by more than 100 American fighters from the Army, Navy and Marine Corps. The enemy lost 107 planes; the Americans, six.

By the end of 1943, Admiral Nimitz was ready to begin his final assault on Rabaul, and the drive up the Solomons ended with occupation of the Green Islands—just 120 miles from Rabaul—on 15 February 1944. As Adm. Arleigh Burke put it, "Behind lay bloody Guadalcanal—an epitaph, and enduring symbol of American bravery and sacrifice."

In January 1943, the USAAF 13th Air Force was formed around the 347th FG, which had been operating over Guadalcanal and adjacent waters since the previous October. The 347th contained one squadron each of P-40s, P-39s, and P-38s. The 13th AF gradually accumulated a hodgepodge of B-17s, B-25s, and other aircraft, including the 8th and 18th FGs equipped with P-38 Lightnings, and the 5th, 42nd, and 307th Bomb Groups (BG) flying B-24 Liberators and B-25 Mitchells. While the bombers went to Rabaul and attacked enemy shipping in the area, the fighters of the 13th AF opposed enemy raids over the Solomons and the advancing ground forces. Australian P-40 Kittyhawks joined in this effort and guarded the "back door" in the southern Solomons and New Caledonia.

Meanwhile, General Kenney's 5th AF on New Guinea was being built up around the

49th, 24th, and 35th FGs, which were equipped with whatever fighter planes Kenney could lay hands on. Early in 1943, Kenney had a total of 330 fighters, of which 80 were P-38s and 72 were the decidedly inferior P-39s. The rest were P-40s, including seven Royal New Zealand Air Force squadrons and eight Royal Australian Air Force squadrons, plus one Dutch squadron. (British and Commonwealth squadrons contained 9–12 aircraft.) Kenney's bomber force would grow from the relative handful of B-17s, A-20s and B-25s of the 7th, 19th, 3rd and 22nd BGs possessed early in 1943 to a total of 11 bomb groups a year later; an eventual total of five USAAF fighter groups after the 475th and 58th FGs were added. General Paul "Squeeze" Wurtsmith was the 5th AF's fighter commander.

The 5th AF, flying from airstrips in the Port Moresby area, made all the difference in the battle of the Bismarck Sea. In fact, that battle was fought primarily between enemy warships and Kenney's airplanes. On 1 March 1943 the Japanese sent a 16-ship convoy from Rabaul toward Lae on New Guinea's north coast to beef up their base there with an additional 6000 troops and thereby keep MacArthur contained in southern New Guinea. But F-5 Lightnings (the recon version of the P-38, fitted with cameras in place of guns) of the 17th Photo Squadron (PhS) discovered the convoy en route. On 2 March, in poor weather, 28 B-17s, escorted by 16 P-38s, sank one of the troop transports in Huon Gulf and shot down two enemy fighters. On the following day, skip-bombing and strafing, 28 Lightnings, with a mixed formation of 5th AF A-20s, B-25s, and some Australian Beaufighters, sent two destroyers and three transports to the bottom. U.S. Navy PT Boats accounted for the rest of the transports. Of the 16-ship convoy, only four destroyers survived, rescuing perhaps half of the enemy soldiers and beating a retreat to Rabaul in deteriorating weather.

It was not a large battle by WWII standards, but taken together with victory in the Solomons and devastating air strikes against the Japanese airfields on New Guinea's north coast that destroyed 200 enemy planes on the ground (made possible by use of a secret jungle airstrip built by U.S. Army engineers only a few miles from the enemy strongholds), the 5th AF over New Guinea, and the 13th AF over the Solomons, gained control of the air—with the help, of course, of the marine Corsair units moving up through the Solomons. That greatly faciliated American strategy in the Pacific.

That strategy was predicated upon three lines of advance: Across the Central Pacific, the USAAF 7th AF in support of naval units via the Gilberts, Marshalls, Marianas, Carolines and Palaus toward the Philippines; in the Southwest Pacific the 5th AF covering, and often leading, MacArthur's march up the north coast of New Guinea toward the Philippines; and the South Pacific line of advance up through the Solomons with the 13th AF, plus navy, marine and RAAF squadrons, to encircle and neutralize Rabaul, which was as important to Japan as was Pearl Harbor to the United States as a Pacific base.

During the first two weeks of April 1943, Admiral Yamamoto moved most of his carrier air groups onto Rabaul for Operation I-go, an all-out attempt to regain control of the air over New Guinea and the Solomons, and in mid-month struck at Port Moresby and Milne Bay with 150-plane raids. But Yamamoto's great aerial offensive was abruptly terminated by a flight of 14 P-38s from 347th FG on Guadalcanal. On 18 April these Lightnings were dispatched by Adm. Bull Halsey, Nimitz' deputy in the South Pacific area, to shoot down a certain Japanese Betty bomber due to arrive at an enemy airfield on Bougainville at a given time.

Halsey's information came from the Japanese themselves, by way of the navy's decoding experts, and the prize was a big one: Adm. Isoruku Yamamoto would be aboard that bomber.

The P-38s flew a long, roundabout route, staying well out to sea to avoid detection. Counting on Admiral Yamamoto's reputation for punctuality, they carefully timed their arrival over Bougainville to coincide with that of their quarry.

Yamamoto was on time. So were the P-38s. The admiral's plane went down aflame under the guns of Capt. Thomas Lanphier, while the remaining Lightnings shot down a second Betty and engaged the escorting six Zeros. One P-38, flown by Lt. Ray Hine, was lost in the fight.

But the enemy's Operation I-go was called off. Japan had lost its greatest military strategist.

## Review questions

1. How many Japanese aircraft took part in the attack on Pearl Harbor? Why were we caught so unaware? Describe our losses in manpower and shipping. How was the attack on our bases in the Philippines a repeat performance? What were some of the unexplained occurrences regarding messages to General MacArthur's headquarters? What was the fate of General Wainwright's forces?

2. What was the significance of the battle of Coral Sea? How was it a unique naval engagement? Why was the battle of Midway such an incredible victory? How come the Douglas SBD Dauntless dive bombers had a clear shot at the Japanese carriers?

3. What was the strategy of the U.S. Joint Chiefs of Staff for the Southwest Pacific? Why was the battle for Guadalcanal such a long and bitterly fought campaign? Describe the battle of the Bismark Sea. What was the significance of this victory?

4. What was operation I-go? How was Admiral Yamamoto killed?

# 12

# The war in Europe

## Objectives

At the end of this chapter you should be able to:

- Summarize the United States position on the war in Europe at the time of the fall of France in June 1940.
- Highlight the purpose of Operation Torch.
- Discuss some of the problems faced by General Eisenhower during the early part of the North African campaign.
- Discuss the importance of the Italian campaign to the allied victory in Europe.
- Describe the combined British and American bomber offensive against Germany starting in January 1943.
- Describe the preparation of manpower and equipment for the Normandy invasion.
- Discuss the importance of tactical and strategic air power during the last year of the war in Europe.

Four days after the surprise Japanese attack on Pearl Harbor, Germany and Italy declared war on the United States, effectively settling any question there may have been in the public mind as to whether or not America would also have to fight in Europe.

President Roosevelt, his military leaders, and perhaps many Americans had accepted that fact long before. As early as 1939 the President had looked the other way as American-built warplanes were pushed by hand across the border into Canada for delivery to England, a practice that supposedly got around U.S. neutrality laws. On the eve of France's defeat in June 1940, the President directed the transfer of large stocks of army WWI weapons, and ammunition and aircraft to France and Great Britain. After France fell these munitions helped to replace Britain's losses in the evacuation of its forces from the Continent at Dunkerque. More aid to Britain was forthcoming in September when the United States traded 50 over-age destroyers for offshore Atlantic bases. The American position was clear by March 1941, when the Congress passed the Lend-Lease Act, sweeping away the pretense of neutrality and by openly avowing that America would become an "arsenal of democracy" against aggression.

Actually, these acts constituted a measure of self-defense, the fundamental purpose being to help contain the military might of the Axis powers—Germany, Italy, and Japan—until the United States could build its own shaky defenses.

American military preparations and actions during the remaining months of 1941 prior to the Japanese attack were steadily toward U.S. participation in the war against Germany. In April, the President authorized an active naval patrol of the western half of the Atlantic Ocean. In May, the United States assumed responsibility for the operation of military air routes across the North Atlantic via Greenland, and across the South Atlantic via Brazil. In May, Roosevelt also proclaimed an unlimited national emergency and ordered the army and navy to prepare an expeditionary force to be sent to the Azores to block any German advance into the South Atlantic.

A few days before the Germans invaded the Soviet Union on 22 June 1941, the president sent U.S. Marines and the 33rd FS to guard Iceland. The 33rd, which belonged to the 8th FG, flew its P-40s off the deck of the aircraft carrier *Wasp* to Reykjavik with orders to attack any Axis aircraft or ship found within 50 miles of shore. By October the U.S. Navy was fully engaged in ship convoy duties in the western part of the Atlantic, and navy ships, with some assistance from army aircraft, were joining with British and Canadian forces in warring against German submarines. During the third

USAF

The P-40s of the 33rd FS, 8th FG, were sent by President Roosevelt to Iceland in August 1941 to forestall the possibility of German seizure of that strategically located island.

week in October, the new U.S. Navy destroyer *Kearny* was torpedoed in the South Atlantic and President Roosevelt declared in indignation. "We have wished to avoid shooting, but the shooting has started, and history has recorded who fired the first shot . . . All that will matter is who fired the last shot!" Actually, the *Kearny* was joining British warships in an attack on a German U-boat when she was hit.

In November Congress voted to repeal prohibition against the arming of American merchant ships and their entry into combat zones, and the stage was set, as Prime Minister Churchill noted on 9 November, for "constant fighting in the Atlantic between American and German ships."

Apparently, all of the overt American moves in 1941 toward involvement in the war against Germany were acceptable to the majority of the American people, with only a small though vociferous minority criticizing the President for the nation's departures from neutrality. America, along with the British and Dutch, had also embargoed oil shipments to Japan and imposed other trade sanctions on the Nipponese for their international misbehavior, and no one questioned the propriety of that. Those embargos forced Japan to do something, even if it was wrong, because it had no oil or certain other strategic materials of its own, and the American/British/Dutch position left it with no face-saving way out, because resumption of normal trade was tied to the condition that Japan get out of China and Indochina and, in effect, renounce her treaties with Germany and Italy. Premier Tojo and his warlords never considered that alternative.

## North Africa and Italy

Once the nation was committed to war, every American, from the President to the humblest

Carrier *Ranger* bound for North Africa with replacement P-40Ls (Merlin-powered) as escorting destroyer drops depth charges over suspected enemy submarine.

USAF

This Bf.109G of JG 27 was shot down during the Tunisian Campaign. Powered with the Daimler-Benz DB 605 of 1475 hp, it had a speed of 403 mph at 21,325 feet. Armament was two 7.9mm machine guns and a 20mm cannon, the latter firing through the prop spinner.

citizen, seemed to possess the same attitude toward it: a strong resolve for quick, direct, and total action. The trouble was that during 1942 the strength of our arms did not match the strength of our will.

Nevertheless, after the Battle of Midway, the weak and exhausted U.S. Navy was completely confident that it would soon own the Pacific Ocean. Although the Joint Chiefs were against it, President Roosevelt confidently placed his finger on a map of the North African coast and told them that, because the Allies were not yet ready to invade Hitler's Europe, we would invade North Africa instead, and then move up through Italy to attack Europe's "soft underbelly."

The invasion of North Africa, Operation Torch, was Churchill's idea, prompted by the fact that Germany's brilliant Field Marshal Erwin Rommel, the "Desert Fox," was then chasing the British 8th Army across Libya and threatening Britain's supply of Middle East oil. Also, with the Germans and their Italian allies in possession of that narrow but strategic strip of the North African littoral between Tunisia and Egypt—the Mediterranean on the north and impassable desert to the south—they denied use of the Mediterranean to Allied shipping and largely diluted the value of the Suez Canal.

Torch was scheduled for 8 November, and just five days before that Gen. Bernard Montgomery's British 8th Army broke out of its defensive position at El Alamein in Egypt (Rommel's Afrika Korps had been stopped just 70 miles short of Alexandria), and was pursuing Rommel westward into Libya. By that time, most of the 400-ship invasion force was at sea, including the U.S. Navy Task Group 34.2 under Rear Adm. E.D. McWhorter with the fleet carrier *Ranger* and the escort carriers *Sangamon, Suwannee,* and *Santee* to provide air cover for the landings. The escort carrier *Chenango* was also along, her deck containing the 33rd FG's 78 P-40s. the 1st and 14th FG's P-38s were waiting at Land's End, England, and would stage through Gibralter after the invasion was underway.

The invasion came off as scheduled, before daylight on the morning of 8 November 1942, with American troops put ashore near Casablanca in French Morocco and in Algeria near the ports of Oran and Algiers. The French fought for their German masters for three days before throwing down their arms. During that time Allied air support for the invasion came

A P-40F Warhawk of the 64th FS, 57th FG, 9th AF, which fought through Egypt, Libya, and Tunisia attached to the Desert Air Force. The 57th later fought in Italy.

from McWhorter's carriers, bolstered by Royal Air Force (RAF) Spitfires from Malta.

On the 10th, airfields near Oran were taken and the 33rd's *Warhawks* immediately moved in, while P-38s of the 1st and 14th FGs began operation the following day from Tafaraoui, Algiers. These USAAF groups were part of Gen. James Doolittle's newly created 12th AF, which also included the 301st, 310th, 97th, 47th, 98th, 319th, 320th, and 17th BGs flying B-17s, B-24s, B-25s, A-20s, and B-26s. The 31st FG, equipped with British Spitfires, also

went into action over North Africa within a week.

The only trouble with Doolittle's 12th AF was that Torch commander Gen. Dwight D. Eisenhower soon had its 800 airplanes (300 fighters, 300 bombers, and support aircraft such as C-47s) spread over 600 miles of desert to serve the presumed needs of the ground commanders, which in both deployment and mission denied the American fighter pilots the opportunity to do their job as it should be done, i.e., first gain control of the air.

The 12th AF—and the troops on the ground depending upon it—paid heavily for Eisenhower's on-the-job training until "Ike," aware that he was doing something wrong, sent to England for Gen. Carl "Tooey" Spaatz (probably America's most able air commander) to tell him what it was. Jimmy Doolittle probably had the answer, but lacked Eisenhower's trust.

Doolittle had been a lieutenant colonel just six months before, and eighteen months before that, a civilian. He had left the Air Corps in 1930, after 12 years' service, and returned in 1940. Then, in April, 1942, he led 12 B-25 Mitchells off the deck of the carrier *Hornet* for the celebrated raid on Tokyo. Twelve medium bombers loaded with fuel—they were launched more than 800 miles at sea—could not deliver sufficient bomb tonnage to

The Junkers JU-87 Stuka, a German dive bomber, was designed for close air support of the mechanized German Army in Europe, but was easy prey for Allied fighters in North Africa.

The P-38J model (foreground) with intercooler radiators beneath the engines was a greatly improved machine, but it did not enter combat until the war in the MTO had moved into Italy. Photo-recon F-5B in background.

greatly damage the enemy, but the Tokyo raid did provide Americans, civilians and servicemen alike, with a tremendous morale boost at a time when all war news was bad. All of the B-25s, and some of their crews, were lost after running out of fuel over China in bad weather, but Doolittle and his surviving crews returned to the United States as heroes, and Doolittle was promoted to the rank of brigadier general by a grateful President. As commander of the 12th AF, Doolittle wore two stars. Later, as boss of the 15th and 8th AFs in turn, he was a lieutenant general—a lot of rank and responsibility for a reserve officer.

General Eisenhower faced several unanticipated problems in Northwest Africa in addition to strong Luftwaffe action. The Germans reacted to the invasion with unexpected speed and began an airlift of troops into Tunisia from across the Mediterranean just one day after the American troops were landed ashore. Initially slowed by the confused French resistance, and then confronted by seasoned German forces,

while depending upon a supply line that reached all the way back to the United States, Eisenhower found his drive toward Tunis slowed until it became bogged in the mud of seasonal rains. He had expected to be in Tunis by Christmas, but Rommel was retreating from the opposite direction across Libya in good order and would, in late January 1943, halt his westward retreat at the Mareth Line, a series of old French fortifications near the southern border of Tunisia, which the British 8th Army would find difficult to penetrate. Meanwhile, 100,000 German and Italian troops, commanded by Gen. Juergen von Arnim, blocked Eisenhower's forces in northwest Tunisia. The Allied plan to defeat von Arnim and Rommel by squeezing them between the American and British armies east of Tunis having failed, Eisenhower had no option but to assume defensive positions in the harsh Tunisian mountains until he could accumulate enough strength to attack in conjunction with a renewed strike by General Montgomery against the Mareth Line.

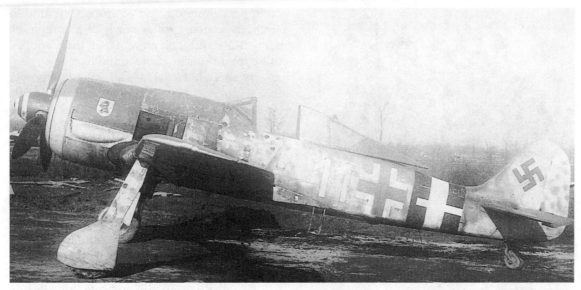

The Focke-Wulf 190 was a formidable enemy, probably the best German fighter of the war. Its 1760-hp BMW twin-row radial gave it a speed of 395 mph at 17,000 feet. Shown here is an FW 190A-8 carrying aft fuselage "defense of the Reich" bands seen in the last days of the war.

In the meantime, the 12th AF was being frittered away in a seemingly endless series of scattered, uncoordinated actions. General Spaatz changed that. He told Ike that all his air units must be commanded by air officers; that the chain of command for all air operations must be through air officers all the way to the top; that the U.S. fighter groups must concentrate on defeating the Luftwaffe and taking control of the air. Then, and only then, could the army move with its communications and supply lines intact and with effective, dependable direct air support, with the air force free to destroy the

enemy's vital communications and transport, whether it be by ship or by air across the Mediterranean.

Eisenhower gave Spaatz a free hand to reorganize U.S. airpower in northwest Africa. Spaatz, coordinating with Britain's Air Chief Marshall Tedder (Montgomery's air boss), formed the Northwest African Air Forces (NAAF) around the U.S. 12th AF, with himself in command, and then placed it in the new Mediterranean Air Command with Tedder's Desert Air Force, and with Tedder in overall command.

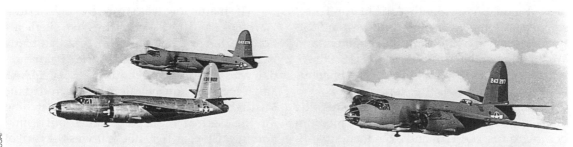

The Martin B-26 Marauder medium bomber had a reputation as a "widow maker," but crews swore by it. The 9th AF contained eight Marauder groups.

Chancellor of Germany Adolf Hitler and Reichs-marschall Herman Goering, boss of the Luftwaffe.

craft, and Brereton had equipped his under-strength bomber groups partly by shanghaiing some B-24s and their crews when they stopped in Egypt for fuel en route to India.

By early March 1943, all Allied airpower in the theater was operating under a single command and run by air officers and the situation in North Africa quickly improved for the Allies. Rommel, badly in need of fuel for his panzers, made an unexpected thrust in the Tunisian mountains against Eisenhower's forces in an attempt to capture NAAF airfield gasoline supplies. The Desert Fox gained Kasserine Pass and took 2000 American prisoners, but failed to reach the fuel he needed. He would undoubtedly have preferred not to have the prisoners because his only supplies came by airlift across the Mediterranean from Italy and Sicily and he was having trouble enough feeding his own troops.

On 7 April, the British 8th Army linked up with Eisenhower's forces in north-central Tunisia after skirting the Mareth Line. The two armies, which had started out nearly 1700 miles apart six months earlier, at last closed the pincer to surround Rommel and back him against the sea in northern Tunisia.

The German commander would hold out there until 13 May 1943 by which time, lacking the means to further resist, Rommel escaped to Italy and surrendered his 270,000 German and Italian troops. Allied airpower had swept the Luftwaffe from the air and severed Rommel's aerial supply lines across the Mediterranean.

The main blow was struck by 46 American Warhawks and 12 RAF Spitfires in a single action on 18 April, Palm Sunday, and that battle has been known ever since as the "Palm Sunday Massacre." Throughout that day, NAAF and Desert Air Force fighters had patrolled the Mediterranean off the Tunisian coast watching for the German transport planes but found nothing. Then, at 1650 hours it was the turn of the 57th FG's three squadrons, the 64th, 65th, and 66th, who could put up only 34 P-40s, so

Air Chief Marshall Tedder's common-wealth Desert Air Force, with complete control of the air, had lead Montgomery's 8th Army all the way from El Alamein in Egypt, because Montgomery as well as Montgomery's superior, Gen. Sir Harold Alexander, Commander-in-Chief, Middle East, understood the proper use of airpower and utilized it wisely, i.e., they listened to Tedder.

Tedder's Desert Air Force mostly consisted of RAF and SAAF (South African Air Force) squadrons flying Hurricanes, Spitfires, and Kittyhawks, along with some Beaufighters and Wellington bombers, plus the small U.S. 9th AF which had been formed in Egypt the previous August by Gen. Lewis Brereton.

Brereton had four Warhawk groups, the 57th, 79th, 324th and 325th FGs; two medium bomb groups, the 12th and 322nd; and two B-24 heavy bomb groups, the 98th and 376th. None possessed its normal complement of air-

they were joined by 12 more P-40s from the 324th FG's 314th Squadron.

The Warhawks stayed low, flying abreast in four-plane formations, stair-stepped from 4000 feet to 12,000 feet. The dozen Spits were at 15,000 feet, just below an overcast watching for enemy fighters.

For an hour, they saw nothing but an empty sea. Then suddenly someone saw the enemy's aerial convoy. The three-engined Junkers Ju. 52s were painted in green and blue camouflage that blended with the water below and were flying just a few feet above the surface. There were 30 of them, then, 60, then nearly a hundred. The Warhawks attacked in pairs.

It truly was a massacre. Some of the 30 or so Bf. 109 Messerschmitt and Macchi C.202 Italian fighters escorting the transports got past the covering Spits above, but the exultant P-40 pilots turned into them and dominated that confrontation as well. At low altitudes, the P-40 gave up nothing to the Messerschmitts or Macchis.

It was all over within ten minutes, and the P-40s, low on fuel and ammunition, turned for home. Six of their number and one Spitfire had gone down, but the enemy's very lifeline in North Africa had been cut. The official score was 58 Ju.52 transports, 14 Mc2O2 and four Bf.109 fighters destroyed, although there

Crew members inspect battle damage to the tail of their B-25 Mitchell medium bomber of the 12th AF in Italy. Mission was to Yugoslavia.

Flight of 9th AF P-38s, returning from a mission against German targets, make the approach to their base at low altitude. Northrop P-61 Black Widows are just visible at lower left.

was little doubt that other Ju.52s, badly damaged, had gone down into the sea unnoticed during the confusion of battle. Three pilots of the 57th FG became "instant" aces that evening: Lts. Richard E. Duffey and Arthur B. Cleveland each got five Ju.52s, and Lt. McArthur Powers shot down four Ju.52s and one Messerschmitt.

The enemy made several more desperate attempts to run the Allied aerial blockade during the following week, with about 20 transport planes each time, and each time suffered disaster. A final attempt, at night, was met by night Beaufighters of the Desert Air Force.

The enemy was allowed no respite. The combined Mediterranean Air Command, ever more fat and sassy with battle experience and receiving new U.S. air groups (including the Lightning-equipped 82nd FG and the P-40-equipped all-black 99th FS), mounted a three-week air offensive against the heavily-fortified Italian island of Pantelleria which lay about 50 miles off the Tunisian coast. Pantelleria surrendered on 11 June—the first bit of enemy territory in history to be taken with airpower alone.

Later that summer, when the Warhawk pilots of the 325th FG (the "Checkertails") felt that they had sufficiently discouraged the Italian defenders on the island of Sardinia, they dropped a note, addressed to the commanding general, suggesting that he surrender the island to the 325th FG. That undoubtedly amused Tedder and Spaatz when they heard about it, but they were forced to pass the word that any such negotiations would be handled at a higher level.

After Pantelleria fell, Sicily was next, a campaign that lasted less than a month after the NAAF destroyed nearly 1000 Axis aircraft, most of them on the ground. During the invasion by 160,000 troops of the U.S. 7th Army and British 8th Army, the Allied air cover extended well into Italy; by 13 July 1943, elements of Tedder's Mediterranean Air Command were making themselves at home on Sicilian airfields. Three weeks later, the Germans retreated across the Strait of Messina into Italy, and the Allies could look across those scant three and a half miles of water to the tip of Italy, toward what President Roosevelt had called "Europe's soft underbelly."

## The Italian campaign

It did not prove to be very soft. Although, with invasion imminent, the Italians disposed of their dictator, Benito Mussolini, and signed a separate peace with the Allies, they remained virtual prisoners in their own country which was occupied by 26 German divisions. The Germans intended to fight for every inch of Italy.

On 3 September 1943 British forces under Montgomery landed in extreme southern Italy, and the U.S. 5th Army under Lt. Gen. Mark Clark followed with an assault on the beaches near Salerno, a point selected because it represented the northern limit of effective Allied air support operating from airfields in Sicily. The ground-based aircraft of the Mediterranean Air Command, mostly the 9th and 12th U.S. Air Forces, provided all air support because all U.S. Navy carriers were in the Pacific.

The Italian campaign would drag out for 19 months, the Germans (under Field Marshal Albert Kesselring) at last surrendering on 2 May 1945, just five days before the war ended in Europe with the German surrender at Eisenhower's headquarters in Reims, France.

Less generally acclaimed than other phases of WWII, the campaign in Italy nevertheless had a vital part in the overall conduct of the war. At the crucial time of the Normandy landings, 25 Allied divisions in Italy were tying down 26 German divisions that might well have upset the balance in France. As a result of this campaign, the Allies obtained airfields useful for the strategic bombing of Germany and the Balkans. Conquest of the Italian peninsula further guaranteed the safety of Allied shipping in the Mediterranean.

North American's Mustang, designed around the Allison V-1710, became a true thoroughbred when re-engined with the Rolls-Royce Merlin, built under license in the U.S. by Packard. This early P-51B shows unusual markings: RAF camouflage and serial and fin flash with red-bordered (mid-1943) U.S. "stars and bar."

Definitive version of the Mustang was the bubble-canopied P-51D, seen here in service with the 8th AF's 20th FG. This early "D" lacks the later-standard dorsal fin. Note the 108-gallon drop tanks that allowed the Mustangs to escort the 8th's "heavies" to even the most distant targets.

General John Cannon's, 12th AF, operating from captured airfields around Naples and Salerno, was a tactical air force, its air groups primarily consisting of fighters and medium bombers. The newly-formed 15th AF contained B-17 and B-24 heavy bombers, along with P-47 fighters and three P-38 groups transferred from the 12th AF, and filled a strategic role under Gen. Nathan Twining. The 9th AF, which had fought from Egypt to Tunisia with Tedder,

joined the 8th AF in England for the air offensive against Germany. Also to England went Generals Eisenhower, Spaatz and Doolittle, with Air Marshal Tedder, to prepare for the cross-channel invasion, and Gen. Ira Eaker replaced Tedder as the top air commander in the Mediterranean Theater of Operations (MTO).

General Eaker had approximately 1200 fighter airplanes in Italy: seven fighter groups in the 12th AF and five fighter groups in the

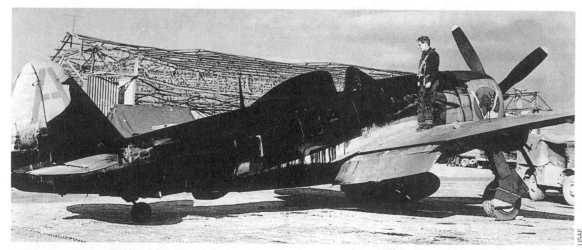

Enemy flak severed the oil line of this Republic P-47 Thunderbolt of the 12th AF, so Lt. Edwin King returned to base thoroughly bathed in oil. He was strafing gun positions near Brascia, Italy.

The Messerschmitt Bf.109F had a top speed of 382 mph at 17,000 feet, and was considered by many Luftwaffe fighter pilots to be the best of the 109 series. The more powerful 109Gs and Ks that followed gained weight and lost maneuverability.

15th AF, plus 16 squadrons of RAF, RAAF, and SAAF fighters. The RAF squadrons were equipped mostly with Spitfires, while the Australians and South Africans went to Italy from North Africa with Kittyhawks. About half of the 12th AF fighters were Warhawks at first, but all were re-equipped with Thunderbolts and, eventually, Mustangs. The 15th AF had three Lightning groups (plus one photo-recce F-5 group), two Thunderbolt and one Spitfire group (31st FG). While the Thunderbolt and Spit groups switched to Mustangs late in the war, the Lightning groups in the MTO kept their P-38s.

Eaker also had 10 medium bomber and light bomber groups in the 12th AF, two flying A-36s (Allison-powered dive bomber Mustangs), four equipped with B-25 Mitchells, and three with B-26 Marauders. The 15th AF, by mid-1944, contained no less than 21 heavy bomber groups and was bombing Germany from its bases in Italy by then. Six of these groups flew B-17 Flying Fortresses, and 15 groups had B-24 Liberators.

The 325th FG, which fought with the 12th AF in North Africa and was transferred to the 15th AF in Italy, flew P-40s, P-47s and P-51s in turn, and provides us with an interesting statistic: They destroyed 3.6 enemy aircraft for each P-40 lost in combat, 3.9 for each P-47, and 3.2 for each P-51. If that doesn't start some arguments, nothing will.

Throughout the winter of 1943–44 the Germans occupied strong defensive positions anchored on the towering peaks around the town of Cassino, about 90 miles south of Rome. On 22 January 1944, American and British troops landed at Anzio, 60 miles behind the enemy's "Winter Line," but the Germans kept this force pinned down on its beach-head, and but for constant Allied air strikes this force could not have survived. The Winter Line was not breached until May 1944, after the 12th AF had methodically destroyed all rail and highway routes of supply to the Germans.

The enemy withdrew to the Apennines in northern Italy and stubbornly remained there until, again, with lines of supply severed by

"... into the valley of the shadow ..." B-17s of the 91st BG, 8th AF, leave the coast of England 27,500 feet below headed for Germany, 4 January 1944.

A B-24 Liberator of the 15th AF is hit by flak while attacking the marshalling yards at Munich, Germany.

Allied airpower, half-starved, and bereft of the means to further resist, surrendered just a few days before the war ended in Europe.

Throughout the final year of the war in Europe, the 15th AF in Italy coordinated its mass attacks on Germany with those of the U.S. 8th AF in England. The 15th's P-38s, because of their long range, always escorted their "Big Friends."

A typical mission was that of 2 April 1944 when 450 B-17s and B-24s of the 15th AF went to Steyr, Austria, to bomb a ball bearing plant and aircraft factory. The 82nd FG furnished initial escort. While still miles from the target, the bombers were attacked by 50 Bf.109s, FW.190s, and Macchi C.202s. The Lightnings fought them off, downing three of the Messerschmitts, and although there was another formation of enemy fighters circling above, the P-38s refused to take the bait and stayed with the bombers.

Fifteen minutes later, at 1045 hours and right on time, the 325th FG's Thunderbolts arrived to relieve the P-38s and to take the Big Friends on to the target area. During the next 45 minutes, the 325th Checkertails warded off an attack on the bombers by 21 Messerschmitts. Then, at 1130 hours, 46 P-38s from the 1st FG arrived, their assignment being to protect the bombers in the target area. But the P-47s, with fuel running low, were scarcely out of sight before the bomber formation was attacked by 70 enemy fighters. That could have resulted in a sticky situation, because there were not enough P-38s on the scene to handle the Messerschmitts and Focke-Wulfs. At that point, any western movie fan could have almost heard the sound of a U.S. Cavalry bugle in the distance, because the 14th FG charged into the melee with 37

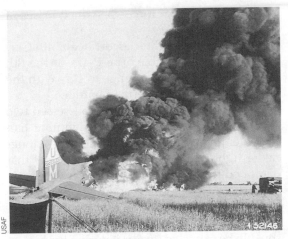

This 8th AF B-17, returning damaged from a mission over Germany, reached its base in England only to crash on landing with its brakes shot away; the crew escaped.

A 9th AF Douglas A-26 Invader hurtles earthward following a direct hit by German 88mm flak, which blasted away one wing.

more P-38s. With more than 80 Lightnings fighting together, only six enemy fighters were able to get through to the bomber stream, two of which went down under the guns of the bomber crews.

The Luftwaffe tried again shortly after 2100 hours as the bombers began coming off their targets and turning for home. Forty twin-engine Messerschmitt Zerstorers (110s and 210s), armed with rockets, struck at the bombers in head-on attacks flying four abreast. The P-38s quickly broke up these formations and, in a 20-minute running battle, destroyed 18 of them.

The 14th FG stayed with the bombers until relieved by a P-47 group just south of Klagenfurt. Later, back at base with no losses of their own to count, the 14th's pilots had a good laugh to drain away the tension when one of them, Lt. Robert Siedman, observed: "I'll bet Hitler would be real mad if he knew that a little Jewish boy had shot down three of his pilots today."

During the early summer of 1944, nine Allied divisions and many 12th and 15th AF units were withdrawn to prepare for the invasion of Southern France that would follow on 15 August against thinly held German positions and almost no Luftwaffe opposition. German airpower had been swept from the skies over Italy, and the decimated Luftwaffe, fighting a desperate, defensive battle against the great Allied bomber offensive that was methodically destroying Germany's ability to make war (and as Eisenhower's armies swept across France following the cross channel invasion the previous June), had lost control of the air over Europe.

## Assault on Fortress Europe

To the American ground forces gathered in England, the shooting war against Germany began with the cross-channel invasion of the Normandy Coast on 6 June 1944. To the U.S. air forces in the European Theater of Operations (ETO), it began long before that.

The buildup of the U.S. 8th AF in England was markedly slowed at the beginning when most of its handful of air groups were taken away by the 12th AF for the North African Campaign. During the summer of 1942, P-38s, B-17s and C-47s were flown across the North Atlantic with refueling stops in southern Greenland and Iceland. Another transatlantic air route was established across the South Atlantic to Africa's Gold Coast with a mid-ocean refueling stop at tiny Ascension Island. Many of these aircraft went to the 12th and 15th AFs. By early 1943, however, warplanes ferried across the North Atlantic remained with the 8th and 9th AFs in England. The South Atlantic ferry route was used to deliver aircraft to the 10th and 14th AFs in the China-Burma-India (CBI) Theater of Operations.

President Roosevelt and Prime Minister Churchill agreed, at the Casablanca Conference in January 1943, that a combined bomber offensive against Germany was a necessary prelude to the cross-channel invasion. The primary aims were the destruction of the Luftwaffe (both in combat and by bombing the enemy's aircraft factories) and Germany's sources of oil. The RAF would bomb by night and the USAAF would bomb by day; around the clock, when the two bomber commands possessed the machines to make that possible.

The biggest problem facing the 8th AF was uncertainty. Airpower had never been used in a massive, coordinated effort to destroy the industrial base, or key parts of that base, of a modern nation. Initially, Arnold and most of his commanders believed that the U.S. heavy bombers, each with nine .50-cal guns were armed sufficiently, that, in large formations at least, they could protect themselves against concentrated attacks by enemy fighters. However, premature raids by two to three hundred B-24s and B-17s, in August 1943, against the Rumanian oil fields at Ploesti and the German ball bearing and aircraft factories at Regensburg and Schweinfurt, without fighter escort, proved the fallacy

of that. The bomber forces sustained losses of nearly 20 percent.

At that time, fighter escort deep into Germany was not possible. The P-47s of the 8th and 9th AFs lacked the range to stay with the bombers beyond the German border.

By October 1943, the 8th AF possessed two groups of P-38s and while the Lightning had the potential of becoming a very effective long-range fighter, the P-38G and H versions that equipped the 55th and 20th FGs were not truly combat-ready aircraft—certainly not for the ETO. Their supercharger system demanded more attention from the pilot than he could reasonably be expected to give it during the heat of battle, resulting in a lot of blown engines. Cockpit heating and windshield defrosting were completely inadequate for the altitudes and temperatures at which the air war over Europe was fought. These craft had no dive brakes, no maneuvering flaps or aileron boost. Not until August 1944 would the P-38J-25 be available in

USAF

Scratch one Messerschmitt. This is how it looked to the gun camera of "Jug" pilot Capt. Floyd Brandt of the 19th Tactical Air Command as he participated in the protection of Patton's exposed southern flank.

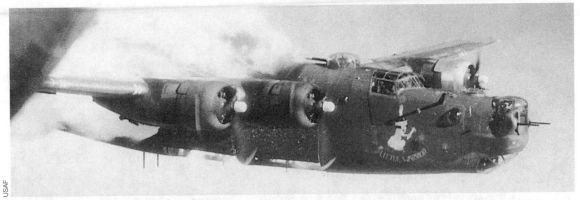

*Little Warrior* takes a direct hit from flak over Quakenbruk, Germany, 29 June 1944. Craft fell out of control a few seconds later. More Liberators were built during WWII than any other American airplane.

significant numbers, the first fully developed Lightning. It and subsequent versions would be the sweethearts of the AAF fighter pilots in the Southwest Pacific, but by that time most fighter groups in the ETO were being re-equipped with the P-51 Mustang, and all but one P-38 group disappeared over Europe.

Nevertheless, throughout the late winter and early spring of 1944, the period during which the Luftwaffe was defeated, the P-38s did the job as assigned to them. Air superiority in the ETO was largely won by the P-47 groups in aerial combat. There were 22 Thunderbolt groups in the 8th and 9th AFs, and seven P-38 groups by May 1944, and many of the P-47 groups were in action months before the P-38s arrived.

By late March 1944, Allied airpower was dominant over Europe (the Luftwaffe lost more than 800 fighters during February and March), and although the P-51 Mustang was probably the best air superiority fighter airplane of the war, it was not in action in large numbers until after the showdown battles with the Luftwaffe in February and March, 1944.

Throughout the winter and spring the P-38s took the bombers into Germany—Bremen, Frankfurt, Munster, Soligen, Berlin—after the P-47s had escorted the bombers across France.

The intelligence summaries of these raids reveal that, more often than not, the German fighters did not attack the bombers while the P-38s were with them, attacking instead while the P-47s were in escort. There is no explanation for this, because the P-47 was certainly a more deadly adversary than the early P-38. Perhaps the Ger-

The concentrated fire of a P-47's eight .50-caliber guns spells doom for any enemy fighter.

America has possessed no greater air leader than Gen. Carl "Tooey" Spaatz, whose career began in 1916 and ended with his retirement in 1948. Today's independent United States Air Force was born under his command.

mans at that time didn't think so; one captured Luftwaffe pilot referred to the P-38s as "those forked-tail devils." In any case, the German fighter pilots were ordered to avoid combat with Allied fighters if possible and to concentrate on the bombers.

## Overlord: The cross-channel invasion

At 0145 hours on 6 June 1944, 9000 paratroopers of the U.S. 101st and 82nd Airborne Divisions began jumping from more than 800 C-47 transports of the 9th AF over France's Cherbourg Peninsula inland from the Normandy

beaches. At the same time, some 200 RAF transports dropped 5000 British paratroopers, while 200 gliders followed with heavy weapons, guided to open fields by flare paths set up by the paratroopers. Concurrently, 8th and 9th AF bombers joined the U.S. Navy bombardment of the enemy's coastal defenses. At daybreak the first of the five divisions of U.S. and British troops began pouring ashore on the Normandy beaches. Behind them, the mightiest sea armada of all time—4000 ships, stretching back to the coasts of England—was bringing more men and guns. Overhead, 11,000 Allied airplanes, hastily painted the night before with special black and white "invasion stripes"

Flames envelop this 9th AF B-26 Marauder after a direct hit on its left engine by German anti-aircraft gunners.

(hopefully, to prevent friendly troops below from firing on them), provided an air umbrella against enemy air attack and fanned out across Normandy at treetop level to interdict enemy movement for miles behind the beachheads. Some 50,000 Allied soldiers were ashore in France before the day—"D-Day"—was over.

After D-Day, most U.S. tactical aircraft and many strategic bombers were diverted from the pure air offensive against Germany to give close air support to the advancing ground forces. The 8th and 9th AFs together possessed 2900 heavy bombers, 3000 fighters, and 400 medium bombers. If some U.S. infantrymen slogging through the mud sometimes wondered where the air force was, they should have been told that it had been there long before, which was why they were advancing without

fear of enemy air attack, and it was presently miles ahead, systematically destroying enemy transportation, communications, troop concentrations, tank farms, and supply lines—in short, going for the enemy's vitals while the ground forces engaged his extremities. Thus, the Allied armies swept across France in almost direct proportion to the effectiveness of their airpower. They were stopped or slowed, usually, for one of two reasons: either when their advance was so rapid that it outstripped their lines of supply, or when weather screened off a sector from their eyes in the sky and allowed the Germans to concentrate sufficient strength for a counterattack.

Although the American tactical aircraft were being efficiently employed, one U.S. General, George ("Blood and Guts") Patton, Jr., a

The Casablanca Conference, January 1943: President Roosevelt and Prime Minister Churchill (seated). Standing, left to right: Gen. Hap Arnold, Adm. Ernest J. King, Gen. George Marshall, Adm. Sir Dudley Pound, Gen. Sir Alan Brooke, and Air Chief Marshal Sir Charles Portal.

tough, bold old rooster, found a way to substitute it for a division or two of mobile ground troops. On 25 July, he sent his U.S. 3rd Army racing through a five-mile breach blasted in enemy defenses along the St. Lo-Periers Road by 8th and 9th AF planes. They dashed toward Germany depending entirely upon American fighters and medium bombers to protect the exposed southern flank. To most veteran ground commanders, such a move bordered upon madness. But the pilots—mostly from Gen. O.P. Weyland's 19th Tactical Air Command—bombed and strafed like demons at altitudes that should have qualified them for Combat Infantryman Badges. They proved so effective

that 20,000 German soldiers, attempting to turn Patton's flank, surrendered directly to the Air Force, without ever engaging the 3rd Army. Later, speaking of tactical air support for his armored divisions, General Patton characterized the relationship as "love at first sight."

A week after D-Day, Hitler began sending his Vergeltungswaffe (vengeance weapons) against London. The first of these was the V-1, a small, unmanned and gyro-stabilized aircraft powered with a pulse-jet engine and carrying a ton of explosives. About 8000 of these flying bombs were sent against London and Antwerp, about half of which were shot down by Allied fighters and anti-aircraft artillery before Allied bombers snuffed out V-1 production and destroyed their launching sites. By September 1944, the V-1 was no longer a threat. Hitler, however, had another and more terrible vengeance weapon, the V-2.

The V-2 was first fired against London and Paris on 8 September 1944. It was a short-range ballistic missile carrying slightly less than a ton of explosive, and, like the German jet fighter could have altered the course of the war in Europe had Hitler possessed enough of them soon enough, and employed them correctly. As it was, the 2500 V-1s, and perhaps 100 V-2s, that struck England killed almost 10,000 civilians and leveled more than 200,000 buildings.

Meanwhile, Allied strategic bombers systematically eliminated the enemy's oil industry. By the spring of 1945, gasoline production in Germany and German-occupied territory had dropped to seven percent of the normal capacity and the Nazi war machine became almost immobile. The mechanized German Army was afoot; panzer units had to hoard fuel for weeks in order to make a single move. New fighter airplanes for the Luftwaffe, produced with supreme effort but in surprisingly large numbers in underground plants, were grounded with empty tanks—and there destroyed by low-flying Allied fighters.

Allied ground forces, moving swiftly beneath skies totally controlled by their own aircraft, swept over the Reich to meet Russian forces at the Elbe River on 25 April 1945. Five days later, Adolph Hitler committed suicide amid the rubble of Berlin. A few days after that, on 7 May 1945, a prostrate Germany, its cities in ruin, surrendered to the Allies' Supreme Commander, ETO, Gen. Dwight D. Eisenhower.

USAF

This B-17 somehow moved directly beneath another as the upper aircraft released its bombs over Berlin. Bomb at lower left struck the stabilizer of the Fortress with this result, and the plane fell away out of control.

This shot-up 358th FG P-47, painted with "invasion stripes," nosed up during landing. Crew chief rushes to aid pilot as others control blaze from the ruptured drop tank and medics stand by.

Consolidated (today, General Dynamics) B-24 Liberator releases bombs over Bielefeld, Germany, 24 February 1945.

A formation of B-24s bound for Ingolstadt, Germany, 1 March 1945

When the end came in the ETO. America had about 13,000 combat airplanes in that theater. The Western Allies had dropped 2.77 million tons of bombs on the continent, of which 1.5 million tons fell from U.S. bombers, largely during the final ten months of that conflict.

Many air commanders today believe that the Allies forfeited a chance at a relatively cheap victory in the ETO during the spring and early summer of 1944, and that invasion of Europe was not necessary. Allied airpower, they point out, was free to destroy all German industry, including Germany's ability to feed her people, after defeat of the Luftwaffe.

They are probably right; General Von Rundstedt, Commander-in-Chief of German Armed Forces in Western Europe, said after the war, "Three factors defeated us in the West where I was in command. First, the unheard-of superiority of your air force, which made all movement in daytime impossible. Second, the lack of motor fuel—oil and gas—so that the panzers and even the remaining Luftwaffe were unable to move. Third, the systematic destruction of all railway communications so that it was impossible to bring one single railroad train across the Rhine. This made impossible the reshuffling of troops and robbed us of all mobility."

A negotiated peace with Germany in the summer of 1944 would undoubtedly have left Germany intact, and the Soviets no farther west than the Polish border, a not unattractive thought today. It would have required the Germans to punish their own war criminals, another attractive thought. But could we, at that time, have accepted that? Probably not. The Nazi excesses were simply too horrible, and in a sense all Germany shared their guilt.

Troop-laden gliders, two towed behind each C-47 of the 439th Troop Carrier Group, carry reinforcements to the U.S. 9th Army for the historic crossing of the Rhine River, 24 March 1945.

# Review questions

1. What was the significance of the Lend-Lease Act? How did the U.S. position on the war in Europe begin to change after the fall of France? Why was North Africa selected for the first invasion by Allied forces? What were some of the early problems faced by General Eisenhower? Describe how Allied air forces were organized for the North African campaign. Why couldn't the German and Italian troops escape from Northern Tunisia in May of 1943?

2. How important was the Italian campaign to the victory in Europe? Discuss why this campaign was so difficult. What was the role of the 15th Air Force?

3. What was the role of the 8th Air Force based in England? How was the P-51 Mustang used? How effective were the P-47s and P-38s against German fighter aircraft?

4. Describe the extent of manpower and equipment assembled for the D-Day invasion. How effective was the use of air power in the allied advance across France and into Germany?

5. What were Hitler's "vengeance weapons?" Describe the situation in Germany by the Spring of 1945.

# 13

# Victory and the unreal wars

## Objectives

At the end of this chapter you should be able to:

- Identify some of the problems encountered during the Aleutian Campaign.
- Describe the role and success of the American Volunteer Group (AVG) known as the "Flying Tigers."
- Discuss the importance of the Air Transport Command (ATC) in supplying Chinese and American forces fighting the Japanese in China.
- Highlight the significance of the retaking of the Philippines and the Battle of Leyte Gulf.
- Identify several of the bloody island campaigns leading to the fire bombing and atomic bombing of the Japanese mainland.

The Second World War demanded that Americans fight in some strange and unlikely places. American troops understood England, France, Italy, and even the German enemy. They are people much like ourselves, with cities and trains and homes and dogs. Even North Africa had towns. But the Aleutians were a different story. So, too, were the airstrips of northern Assam, the awesome Himalayas, China. There, as in the rain forests of the Solomons and New Guinea, the young American in uniform was prone to demand: "What am I doing in this stinking hole? Tojo can have it as far as I'm concerned!"

## The Aleutian campaign

Nowhere did the American serviceman have a better right to gripe than in the bleak Aleutians. Of all the unreal, "lesser" wars contained in WWII, it was, perhaps the "unrealest." Americans had to be there to prevent the Japanese from grabbing bases from which the enemy could strike at the North American Continent. But the Japanese were not the primary enemy in that cold, mist-shrouded and desolate land. Weather was the most dangerous foe to the pilots of the 11th AF who had to fly in it. Navigating through the icy mists was likened to "flying inside a bottle of milk," and violent winds could sweep the lifeless tundra with unsuspected suddeness. Distances were great. The Aleutian chain arcs across the extreme North Pacific from the Alaskan Peninsula to within a few miles of Soviet territory. Japan is closer than Seattle.

At the time of the attack on Pearl Harbor, the U.S. had a dozen old Douglas B-18 Bolo bombers and 20 even older P-26 fighters in Alaska. Not until a month before the Battle of Midway, and the Japanese occupation of Kiska and Attu in the western tip of the Aleutians,

Warhawks of the 11th AF prepare for a patrol on a typical mist-shrouded day in the Aleutians.

did the first P-39s and P-40s arrive at Otter Point and Cold Bay on Umnak Island to protect the U.S. Navy base at Dutch Harbor. Later that summer, a squadron of P-38s would arrive and the 343rd FG would be organized, each of its three squadrons flying a different aircraft. The 407th BG, equipped with B-24s, made up the balance of the 11th AF's combat units.

When the Japanese attacked Dutch Harbor in a diversionary thrust immediately preceding the Battle of Midway, the P-40s shot down six of the enemy's carrier-based planes, but thereafter aerial combat over the Aleutians was extremely rare. The Japanese never had more than two or three squadrons of Rufes (a floatplane version of the Zero) and some Kawasaki Ki-97 flying boats in the Aleutians, and they were not aggressive. But airstrips were difficult to build on the spongy tundra, and because the enemy seemed content to remain where he was—a thousand miles from Umnak—new airstrips had to be built, because only the P-38 fighters could reach him, barely.

A new strip at Adak, 375 miles closer to Kiska, allowed the fighters to accompany the 407th's Liberators on raids against the enemy bases. Because of the lack of enemy air opposition, the P-38s carried bombs. Flying in the Aleutian weather, the fighters tucked in close to the bombers and followed their lead. The Army's WWII fighter pilots, being hastily trained, were not particularly noted for their navigational and instrument-flying skills.

Throughout the winter and early spring of 1943 (though it's hard to tell the difference in the Aleutians) the 11th AF flew bombing and strafing missions to Kiska and Attu. Then, on 11 May, a small task force of the U.S. Navy operating with the escort carrier *Nassau* put the U.S. Army 7th Division ashore at Attu and the 2300 enemy troops on the island were soon overwhelmed. Navy and marine aircraft from the *Nassau* added their muscle to that of the 11th AF in providing close air support for the men of the 7th Division fighting in the snow-covered mountains of Attu.

Two months later, American troops invaded Kiska, only to find that the Japanese had already slipped away in the fog.

The 343rd FG, completely equipped with P-38s, moved westward to the island of She-

Lightning pilots of the 343rd FG at Adak are briefed during the battle for Attu.

The P-40 of AVG pilot Charles Older, a marine reserve officer who achieved 10½ kills with the Flying Tigers. Older later ran his score to 22½ with the 14th AF and became a Los Angeles Superior Court Judge.

mya, where its hapless pilots and support people were doomed to stand guard for the rest of the war, fighting the weather and boredom in a "stinking hole" that each would gladly give to the Japanese if only he could be sent somewhere else to fight. The U.S. Navy also set up an air station on Attu, from which planes of Fleet Air Wing 4 henceforth patrolled the North Pacific.

## Over the hump with the AVG and the 14th AF

The American Volunteer Group (AVG), more popularly known as the "Flying Tigers," is not easy to accurately describe. It was organized under the direction of Claire Lee Chennault, a retired U.S. Air Corps captain who had been in China since 1937 attempting to train and lead Chinese pilots against the Japanese invader. The AVG's personnel was recruited and its aircraft purchased through the Central Aircraft Manufacturing Company in Burma. This was actually an assembly plant for Curtiss-Wright

fighters (fixed-gear versions of the P-36 up to that time) sold to China by wheeler-dealer William D. Pawley. Pawley did not work directly for Curtiss-Wright. He may be more accurately described as an international promoter who collected highly placed friends, thought

Robert "Duke" Hedman's airplane. Chinese insignia is painted over the original RAF roundel on wing. The AVG P-40s actually were Curtiss H81-A2 Tomahawks ordered by Britain.

*Over the hump with the AVG and the 14th AF*   229

Colonel David "Tex" Hill, a Flying Tiger double ace and ex-navy dive bomber pilot, also transferred to the 23rd FG, 14th AF, and ended the war with 18¼ official victories in P-40s.

lots and most of the supporting personnel were American civilians. That made them, by definition, mercenaries. But that is an oversimplification. Almost all were reservists in the USAAF, the U.S. Navy or Marines. Most of them believed that war with Japan was imminent. So they were patriots and adventurers, and their reasons for agreeing to go to China to fight the Japanese months before Pearl Harbor were as varied as the men themselves. Their story belongs here because the U.S. 14th AF in China grew from the AVG, and because, after the Tigers were disbanded in mid-1942 and the U.S. 23rd FG was born in their place, most of them returned to duty with their respective branches of service.

The release of U.S. military reservists for combat under a foreign flag—an active combatant—was probably about as legal as pushing American warplanes across the border into Canada, but President Roosevelt signed an executive order, without publicity, on 15 April 1941 permitting Pawley's representatives to recruit the 350 pilots and support personnel. This had clearly been agreed upon earlier because Curtiss-Wright billing records reveal that the 100 P-40s needed to equip the AVG were billed "to China" three months earlier. (That transaction is fascinating because C-W billed Madame Chiang Kai-Shek's "China Defense Supplies," a

big, and had the guts to back his schemes with action.

The AVG flew under the flag of China, and its airplanes carried Chinese insignias. The pi-

The Chinese-built bamboo-and-paper P-40s that served as decoys for Japanese raiders of the Flying Tigers' field at Kunming.

duly registered Maryland corporation, for only 87 airplanes, although 100 were actually delivered. Those machines were H81-A2 Tomahawks built for the RAF, essentially the same as the USAAF P-40B.)

The AVG's three squadrons flew from improvised airstrips near Rangoon, Burma, and Kunming, China, their primary mission being to protect Generalissimo Chiang Kai-Shek's supply routes through Burma. The Chinese Nationalist leader had been fighting the Japanese invader for years, and was the only force standing between advancing Nipponese and weakly-held British positions in Burma and India.

Generalissimo Chiang Kai-Shek and Maj.Gen. Claire Chenault after the AVG was disbanded and the 23rd FG born in its place as part of the new China Air Task Force, later the 14th AF.

Contrary to popular belief, the AVG did not enter combat until after the attack on Pearl Harbor, their first air battle coming on 10 December 1941. But during the winter of 1941–42, the "Flying Tigers" (apparently named by a *Life* magazine correspondent) provided the American public with the only heartening news to come out of the war during those months. During their first ten weeks of combat the AVG shot down 217 Japanese planes and claimed another 43 as probables while losing 16 P-40s and four pilots.

The Tigers, including Papa Tiger Chennault, earned all the acclaim they received. Never at any time did they have more than 55 flyable P-40s while the enemy had more than 600 combat aircraft in the area. They had no spare parts, an uncertain supply of fuel, faulty ammunition, poor food, and worse housing.

Because they were civilians, they were somewhat on the undisciplined side—23 quit and went home as the result of an argument with Chennault over mission assignments, and Chennault "dishonorably discharged" a few others, including Greg "Pappy" Boyington. On the ground they were individualists, typical young Americans, with names such as Laughlin, Dupouy, McGarry, Schiller, Rossi, and the usual complement of Smiths. In the air they were as deadly a team of fighter pilots as has ever been assembled.

The AVG was disbanded on 4 July 1942, with the USAAF 23rd FG born in its place. At that time, 87 pilots and 164 support personnel remained of the original 350. During its 30 weeks of combat, the AVG had 297 confirmed air victories and 240 unconfirmed, plus 40 enemy aircraft destroyed on the ground. Four AVG pilots died in combat: three were taken prisoner by the Japanese. Only five pilots and 17 mechanics chose to remain in China and accept induction into the 23rd FG, although 55 volunteered an additional two weeks duty to help the 23rd get into operation. These, and the rest of the Tigers returned to the navy, marines, and to service elsewhere with the USAAF. The AVG produced 26 aces.

# The Assam Trucking Company

In March 1942, while Americans and Filipinos were holding out on Bataan and the AVG was fighting over China, AAF Col. Caleb Haynes was dispatched across the South Atlantic in command of 15 bombers on a secret mission to bomb Tokyo from a base in China. Haynes got as far as Karachi, India, when his mission was

Warhawks of the 23rd FG near their base at Chengkung, China, late in 1943.

A Douglas C-54 transport (DC-4 in civilian dress) of the Air Transport Command landing at Kunming, China, after a flight over the Himalayas from northern India.

cancelled. Doolittle's raiders had struck Tokyo the day before from the carrier *Hornet*.

General Lewis Brereton had taken his surviving B-17s from the Philippines to Australia, and had been ordered to India to form the U.S. 10th AF from whatever he could scrounge. He grabbed Haynes's B-17s and sent Haynes to Dinjan, in the Assam Valley, close to India's northeastern border with Burma. Haynes's new mission was to form the Assam-Burma-China Ferrying Command, a shoestring operation that would supply fuel and ammunition to

the AVG in China. Haynes was given two C-47s and promised more. His pilots were several air force fliers with "midnight" order changes and some Pan American Airways personnel. These were the first "Hump" pilots, forerunners of a legendary breed who would fly the awesome Himalayas in ever-increasing numbers to supply not only the Flying Tigers but the 23rd FG, Chiang Kai-Shek's forces, and the 14th AF. The idea was to allow the Nationalist Chinese to continue fighting after the enemy had cut their overland supply route, the torturous 800-mile Burma Road which had linked Kunming with Lashio and the road to Mandalay in central Burma.

Aided by China's airline, China National Aviation Corporation (CNAC, established and partly owned by Pan Am), Colonel Haynes had a trickle of supplies reaching the AVG and Chiang Kai-Shek by early May 1942, although the capacities of his C-47s were limited by the need to climb above the 16,000-foot peaks of the Himalayas in northern Burma.

But the promised additional airplanes did arrive: first, some 10th AF B-24 bombers hastily converted to cargo carriers, then the Curtiss C-46 which, though untested, had been ordered into production by General Arnold because of its great cargo capacity and the pressing need. By December 1942, the ABC Ferry Command became part of the newly-created (everything

Workhorse of the "Hump," the Curtiss C-46 Commando.

The war was also won on the production lines back home. The Curtiss plant at Buffalo, New York, is pictured in mid-war producing P-40s and C-46s.

On the China side of the Himalayas there was always plenty of hand labor to fill bomb craters and keep the airstrips open.

seemed to be newly-created during the desperate days) Air Transport Command (ATC), often referred to by the air crews in India as the "Assam Trucking Company." ABC Ferry Command was delivering 2500 tons of supplies to China per month by early 1943.

They accomplished this by flying from the broiling sun of Assam, over fetid jungle and enemy occupied territory, above the world's highest mountain range, to the improvised airstrips in China. Navigational aids were few and unreliable; as often as not the flight was in or above cloud, clouds that were welcome when enemy fighters were about. Their life-giving cargos were delivered regularly despite the eight months of monsoon rains and the four months of violent winds that followed each year, despite dysentery and malaria and fitful rest beneath mosquito netting in oppressive heat. Under the direction of Gens. Hoag, "Black Bob" Hardin, and later, William Tunner, the Hump airlift, in defiance of all reason and common sense, was delivering 71,000 tons of supplies monthly by mid-1945.

As the Japanese were at last pushed back in Burma by Allied troops under Lord Mountbatten (including a U.S. Army regiment known as "Merrill's Marauders"), the Hump routes moved south to lower terrain and Douglas C-54s took over much of the load, some of them belonging to the Navy Air Transport Service.

A total of 1314 airmen died flying the Hump while delivering more than three quarters of a million tons of cargo.

## The CBI fighters

The 10th AF in India was made up of just seven combat groups: the 7th BG with B-24s, the 12th and 341st BGs with B-25s, and the 33rd, 51st, 80th and 311th FGs, the first three of which were equipped with P-40s, while the 311th flew P-51s.

The veteran 33rd FG, having fought in North Africa and Italy before going to India, finally ended up in China, flying P-47s with Chennault's 14th AF while the 51st FG, after a stint in India, also joined the 14th AF in China where it eventually received P-51s, though it had a fourth squadron attached to it (the 459th FS) flying P-38s. The 80th FG, based in Upper Assam, also had one squadron of P-38s.

While based in India, these fighter groups saw little aerial combat, but were kept busy bombing and strafing in an attempt to stop the Japanese advances in Burma. Not until Col. Phil Cochran, who had come to India with the 33rd FG, led a daring glider assault deep into Burma behind enemy lines to cut the enemy's supply lines, did the Allies break Japan's grip on Burma.

In China, Chennault, who had assumed the rank of colonel in the Chinese Air Force as leader of the AVG, became a Brigadier General in the USAAF when the AVG was disbanded, and was given command of the China Air Task Force (CATF), originally consisting of the 23rd FG and a group of B-25s commanded by Col. Caleb Haynes. Early in 1943, the CATF became the U.S. 14th AF, which steadily grew in strength during the following two years as it received air units from the 10th AF, and as the ATC was increasingly able to supply it.

Warhawks and Marauders share this base in New Guinea of the 5th AF.

White-tailed Warhawks of the 44th FS on Munda Airstrip, late summer 1943

The 14th AF fought a makeshift war at the end of an incredibly long supply line. Until the final year of the war, the P-40 was its main fighter airplane, and the 23rd FG alone accounted for 941 enemy aircraft destroyed, although most of its missions were against ground targets.

Perhaps the best assessment of the 14th AF was offered at war's end by General Takahashi, Chief of Staff of the Japanese Armies in North China: "But for the 14th Air Force, we could have gone anywhere we wished in China."

## The final thrust

MacArthur's return to the Philippines was something the people back home could at last identify with impending victory. For almost three years Americans had died taking a series of Pacific islands that most had never before heard of, and the newspapers reported great sea battles in which only the enemy ever seemed to lose any ships. (Censorship was something else the American people endured during WWII, but it was counterproductive in the sense that the people quickly lost confidence in official military bulletins and most felt that they never really knew how the war was going.) But here, finally, was the kind of evidence of success that everyone understood.

Bell P-39s and P-400s (the latter a P-39 fitted with a 20mm cannon, the former with a 37mm gun) served in all theaters but were decidedly inferior to all enemy op-position in the air. Bell's follow-on design, the P-63 shown here, used a laminar-flow wing. Most P-63s built went to Russia under Lend-Lease. USAF

General Arnold meets with military leaders in the CBI; from left: Arnold, Gen. Chennault, Gen. Joseph "Vinegar Joe" Stilwell, Gen. Sir John Dill, Gen. Clayton Bissell. Chennault was normally at odds with all but Arnold.

Militarily, the retaking of the Philippines held far more than psychological significance. It provided a major base of operations both for ships and land-based aircraft. Admiral Nimitz's Central Pacific forces, which included the 7th AF and the recently-created 20th AF, had moved 4000 miles across the Pacific, taking bases from Tarawa through the Gilberts and Marshalls to the Marianas, while MacArthur (whose command contained a high percentage of Australians and New Zealanders) had fought 1300 tough miles from Port Moresby to Hollandia on New Guinea's north coast and beyond to the island bases of Wakde and Biak. Admiral Halsey had moved northward through the Solomons to neutralize the great enemy base at Rabaul. With Rabaul encircled and cut off from supply, it was left to "wither on the vine." After its air units were destroyed, invasion by Allied troops was unnecessary.

As the two forces under MacArthur and Nimitz came together southeast of Mindanao, with MacArthur on the island of Morotai and four strong U.S. Navy task groups operating from the Palaus, Yap, and Ulithi, their power was merged for the invasion of the Philippines at Leyte on 20 October 1944.

By early March 1945, Manila Bay was open to Allied shipping and Gen. Douglas MacArthur and Filipino states-man/soldier Carlos Romulo (standing) made a symbolic return aboard a U.S. Navy PT boat.

The 13th and 5th AFs were combined into the reborn Far East Air Forces (FEAF), and these fliers, together with land-based marine air and carrier-based navy air units, soon took possession of the air over the Philippines and led the allied invasion of Luzon at Lingayen Gulf on 9 January 1945. Manila was liberated a month later.

Meanwhile, the Imperial Japanese Navy was decisively defeated attempting to turn back the Leyte landings. The Battle of Leyte Gulf, actually a series of actions from 10 through 29 October 1944, cost the enemy 1046 aircraft destroyed by carrier-based U.S. Navy planes alone, along with 26 major combatant ships, including three battleships, three heavy cruisers, and four aircraft carriers, the *Zuikaku*, *Chiyoda*, *Zuiho* and *Chitose*. The U.S. Navy lost the escort carriers *Gambier Bay* and *St. Lo*, the latter to kamikaze attack. Kamiazes also damaged the carriers *Intrepid*, *Franklin*, and *Belleau Wood*.

The kamikaze attacks would continue as the U.S. Navy operated close to the Japanese home islands, and although the censored press reports at the time minimized their effect, the truth is that this desperation tactic accounted for at least half of all U.S. Navy ships damaged and a fifth of those sunk throughout the war, most of the attacks coming during the final 10 months of the Pacific War. The kamikazes also struck at important shore installations. Had the war not ended as it did, another seven to nine thousand kamikazes were waiting for the expected invasion of Japan.

Grumman F6F Hellcat escorts TBFs and SBDs from the new *Yorktown* in the Philippine Campaign, October 1944.

tions. Iwo Jima was not secured until 16 March and at the cost of 4590 marine dead, plus the loss of the escort carrier *Bismark Sea*, sunk by kamikazes, along with serious damage to the *Saratoga*.

The price paid for Iwo Jima was said to be justified by its location. It gave the United States airfields halfway between Japan and the 20th AF's B-29 bases in the Marianas, and was later claimed to have saved no less than 2400 B-29s and their crews that would not have made it to the Marianas after missions to Japan. But that would seem to be an overstatement since fewer than 1200 B-29s went to the Pacific before the war ended.

The B-29 air offensive against Japan began in mid-1944 when the 58th Bomb Wing of the 20th Bomber Command (the 20th and 21st Bomber Commands were part of the new 20th AF which operated directly under the Joint Chiefs as a Global Air Force) began operations from Chengtu in west central China. But that was a premature effort that served mostly to prove that meaningful numbers of Superfortresses could not be supported by the ATC airlift over the Hump. By October, however, bases taken from the enemy in the Marianas were ready to handle the B-29s and the Superforts were concentrated there on five big airfields, two each on Guam and Tinian and one on Saipan.

While Allied troops were mopping up in the Philippines, U.S. Navy Task Group 52 with 12 carriers under Rear Adm. C.T. Durgin, and TG 58 containing 17 carriers and commanded by Vice Adm. Marc Mitschner, carried two marine divisions to landings on Iwo Jima 19 February 1945. The marines faced 23,000 Japanese in exceptionally strong defensive posi-

Warhawks of the 80th FG at Nagahuli Airstrip in Upper Assam, India, 1944

PBY-5A Catalina patrol plane drops depth charge over enemy submarine in Philippine waters.

The 51st FG in India had a different idea for painting their P-40 air scoops.

The air assault against Japan was resumed in November 1944, but too many B-29s were lost to enemy defensive fighters and to fuel starvation on return to base, while results of the raids were disappointing. High level precision bombing was not markedly affecting the production of the thousands of small shops that made parts and subassemblies for the Japanese war machine.

In January 1945, Gen. Curtis E. LeMay was sent to take command of the B-29 wings in the Marianas and was informed by Arnold that the Joint Chiefs expected the same kind of job that LeMay had done over Europe as a bomber commander where he had earned the sobriquet "Iron Pants."

By early March, LeMay had all his problems sorted out. He ordered his planes loaded

Fire rages on the forward deck of the *Saratoga* after hit by kamikaze off Iwo Jima 21 February 1945.

with incendiary bombs, stripped of guns and ammunition, and told his crews that they would raid Tokyo at night from an altitude of 7000 feet.

Most of the crews were incredulous. The pressurized B-29 with remote controlled guns was a high-altitude strategic bomber; ol' Iron Pants was asking them to take it over the enemy's capital unarmed at low altitude and at night! Still, if one thought about it, it just might work. The enemy certainly would not expect them at low altitude and their heavy anti-aircraft guns would be set up to fire high above them. Intelligence reports indicated that the enemy had relatively few night fighters, and if the B-29s carried no guns, that would eliminate the danger of firing upon one another in the darkness, additionally, the weight saved would lower fuel consumption for the trip home. The bold plan just might work.

It did. Almost 16 square miles of Tokyo were destroyed by fire that night by 323 Superforts. During the next ten days Nagoya, Osaka, and Kobe were struck with similar raids to add another 15 square miles of fire-blackened ruins to those cities. The cost was 21 B-29s lost in 1489 sorties, a sortie being one mission, one airplane.

USN

Marine F4U-1 Corsair takes off from the carrier *Essex* for a strike against Formosa.

Late in March 1945, LeMay was ordered to temporarily halt the aerial destruction of Japan's major cities and to aid in the invasion of Ryukyu Islands and Okinawa, in which the B-29s were used as tactical aircraft, attacking enemy airfields and sowing mines in the Shimonoseki Straits.

The Ryukyus were but 400 miles from Japan and the enemy resisted with everything it had. The American force of four army and two marine divisions, accompanied by Admiral Durgin's TG 52 and Admiral Mitschner's TG 58, along with AAF air units, were met by mass kamikaze attacks—up to 400 at a time—despite American air superiority. During the 83 days of the Okinawan campaign, kamikazes sank 35 U.S. ships and damaged 288.

Okinawa was finally secured on 21 June 1945 at the price of 12,500 American lives and 763 aircraft. The enemy, fighting from a maze of tunnels and caves that were largely immune to air attack, lost 110,000 soldiers who refused to surrender.

The Okinawan campaign was the last and most violent for the U.S. Navy. Mitschner's and Durgin's task groups, fighting with a smaller British task force containing four carriers, were constantly on station in the battle area, and most of their ships logged more than 60 days of consecutive combat duty. Nine U.S. aircraft carriers were damaged, some seriously, although none were sunk.

USN

The TBM torpedo bomber was the Grumman design (TBF) built by the Eastern Aircraft Division of General Motors. TBM above is aboard the carrier *Bunker Hill* during the Battle of the Philippine Sea.

The U.S. Navy's leading ace in WWII was Comdr. David McCampbell, shown here in his F6F Hellcat aboard the *Essex*.

Landing signal officer brings a Hellcat aboard the *Essex*.

After Okinawa was taken, the Superforts of the 20th AF resumed their assault on Japan, and by the end of July had devastated more than 100 square miles of the enemy's six largest cities. With both USAAF and navy/marine fighters ranging at will over the enemy's homeland, B-29 losses dropped to near zero, and General LeMay began announcing in advance where he would strike next in order to cut civilian casualties.

The enemy was defeated. Its navy was gone, along with most of its merchant shipping. Allied airpower was free to destroy whatever it chose to attack in the Japanese island nation. True, thousands of kamikazes (planes of all types, including trainers) were held in reserve, and a well-equipped army was prepared to resist invasion. But an army that cannot maneuver, that cannot be supplied or fed, cannot long exist. General LeMay, unaware that the U.S. possessed an atomic device, recommended against the presumed invasion of Japan, telling his superiors that the enemy's unconditional surrender was only a matter of time. He judged it at "several weeks."

Iron Pants may have been right, but President Truman, who had assumed office on 12 April upon President Roosevelt's sudden death, was not willing to wait several weeks. He said Americans were dying every day, and therefore, if he could shorten the war by one hour, it was his duty to do so.

At 0245 hours on 6 August 1945, the *Enola Gay*, a B-29 from the 509th Composite Group, 20th AF, took off from Tinian in the Marianas and headed for Hiroshima with an atomic bomb in its bays. The *Enola Gay* (named for the mother of the aircraft commander, Col. Paul Tibbets) loosed her terrible weapon above the Japanese city at 0816 hours, and four square miles of Hiroshima were obliterated. The number of human casualties was unknown at the time, but are given today as 78,150 dead, 13,083 missing, and 37,425 injured.

Three days later, the B-29 *Bock's Car* dropped the second A-bomb on Nagasaki, killing 73,884 people, and Japan sued for peace.

USAF

The Northrop P-61 Black Widow night fighter appeared late in the war but saw extensive action with air force units over the Philippines and subsequent battles; 9th AF also used the type late in the European war.

USN

The Chance Vought F4U-4 Corsair, powered with the P&W R-2800-18W Double Wasp of 2325 hp, had a maximum speed of 424 mph at 23,000 feet. The reason the marines got such a fine fighter first was because the navy didn't clear the Corsair for carrier operations until April 1944. The marines, however, regularly few Corsairs from land bases throughout the war.

*The final thrust* 243

This kamikaze, although burning from hits by navy gunners, held determinedly to its final attack, smashing onto the deck of the *Essex* during the Philippine campaign.

The flight deck of the *Randolph* after a night kamikaze attack 12 March 1945

Sixty-one squadrons of B-29s Superfortresses were activated in the 20th AF by war's end. Superfort engines were Wright R-3350s of 2430 war emergency hp; cabin pressurization and remote control of the ten .50-caliber and one 20mm guns were innovations.

General Curtis E. LeMay.

On 2 September 1945, in Tokyo Bay, formal surrender documents were signed aboard the battleship *Missouri*. The U.S. Navy has yet to explain why the ceremony did not take place on an aircraft carrier, the true symbol of victory in the Pacific.

## Review questions

1. What was the purpose of the Aleutian campaign? What were some of the geographical and environmental problems encountered?

2. Who was Claire Chennault? Why was he in China? What was the role of the "Flying Tigers?" Were they successful? What happened to this group?

3. What was the function of the Air Transport Command (ATC) under Colonel Haynes? How successful was the "Assam Trucking Company" in carrying out their mission?

4. Describe the psychological and strategic importance of retaking the Philippines. Why did the Battle of Leyte Gulf virtually put an end to the Imperial Japanese Navy as a fighting force? Were the kamikaze attacks effective? What was the importance of taking Iwo Jima?

5. Describe the fire bombing campaign ordered by General LeMay in the spring of 1945. Why did the kamikaze attacks increase during the Okinawan campaign? Why was General LeMay against the invasion of Japan?

Corsairs of the 2nd Marine Air Wing over Okinawa.

Near the end, defeated Japan could no longer challenge the B-29s, seen here passing Mt. Fujiyama, and LeMay announced in advance where they would strike in order to spare civilian lives.

USN

Symbolic of peace in the Pacific and the end of countless tragic days, these Curtiss SB2C Helldivers return to their carrier, cruising serenely in the South China Sea.

# 14

# Uneasy peace
# and another war

## Objectives

At the end of this chapter you should be able to:

- Give the reasons for and results of the Berlin Airlift.

- Explain why the B-52 was developed and how it became such a good investment.

- Describe our response to the invasion of South Korea by North Korea and subsequently Chinese troops.

- Give President Eisenhower's ultimatum to the Communists in 1953 regarding the continued fighting in Korea.

- Describe the type aircraft and source of manpower for the Korean War.

- Give the reason for President Truman recalling General MacArthur in 1951.

- Describe some of the results of the Korean War regarding military preparedness.

World War II changed the world, and the peace that followed was an uneasy one. For a brief period, America felt secure. The United States was the sole possessor of the atomic bomb and had the means to deliver it anywhere in the world. Surely, the threat of such massive retaliation would deter the most ambitious aggressor.

The potential aggressor was, of course, the Soviet Union. Few Americans ever doubted that. At the end of WWII, while the United States and its Allies demobilized (the U.S. Army went from 8 million 1945 to 684,000 by 1950), the Russians kept much of their military intact, and repeatedly demonstrated their allegiance to the communist canon that holds that "political power comes from the barrel of a gun."

Their national character was bared to the world by their acts immediately following Germany's surrender. In Poland, and in that part of Germany occupied by the Soviets, the only women who were not raped were those few who successfully hid for months. Everything of value was stolen. Millions of German "prisoners" disappeared into Soviet Siberia. Even the railway tracks were ripped up and shipped back to the Soviet Union. The terror and pillage that came in the wake of the Soviet army was little different than that practiced by the Mongol hordes of Genghis Khan 700 years earlier.

So the Free World knew its godless enemy and watched in apprehension as the Soviet Union hammered its Iron Curtain around Eastern Europe. President Roosevelt—sick and debilitated—just a month before his death had

USAF

The USAF's first operational jet fighter was the 550-mph Lockheed F-80 Shooting Star, which appeared in 1945. The F-80C, which entered service in 1948, had a thinner wing, allowing a higher critical Mach number. Two-seat versions became the T-33 jet trainer.

believed that he could deal with the Soviet dictator Stalin at the Yalta Conference. However, agreements made in good faith by FDR were to be regarded by the Soviets merely as positions of advantage from which to expand their communist dominion.

## Berlin big lift

Among those agreements, which greatly affected us all for more than 40 years, was the supposedly temporary occupation of Germany by the Allies. The Soviets were allowed to occupy East Germany and a portion of East Berlin (Berlin is 110 miles inside what was the Soviet sector). Britain, France, and the United States occupied the remainder of Berlin and West Germany, and were guaranteed access to Berlin by rail, the autobahn (German express freeway), and three 20-mile wide air corridors.

By 1948, however, the Soviets possessed the secret of nuclear fission (by espionage), and were ready to test the will of the United States in Germany. It should have come as no surprise. From the start, the Soviets had refused to cooperate in Allied efforts to establish a new government that the Germans could run themselves and to begin rebuilding the German economy.

On 24 June 1948, the Russians stopped all surface transportation into the western sectors of Berlin, suspended parcel post service,

The Bell X-1A was a rocket-powered research aircraft; X-1 was the first airplane to exceed the speed of sound, 14 October 1947.

Lawrence Bell (left), who began his career as a designer of the 1919 Martin GMB bomber and saw a Bell aircraft break the sound barrier only 28 years later, congratulates X-1A pilot Capt. (later General) Charles Yeager.

and cut off electric power. They stopped barge traffic on the rivers, destroyed bridges, and tore up the tracks of the remaining railroad into the city from the west. Berlin was isolated.

Almost. The Soviets faced one problem with their blockade: Iron Pants LeMay was the commander of the U.S. Air Force in Europe (USAFE). The Joint Chiefs under Truman also made some pretty good choices.

Within 48 hours, General LeMay had all his C-47 transports ready for duty with Operation Vittles. Almost immediately they began flying milk, flour, medicines and coal into the beleaguered city from Frankfurt, carefully staying within the prescribed air corridors. There was nothing the Russians could do about an airlift short of shooting down the unarmed transports, and that, of course, would have been a clear act of war.

The C-47s carried 80 tons of cargo to Berlin that first day. Meanwhile, orders went out around the world calling in air force C-54 four-engine transports for duty with Operation Vittles. Within a month a steady stream of U.S. and British transports were delivering 1500 tons of life-giving supplies to West Berlin daily. After the new Military Air Transport Service (MATS)—successor to the wartime Air Transport Command and Naval Air Transport Service—took over with old "Hump" commander Gen. William Tunner running the show, the tonnage exceeded 5000 per day. It even included candy for Berlin's children.

During the 13 months the Berlin Airlift was in operation, MATS delivered 2.2 million tons of essential cargo into that city and averaged 700 flights daily, to thwart the Soviet attempt to force the Western Allies out of Berlin. In so doing, MATS also administered a sound—and responsible—diplomatic/strategic defeat to the communist aggressor. The Soviets could find no face-saving way out. They simply lifted the blockade, and contented themselves with an ultimatum to Czechoslovakia that forced the Czechs into the Russian orbit, and announcement of the detonation of the first Soviet A-bomb.

## Birth of the B-52

The fallout from the Berlin blockade was far more significant than the Russians could have foreseen when they recklessly imposed it. Among other things, it was indirectly responsible for America's B-52 global bomber program, plus a lot of rethinking of the U.S. defensive posture vis-a-vis Russia's newly-obvious expansionist policies.

Actually, air force brass had sent a new strategic bomber specification to the aircraft industry seeking proposals in mid-1946. They were looking ahead 10 years, by which time it was reasonable to assume that the United States would need a fast, high-flying nuclear carrier of extra-long range. There was, however, significant opposition to the concept within the air force.

The Strategic Air Command (SAC) had been organized on 21 March 1946 with Gen. George Kenney as its first commander. At that time, Kenney was given 36,000 men, 18 bases and 600 aircraft—B-17s, B-29s and B-25s. The air force was ready to substantially restructure in anticipation of legislation that would separate it from the army and make it an indepen-

MATS C-54s (R5D in navy dress) were the backbone of the Berlin Airlift, which averaged 700 flights daily to keep the city alive—and from total Soviet control—for 13 months.

Convair B-36 (in background) had a span of 230 feet, six 3500-hp engines driving pusher props, and four turbojets of 5200 pounds thrust each. SAC had 33 squadrons of B-36s to enforce the peace until the B-52 began entering service in 1955.

This unlikely critter was the McDonnell XF-85 parasite fighter, which was to be carried by the B-36 for protection against enemy fighters—one of those good ideas that didn't work out.

dent and co-equal branch of the U.S. military, the dream of Billy Mitchell and all other army airmen since the First World War. That act was passed by the Congress and signed by President Truman in mid-1947, becoming law on 18 September of that year. The National Security Act of 1947 also created the CIA, another security measure long overdue.

The early B-52 proposals from Boeing were for large propjets that lacked the performance envisioned by the air force. In any case, the B-52 concept had some strong opposition in the

Boeing XB-52 had pilot and copilot sitting in tandem in blister atop the nose. The first B-52 flight came on 15 April 1952.

persons of Gen. George Kenney and Gen. Lauris Norstad, Deputy Chief of Staff for Operations. Kenney felt that the B-50 (essentially, the B-29 with bigger engines) would be a lot cheaper, and that, therefore, he could have more of them. Also, the B-52, if it had the performance being asked for, would require technological advances that could take years to attain. There was no engine then available that would furnish the power such a machine would require.

Meanwhile, Convair wanted to go ahead with the mammoth B-36, a 1941 program that had been sidetracked by the war. The technology was available to build the B-36 at once, but Kenney and Norstad opposed the B-36 for the same reasons they were against the B-52. Assured of plenty of overseas bases, there was no reason the B-50 couldn't do the job.

In favor of the B-36 and the follow-on B-52 was Gen. "Tooey" Spaatz, Air Force Chief of Staff, but Spaatz knew he'd have a hard time getting money from Congress for them without the support of Kenney and Norstad. Then

the Soviets blockaded Berlin and literally saved both new bomber programs.

One day after the blockade went into effect, Gen. Hoyt Vandenberg, just recently appointed Air Force Chief of Staff upon Spaatz' retirement, met with Air Force Secretary Stuart Symington. With Kenney and Norstad in agreement, Vandenberg determined that a fleet of B-36s would be built to ensure the capability of a U.S. nuclear deterrent strike force until the B-52 could be brought along in the mid-'50s.

The Pratt & Whitney jet engine (the J-57) that made the B-52 possible was under development by late 1948, and the first B-52 prototype made its maiden flight on 15 April 1952. Deliveries of the B-52 Stratofortress to SAC began three years later.

The air force should be very proud of the B-52 program. It reflected high competence upon the several commands that planned and administered it. Boeing engineers, led by Edward Wells and Art Carlsen, produced an airplane that logically should not have appeared for another ten years. The air force knew ex-

Drag chute deployed upon landing greatly aids in braking the 200,000-pound (488,000-pound fully loaded) Stratofortress to a safe stop.

Wings flex upward as B-52D takes off and outrigger wheels retract. Approximately 75 B-52Ds remained in service during the early '80s, along with the G and H models.

actly what it needed, and the senior officers stuck to their guns through many frustrations and the long gestation period required to get it.

A total of 744 B-52s were built during the plane's nine-year production run, the last being delivered to SAC in 1962. Throughout its service life, the B-52 Stratofortress has represented one critical leg of America's nuclear deterrent triad, along with the ICBMs and nu-clear-armed submarines. In 1980, after 25 years as a first-line defender of the United States and the Free World, 300 B-52s continued in that role. In the absence of a new nuclear carrier to replace them, they were expected by the air force to serve until the year 2000. The B-52s originally cost slightly less than $6 million each, and perhaps an equal amount has been spent on each of those still flying for updated

The B-52G and H versions were the prime nuclear carriers through the 1980s, the Gs and Hs having a cut-down vertical tail. The G model is easy to differentiate from the H because the H model is equipped with turbofan engines and fatter engine pods than the G (above).

electronics and weapons systems. Considering that this fleet of global bombers has contributed nearly 40 years of service to the security of this nation, it is safe to say that seldom has the overburdened American taxpayer received so much for his hard-earned money.

## The Korean War

If the Berlin blockade pushed the B-52 program off dead center, other threats to the Free World during the early '50s provided the impetus to keep it moving. By early 1949 it was obvious that a Chinese communist army, supported by the Soviets, would defeat Chiang Kai-Shek's Nationalist forces and take possession of that vast land, while the Soviets had installed a former Russian army officer as premier in North Korea and supplied the North Koreans with arms and the belief that they should rule all of Korea, which had been divided between U.S. and Russian occupation forces in 1945, with separate republics proclaimed in August and September 1948.

At 0400 hours on 25 June 1950, 60,000 North Korean troops, spearheaded by 100 Russian-built tanks, swept across the 38th parallel (the border between North and South Korea) and drove rapidly southward, overrunning the South Korean capitol of Seoul four days later.

The South Koreans were, of course, unprepared for the invasion. U.S. occupation troops, who had supervised the withdrawal of the Japanese at the close of WWII, had stayed in South Korea only long enough to allow those gentle people to establish a government of their own under Korean statesman Syngman Rhee.

On the afternoon of the surprise invasion (it was 24 June in the United States), the United Nations Security Council met in emergency session to condemn the act, and President Truman ordered the 5th AF, which had planes in Japan and Okinawa, to evacuate U.S. citizens. Two days later, as the invaders approached Seoul, Truman directed that U.S. Air Force and Navy planes give assistance to the South Koreans, and ordered General MacArthur to take command of the troops being sent from 15 Free World nations (mostly the United States) to fight under the flag of the United Nations. President Truman termed the UN response a "police action."

F-51 Mustangs were taken from mothballs and Air Guard units for service in Korea. Shown is an F-51 supplied to the Republic of Korea Air Force (ROKAF).

F-82 Twin Mustangs were basically stretched F-51H fuselages joined at a common wing center section and fitted with V-1710 Allison engines. F-82s pictured were radar-carrying night fighters.

Actually, that was an accurate description of the UN's intent, because the United States, and other countries that sent troops, had no objective except to push the communists back across the 38th parallel and restore peace. Most also undoubtedly saw it as a test of the effectiveness of this new (1945) world organization in dealing with "brushfire" wars that could escalate into big wars.

U.S. airpower played a major role in the Korean War. American warplanes dominated the air and provided close air support that was the decisive factor in UN successes on the ground. There were four major offensives and counteroffensives in the Korean War: (1) The initial North Korean thrust that carried all the way to the southern end of the country by 15 September 1950, with the South Korean and UN troops backed into a pocket around Pusan; (2) A UN counteroffensive with an amphibious landing by the U.S. Marines at Inchon, just south of Seoul, that trapped half of the invader's army between the UN forces in the south and the marines closing from Inchon. This done, the UN troops drove north across the 38th parallel, entered the North Korean

Another retread; the T-6 Texans, armed with rockets, served as forward air control craft, spotting targets for the heavy ordnance carriers. The T-6 was an advanced trainer in WWII.

Lockheed F-94 Starfire saw service in Korea, primarily as a night fighter. The F-94 was a member of the F-80/T-33 family with thinner wing, afterburner, and nose-mounted search radar.

capital of Pyongyang, and totally defeated the North Koreans as the drive reached the Yalu River that separated North Korea from Manchuria. The next day, on 3 November 1950, (3) Communist China entered the war by sending 300,000 troops across the Yalu and pushed the UN forces back below Seoul again by late January 1951. (4) The UN forces counterattacked and once again advanced into North Korea, halting along a line that stabilized by November, averaging about 20 miles north of the 38th parallel. That would be the positions of the opposing forces when a truce was at last agreed upon on 27 July 1953.

Negotiations to end the fighting had been going on for two years when the agreement was finally reached. The unrepentant aggressors had stalled and seized upon any excuse to

The 670-mph North American F-86A Sabre appeared in 1949, and in December 1950 the USAF 4th Fighter Interceptor Wing went to Korea equipped with Sabres. Normal armament was six .50-caliber machine guns; later (H) versions sometimes replaced the machine guns with four 20mm cannons.

The Douglas A-26 Invader of WWII was redesignated B-26 in 1948 after the Martin B-26 Marauder was no longer in inventory. The Invader served in Europe and the Pacific in WWII, in Korea, and (shown here) in Vietnam.

delay a settlement, apparently hoping to gain something from the war. But Dwight Eisenhower became President of the United States in January 1953. Immediately after taking office, Ike sent a message to Moscow, Peiping, and Pyongyang saying that if satisfactory progress toward an armistice was not forthcoming, ". . . we intend to move decisively without inhibition in our use of weapons, and will no longer be responsible for confining hostilities to the Korean peninsula."

That was the kind of "negotiation" the communists understood, and it achieved the desired results.

At the outbreak of hostilities in Korea, the FEAF, made up of the 5th and 13th AFs, greatly reduced from WWII levels, had 535 operational aircraft, including 365 F-82 Twin Mustangs. The Lockheed F-80 was America's first operational jet fighter, appearing in 1945, and was obsolescent by 1950 as the result of the pace of jet engine development and new lessons learned in the field of aerodynamics as jet and rocket-powered U.S. research aircraft attained ever-higher speeds. (USAF Capt. Charles Yeager had exceeded the speed of sound on 14 October 1947.) The North American F-82 was, literally, a "Twin Mustang," two stretched P-51H fuse-

USN

The Black Sheep were back in Korea, operating off the escort carrier *Sicily*, and still flying Corsairs. Shown is a cannon-armed F4U-4.

lages (F-51s after the USAF changed the army's "P" for "pursuit" to "F" for "fighter" in 1948) joined together on a common wing center-section to make a single twin-engine aircraft. It was, however fitted with Allison rather than Rolls-Royce engines.

A month after the war started, 764 national guard F-51s were called to active duty, and 145 of them rushed to Korea aboard the carrier *Boxer*. WWII's illustrious 4th FG, now designated the 4th Fighter Interceptor Wing and equipped with F-86A Sabrejets, followed in December 1950 to take on the Chinese MiG-15s.

Actually, the United States was in the process of rebuilding the air force into a new all-jet air force to meet America's defense needs of the '50s. At the end of WWII, the USAAF contained a whopping 218 air groups with nearly two and one quarter million men. Demobiliza-

tion was so rapid and so thorough that the Army Air Forces were down to 52 groups on paper, with only two groups fully operational, by mid-1947. Thousands of WWII combat aircraft—many of them brand new—were sold for scrap. Movie flier Paul Mantz bought 500 war surplus airplanes for $50,000, sold the fuel in their tanks for $55,000, and still possessed the world's seventh largest "air force". A small percentage of the latest models were "moth-balled" at Davis-Monthan Air Base near Tucson, Arizona, where the dry desert air contributed to their preservation.

However, the United States had trained more than a quarter of a million pilots during WWII and many remained in the national guard or air force reserve. These were the pilots called back to active duty to augment the relatively small FEAF in Korea; since most of

This frosted Mustang crash-landed after being hit by enemy ground fire. Foamite controlled the fire and the pilot was not injured.

the regulars were also WWII vets, the air force, navy and marine fliers over Korea were often called "retread tigers."

Retreads they may have been, but there is no substitute for experience, and the Americans' ten-to-one kill ratio over the North Koreans and Chinese pilots established that the old hands were quite as effective as the new breed. WWII aces became double aces in the skies over Korea, and the old saw which held that fighter pilots should be under 25 years of age was confounded by many a 30-plus retread at the controls of an F-86, F9F or F4U.

During the first enemy offensive, the F-80s and F-82s of the 5th AF shot down 7 of 13 Rus-

sian-built YAK fighters and IL-10 attack planes attempting to shoot up Seoul's Kimpo Airfield, Lts. William Hudson and Charles Moran and Maj. James Little being officially credited with the first U.S. air victories over Korea.

The North Koreans apparently had but 70 of the propeller-driven YAKs and 62 IL-10s. The 5th AF quickly destroyed them all, mostly on the ground. In November 1950, when the Chinese entered the war, they had approximately 500 Russian-built MiG-15 jet fighters, some apparently manned by Russian pilots.

On 3 July the U.S. Navy attack carrier *Valley Forge*, operating with the British carrier *Triumph* in the Yellow Sea, joined the FEAF aircraft in at-

Soviet MiG-15 was the standard fighter for the Soviet-bloc air forces during the '50s. In Korea, despite the fact that American pilots were not allowed to pursue the MiGs beyond the Yalu River, the F-86 pilots shot down 10 MiGs for every F-86 lost in combat.

Staff Sergeant Jerry Webb, B-29 tailgunner, points to a cannon hole close to his head after attack by *MiGs*. Sergeant Webb shot down one MiG; another gunner on this Superfort downed a second. The B-29's rudder controls were shot out, but it landed safely at its base on Okinawa.

tacks on airfields and the enemy's lines of supply around Pyongyang. Navy Panther jets (F9Fs) of VF-51 shot down two YAK-9s. The two carriers worked with the air force to slow the communist advance. Late in the month, the attack carriers *Philippine Sea* and *Boxer* arrived, along with the escort carriers *Badoeng Strait* and *Sicily*. Eventually, the air groups from 11 U.S. aircraft carriers would operate in Korean waters, coordinating their air strikes with those of the FEAF aircraft in a ground support role, attacking enemy airfields, railroads, factories, oil refineries, and enemy troop concentrations. Marine Fighting Squadron 214, flying Corsairs from the deck of the *Sicily*, and VMF-323 aboard the *Badoeng Strait* began operations over Korea on 3 August.

Although the navy and marines were unhappy over the fact that MacArthur and his air commander, Gen. George Stratemeyer, were bosses of all UN air units (what did the army know about the logistics of maintaining a navy task force in constant touch with hostile forces for three years?), navy and marine air nevertheless performed as usual. After

ROKAF Mustangs operated under command of the 5th AF. Mustang #18 at left is flown by Maj. Dean Hess, ROKAF pilot training program commander.

A North Korean YAK fighter shot down by an F-80 14 miles north of Suwon, 15 August 1950.

the highly successful Inchon landing (MacArthur's idea, opposed by most of the Joint Chiefs), and the resulting defeat of the North Koreans, the U.S. Army commander, Gen. Walton Walker, declared that, except for U.S. airpower, the UN troops could not have stayed in Korea—a selfevident fact, of course, but the kind of fact that ground commanders are often slow to acknowledge.

After the line of battle stabilized, just inside the North Korean Border in the fall of 1951, and the primary enemy was the Chinese Communists ("Chi-Coms"), the ground war became a series of small battles for advanta-

USAF

A Vultee (Stinson) L-5 liason plane delivers mail to G.I.s at a forward gun position. The unarmed L-5s and Cessna L-19s performed many such unglamorous duties in Korea.

USMC

Marine helicopters of HMR-161 carried 60,046 passengers, including almost 10,000 wounded. This front line evacuation of wounded by marines and army choppers proved not only lifesaving, but morale-building.

geous outpost positions, artillery duels and reconnaissance patrols. Navy and air force planes continuously struck at the enemy's supply lines and prevented a buildup of enemy forces. Negotiators at Panmunjon argued fruitlessly over side issues such as the repatriation of one another's prisoners.

Meanwhile, General MacArthur had been fired by President Truman on 11 April 1951. Gen. Matthew Ridgeway was sent to replace him after MacArthur made statements considered by the President to be at cross-purposes with the UN (and U.S.) policy in Korea. MacArthur wanted a naval blockade of the China coast, air attacks on China's war industries, and an invasion of China by Chiang Kai-Shek's Nationalist Chinese forces from Taiwan. MacArthur said that he believed in meeting force with maximum counterforce, and that ". . . if we lose this war to communism in Asia the fall of Europe is inevitable; win it and Europe most probably could avoid war . . . there is no substitute for victory . . ."

President Truman had no intention of going to war with Red China—all-out war, that is. He kept U.S. Navy and Air Force pilots on a tight leash, giving strict orders that they could not fly across the Yalu River even if in "hot pursuit" of enemy *MiGs*—a circumstance the Chi-Com pilots soon learned to exploit—and no targets could be bombed north of the Yalu. The "police action" was not to be carried into Chinese territory. Truman was undoubtedly right; it's better to talk than fight, even if it takes years for the talks to get anywhere. In any case, the American people would not have united behind such an action. They were already showing signs of discontent with a war that was, for most, difficult to identify with America's best interest. Strangely, most Americans seemed to sympathize with MacArthur—there was a lot of controversy in the press and in Congress over his dismissal—although no one questioned the Commander-in-Chief's right to fire any general or admiral for cause. Civilian control of the military is essential in a free society, and is spelled out in the Constitution.

MacArthur's removal from command probably had no effect on subsequent events in Korea. UN field commanders had little latitude of action, particularly after the battle lines stabilized in November 1951.

When the final casualty report for the 37 months of fighting was prepared, total UN casualties reached more than 550,000, including almost 95,000 dead. U.S. losses numbered 142,091, of whom 33,639 were killed, 103,284 wounded, and 5178 missing or captured. The bulk of these casualties occurred during the first year of fighting. The estimate of enemy casualties, including prisoners, exceeded 1.5 million of which 900,000 were Chinese.

The war's effect reached far beyond Korea. The primary result for the western bloc was a decided strengthening of the NATO alliance. Virtually without military power in June 1950,

USAF

Lieutenant Colonel Glen Eagleston, 4th Fighter Interceptor Wing's group commander, inspects damage to his Sabre after an air battle with MiGs.

The Grumman F7F Tigercat was a 435-mph all-purpose fighter delivered to the marines in 1945 and 1946. Most of the 364 produced were night fighter versions armed with four cannons and radar in the nose as shown. Engines were P&W R-2800s of 2100 hp each.

NATO would call on 50 divisions and strong air and naval contingents by 1953, a buildup directly attributable to the increased threat of general war seen in the outbreak of hostilities in Korea. The relative positions of West and East also had been affected during the war by the development of thermonuclear devices. The United States exploded its first such device in 1952, the USSR (Union of the Soviet Socialist Republics) in August 1953. The exact consequences of all these changes were incalculable; but it was certain that the cold war would continue and that both power blocs would face new challenges and new responses.

## Review questions

1. What was the primary reason for the Berlin Airlift? How was Berlin supplied? Why was the blockade lifted?

2. What is the function of the Strategic Air Command (SAC)? Why were the B-52 and B-36 concepts opposed by Gens. George Kenney and Lauris Norstad? How many B-52s were eventually built? Why have they been a good investment?

3. What was President Truman's reaction to the North Korean attack on South Korea? What were the four major offensives and counteroffensives in the Korean War? How did U.S. air power play a major role in the war? What was President Eisenhower's message to Moscow in January 1953? What role did WWII aircraft and pilots play in the war?

4. Why did President Truman recall General MacArthur? Describe President Truman's position. Discuss the impact of the war on military preparedness.

# 15

# Johnson's war—and after

## Objectives

At the end of this chapter you should be able to:

- Define the theory of flexible response as it pertained to the military during the 1960s.
- Explain why the U.S became involved in Vietnam.
- Describe the Geneva Accords.
- Describe the powers given President Johnson under the Gulf of Tonkin resolution.
- Compare and contrast the Vietnam War with WWII and the Korean War.
- Describe the important role played by the helicopter in the Vietnam War.
- Discuss Secretary McNamara's policy of cost effectiveness regarding military procurement.
- Describe some of the aircraft that entered service with the United States in the 1980s.

If it is true that those who fail to learn the lessons of history are doomed to relive it, Americans should demand that every congressman and every presidential candidate be required to pass a comprehensive examination to establish that each possesses detailed know-

ledge of all the contributing factors that led to America's involvement in the Vietnam War.

Although U.S. involvement in Southeast Asian affairs actually began during the Truman Administration, the tragic bungling of America's role in the war that evolved there must be laid at the doorstep of the Johnson Administration. The indictment is especially severe because never before in history were U.S. military forces so totally misdirected on so grand a scale or the President's responsibility to the American people so incompetently performed.

The decisions faced by Lyndon B. Johnson regarding the American presence in South Vietnam when he was thrust into the presidency by President John Kennedy's assassination were basic and entirely manageable. Kennedy had increased the number of U.S. military advisors in South Vietnam from 700 to approximately 16,000. They were noncombatants, ordered not to participate in the fighting, their mission being to train the South Vietnamese Army. Therefore, the questions that President Johnson had to address were: (1) Assuming that the American assistance program to the South Vietnamese was both morally defensible and in the best interest of the United States, what should be the maximum limit of that assistance? And, (2) assuming that maximum assistance led to American involvement in hostilities, what should be U.S. policy in bringing the fighting to a quick end?

## Airpower and the flexible response

Johnson's decision was to continue with the open-ended and heretofore untried theory of "flexible response" bequeathed by the Kennedy Administration.

The theory of flexible response sounded logical. It was a term coined by President Kennedy's Secretary of Defense Robert McNamara, a former professor of economics at Harvard University and Ford Motor Company president. It was born of the proposition that America needed a balanced combination of conventional forces available that would provide alternatives to deal with aggression other than the unhappy choice between massive nuclear retaliation or no retaliation at all.

Few would argue with that. However, the Kennedy/McNamara corollary was that, possessing a varied mix of forces, the amount of force used by the United States should always be commensurate with the threat. That was flexible response; that is what led President Johnson into a war in which the enemy could choose the kind of conflict best suited to its resources, could pick the areas of confrontation, and decide the level of the fighting. Vietnam was a war fought on the enemy's terms and at its convenience.

USAF

Republic F-105 Thunderchiefs refuel from a KC-135 tanker on their way to tactical targets in North Vietnam, December 1965. Note that only two of the "Thuds" have received the new camouflage.

It was, of course, impossible to win such a war militarily, and because this enemy possessed a quasi-political organization trained in the arts of propaganda and terror, and effectively infiltrated it throughout the defended area, no stable political settlement was possible except in its favor.

President Johnson was well aware of the alternatives to flexible response. General MacArthur had already stated the most obvious a decade earlier in Korea: Meet force with maximum counterforce. If America must fight, do so to win and get it over with as quickly as possible.

Johnson had the means at his disposal to do just that without the use of nuclear weapons. The USAF and the navy's air strike forces could have, in a matter of weeks, destroyed the enemy's ability to make war or feed its people, while few, if any, American ground troops need be risked. North Vietnam was especially vulnerable to a massive strategic air offensive. The destruction of its Red River Dam complex alone would have denied to that country 90 percent of its domestic food supply. A sea blockade of the enemy's coasts, the aerial mining of its harbors, and aerial interdiction of its supply line from China would have severed its source of military and other war-essential materials. Meanwhile, industries, transportation routes, electric generating plants, and troop concentrations could have been pounded into the earth by SAC's B-52s. Johnson could have told the enemy exactly the same thing that President Eisenhower told the North Koreans, China and Russia in 1953.

Instead, Johnson decided to commit ". . . our American boys to a land war in Asia," an act he had promised, during the 1964 Presidential campaign, that he would never consider. He was unwilling to unleash American airpower, with no target restrictions, for fear that it would lead to nuclear war with the Soviets. He chose instead to fight a war that would not offend the enemy too much—an incredible stance for the world's most powerful nation (or the world's weakest, for that matter).

The United States possessed a clear five-to-one nuclear advantage over the Soviets when President Eisenhower left office. Although that superiority had eroded some as a result of the Kennedy/McNamara adventure into "cost effectiveness" in the acquisition and maintenance of American arms, the Soviets did not have a numerically superior ICBM force in place until 1969 (1054 American; 1100 Russian).

To understand the United States' presence in Vietnam, we must go back a bit. Prior to WWII, the French had ruled Vietnam, then called Indochina, which included Laos and Cambodia, for nearly 100 years. Even before that the country had been divided, the people of the north ruled from Hanoi, while the people in the south were ruled by emperors in Hue. The Japanese occupied Indochina during WWII. When the French returned after the war, President Truman felt that he had to aid the French in their "recolonization" partly because Truman saw the French presence there as a barrier to Soviet moves in that direction, and also because French cooperation in the formation of the North Atlantic Treaty Organization (NATO) was needed.

Meanwhile, a typical communist organization, originally formed in 1930 by Ho Chi Minh, and which had no success opposing French rule in northern Indochina before WWII, grew in strength during that war by playing down its communist ideology while recruiting young people for the avowed purpose of ousting the Japanese. They called themselves the Viet Minh, and with Soviet and Red Chinese money and arms during the early '50s, fought a guerilla war to expel the French, a task they accomplished in 1954 after the famed seige of the French garrison at Dienbienphu.

Following the French defeat in North Vietnam, a multination conference in Geneva produced the Geneva Accords that established conditions for a cease-fire in Indochina, provided for the independence of Laos, Cambodia, and Vietnam, while a political dividing line was drawn at the 17th parallel across Vietnam in

recognition of the centuries-old differences between the people of the north and those of the south. Although the Geneva Accords called for free elections throughout Vietnam by July 1956, that provision, cleverly backed by the Soviets and Red China, embarrassed the United States because it resulted in President Eisenhower's refusal to sign the accords. The CIA had informed Secretary of State John Foster Dulles that the Viet Minh had terrorist agents in almost every South Vietnamese hamlet, and that the "free election" bit would be a farce until stable government in the south could root out the northern infiltrators.

Aware that the Geneva Accords would do nothing to ensure the independence of Southeast Asian nations, the Free World nations had already met in Manila to form the Southeast Asia Treaty Organization (SEATO), and signed an agreement on 8 September 1954 pledging aid to any Southeast Asian country that asked for it if attacked. It was under terms of the SEATO pact that President Eisenhower sent

The attack carrier *Forrestal* in the Gulf of Tonkin, 29 July 1967

CH-21 Shawnee ("Flying Banana"). These craft served in Korea and saw limited service in South Vietnam.

*Airpower and the flexible response* 269

An Air Force F-4C Phantom, a Mach 2-plus fighter originally procured by the U.S. Navy in 1960 and added to air force inventory because of its outstanding performance. It was used extensively in Vietnam.

some 400 U.S. military advisors and military equipment to South Vietnam when the French pulled out the last of their troops in 1956 in compliance with the Geneva Accords.

Ho Chi Minh counted upon the 1956 elections to give him all Vietnam, but a general of the South Vietnamese Army (ARVN), Duong Van Minh ("Big Minh") led a coup d'etat against the tottering Bao Dai government and repudiated the Geneva Accords.

As a result of a revolt within his own ranks, Ho was not able to increase the terror campaign by his agents in the south until 1961. At that time, he announced the formation of the "Na-

With tail hook engaged, a Douglas A-4 Skyhawk of VA-12 returns to the attack carrier *Franklin Roosevelt* operating in the Gulf of Tonkin, 10 August 1966.

An ordnanceman wheels Sparrow missiles to F-4 Phantoms aboard the U.S. 7th Fleet attack carrier *Midway* as the aircraft are prepared for a strike against Viet Cong positions in South Vietnam.

tional Liberation Front" (Viet Cong), and began escalating his war below the 17th parallel. The Viet Cong, organized around hardcore Red guerillas of the old Viet Minh, murdered 1719 and kidnapped 9688 South Vietnamese that year. About 6200 Viet Cong slipped into South Vietnam during 1961, and in much of the south the Viet Cong were sufficiently in control to levy taxes in rural regions. Even though ARVN troops might control many areas in daylight, it was generally accepted in much of the countryside that "the night belongs to the VC."

President Kennedy responded with more U.S. military advisors to help train and direct the ARVN's 200,000 men, and appeared less-than-surprised when the third corrupt and ineffective South Vietnamese government fell to still another coup, which some believed was CIA-inspired.

That was the Southeast Asian bucket of eels inherited by Lyndon Johnson when he assumed the presidency in November 1963. By that time, the VC were boldly launching day-

Heavily-laden Grumman A-6 Intruder just prior to catapult launch from the attack carrier *Independence*. The A-6's electronics allow crew to "see" at night and through clouds for accurate bombing.

An F-4B Phantom of VF-102 stretches out the arresting cable as it lands on the attack carrier *America*.

light attacks against ARVN forces, and U.S. advisors began to die: 42 in 1963, 118 in 1964.

On 2 August 1964 North Vietnamese torpedo boats attacked the U.S. Navy destroyer *Maddox* cruising in international waters in the Gulf of Tonkin. They were damaged and driven off by aircraft from the carrier *Ticonderoga*.

Two days later, Johnson told a nationwide TV audience that a second attack had occurred and that, as a result, retaliatory air strikes were underway.

There is no evidence that a second attack took place, but on 5 August, on orders from the President, 64 aircraft from the 7th Fleet carriers *Constellation* and *Ticonderoga* struck at motor torpedo boats and their supporting facilities at five points along the North Vietnamese coast and sank 25 boats along with their petroleum stores.

On that same day, Johnson used the "two" attacks on U.S. ships as his reason for asking Congressional support for ". . . all necessary action to protect our armed forces and to assist nations covered by the SEATO treaty." Congress gave him a signed, blank check. The exact wording of the Congressional resolution was: ". . . take all necessary steps, including the use of armed force, to assist any member or protocol state of the Southeast Asia Collective Defense Treaty requesting assistance in defense of its freedom." It was adopted by a vote of 416 to 0 in the House, 88 to 2 in the Senate. Johnson's War was to have a lot of sponsors.

North American F-100 Super Sabre was designed as an 800-mph superiority fighter. It appeared in 1954 and saw extensive use in Vietnam as a fighter-bomber. A total of 2294 were delivered to the air force.

When President Johnson obtained the Tonkin Gulf resolution, endorsing in advance whatever he decided to do in Vietnam, the Viet Cong had approximately 115,000 guerillas in the south; they had murdered an estimated 5587 and kidnapped an estimated 26,504 South Vietnamese civilians.

With North Vietnam escalating the war (whether or not it was a "civil war" is an arguable point, because the people of Indochina had never been united), and the sketchily-trained and often poorly motivated ARVN forces clearly unable to effectively oppose the enemy, it was obvious by 1965 that the United States would determine whether or not South Vietnam, Laos, Cambodia—and after that, perhaps, all Southeast Asia and peripheral nations—would fall to communism or mark the time and place where red aggression was contained in that part of the world.

An air offensive of sorts against North Vietnam was begun in March 1965, although it was limited to indecisive targets selected by the Joint Chiefs, who in turn were fettered by the Johnson/McNamara policy of placing important strategic targets off limits. On 26 March, F-4 Phantoms from the 7th Fleet's carriers *Hancock* and *Coral Sea* struck at radar sites in the vicinity of Vinh Son, while air force F-100 Super Sabres and F-105 Thunderchiefs began a series of sustained attacks on bridges and the "Ho Chi Minh Trail," the collective name for several routes of supply through eastern Laos used by the invader to funnel men and supplies into the south. The air force fighters were based in Thailand.

Air action was all the United States was capable of for a time, as the buildup of American combat ground forces did not begin until September 1965, with the arrival of the 1st Cavalry.

On 18 June, 27 B-52F *Stratofortresses* from Anderson Air Force Base on Guam began a 10-month operation against Viet Cong troop con-

Douglas AD Skyraider series went into production in 1945. Its Wright R-3350 engine of 2700 hp gave it exceptional load-carrying ability. A total of 3180 were built in 28 different versions with production ending in 1957. U.S. Navy used the Skyraider until 1968.

An A-4 Skyhawk approaches for landing on the attack carrier *Hancock* in the South China Sea.

centrations in jungle hideouts in South Vietnam. Each aircraft carried 750-pound "iron" bombs—27 internally and 24 on external wing pylons. The B-52 operations were code-named Arc Light while the overall air offensive was known as Rolling Thunder.

Two weeks earlier, the U.S. Marines had an airbase in operation at Chu Lai, 52 miles south of the major U.S. base in Danang, and the attack carrier *Independence* arrived in Subic Bay for duty with the 7th Fleet, making a total of five U.S. aircraft carriers operating off Vietnam. The nuclear-powered attack carrier *Enterprise* joined the action in December.

Within three years, U.S. military strength gradually built up in South Vietnam from less than 25,000 to more than 500,000, including two marine divisions. Regular ARVN forces meanwhile grew to more than 340,000. South Korea sent 48,000 men; Australia, Thailand, New Zealand and the Philippines committed token forces. Despite nearly 180,000 communists killed and 70,000 captured during this period, the invader still managed to build its strength to nearly 240,000 men in the south, a feat accomplished by recruitment through terror and intimidation, and by sharply increasing the number of North Vietnamese regular army troops sent to VC units.

Death of a MiG. An F-105's camera gun records this air victory over a Soviet-built MiG-17 near Hanoi.

It was an unusual war by any standard. There were no front lines. The enemy could be anywhere and everywhere, and was often indistinguishable from the native population.

Army CH-37 helicopter delivers a field piece to a new firing position.

The U.S. ground forces were spread around in fortified base camps from which they would strike out in search-and-destroy missions. On many such missions, particularly in the thick jungles of the highlands, companies and battalions would be far from any road and wholly dependent upon helicopters for resupply and evacuation. Most battles were fought at the platoon or company level. Ambush and coun-terambush were familiar tactics on both sides. The helicopter and good radio communications were the two essential ingredients that made it possible for the U.S. Army and Marines to engage in that kind of combat successfully, while the B-52s, air force and navy fighters—despite the frustrating limitations placed upon them—limited the enemy's ability to fight and denied it the opportunity to concentrate resources for attacks in strength. Enemy air opposition was rare except over especially sensitive targets in the north.

The first helicopter to fly in large numbers in South Vietnam was the CH-21 Flying Banana, followed in 1963 by the faster and more versatile UH-1 Huey. The helicopter became the symbol of this new kind of war, a checkboard campaign in which units might be picked up and set down swiftly almost anywhere from the forested highlands to the fertile, densely-popu-

A pair of F-105 Thunderchiefs with an F-100 Super Sabre enroute to strike at Viet Cong positions.

*Airpower and the flexible response*    

USAF

A fearsome foursome of F-105s over Vietnam. The Thunderchief's radar system allowed it to attack enemy ground positions through clouds from any altitude.

lated river bottoms along the coast and the largely inundated rice paddies of the Mekong Delta region in the extreme south. As the enemy reacted by increasing its antiaircraft capability, the Huey Cobra appeared, a heavily armed gunship version of the UH-1.

The Huey Cobras were mostly employed in an attack role and were especially effective in close air support situations. Ground troops in radio contact with the Cobras could direct them with extreme accuracy to nearby targets. During street fighting in Hue, a U.S. Army platoon leader marvelled that: "Those chopper guys would come in just a couple of feet over our heads and we could tell'em, not which building we wanted hit, but which doorway. Man, that's close air support!"

Directing the war from Washington, the Johnson/McNamara planners, believing that the limited air strikes on North Vietnam had seriously hurt the enemy, decided that a major cutback in the air offensive could encourage the North Vietnamese to sit down in good faith at a meeting in Paris to negotiate a cease-fire.

It was true that Ho had been seriously hurt by the air attacks. By early 1968 all major railroad bridges in the north were down, petroleum storage facilities were destroyed, war material could move southward only at night, and even then the trucks were in constant danger from U.S. night fighters. All consumer goods, including food, were strictly rationed, and 300,000 people (including many Chinese "volunteers") were fully employed repairing bomb damage to roads and rail tracks.

Therefore, President Johnson announced on 31 March 1968 that 80 percent of the area north of the 17th parallel (containing 90 percent of all North Vietnamese people) would be spared further attack by U.S. aircraft. Johnson had tried short bombing moratoriums during the previous two years, but this one was tied to the Paris negotiations.

But Ho Chi Minh had no reason to seriously negotiate with Johnson offering such a major concession, and all the Paris talks accomplished at that time was to provide Ho with a breathing spell while he rebuilt his shattered supply lines to the south.

Nevertheless, on 1 November 1968 (on the eve of the elections), Johnson halted all bombing of North Vietnam. He said at the time that Ho had agreed to some reciprocal measures of de-escalation. If Ho did so, there was never any evidence of it.

That was the situation when Richard M. Nixon took office in January 1969. The United States had half a million men in South Vietnam, American combat deaths were approaching the 33,000 mark, and although the Viet Cong and North Vietnamese People's Army had lost 500,000 men, they seemed prepared to lose that many more. Indeed, Ho declared that he was willing to fight for another 20 years if necessary.

Nixon, of course, was not. Nor were the American people. The average American found it difficult to understand a war with such confused beginnings fought—seemingly endlessly—for no clearly defined purpose affecting America's vital interests, and offering no chance of victory.

A month after taking office, President Nixon, acting on the advice of his new army commander in Vietnam, Gen. Creighton Abrams, secretly authorized B-52 strikes against enemy sanctuaries in Cambodia. He later ex-

Bob Dean

The army's Bell Huey helicopter became the symbol of the hit-and-run war in Vietnam, serving as ambulance, troop transport, gunship—name it, the Huey could do it.

Many Hueys were fitted with the 7.62 Gatling gun mounted above a 2.75-in rocket launcher. Such aircraft were designated UH-1Bs and UH-1Cs.

tended that authorization to include Laos as well, since those "neutral" countries had from the beginning not only been used by the North Vietnamese as bases from which to conduct the war in South Vietnam, but eventually became victims of communist "wars of liberation" themselves.

But Nixon, too, had to learn that impressive "enemy body counts" reported by U.S. Army commanders was not a measure of progress in this strangest of wars. The enemy knew that time was on its side, and to it life was cheap.

By May 1972, a total of 200 B-52s were committed to the war in Southeast Asia, along with their KC-135 tankers (the "tanks" also served as aerial filling stations for the fighters), but Nixon ordered that no air strikes be made north of the 20th parallel. However, after the North Vietnamese walked out of another fruitless round of cease-fire talks in Paris on 13 December 1972, Nixon lifted that ban and authorized an air offensive against selected military targets in the Hanoi/Haiphong area. Navy A-6 Intruders, operating from carriers in the Gulf of Tonkin, and air force F-111s from Takhli Air Base in Thailand joined the B-52s in the round-the-clock all-weather offensive (Linebacker II) that came to be known as the "Eleven-Day War."

At 1451 hours on 18 December 1972, the first of 87 B-52s lifted off the runway on Guam bound for Hanoi. They would be joined by 42 more flying from U-Tapao Air Base in Thailand, along with some 400 fighters, including marine F-4s escorting the KC-135 tankers.

Over their targets at 35,000 ft., the bombers were met by hundreds of surface-to-air (SAM) missiles and a few MiG-21 fighters; the F-111s and A-6s going in low faced the greatest concentration of antiaircraft artillery ever assembled. But losses were remarkably light: 15 B-52s and six F-111s. With only a 36-hour pause for Christmas (during which time the North Vietnamese stridently charged that the Americans were bombing schools and hospitals and spoiling all chance for a negotiated cease-fire), the air offensive continued, loosing more than 20,000 tons of destruction on the enemy's transportation and oil facilities. On 30 December Hanoi wanted to talk again.

While the Eleven-Day War represented but a fraction of what an all-out strategic air offensive could have been, it was more than enough to force an agreement on cease-fire, effective 27 January 1973. Violations of the agreement by communist guerillas in Laos and Cambodia caused President Nixon to send the B-52s back into limited action until 15 August 1973, when the war in Southeast Asia ended—for the United States.

During the eight years the B-52 strategic bombers were in action over Southeast Asia, just six percent of their total missions were directed at decisive strategic targets.

Almost anyone who had read the U.S. Strategic Bombing Survey, commissioned by President Truman at the end of WWII, could have successfully planned a quick end to the Vietnam conflict in 1965. U.S. military leaders offered such a plan to President Johnson early that year, and fully explained it to the Senate Preparedness Investigating Subcommittee in mid-1967, but Johnson opted for the McNamara doctrine of flexible response, a policy not of action, but of reaction (the "knee-jerk syndrome"). The total cost of that to America and the free world has not yet been paid.

## McNamara's brand

Robert McNamara ran the U.S. Department of Defense just as he had the Ford Motor Company. His watchword was "cost effective," bureaucratic code for "get your money's worth," and in pursuit of his cost-effective programs, McNamara successfully wrested control of weapons selection and the U.S. defense posture from the generals and admirals.

The Vought Corporation

The A-7A Corsair II light attack bomber was built by Vought and developed from the earlier F8U Crusader. The A-7 series entered squadron service in October 1966.

The USAF also used Skyraiders over Vietnam and provided some to the South Vietnamese Air Force (VNAF).

A Kaman HH-43F Huskie rescue helicopter with fire bottle is first on the scene as an A-1E Skyraider crash-lands at Da Nang.

There was just one critical factor in the defense equation that McNamara's textbook efficiencies did not include: A dollars and cents appraisal of freedom itself.

In the name of fiscal responsibility, McNamara closed a number of airbases, cancelled the Skybolt air-to-air missile program (which weakened NATO because it forced retirement of Britain's Vulcan bomber force), cancelled the B-70 supersonic strategic bomber program and the Nike-Zeus anti-ballistic missile that was planned to intercept Soviet ICBMs approaching targets in the United States. He expected to retire the B-52s, and planned to equip the air force and navy with a single fighter airplane—one that would also serve as a strategic bomber. ("There's no use trying," Alice said, "One can't believe impossible things." "I dare say you haven't had much practice," said the Queen).

That airplane was then called the "TFX" for "Tactical Fighter, Experimental." It had been in the works for about 18 months when McNamara took charge of the Pentagon with John F. Kennedy's inauguration as President in January 1961. The TFX was originally conceived as the air force's new 1700-mph long-range tactical fighter, and the idea went through the usual channels: Once Tactical Air Command (TAC) settled upon the performance parameters required of the new fighter it would need during the late '60s and '70s permission to proceed with the project was obtained from Air Force Headquarters. Then, Air Force Systems Command took over to decide whether or not such a plane was feasible. Next, detailed specifications were drawn up to be sent to the aircraft manufacturers which, in turn, would produce plans showing just how they would design and build such an airplane. Finally, with input from the several commands concerned, air force brass would get together to select the design they liked the best and, through the Secretary of the Air Force and Secretary of Defense, ask Congress to fund it. (Since 1974 the Air Force Test and Evaluation Center at Kirtland, AFB, N.M. evaluates the prototypes, and the Defense Systems Acquisition Review Council makes the decision as to whether or not the new hardware is recommended for acquisition to the Secretary of the Air Force.)

Meanwhile, the navy, too, had a new fighter proposal in the mill, and therefore, when these proposals appeared on the desk of Defense Secretary McNamara, scarcely before he had time to warm his chair, McNamara made his incredible decision: The TFX would be redesigned, in two versions, employing at least 90 percent "commonality of parts," to serve both the air force and the navy! Five hundred million dollars could be saved, he said, by developing one airplane rather than two.

At that time, the Air Force Chief of Staff happened to be Gen. Curtis LeMay, but LeMay held his fire and waited for the navy's reaction, which wasn't long in coming.

The navy pointed out that it needed an entirely different kind of aircraft than that required by the air force because their missions

An A-4 Skyhawk approaches the flight deck of the *Ranger* in the South China Sea.

USAF C-130 Hercules drops South Vietnamese paratroopers into Viet Cong stronghold southwest of Saigon.

were different. The air force tactical fighter would have to be a large, heavy, offensive machine (90 ft. in length and weighing 90,000 lbs.), while the navy needed a much smaller, lighter defensive fighter to ride shotgun for the fleet.

But McNamara was adamant. The TFX—by then designated the F-111—would proceed as decreed.

Boeing and Convair (the latter with Grumman as a sort of junior partner) responded to McNamara's specifications, and in November 1962 the services chose the Boeing proposal. Eight air force generals and three admirals, plus the Chief of Naval Operations, Admiral Anderson, and Air Force Chief of Staff General LeMay, picked the Boeing designs.

However, McNamara overruled them all because, he said, the Boeing designs contained only 34 percent commonality of parts (by weight), while the Convair designs used 92 percent identical parts. Backing the McNamara decision were Secretary of the Air Force Eugene Zuckert and Secretary of the Navy Fred Korth, who were also Kennedy appointees.

An A-4 is launched from canted deck as F-4Bs prepare to follow from the main deck.

General Dynamics

Convair F-111, originally planned as a superior tactical fighter, was downgraded by McNamara's naive theory, and the resulting airplane met none of the original design specifications.

General Dynamics

The F-111's terrain-following radar and other sophisticated systems are praised by its pilots, but the airplane itself, compromised by a multi-mission requirement, performs marginally in each role. As General (ret) Eaker pointed out, it's not possible to mate a sports car and a four-ton truck.

In the end, the Navy decided to stonewall it, saying that the F-4 Phantom, which it already had, was better suited to the navy's needs than the Convair F-111B.*

---

* Ironically, the air force also began buying F-4s in 1963. McDonnell's versatile Phantom proved to be one of the star performers of the Vietnam war in the air superiority, fighter-bomber, interceptor, ground support, tactical strike, and reconnaissance roles.

The air force, however, ended up with 270 F-111 tactical fighters (which fell short of all original performance specifications, and was grounded a number of times until the wing carry-through structure and other weaknesses were modified), and 70 FB-111 "strategic bombers," acquisitions that were considerably eased by the retirement of General LeMay in February 1965, a few days after the F-111 pro-

The navy managed to prove that the F-111 was unsuited to navy needs and did without a new fighter until the political climate changed in Washington. Then it got the fighter it wanted, the F-14 Tomcat, seen here during initial tests early in 1974.

The Convair F-106A was a 1500-mph USAF fighter with a service ceiling of 60,000 feet. It was in operation since 1959 as a home defense weapon in the United States. It was automatically directed to its targets by advanced ground radars.

totype began its flight tests. LeMay had characterized the F-111 as a "jury-rigged . . . inferior stop-gap weapon system." But LeMay could not have remained as Air Force Chief of Staff in any case, because he was bitterly opposed to the policy of flexible response.

The Mitchells, MacArthurs and LeMays must always risk the foreshortening or termination of their military careers—however right they may be—because they cannot be allowed to publicly challenge the decisions of the Commander-in-Chief—however wrong he may be.

The Lockheed F-104 Starfighter was introduced in 1958 and seemed slightly unbelievable with a razor-thin wing of only 22-foot span and a gross weight of 20,000 pounds. Top speed was 1600 mph, but it was an unforgiving machine and generally unpopular with pilots.

## Faith, hope, and parity

Throughout the '60s and '70s, American defense forces, including the nuclear deterrent forces, steadily eroded in comparison to those of the Soviets; and four different Presidents—Johnson, Nixon, Ford and Carter—sought solace in a series of code words when forced to defend the decline of American arms. Equivalency, sufficiency and parity were imprecise terms used to imply that, even if the Soviets had more intercontinental ballistic missiles (ICBMs), there was no need for alarm because, all things considered, the two powers actually were about even in nuclear might. The Congresses of these two decades endorsed this position.

But the assumption that nuclear confrontation is thwarted by this presumed balance of terror is meaningless if the balance exists only in presidential rhetoric. As valuable as the U.S.

The Lockheed TR-1 is a larger and improved version of the famed U-2 "Spy Plane". It has a wingspan of 103 feet and cruises more than 430 mph above 70,000 feet with a range of 3000 miles. The USAF had 35 of them in mid-1986.

The Strategic Air Command's SR-71 Blackbird can cruise at 2000 mph at 80,000 feet, and is a product of Kelly Johnson's "Skunk Works" at Lockheed.

spy satellites may be, they cannot probe the contents of roofed structures, and therefore U.S. defense planners cannot know how many ICBMs the Soviets have in standby storage to give them a multiple reload capacity for the ICBMs that are detectable.

At the beginning of the '80s, the U.S. possessed 1053 ICBMs: 53 Titan IIs in silos at three locations in Arkansas, Arizona and Kansas; 450 Minuteman II solid-propellant missiles; and 550 Minuteman IIs fitted with multiple independently targetable reentry vehicle (MIRV) warheads. The ICBMs, with a range in excess of 6000 miles, were preprogrammed to strike strategic targets in the Soviet Union.

The second leg of America's nuclear deterrent triad was the nuclear-powered submarine fleet armed with some 640 nuclear-tipped missiles of medium range.

SAC's manned bombers represented the third leg of the U.S. strategic retaliatory force—290 B-52G and H nuclear missile carriers, 70 FB-111s and 600 supporting KC-135 tankers.

The manned bomber had one very important advantage over the ICBM: It could be launched at the first suspicion of attack and then recalled for several hours thereafter if no attack materialized. The ICBM could not be called back once launched. Indeed, it would have reached a target—at that time the Soviet Union—in slightly over 20 minutes. Or it could be destroyed in its silo if for any reason (including a delayed order from the Commander-in-Chief as he agonizes over the decision) it was not launched within the 15-minute warning period provided by satellite and radar surveillance.

The manned bomber is more vulnerable to enemy defenses, which is why—had there had been a confrontation with the USSR—the B-52s would have penetrated Soviet airspace at 400 mph and only 400 feet above the surface to launch their stand-off nuclear missiles hundreds of miles from their targets.

In 1980, the stand-off nuclear missile carried by the most B-52s was the SRAM (Short Range Attack Missile), as many as 20 per plane (or, more often, depending upon each B-52s preselected targets, a mix of SRAMs and nuclear gravity bombs). The SRAMs may be launched with the aircraft on any heading, even 180 degrees away from the targets. It flies at 2000 mph and its 18-inch diameter gives it a very poor signature on enemy radar. In tests, the SRAM has repeatedly impacted within 100 ft. of its programmed targets. Its only weakness is its short range—about 100 miles. It has been operational since 1972.

The Air Launched Cruise Missile (ALCM) is subsonic, but has a much greater range and therefore significantly increases the B-52 survivability factor. The Cruise Missile program was delayed by the Carter Administration, and as a result full deployment of the ALCM could

not be accomplished before 1986. Carter also delayed development of the improved Trident II nuke missile for U.S. submarine strike force, cancelled the B-52's replacement, the B-1, and delayed the MX (mobile ICBM) for three critical years. At last faced with the consequences of these acts—along with those of previous administrations—and a re-election campaign, President Carter endorsed an enormously expensive, environmentally destructive and embarrassingly ridiculous MX railway system in which the missiles were to be shuffled about in a massive shell game that, hopefully, would leave the Soviets guessing as to which shelters contained missiles at any given time. Meanwhile, Carter voiced the belief that an eventual nuclear arms limitation agreement with the So-

General Dynamics

The Convair B-58 Hustler was intended as a replacement for the medium-range Boeing B-47 bomber and entered service in 1960. With a speed in the 1600-mph range, it was impressive for its time. But changing requirements, and the fact that SAC was stuck with the FB-111s, caused a phase-out of the 80 Hustlers by the end of the '70s.

The Military Airlift Command delivers whatever needs to be delivered by air, anywhere in the world, at any time, for the military services. Pictured is one of MAC's emergency hospital aircraft, a Douglas C-9 Nightingale.

Lockheed C-130 Hercules is the air force combat transport, designed to operate from unimproved airstrips. It does everything from iceberg patrol (for the Coast Guard) to paratrooper drops.

viets was possible. The Soviets, no more concerned with adherence to their future promises than to their past ones, claimed support for such an agreement while going forward with a mobile ICBM program of their own, and concurrently installing new SS-20 medium-range, semi-mobile missiles in Western Russia aimed at targets in Free Europe.

Each SS-20 is fitted with three independently-targeted warheads, and a total of 300 SS-20 boosters (900 warheads) were in place by early 1982, giving the communists a clear six-to-one advantage in nuclear weaponry deployed for any kind of a so-called "limited" nuclear confrontation in Europe.

That advantage was, of course, measured against the combined nuclear strength of the NATO partners. This situation so alarmed President Reagan when he took office that it prompted him to seek deployment of ground-

The Lockheed C-5A Galaxy of MAC is shown with a typical load. It can carry 256,000 pounds 2900 miles non-stop at a speed of 530 mph and land in a distance of 5000 feet. Improved C-5B version was ordered in 1982.

launchable cruise missiles in Western Europe to counter this threat. The cruise missile program, along with that of the B-1 bomber, went forward in the Reagan administration.

Earlier, on the eve of the 1980 elections, in an apparent attempt to gloss over the weaknesses in America's defenses, Carter's secretary of defense, Harold Brown, decided it was time to reveal the air force's "Stealth" bomber program, which had been in the works since late in the Nixon administration. The Stealth bomber, Brown said, would be virtually "invisible" to current Soviet radars.

Brown's revelation impressed the news media and surely sounded reassuring to the taxpayers. But what Brown did not say was that the Soviets already had some of the key engineering data on the Stealth's radar-eating systems. It had been sold to a Polish intelligence agent for $100,000 by an engineer working for Hughes Aircraft.

As the USAF Tactical Air Command entered the '80s, it possessed some excellent new aircraft. The F-15 *Eagle* had been entering squadron service since the mid-'70s. The first of a planned buy of 733 A-10 ground support planes had come along in the late '70s, and the F-16 lightweight fighter, 650 of which were replacements for the 675 F-4s acquired during the '60s, was entering service. The F-15 has a top speed in excess of Mach 2, a combat thrust-to-weight ratio of 1.4 to 1, and is superior to anything the Soviets could put into the air during the '80s. It carries four medium-range missiles and two short-range missiles, along with 900 rounds of ammunition for its 20mm cannon. The F-16 is not as fast or as well armed as the F-15, but is much lighter and more maneuverable.

The F-16 was originally justified as an "economy" fighter, one almost as good as the F-15 for a lot less money. But the initial cost turned out to be $14 million each, while the F-15 is $17 million. The necessary spares and maintenance equipment add significantly to these figures, not to mention that highly trained technicians are required to keep them flying.

*Faith, hope, and parity* **289**

Francis H. Dean

A navy Tomcat fighter of the "High Hat" squadron, a unit that dates back to the mid-'20s; nowadays part of the air group on the attack carrier *John F. Kennedy*.

USN

U.S. Navy's P-3 Orion anti-submarine warfare (ASW) aircraft makes a mock run on an American sub during exercises held in the Sea of Japan. A perimeter of P-3 bases, extending from Sigonella and Souda Bay in the Mediterranean to Norway, Iceland, United States, Japan, Okinawa, the Philippines, Thailand, Australia, New Zealand, Guam, and Hawaii, made any area in the world accessible to the Orion within 30 minutes' flying time. More than 400 are in service.

While such aircraft are capable of some truly amazing performances in the delivery of their ordnance against an enemy, the complexity of these high-technology combat machines is in itself a limiting factor. No matter how miraculous their systems, those out of service for high-tech maintenance have an effectiveness factor of zero. And if no more than half of these machines in squadron service can be put into the air at any given time because of the amount of expert care demanded by their mag-

ical black boxes, then our air commanders must plan accordingly.

One lesson learned about airpower in WWII was that the "best" and most effective combat airplanes were simply those that were airborne and ready to fight when needed—a principle clearly established by the pilots flying the unremarkable Douglas Dauntless at Midway, the obsolescent P-40 over North Africa, and the inadequate F4F Wildcat at Guadalcanal and the Coral Sea.

The newest air force fighter during the '80s was the McDonnell F-15 Eagle, believed by the air force to be superior to anything the Soviets put in the air.

The General Dynamics F-16 USAF fighter is a lightweight air combat fighter that performs so well that the gadgeteers and Pentagon pilots added air-to-surface and all-weather radar and navigation capabilities to broaden its mission. Predictably, the new goodies forced a quantum leap in cost.

This is a relevant consideration because, currently, the air force and navy are short of the technical people needed to maintain the sophisticated systems in our first-line combat aircraft.

## Anytime, Gaddafi Baby

On 19 August 1981, two Soviet-made Su-22 "Fitter" fighter-bombers of the Libyan Air Force were shot down by a pair of U.S. Navy F-14 Tomcats above the Gulf of Sidra in international waters. The fight started when the Libyan aircraft fired a missile (presumably, a Soviet Atoll) at the Americans, who were flying combat air patrol protecting the carrier *Nimitz*, participating in maneuvers with the U.S. 6th Fleet. The Tomcats, armed with Sidewinder missiles, made short work of the Fitters.

The Tomcats were flown by Comdr. Henry Kleeman and Lt. Larry Muscyznski, and their Radar Intercept Officers (called GIBs in the navy, for "Guys in Back") were Lt. Davis Venlet and Lt. James Anderson. Later, one of the F-14s seen aboard the carrier had an appropriate victory symbol painted on its fuselage above the legend: "Anytime, Gaddafi Baby."

The "Gaddafi" referred to was, of course, the Libyan dictator Muammar Gaddafi, who gained power in 1969 (at age 27) by way of a coup d'etat, deposing the aged King Idris. A strutting, desert dandy, Gaddafi was a supporter of Uganda's mad Idi Amin, provoked the destruction of the U.S. Embassy in Tripoli in 1979, and was to contribute more to world terrorism during the 1980s than the Soviets, Iranians, and Syrians combined. He claimed the entire Gulf of Sidra to be Libyan waters (150 miles off the Libyan Coast), declaring that any unauthorized entry into the Gulf was to cross his "Line of Death."

President Reagan, aware of the 20 terrorist training camps in Libya, and frustrated by the fact that a great many Americans, and cit-

Fairchild's A-10 ground support aircraft was literally designed around its tank-killing General Electric seven-barrelled cannon.

izens of America's allies, had been victimized by hijackings and terrorist bombs, nevertheless would take no direct action against Libya until he possessed incontrovertible evidence of Gaddafi's involvement in a specific terrorist act. He would eventually have it.

Meanwhile, on 23 March 1986, the U.S. 6th Fleet, containing the attack carriers *Saratoga*, *Coral Sea*, and *America*, began exercises in the Mediterranean. On the following day, three U.S. ships crossed Gaddafi's so-called "Line of Death," the Libyans launched at least five SA-2 and SA-5 surface-to-air missiles at U.S. aircraft. Grumman EA-6 Prowlers diverted the SAMs with their electronic countermeasures

devices, and the Libyan missiles fell harmlessly into the sea. But having been fired upon over international waters, the Americans reacted as they had five years earlier. A pair of A-7 Corsairs took out the SAM site's radar with HARM missiles (the HARM homes on the enemy radar signal), while A-6 Intruders destroyed two enemy gunboats, and the cruiser *Yorktown* blasted a third Libyan attack boat. Two Libyan MiG-25s charged toward the fray, but suddenly decided that they had something more important to do back inside Libya.

Less than two weeks later, on 5 April 1986, a terrorist bomb exploded in a West Berlin nightclub frequented by U.S. servicemen. One Amer-

Approximately 90 B-52 nuclear carriers were on alert at all times during the '80s. Quick-start ability allowed simultaneous starting of all engines and a five-minute elapsed time from the scramble order to liftoff.

ican soldier died (along with a 28-year-old Turkish woman), and 79 Americans were among the 230 injured. This time, U.S. intelligence people could provide the President with the hard evidence of Libyan planning and execution that Reagan had demanded. He immediately approved a retaliatory air strike against Gaddafi.

The attack was carried out at 2 A.M. on the morning of 15 April (7 P.M. on the 14th EDT) by 12 A-6 Intruders from the *America* and *Coral Sea*, that struck at targets in the Benghazi area, and by 13 F-111s from bases in England that attacked Gaddafi's headquarters/residence and the international airport in the Tripoli area.

The F-111s destroyed five Libyan transport planes and damaged Gaddafi's compound. The A-6s shot up four enemy airplanes on the ground at Benghazi and inflicted an undetermined amount of damage on a military barracks. One F-111 was lost shortly after leaving the target area. Five additional F-111s were unable to bomb because of to mechanical malfunctions.

The attack unquestionably shook Gaddafi—he maintained a low profile for weeks afterward—but actual damage was relatively slight. However, there were some useful truths to be gleaned from the action:

The Titan II ICBM was liquid-fueled and required extensive maintenance. America's ICBM force consisted of 53 Titans and 1000 Minutemen in 1980, a figure that had remained static throughout the '70s. By 1986 the count was 1008 Minutemen IIs, and the Titans were being deactivated.

tack, France and Spain going so far as to deny the American planes right of transit through their airspace.

2. The Paveway 2000-lb. laser-guided bombs carried by the F-111s were less accurate than expected. Sixteen were delivered and, had they been squarely on target, would have left a grease spot where Gaddafi's headquarters had been. No direct hits were made.

3. The F-111s probably required more support than they were worth. A total of 17 F-111s, plus five EF-111s (countermeasures aircraft with radar jamming equipment and infrared decoys), required 28 tankers for their six airborne fuel stops during the 5600-nm round trip. The F-111s were selected because they were equipped to deliver the laser-guided bombs, and because the air force insisted upon grabbing a piece of the action. The navy could have done it all, flying 400-nm round trips from their carriers.

4. The politics of defense did not serve this mission well. It was clearly not an air force caper, but a job for the 6th Fleet. This mission suffered from overplanning, with input from the National Security Council, the Joint Chiefs, and others close to the President.

1. Underscored once again was the uncomfortable fact that America has no dependable allies. True, Britain's "Iron Lady," Prime Minister Margaret Thatcher, backed the U.S. play all the way, but she faced substantial criticism in Parliament for allowing the Americans to operate from British bases. West Germany, France, Italy, and Spain opposed the at-

No one believed that the U.S. air strike against Gaddafi would mark the the end of world terrorism. The Soviet Union's surrogates—Bulgaria, Cuba, Nicaragua—would continue to aid and abet violence in the West, while Syria's ambitious King Assad, along with Iran's fanatical Ayatolla Khomeini were intent upon savaging any prospect of a mid-East peace with their own hired guns. Nevertheless, the United States had put the world on notice that it would make terrorism as costly as possible for its sponsors, with or without the support of America's allies.

The U.S. Navy's nuclear submarine fleet contained 41 vessels in 1980, each armed with 16 nuclear missiles with a 2500-mile range. Test firing shown is of a Polaris A-3, launched while the submarine was submerged. The Carter Administration refused to update with the more advanced Tridents. New Trident subs entering service late in the '80s each carried 24 Trident missiles.

## Carrier power

By 1982, the U.S. Navy had 14 aircraft carriers, ranging in size from the 40 year-old 45,000-ton *Midway* to the 91,000-ton nuclear-powered *Carl Vinson*. Three new Nimitz-class carriers were expected to join the fleet by the early 1990s. Aircraft complements are typically 50 to 80 aircraft, with up to 24 Tomcat fighters, 36 Intruder and Corsair attack craft, plus a handful of Prowlers and Hawkeyes, four to six SH-3 helos and, on the larger attack carriers, up to 10 S-3 Viking anti-submarine aircraft.

The Pershing was a short-range tactical missile with a low trajectory. Based in Western Europe during the mid-1960s, and supplemented with the surface launched cruise missile in the mid-1980s. This kind of weapon was most affected by arms-reduction talks between the superpowers.

There has long been substantial opposition to operation of the supercarriers. They are expensive—$2.5 billion for the Nimitz-class *Carl Vinson*—and critics charge that, in all-out nuclear war, the big flattops would be vaporized in a matter of days, or even hours. However, in an all-out nuclear war, the fate of our carriers wouldn't much matter. In a non-nuclear war, the big carriers would be vulnerable to any power having a fleet of attack submarines. Still, the navy's ability to send these self-contained mobile airfields throughout the world to show the flag and serve U.S. policy is probably worth the cost. An enemy must assume that each American aircraft carrier possesses a stock of nuclear weapons, while the flattops' ever-present escorts, which can include a modernized battleship, is a formidable force in itself.

The Lockheed S-3B Viking, fitted with Harpoon missiles, is a sub-hunter, and its electronic support measures and countermeasures systems make it a valuable escort for carrier-based strike aircraft.

*Lockheed-California photo by Bob Ferguson*

## ATF and ATA

The USAF expected to replace its F-15 Eagle fighters with a machine that, in development, was referred to as the Advanced Tactical Fighter (ATF). This was to be a supersonic air-superiority fighter, rather than the slow-and-sneaky F-117A Stealth out of Lockheed's famed "Skunk Works," a number of which were flying (only at night) from a super-secret airstrip near Tonopah, Nevada, in mid-1986. The Air Force also asked Congress to fund a secret airplane, code-named "Aurora", early in 1985.

At least seven aerospace companies worked on the ATF design, which certainly incorporated Stealth technology. Stealth technology consists of engines mounted inside the aircraft, a well-rounded airframe (no sharp corners), at least 40 percent composite construction, and a radar-absorbing finish, probably a ceramic. On 23 April 1991, the Lockheed F-22 was chosen to become this next-generation fighter.

In the meantime, the U.S. Navy also wanted a new fighter for delivery in the early '90s. Designated the Advanced Tactical Aircraft (ATA), it would also possess Stealth characteristics. The ATA became the A-12, cancelled and eventually incorporated into the A-X strike aircraft, a replacement for the A-6 Intruder. The new F/A-18s, meanwhile, would replace the aging A-7s.

Northrop's Stealth bomber was due to appear in the same time frame. During the early fall of 1986, the first 15 B-1B bombers were delivered for service to Dyess AFB, Texas. At the time, the air force planned to buy 100 of the B-1Bs pending delivery of the Stealth bombers in the '90s.

In addition to a more extensive use of composite materials in the airframes of the ATF /ATA/Stealth machines, the newer aircraft have "heads up" cockpit displays, which project flight, navigation, and weapons delivery data onto transparent screens directly in front of the pilot. The most significant advance, however, will come—as it always has—in the new generation of engines. The Pratt & Whitney PW5000 and the General Electric GE37 may have up to 50 percent fewer parts, 40 percent less fuel consumption at supersonic speeds, and 25 percent higher thrust-to-weight ratios than the best fighter engines of the '80s.

## The balance of power, United States versus USSR

Despite the fact that the U.S. enjoyed a clear 10-to-1 advantage in deliverable nukes over the Russians at the end of the Eisenhower Administration, John F. Kennedy won the presidency claiming a dangerous "missile gap" in favor of the Soviets. The missile gap did indeed develop during the Kennedy and subsequent administrations, until President Reagan began repair of America's leaky defenses and regained, if not military superiority, at least a thoroughly credible deterrent force.

In October 1986, as President Reagan prepared to talk about nuclear arms reductions with Soviet General Secretary, Mikhail Gorbachev, in Reykjavik, Iceland, the Soviet Union possessed a total of 15,206 known nuclear warheads vs. 12,564 U.S. nuclear warheads. Having recorded that bit of insanity, we should now crank-in the "howevers":

However, the U.S. had 1008 land-based inter-continental ballistic missiles (ICBMs), fitted with a total of 2108 independently-targeted warheads, while the USSR had 1398 ICBMs fitted with a total of 6420 warheads.

The U.S. had 100 submarines set to fire 5632 warheads from 640 missiles, and the Soviets had 300 submarines, carrying 940 missiles fitted with a total of 3100 warheads.

The U.S. could deliver 4200 nuclear devices with 260 B-52s, one B-1B, and 280 FB-111s, while the Soviet Union had 950 bombers (mostly short-range) carrying 3200 nuclear bombs and missiles.

In Europe, the U.S. had 220 short-range land-based missiles, vs. 1250 for the USSR. The Soviets also had a reported 170 SS-20 triple-warhead intermediate-range missiles aimed at China.

America's Minutemen ICBMs, scattered in underground silos in nine states in the Midwest, South, and West, fitted with up to three warheads, were to be at least partially replaced by the MX Peacekeeper, each carrying 10 warheads. President Reagan asked for 100 MXs, but the Congress had agreed to only 50 late in 1986.

## Midgetman

The appearance of the single-warhead Midgetman ICBM clouded the defense picture. Midgetman was mobile; it could be driven about the U.S. mounted on specially-built trucks and fired from wherever it happened to be if the President ever pushed the Doomsday button. Midgetman's mobility provided the protection against destruction by an enemy first strike that the MX originally promised but never achieved. The Pentagon big-rocket people opposed Midgetman, and when it appeared to be gaining adherents in the Congress, suggested that Midgetman be more than doubled in size (from 38,000 to 90,000 pounds) and fitted with at least three independently targeted warheads.

Meanwhile, arms reduction talks with the Russians, and President Reagan's so-called

A Grumman A-6A Intruder comes aboard its carrier. The Intruder is an all-weather attack aircraft, equipped for aerial refueling and nighttime delivery of its ordnance; in service since the mid-1960s.

"Star Wars" research program, introduced more uncertainty into the nuclear arms standoff.

## The Strategic Defense Initiative

On 23 March 1983 President Ronald Reagan proposed that the United States embark on a research program that would lead to a defense system designed to intercept and destroy ICBMs before they could reach American soil or that of our allies. Reaction to this bold announcement was instantaneous and varied, at home and about the world. The Soviets and their apologizers cried "Foul," claim-

ing that effective protection against nuclear attack would be "destabilizing," the balance of terror would be upset, and the United States would have a first-strike advantage (perhaps an only-strike advantage) if such a system were in place. The president, anticipating that objection, said that America would share SDI technology with the Soviets, although no one could—or should have—believed that. If both superpowers were protected against nuclear destruction, the Soviets' massive military, equipped with conventional weapons, would have a "first-strike" capability of another kind.

In the beginning, much opposition to the SDI project in America was rooted in the belief that such a system was either impossible of attainment, or, if possible, would require decades to develop at an astronomical cost. Late in 1986, after spending more than three years and almost $5 billion on the project, SDI researchers could offer no absolute assurance of their ultimate success.

However, their efforts had sufficiently impressed the Soviets that Mikhail Gorbachev was eager to swap some Russian warheads for a curb on the American SDI program. Whether the Communist Party's General Secretary feared America's high-tech potential, or whether it was the enormous cost of attempting to circumvent an effective nuclear shield, Gorbachev appeared to be, prior to the October "Mini-Summit" in Iceland, eager to talk about nuclear arms reductions, beginning with the European-based missiles.

## Lasers

SDI research focuses on a system that would employ submarine-launched X-ray lasers. The X-ray laser is generated by the detonation of a small nuclear device—small enough that it can be lofted into space by a submarine-launched missile. As it began with the USSR the primary potential enemy, it had to be submarine-launched to be close enough to the Soviet Union to zap their ICBMs during their five-minute launch phase—before each missile's multiple warheads, and 100 or so decoys, have separated from the missile's "bus" and greatly multiplied the problems of interception. Clearly, the big rockets would be easier to track while in their boost phases, and it is more effective to kill 10 warheads at a time than to search them out in space among their decoys.

The alternative to submarine launch of the defensive lasers would be nuclear devices in earth orbit, but there would seem to be no ad-vantage to that from a purely technical standpoint, and world opinion would surely argue against it.

Why the X-ray laser? Because it seems to be the only weapon, not based in space, that may be effectively hidden and capable of intercepting Soviet ICBMs during their boost phase. Plus, an X-ray laser beam, nuclear-generated, will destroy its target with a mere one-second dwell. Other forms of lasers, and particle beams—which are greatly weakened passing through the earth's atmosphere—must remain exactly focused on their targets for as long as seven seconds to cause significant damage, are much too unwieldy to be placed in earth orbit, and require complex mirror systems to relay their beams against Soviet ICBMs during boost phase.

When President Reagan proposed SDI, he recognized that it was a ". . . formidable task, one that may not be accomplished before the end of this century." Whatever the outcome, the fallout from such an effort, in terms of jobs, technological advances and, perhaps, a substantial shove toward nuclear disarmament, may alone justify the great cost.

Interest and funding for SDI lessened in the late 1980s as the USSR crumbled under the failed socialistic system and the dedication of an expremely high percentage of its limited economic resources to military expenditures.

The break-up of the USSR greatly eased America's concerns over a nuclear war. However, there still remained the remnents of the USSR nuclear arsenal that now was in the hands of some independent states.

## Review questions

1. What was the theory of flexible response? Did President Johnson have any other choice but to commit U. S. troops to a land war in Asia? How did the Viet Minh get started? What were the Geneva Accords? What was the purpose of the Southeast Asia Treaty Organization (SEATO)? Who were the Viet

Cong? Why were the South Vietnamese governments so ineffective?

2. Describe the events leading up to the Gulf of Tonkin resolution. What powers did this resolution give to the President?

3. How was the Vietnam War different from WWII and the Korean War? Why was it difficult for the average American to understand the war? Why can it be said that time was on the side of the North Vietnamese?

4. Why was the helicopter such an effective vehicle in this conflict?

5. What was the situation when President Nixon took office in January 1969? Why did he authorize B-52 strikes on neutral countries?

6. Discuss the implications of Secretary McNamara's cost effectiveness policy. List some of the aircraft which entered service with the U. S. Air Force during the 1980s.

# 16

# Gen-av and fun-av

## Objectives

At the end of this chapter you should be able to:

- Describe the private flying market in the immediate postwar period.
- Summarize the history of air racing in the United States.
- Define the purpose of the Experimental Aircraft Association (EAA).
- Describe the FAA position regarding ultralights.
- Describe how Piper Aircraft Corporation was formed and the role of the J-3 Cub in its history.
- Identify some of the successful early aircraft developed by Beech Aircraft Corporation and Cessna Aircraft Company.
- Discuss some of the uses of general aviation aircraft.
- Summarize the brief history of helicopters and describe some of their uses.

Sensibly regulated by the Civil Aeronautics Act of 1938 and the Federal Aviation Act of 1958, private and commercial flying steadily advanced after WWII. Sport and pleasure flying grew apace, embracing such activities as air racing, homebuilt aircraft, and the rest-oration of antiques. Meanwhile, the lightplane manufacturers increasingly prospered as United States businessmen discovered the several advantages of airplane ownership. The helicopter took its unique place in the workaday world. The past was prelude.

## WWII surplus

The late 1940s was a time of readjustment, for the nation as well as for aviation. As soon as the shooting stopped, America dismantled—almost overnight—the mightiest military force the world had ever seen. Fighting men and women were brought home and mustered out of uniform as fast as transport for them could be provided; the streets at home were filled for a time with members of the "52-20 Club" ($20 per week for 52 weeks; an immediate postwar measure that put a few dollars in vets' pockets while they sought jobs and reassembled their lives), each proudly wearing the little gold-colored emblem of honorable service irreverently known as the "Ruptured Duck."

Private flying returned in boom proportions after the war, at least for a time. It was helped along by the "G.I. Bill," legislation that offered a wide range of educational benefits, among other things, to WWII vets, including civilian flight training.

Randall Brink

The Aeronca Champion series appeared in 1945. The first ones, Model 7AC, had 65 hp; later versions, such as this 1947–49 7DC, had 85 hp. All were fabric-covered and seated two in tandem. After the cost of personal flying began escalating in the late '70s, such craft were sought on the used market and refurbished for economical personal flying while the investment appreciated.

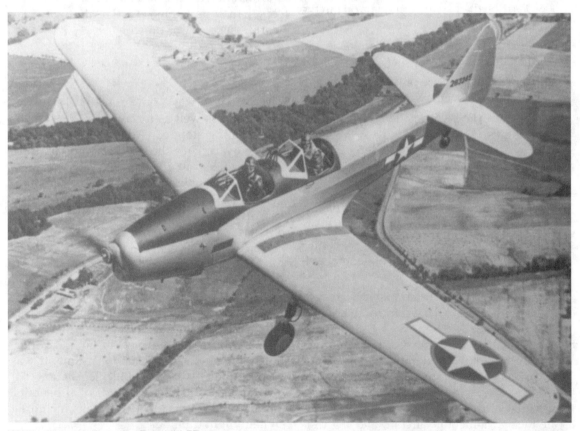

WWII primary trainer, the Fairchild PT-19, was available in the immediate postwar surplus market for very little money, but most soon disappeared because of maintenance problems with internal wooden wing structure.

The Boeing-Stearman PT-13/PT-17 (or its naval equivalent, the N2S-5, above), was another WWII primary trainer. Most that were purchased as surplus were converted to use as ag-planes. Nowadays, those that remain are being refurbished to their original configuration by warbird addicts.

## Postwar ag-planes

During this period the general aviation fleet was dominated by Aeronca Champions, Piper Cubs, and Taylorcrafts, sprinkled with war surplus trainers, mostly Fairchild PT-19s and Stearman PT-17s. A lot of Vultee BT-13s were to be seen at first, but most gave their engines (450-hp R-985 *Wasp* Juniors) to the Stearmans, which combination became the backbone of the aerial dusting and spraying businesses

Stearman spray plane with 600-hp P&W Wasp engine. Both maneuverable and ruggedly built, the Stearman was well suited to ag-flying.

that rapidly spread throughout the country's agricultural areas. Later, the same fate befell many of the surplus AT-6s, their P&W R-1340 Wasp engines of 600 hp transforming the sturdy Stearman (actually, Boeing-Stearman) biplane into an excellent duster/sprayer (the Stearman military trainers were originally fitted with 220-hp Lycoming or Continental radials, R-680s and R-670s respectively). Eventually, the commercial aircraft manufacturers offered aircraft especially designed for agricultural work, beginning with the Piper Pawnee introduced in 1959. Ever-larger loads (hoppers grew to 400 gallons or more), and the aging of big radial engines that had been out of production since the early 50s, led to the introduction of turboprop engines on ag-planes, such as the Turbo AgCat, Turbine Thrush and Air Tractor.

In the early '80s, one could still find a few Stearmans working for "aerial applicators," as the dust/spray operators prefer to be called. However, many of the Stearmans that survive today have been returned to their original

Jim Larsen

Popular warbird is the F4U series Vought Corsairs, which served in both WWII and the Korean War with the navy and marines. This one is an F4U-7, originally built for the French.

Dustin Carter

Restored P-51D Mustang. Many warbirds are painted to represent a particular WWII fighter, and many present-day owners are younger than their airplanes.

"two hole" configuration and painted as they looked when in military colors.

## Warbirds

The restoration of WWII aircraft is hardly limited to Stearmans. It is an activity that started,

almost imperceptibly, in the early '60s after the surplus warbirds had become scarce. It apparently began as a nostalgia trip for former military pilots, and was spearheaded by a group of aging tigers in South Texas who loosely banded together as the "Confederate Air Force" in order to locate, finance, and re-

A restored North American T-6, photographed at Willow Grove, Pennsylvania, in 1974.

Curtiss P-40 Warhawks at the annual EAA fly-in, Oshkosh, Wisconsin. Airplane in foreground has Flying Tiger (American Volunteer Group) paint scheme, although the actual Flying Tiger aircraft number 47 was an earlier model.

furbish the old fighters and bombers. Before long, the CAF colonels (everyone in the CAF is a "colonel") had been joined by others who tracked down the vintage fighters, bombers, and trainers in the smaller Latin American countries, the limited air forces of which had been so equipped near the end of WWII. With the supply of such craft virtually exhausted, prices reached $500,000 and up. Most were in the hands of affluent men, as yet unborn when these machines were built, who regarded them as investments, and who obviously enjoyed the macho image that attached to the operation of such airplanes.

## Air racing

A number of WWII-era fighters have constituted the Unlimited class in civilian air racing since 1945. The most successful have been highly-modified F8F Bearcats and P-51 Mustangs (F-51 after the air force redesignated its aircraft in 1948).

Air racing in America began as soon as it was possible to gather a few flying machines together that could remain airborne long enough to complete such an event—which is to say, 1910. A top speed of less than 50 mph was sufficient to win, and that was quite

Walter Beech's Travel Air Model R, commonly called the "Mystery Ship," returned air racing to civilians in 1929 after military domination of such events throughout the '20s.

Matty Laird's "Super Solution" of 1931 averaged 223 mph between Burbank, California, and Cleveland, Ohio, in the transcontinental Bendix Trophy race with Jimmy Doolittle as pilot.

The Gee Bee R-1 racer of 1932, built by the Granville brothers in Springfield, Massachusetts, established a world's speed record for landplanes at 296.28 mph. Jimmy Doolittle was the pilot.

enough for the spectators at Compton, California, many of whom still doubted that man could fly when the event was announced.

The air races of the '20s were dominated by the military until 1929, when Walter Beech's Travel Air "Mystery Ship" appeared at the Cleveland National Air Races and ran away from the best military fighters. Then, until the mid-'30s, a succession of civilian racers, most of them built on a shoestring, led the United States and the world into the realm of high-speed flight and returned to America (from France) the world's landplane speed record.

Beech's 220-mph racer, fitted with a 420-hp Wright R-975—souped-up from its normal 300 hp—was eclipsed the following year at Chicago's National Air Races by Matty Laird's LC-DW300 "Solution" ("solution" to Beech's mystery), which was approximately 10 mph faster.

In 1931, the first of the 300-mph Gee Bee racers appeared, and a year later, Jimmy Doolittle won the Thompson Trophy Race in the Gee Bee R-1, then took the world's landplane speed record, averaging 296.28 mph in four passes over the three-kilometer course.

From 1932 until WWII suspended air racing, James Wedell's Wedell-Williams racers shared the Unlimited class purses with similar machines, fitted with engines of up to 1000 hp. All of these would be classed as "homebuilts" today except for a couple of new Severskys, prototypes of the P-35 air corps fighter that eventually evolved into the P-47 Thunderbolt of WWII.

After the war, the 400-mph surplus fighters took over Unlimited class air racing. In 1979, Ed Browning's highly modified Mustang, flown by Steve Hinton, established a new world's speed record for piston-engine airplanes at 499.059 mph, while closed-course speeds for this class were in the 430 mph range. The engine in Browning's machine was a Rolls-Royce Griffon, normally rated at 2375 hp but certainly producing more power than that for the assault on the record. On 21 August 1989, Hinton's record was eclipsed by veteran race pilot Lyle Shelton in an F8F-2 Bearcat, pacing 528.329 mph over a 3 kilometer course.

Shelton, a six-time winner at Reno, replaced his much-modified Grumman Bearcat's Pratt &

Jim Larsen

John Wright in his P-51D Mustang at Reno, 1976

Whitney R-2800 with a Wright R-3350 turbo-compound engine, used in the Douglas DC-7 and Skyraider. His "Rare Bear" is the most-winning aircraft in the Unlimited class, with a record 481.618 mph pace in the 1991 Reno race. A few notable homebuilt Unlimited racers have crept into the Bronze and Silver heats, such as Burt Rutan's twin-Nissan racing engine powered Pond Racer. Built for industrialist Bob Pond, it qualified at 400.10 mph in 1991. It crashed in 1993, killing pilot Rick Brickett.

The T-6 racing class is nearly as noisy as the Unlimited class, as the nearly-stock North American trainers bellow around the pylons at speeds up to 235 mph, an unheard-of pace in military service. Other racing classes included the Formula I machines, tiny homebuilt monoplanes that somehow achieved closed-course racing speeds of more than 230 mph with engines originally rated at 100 hp, and a confused Sport Biplane class, also homebuilts, in which three or four professionally designed machines have taken all the money in recent years with average speeds around 200 mph while the amateurs trail along for the ride at 150 mph.

Formula V racing, using Volkswagen-powered miniature versions of Formula One racers, has gained popularity at the small airshows, where race courses of 2 miles or less in length allow spectators to see most of the action. Speeds of 150 mph provide ample thrill, seen up close.

Air racing is a spectator sport, and the largest annual meet is the National Air Races held at Reno, Nevada, which embraces many

Dustin Carter

A typical Formula 1 racer at Reno, flown by Thurman Rock and built by Dick Minges.

other aerial activities such as aerobatic competitions, parachuting, etc. Air racing itself is not economically significant to the overall general aviation industry, and some feel that it promotes a negative impression of civilian flying. It should not. Man will race whatever vehicles he may possess, and that is less a commentary on our machines than on the nature of man.

## Homebuilts

That adventurous and creative nature finds other outlets in private aviation. Many free spirits build their own airplanes. That is just about the only discernible thing they have in common, because amateur plane builders are otherwise as diverse as the feathered denizens of a tropical rain forest. Homebuilt airplanes are constructed by all kinds of people, male and female, of all ages, from every economic level. Some get their creations into the air within a few months; some take years. It is possible for all because, as plane builder Peter Bowers once pointed out, building an airplane in one's garage is not a big job, but a collection of little jobs.

Today the cost of a ready-to-fly homebuilt airplane will range between $10,000 and $20,000 if one's labor is counted as fun. Some designs can easily cost $100,000 or more, if a goodie-filled instrument panel is included. The emergence of fast-built aircraft kits, with every nut and bolt supplied and many prefabricated components included, has boosted completion rates for homebuilt projects immensely.

The two greatest advantages to be taken from such a project are: 1) purchasing materials or kit components as needed, the airplane is paid for when completed, and 2) one has a machine tailored to his/her own personal need/preference/dream that is unavailable in the high-priced commercial market. Other benefits include the deep satisfaction that comes with the knowledge that one is transiting the skies with wings of one's own creation.

There are pitfalls. The four greatest obstacles to a successful homebuilt airplane project are: 1) a spouse who is against it; 2) finding a proper engine at a reasonable price; 3) maintaining one's dedication to the task over the protracted period of time required; and 4) friends and neighbors who make the builder's garage-workshop a gathering place, drink his or her beer, and keep him or her from working.

## The EAA

No special skills are required, except that some welding is usually needed, and that may be done by a professional or another amateur

The Williams-Cangie sport biplane racer, *Sundancer*, flown by Dr. Sidney White at Reno and Mojave air races.

Airshow performers combine skill with the spectacular, and the Cole brothers, headed by champion Duane Cole and his wife, Judy, were unsurpassed in this field.

Don Downie

In recent years, homebuilt airplane constructors have increasingly turned to foam and fiberglass, as in this advanced design by Burt Rutan of Mojave, California. Rutan's Long-EZ (above) flew nonstop from California to the Oshkosh fly-in; it was being built in large numbers by others.

plane builder who possesses that skill. One should become acquainted with other builders before starting a project, because they can be very helpful, and the best way to contact such people is through membership in the Experimental Aircraft Association (EAA). This nonprofit organization was founded in 1953 and has approximately 130,000 active members in more than 740 local chapters and is still growing. Its primary purpose is the promotion of sport aviation. While the EAA embraces all forms of recreational flying—the restoration of classic and antique airplanes, warbirds, ultra-lights—the hard-core membership is made up of those who build their own flying machines, and who have banded together for mutual support.

The EAA has been deftly guided by Paul Poberezny from the time that he and a handful of other homebuilt airplane enthusiasts obtained its charter in Milwaukee back in 1953. Poberezny was an air force pilot who had already constructed his first airplane at home. Under his leadership, the EAA soon had members nationwide and, by 1969, Paul left the air force to devote full time to it. Over the years,

Homebuilt copy of the Travel Air Mystery Ship in flight at the Oshkosh fly-in. At right is homebuilt replica of Lindbergh's *Spirit of St. Louis.*

The antiques go to Oshkosh, too. The antiquers have a division within the EAA, and also an Antique Aircraft Association, headquartered in Ottumwa, Iowa, presided over by Bob Taylor. Pictured is Pete Ettinger of Albuquerque in his 1929 Fleet.

A portion of the crowd at the annual EAA fly-in at Oshkosh, Wisconsin. The EAA headquarters and museum are located there after years in Hales Corners, Wisconsin, a suburb of Milwaukee.

aided by wife, Audrey, and son, Tom (a champion aerobatic pilot), Poberezny directed the EAA into a significant place in general aviation. After 37 years at the helm, Paul turned the EAA presidency over to Tom Poberezny in 1989, continuing as Chairman.

The EAA's annual fly-in and convention at Wittman Field, Oshkosh, Wisconsin, is far and away the single largest aviation event in the world, with an attendance of close to one million. During this week-long event each August, Wittman Field is the busiest airport in the world, with 15,000 airplanes from antiques to mini-jets, in a constant state of arrivals and departures, fly-bys, and demonstrations, all concurrent with countless activities on the ground from seminars to "fly markets."

Poberezny and his board of directors preside over a multimillion dollar budget that has allowed the purchase of 500 acres on Wittman Field for an extensive EAA headquarters, museum, and research facility. The money comes from members; $35 annual dues (estimated at $2.75 million), an equal amount from the fly-in, and revenues from EAA publications, museum admissions, etc.

## Ultralights

As with EAA's Warbird, Aerobatic, Antique/Classic divisions, the ultralight aircraft people have found a warm welcome within the EAA. The ultralights have been called a phenomenon of the early '80s recession, but that

The EAA Aviation Center adjacent to Wittman Regional Airport at Oshkosh, Wisconsin. Opened in 1983, the complex houses the headquarters of the Experimental Aircraft Association and the world-class EAA Air Adventure Museum. Restored vintage hangars and grass runway of the Pioneer Airport are at top.

was not entirely true. These minimum aircraft are not substitutes for small, private airplanes that have become too expensive for too many; they are not substitutes for anything. The ultralight is a distinct new class of aerial recreational vehicle, fun machines with roughly the same practical value as small sailboats.

The modern ultralight aircraft was developed from the modern hang glider. The Wright brothers began their experiments with a hang glider, and this most primitive of the heavier-than-air flying machines was reinvented in the '70s in two forms: the conventional monoplane or biplane with rigid wings, and the flexwing, or Rogallo wing, the latter being, essentially, a man-carrying kite. These were "modern" in the sense that they employed modern materials in their construction and, in the case of the rigid-wings, perhaps a more efficient airfoil shape than that worked out by the Wrights. All were/are controlled, to

a degree, by the operators' shifting weight. The addition of small two-cycle engines to the rigid-wing hang gliders resulted in the first modern "ultralight aircraft"—a term adopted for the lack of a better one, since tiny airplanes weighing less than, say, 500 pounds had been called ultralight since the late '20s.

Inevitably, the powered hang gliders quickly grew in weight and power as their builder/pilots sought better performance and increased control. Movable control surfaces became necessary because the heavier the structure, the less effective the shifting weight of the operator in controlling it. And dissatisfied with chainsaw and other tiny gasoline engines, the proponents of this sport went to snowmobile and larger engines. By 1982, 30-hp ultralights were common.

The question was, at exactly what point did such a contrivance become an airplane? That was important because, as long as such ma-

The ultralights evolved from hang gliders, such as this Rogallo Wing type, as well as the rigid-wing designs.

The Mitchell P-38 illustrates the evolution from ultralight to "real airplane."

chines remained "foot launchable," the FAA had a good excuse to ignore them. Their construction and operation were completely unregulated, their pilots unlicensed, and those involved in the sport regarded that as a highly desirable state of affairs.

But again, the nature of man being as it is, he will never, as the saying goes, leave well enough alone. The use of one's legs for a landing gear became next to impossible as the machines acquired weight and more power. They had to have wheels.

Still, the FAA left them alone as long as possible, although everyone knew that some sensible regulation would have to come, especially, after a couple of dimbulbs flew ultra-

The twin-engine Lazair ultralight is a Canadian design.

lights coast-to-coast, and began taking them to altitudes as high as 14,000 feet.

The FAA acted with remarkable restraint. It decreed, in 1982, that ultralights must not: exceed 254 pounds in empty weight; carry more than five gallons of fuel; exceed 63 mph in top speed or 28 mph in stall; operate in controlled airspace; or fly during the hours of darkness or over populated areas. For the time being, pilots and machines would remain unlicensed by the federal government, except for two-place ultralights, which required N-numbers and pilot licenses unless operated under a training exemption. So, under Federal Air Regulation Part 103, a slim two pages in length, the ultralighters got off light.

# Piper

The Piper J-3 Cub did not burst upon the avscene overnight. The concept awaited the appearance of a proper engine—and Bill Piper.

Oilman William T. Piper, Sr., at age 48 became involved with airplanes sort of by accident when, along with several other Bradford, Pennsylvania, businessmen, he invested $600 in the Taylor Brothers Aircraft Corporation a few months before the stock market crash of

1929. The Taylor Brothers company consisted of Gilbert Taylor (his brother had died in a plane crash the year before), two employees, and a parasol monoplane fitted with a 90-hp Kinner engine, which Taylor expected to produce priced at $4000.

Taylor's airplane found no buyers at the beginning of the Great Depression and, at Piper's suggestion, Taylor designed and built a smaller, much lighter airplane, powered with a 20-hp Brownbach engine. That craft, designated the Model E-2 Chummy, barely flew with such an anemic power-plant, and Taylor's backers allowed the company to slide into bankruptcy early in 1931.

But Piper retained his faith in the E-2's concept—a minimum airplane that could be sold at a minimum price. He purchased the Taylor company's assets for under $1000, and cast about for a suitable engine.

Piper's timing could not have been better, for late that year Continental Motors introduced a little 4-cylinder, four-stroke, air-cooled engine of opposed configuration rated at 37 hp. It was called the A-40, and it would establish the basic lightplane engine configuration for at least the next 60 years. Mated to the Taylor E-2 Cub, the A-40 al-

The gentle, versatile Piper J-3 Cub. As an Army Air Force liason aircraft it was known as the L-4. Pictured is a flight of L-4s in service with the South Korean Air Force.

Piper's successful Cherokee series first appeared in 1960. The Cherokee 235 Pathfinder, above, was a 1974 model. Cherokees range from two-place to six-place.

lowed Piper to sell that airplane for $1325. Piper sold 17 Cubs in 1933, 71 the following year, and 210 in 1935.

At that point, Gilbert Taylor, aware that he had something going, left Piper and moved to Alliance, Ohio, where he introduced a similar airplane in 1937 known as the Taylorcraft B12. The Taylorcraft would have the improved Continental A-65 (65 hp) by 1941, and as the BC-12D reintroduced after WWII, about 3000

"T-Crafts" would be built before the company folded in 1947.

A lot of T-Crafts have been restored and are flying today, along with some new ones. In 1974, a new company was formed in Alliance to produce the F-19 Sportsman, a re-engineered version of the BC-12D, fitted with the Continental O-200 engine of 100 hp. It was initially priced at $9500, and was later developed into the F-21 with a Lycoming O-235 engine.

In the meantime, Bill Piper had moved to Lock Haven, Pennsylvania, changed his company name to Piper Aircraft Corporation, and introduced the Piper J-3 Cub powered with a 50-hp version of the A-40. Piper sold 736 of these machines priced at $1617. His 1938 models were the first to standardize on the now famous "Cub Yellow" paint scheme, and that finish, like Henry Ford's "Model T black," stayed with the Cub until the last J-3 was built in 1947. Altogether, 14,125 J-3 Cubs were produced.

In 1940, the J-3 was certified with the 65-hp Continental and Lycoming, and production jumped to more than 3000 per year as the Civilian Pilot Training Program (CPTP; later, the War Training Service) was begun in colleges across the country to give primary flight training to thousands of American youngsters. When this program ended in mid-1944, 1132 educational institutions had trained 430,000 primary flight students and, according to an FAA publication (GA-20-84), "Three-quarters of those trainees had their first flights in Cubs, soloed in Cubs, and were certificated in Cubs." Just how many others earned their wings in the gentle, pokey J-3 before and since that time will never be known.

The Piper Tomahawk was a popular two-place sport/trainer. The T-tail gives it a modern look, but offers no aerodynamic advantage to offset its disadvantage on a small, piston-powered airplane.

The second generation of Pipers, metal-framed and fabric-covered like the Cub, appeared immediately after WWII, and the Piper Cruisers, Clippers, Pacers, Tri-Pacers, and Colts, all in the 100- to 160-hp class, continued the Piper success story throughout the '50s. All were two- to four-place, with the two-place Vagabond of 1948 being the best compromise between performance and cost at $1995.

The Cub reappeared in 1949 as the Super Cub with a red paint scheme and 90 hp. It soon went to 108 hp, 115 hp, 125 hp, and was sold in later years mostly with 150 hp, remaining in production until 1992, at which time Piper supposedly closed out the line with the last 19 going to Muncie Aviation in Indiana. Later Piper relented to produce several more in 1993–1994.

The third generation Pipers represented a clean break with the past; they were all-metal low-wingers, beginning with the Comanche in 1958, and followed by the Cherokee series in 1961. But Piper, with production facilities at Lock Haven and in Vero Beach, Florida, had reorganized in 1948 to acquire fresh capital, and that led to loss of control of the company by the Piper family.

Both the company's founder, and his son, William T. Piper, Jr., are gone from the company now, and it continues, seemingly always a little different from its competitors in its marketing practices. In 1986, Piper—by then a subsidiary of the Lear Siegler Company—offered the *Malibu* and the *Archer* single-engine craft, along with a couple of twins. The Lock Haven facility had long since been sold. Oddly enough, in 1990 the revitalized Taylorcraft company, under new ownership, put its flap-equipped F-22 model into production in the former Piper factory at Lock Haven.

Meanwhile, both Beech and Cessna struggled in the changing market of the '80s, both counting on corporate customers for survival.

## Beechcraft

Walter Beech appears to have leaned to corporate customers from the beginning. After

The Piper Cheyenne III is a cabin-class turbine-powered business airplane, representative of the big-buck market that outpaced the once-strong demand for single-engine privately owned airplanes.

selling Travel Air to Curtiss-Wright in mid-1929, Walter served as president of the C-W Airplane Division until 1932. Then, at the lowest point of the Great Depression, he and wife Olive Ann (nee Olive Ann Mellor, Travel Air's office manager, whom Walter married in 1930), left Curtiss-Wright, returned to Wichita, and formed Beech Aircraft Corporation. At first working in rented space in the idle Cessna plant, Walter brought in engineers Herb Rawdon and Ted Wells, and sent them to their drafting tables with, reportedly, the admonition to design a reverse stagger (lower wings placed forward of the upper ones) cabin biplane that would seat four and "go like hell."

The first four Beechcraft Model 17 Staggerwings had fixed, fully enclosed landing gear; it entered the market in 1932. A total of 781 Staggerwings were built before the last one left the factory in 1949, two years after introduction of the Model 35 Bonanza.

The Beechcraft Model 18 appeared in 1937. Commonly called the "Twin Beech," the Model 18 remained in production until the last Super H18 left the factory in Wichita in January 1969.

Walter got what he asked for, the classic Model 17 Staggerwing that despite its high price—$14,000 to $17,000, depending upon engine installation, which ranged from 225 hp to 420 hp—found 332 buyers prior to WWII. The military purchased an additional 427 Staggerwings, and 16, fitted with 450-hp Wasp junior engines, were produced on special order, 1946–1948, for civilian customers who preferred to pay $29,000 for a new Staggerwing rather than accept the promise of a new Beech Bonanza for less than $10,000.

The model 35 Bonanza was introduced in 1947, fitted with a 165-hp E-185 Continental engine. It was priced at $8945, weighed 1460 pounds empty, and cruised at 172 mph. Thirty-five years and more than 10,000 Bonanzas later, when V-tail Bonanza production ended, the Bonanza cost eighteen times more, had gained 800 pounds in weight, possessed 120 more horsepower, and cruised about 20 mph faster. By then, it had been in continuous production longer than any other airplane.

The Bonanza V35B was priced at $126,500 in 1983; none were delivered. Non-Bonanza owners charged that part of that price was for the aircraft's "snob appeal."

Beech's radical twin-pusher Starship, built entirely of carbon graphite composites and equipped with a variable-sweep canard for pitch control, was an attempt to market advanced technology, as was done with the Stagger-wing and Bonanza in their day. Certificated in 1988, the Starship flew 10 persons at 385 mph in the comfort of a 21-foot long pressurized cabin; equipped price was just over $4 million in 1991.

There are, and have been, many other Beechcrafts, but the only civilian aircraft known to Walter were the Staggerwing, V-tailed Bonanza, and the Model 18 Twin Beech that entered the market in 1937. Walter died in 1950, and Olive Ann, along with Frank Hedrick and other top management people who were there when Walter was, ran the company until after it became a subsidiary of the Raytheon Company in 1980.

Raytheon brought in its own management people and announced plans to market several new turboprop twins for the early 1990s, following certification of its radical all-composite Starship canard-equipped pusher on 14 June 1988.

## Cessna

When Walter rented space at Cessna in 1932, aircraft production had halted there. Three years earlier, Clyde had purchased 80 acres at Cessna's former main plant site on Pawnee Road, constructed five buildings, and had 80 employees. His products were the Cessna Model A series—clean, four-place cantilever monoplanes powered with a variety of engines—the most popular of which was the Model AW, fitted with a 125-hp Warner or 200-hp Wright Whirlwind. These Cessnas were Clyde's own designs, and were so basically sound that one can still see some Model AW in single-engine Cessnas today.

Beech Aircraft Corporation

Deliveries of the Beech 1900 regional airliner began in 1983. Seating 19 passengers, this pressurized turboprop cruised at 300 mph and has a range of 850 nautical miles. Shown is the larger 1900D, offering stand-up headroom, which replaced the basic 1900 in 1991.

By 1932, however, Clyde was nearing retirement age, and had he not given an airplane ride to this 12-year-old nephew, Dwane L. Wallace, in Clyde's new Laird Swallow back in 1923, the Cessna story would be somewhat different.

From that time forward, young Wallace knew that his future would be in aviation. He soloed an OX-5 Travel Air in 1932, and was graduated from Wichita State University in 1933 with a bachelor's degree in aeronautical engineering. Since Cessna was closed, Dwane worked briefly for Beech, then persuaded his uncle to reorganize the Cessna Aircraft Company and reopen the plant, producing a new four-place monoplane based on the Model A series. The resulting Cessna Airmaster kept the company alive for the next five years, an average of 30 per year finding buyers.

Clyde retired to his farm in 1936 (he died in 1954), and Dwane Wallace, at age 25, became president of the company, as well as the test pilot, engineer, and salesman.

Cessna's first twin-engine airplane, the T-50, was introduced in 1939, shortly before Hitler marched into Poland. Although intended for the civilian market (as an economy version of Beech's Model 18), the T-50 achieved a degree of success as a military trainer that Wallace had not envisioned. There was exactly $5.03 in the company's bank account when Canada bought 180 of these machines, and during WWII more than 5400 were built as the USAAF AT-8, and UC-78. Cessna called it the Bobcat, but to the cadets who transitioned to multi-engine airplanes in it, the Bobcat was irreverently known as the "Useless 78" or the "Bamboo Bomber."

Also during the war, Cessna (along with Beech, WACO, and other general aviation plane makers who had survived the depression) produced troop-carrying gliders and subassemblies for bombers and fighters.

When the war ended, Cessna again turned to the commercial airplane business, its first postwar models being the two-place 120 and 140, 4000 of which were built in 1946.

A total of 185 C-165 and C-145 Airmasters were built 1935–1941 inclusive.

The Cessna 190 and 195 were essentially all-metal versions of the prewar Airmasters, albeit with more power. The 190/195 appeared in 1947, and 1177 were produced, including 83 for the military, which were designated LC-126s.

Cessna broadened its market in 1947 with introduction of the five-place 190 and 195, essentially all-metal Airmasters with more horsepower. And the following year production was begun on the new four-place Cessna 170.

The Korean War claimed a large portion of Cessna's production capacity, turning out subassemblies for Boeing, Lockheed, and Republic, but in 1954, along with the T-37 jet trainer, the five-place twin-engine Model 310 was in-

troduced. The Models 172 and 182 came out in 1955, and then, when the two-place Model 150 was added in 1959, the foundations of the modern Cessna company were complete.

## Business flying

Meanwhile, the American businessman had begun to recognize that the airplane could be a valuable business tool, and as such was subject to the same kind of tax writeoff as other

The classic Cessna 120/140 series of two-place personal/trainers each sell for far more today in the used market than when new. Produced 1946–1950 inclusive, with 85 or 90 hp, these craft cruised at 105 mph on five gallons of fuel per hour.

The two-place Cessna 152 cruised at 120 mph with 108 hp.

business machines. By 1975, an estimated 40 percent of the general aviation fleet was used for business purposes, either full- or part-time, and with the exodus of factories to the Sun Belt from less gentle climes, company airplanes represented an everlarger percentage of the new civil aircraft sold each year.

That, along with the rapidly rising cost of flying, changed the look of general aviation. The demand for new single-engine airplanes steadily eroded, while the market for twin-engine airplanes and corporate jets remained strong. The lowest-priced single-engine craft suffered the greatest loss in sales during the early '80s, while the costliest twins suffered the least during that recession. Cessna 152 and 172 production lines were shut down in 1985 at a time when there was a backlog of orders for the Cessna Citation business jet.

Production of the single-engine Cessnas had been completely suspended by 1986, except for the turboprop Caravan, an ungainly freight-hauler. In November 1986, Cessna offered three versions of its successful Citation

Cessna Aircraft Company

The Cessna Skyhawk, the most successful lightplane ever produced; 33,629 were built before it went out of production in the mid-1980s. Basic list in 1983 was $48,940 with essential avionics. Engine is the 160-hp Lycoming O-320-D2J.

Cessna Aircraft Company

The Cessna Pressurized Centurion II cruised at 191 kts at 20,000 feet, and had a 660 nautical mile range. List price in 1983 was $207,000.

bizjet, two of its twin turboprop Conquest, and two models of the Caravan.

Cessna became a subsidiary of General Dynamics in 1985, at which time its boss was Russ Meyer, who moved into the top slot following Dwane Wallace's retirement.

The general aviation ("gen-av") airplane manufacturer increasingly looks to the businessman, who sees the airplane as a means of multiplying the effectiveness of key management and technical personnel, especially in corporations with scattered facilities. As an efficient compressor of time and distance, the airplane places a company's decision-makers on-the-scene in several places hundreds of miles apart in a single day and will still have them home that evening. The electronic age notwithstanding, it is apparent that the most crucial determinations often demand on-the-spot analysis by management. And in competitive markets, time is often the most important single factor to correct decisions, because management decisions are not a storable commodity, but are the products of informed intellects constantly faced with changing conditions, and who are most effective when eyeball-to-eyeball with the knottiest challenges.

Company-owned airplanes are seldom identifiable as such because management often suspects that stockholders doubt the true usefulness of such machines. Therefore, most corporate airplanes do not carry the company name or logo.

Nevertheless, scheduled airlines serve only five percent of the nation's 13,000 airports, and offer multiple, daily schedules, without plane-change service, to only a fraction of those. In other words, the scheduled airlines do not—and cannot—provide the on-demand air travel that thousands of corporations often need.

The economics of the situation are not hard to grasp. A middle-level executive paid $48,000 per year is earning $25 per hour. He/she is assumed to be worth twice that to the company, and therefore the company cannot afford to have such a person sitting in an airport terminal waiting for an airplane during the productive hours of a business day, or on the highway somewhere at 55 mph in a rented automobile enroute to a place not served (or with limited service) by a commercial air carrier. It is the on-demand, make-your-own-schedule flexibility of the company-owned airplane (or fleet of planes in some cases) that makes economic sense to corporations.

The corporate airplane offers other less tangible competitive advantages, including the progressive company image it projects to a company's customers. Imaginative executives may use it to gain the undivided attention of a client who has been difficult to see: "You're going to New York on Tuesday? As it happens, so am I. Why don't I stop by in our company airplane and pick you up? Our pilots will take you back to Booneyville whenever you are ready." It happens all the time, and a surprising amount of business is transacted in the posh cabins of the nation's corporate airplanes. And, yes, just as the office copier is sometimes switched on for personal use, so is the corporate airplane—and that fact won't surprise anyone, including the IRS.

The turbocharged Mooney TLS offers 256-mph cruise at 25,000 feet with a range of more than 1200 miles. Engine is the Lycoming TIO-540-AF1A of 270 hp.

Mooney Aircraft Corporation

The Cessna AgTruck, built from 1972 through 1983, had a 280-gallon hopper capacity; was powered by the Teledyne-Continental IO-520-D engine of 300 hp.

The manufacturers of corporate airplanes have long since learned how to sell their products. The corporate airplane salesman is well-educated, well-dressed, and low-key. He is backed by a top accountant or two, ready to sit down with the prospect's comptroller and investigate the dollars-and-cents reality of airplane ownership/operation as it would apply to that company's particular situation. Usually, cost-benefits projections will be prepared for several types of airplanes, with varying degrees of aircraft utilization rates cranked in. Since the fixed costs of airplane ownership (hangar, insurance, crew salaries, normal maintenance) are the same whether the airplane is flown or not, its cost per hour of operation goes down with increased utilization. The one thing the aircraft manufacturers have learned not to do is oversell in this market. There is no room for hype, and not every busi-

Cessna Crusader, built 1982–84, had turbocharged engines for cruising speeds above 250 mph between 10,000 and 20,000 feet. Single-engine service ceiling was 13,000 feet.

The Cierva Autogiro of 1929. Principal U.S. builders of these craft, which flew with free-turning rotors, were Pitcairn and Kellett. The fixed wing disappeared on later models before the appearance of the helicopter-ended autogiro/autogyro development.

ness can profitably employ an airplane. Some are best served with a pure jet, and some with a medium-sized twin, while at the bottom of the scale a ladies' hosiery salesman may profitably extend his territory with a single-engine Cessna.

## Helicopters

In recent years the corporate helicopter has begun to find buyers. In 1989, a look at the top 500 U.S. industrial firms as compiled by Fortune magazine reveals that 336 companies owned 1285 aircraft, and helicopters represented 11.9 percent of the total, or 153 corporate copters.

Actually, almost all helicopters work for a living, and they are spread throughout the business community. The central fact about the helicopter is that it is a unique machine, capable of performing tasks that no other machine possessed by man can do. It can fly backwards or sideways, straight up or straight down. It can hover motionless in the air while lifting all sorts of loads—including people—and it can operate from any reasonably level cleared space barely larger than the diameter of its rotors. Its place is secure in the modern world. Developed as a military vehicle, the helicopter is indispensable to a modern army, and in civilian dress daily transforms the impossible into the commonplace.

The concept of vertical flight, induced by rotating wings, was understood at the time of the Wrights, and a great many experimenters tried to build a controllable helicopter without significant success, until the Focke-Achgelis FA-61 at last flew in Germany in 1937.

The autogyro was developed in the meantime, initially by Juan de la Cierva in Spain, who first flew such a machine on 9 January 1923. The Cierva autogiro (the copyrighted spelling attendant to Cierva's patent; otherwise, "autogyro") was essentially a conven-

Igor Sikorsky at controls of the first successful U.S. helicopter, 14 September 1939.

tional airplane—fuselage, engine and propeller, tail, stubby low wing—to which was added freely rotating long and narrow wings mounted on a pylon above the fuselage. These wings, or rotors, were turned by the aircraft's forward motion, and were not connected to a power source. About 500 autogiros (and autogyros) were produced during the '30s, largely by Kellett and Pitcairn. (Harold Pitcairn disposed of his airline stock and the airplane manufacturing firm to concentrate on the marketing of autogiros. He later took his own life.)

In the United States, the first successful helicopter was designed by Igor Ivanovich Sikorsky, and first flew, with Sikorsky himself at the controls, on 14 September 1939.

Sikorsky was born in Kiev, Russia, 25 May 1889, and was educated at the Naval College in Petrograd (later, Leningrad, now St. Petersburg). He designed and built two helicopters in 1909-1910 that did not fly.

Between 1912 and 1918, Sikorsky worked as engineering manager for the Russian Baltic Car Factory and designed four-engine bombers for the Czar. He fled Russia during the Bolshevik Revolution and reached the United States in 1919. He founded Sikorsky Engineering Corporation on Long Island in 1923 and produced a series of amphibians and flying boats. His company became a subsidiary of United Aircraft in 1929, was merged with Chance Vought's company, another United acquisition, and was known as Vought-Sikorsky for a time. Later, it was simply the Sikorsky Division of United.

More than 400 of the R-4 through R-6 series Sikorsky helicopters were produced for the military during WWII. But those machines were the Curtiss Jennies of rotary-winged flight, and it was the Bell H-13 (Model 47), designed by Arthur Young and Bartram Kelly, that convincingly demonstrated the helicopter's great potential during the Korean War (M*A*S*H television show fans will be familiar with that machine).

During the '60s, another war would greatly advance helicopter technology, and the major U.S. manufacturers would be those who started early: Sikorsky, of course; Hiller, 1942, later merged with Autolite; Hughes, 1948, later part of McDonnell-Douglas; Bell, 1941, became a Textron company in 1960; Ka-

No, this is not a scene from a *M*A*S*H* television episode, but the real thing. A Bell H-13 lifts wounded in Korea, 23 July 1953.

man, 1945; and the original Piasecki company, 1945, which became the Vertol Aircraft Corporation in 1956, and the Vertol Division of Boeing in 1960. There were many others, most of which disappeared, while some still limp along on short rations.

The high-water mark for commercial helicopter production in the United States was 1980, when 1425 units were produced. Then the early '80s recession took its toll and only 637 helicopters were delivered to the civilian market in 1982, by which time the sale of fixed-wing aircraft was also markedly down.

There is almost no competition between the helicopter and the airplane; each does its own thing. Each is limited to a role that no other machine can do better or more efficiently. Our vehicles define their own spheres of service. Therefore, the helicopter will continue to earn its keep in the workaday world. Velvet seats won't alter its character.

## Minority group

There are about 850,000 licensed pilots in the U.S., although no more than 700,000 are considered active at this writing. By category, approximately 35 percent are student pilots (a slowly diminishing number during the '80s); 43 percent are private pilots; 14 percent hold a commercial rating; 5.6 percent are airline transport rated, and 4 percent are rated on helicopters. That will total more than 100 percent because some are rated on both fixed-wing and helicopters.

Women pilots constitute six percent of the total.

Twin-turbine Sikorsky S-64 demonstrates its potential as a heavy lifter.

The 30-passenger Sikorsky S-61 in service for Los Angeles Airways, a pioneer passenger helicopter operator that began operations 1 October 1947.

## Rutan Voyager

Most persons in general aviation first heard the name Rutan in 1974, when an odd-looking homebuilt airplane, constructed of foam and fiberglass, with its propeller in back and its tail in front, won the award for the Outstanding New Design at the EAA's Oshkosh Fly-In. This improbable machine was the creation of Elbert L. "Burt" Rutan, a 31-year-old pilot and aeronautical engineer on leave from the flight test section at Edwards AFB, California.

Burt sold plans for this airplane—the VariViggen, named for a Swedish fighter it vaguely resembled—set up shop on the high desert airport at nearby Mojave, California, and then designed a series of outstanding homebuilt aircraft with such names as VariEze ("very easy") and Long-EZ, all of which were of composite construction (foam, fiberglass, and epoxy), pusher configuration, and fitted with a horizontal lifting surface in front in addition to the main wing in back.

These were very efficient airplanes, and they were flown to a number of speed and distance records for machines in their class, mostly piloted by Burt's elder (by five years) brother, Dick Rutan, a much-decorated former air force fighter pilot, and Dick's "constant companion" at the time, petite Jeana Yeager, who was Dick's junior by 14 years. Jeana had several years' experience in design drafting and management with an aerospace firm before joining Dick at Mojave in 1980 to form a

The Rutan *Voyager*, flown around the world nonstop and unrefueled by Dick Rutan and Jeana Yeager between 14 December and 23 December 1986.

partnership, Voyager Aircraft, a loose-knit organization consisting largely of EAA-type volunteers, and allied with Burt's Rutan Aircraft Factory for the purpose of designing, building, financing (lots of donations from private individuals), and—finally—flying an airplane around the world ("around the fat part") nonstop and without refueling.

Meanwhile, in 1983, Burt formed another company, SCALED Composites, with Herb Iversen, to provide aerospace companies with a complete engineering, technical, and flight test staff to develop and test scaled-down, manned prototypes of new airplanes, a concept that promised to cut development costs,

while taking advantage of Burt's talent as a designer, and his experience with canard ("tail first") airplanes, as well as composite airframe construction. The Beechcraft Starship proof-of-concept vehicle was built and tested in 85 percent scale by SCALED Composites—whereupon Beech purchased SCALED Composites in 1985, and Burt became a Beech v.p. for a time, in his capacity as president of SCALED Composites. Beech subsequently sold the company back to Rutan, ending their relationship.

The *Voyager* was completed early in 1985. It had a span of 111 feet, weighed 1800 pounds empty, and was designed to hold approximately 1800 gallons of fuel, mostly in the two 30-foot "outrigger" fuselages. The two-place craft was constructed of quarter-inch-thick panels of Hexcel honeycomb, a resin-coated paper-like polymer, covered with graphite fibers embedded in epoxy, a construction system said to be one-fifth lighter but seven times stronger than aluminum. Burt designed *Voyager*'s wings with a high aspect ratio (long and narrow) and capable of flexing at the tips as much as 30 feet in either direction—a condition evident to the TV viewers who watched the historic takeoff from Edwards AFB. Fully loaded with fuel, *Voyager*'s gross weight was in the neighborhood of 11,000 pounds (gasoline weighs six pounds per gallon), and that allowed the wingtips to drag on the runway during the early part of the takeoff roll, grinding away as much as a foot of each. With this type of construction, that did not weaken the structure, but did add some drag.

Voyager was built behind locked doors, and after its inspiring flight many of its specifications and construction details were not immediately released. That may have been because Dick and Jeana reportedly owed some $300,000 for expenses directly related to the project, and wanted to pay off their creditors with, among other things, book and perhaps even movie rights to their story. They complicated their financing because they refused to endorse products they did not actually use, and never considered tobacco advertisements ("There'll be no narcotics in our airplane!").

Voyager had made more than 40 test flights by mid-1986 when Dick and Jeana combined the final, most realistic test with an assault on the closed course distance record. They established a new record by remaining aloft for 111 hours and 44 minutes—2:42 P.M. 10 July, to 5:15 P.M. 15 July—flying 20 laps around a 503.73-mile course off the coast of California.

If some Rutan-watchers had expected the *Voyager*'s round-the-world flight to be little noted in the press, they were surprised. By the time *Voyager* had crossed the Pacific during its second day after takeoff, much of the Free World was clearly enthralled with the brave venture, and Dick and Jeana had acquired a cheering section of millions.

They had taken off at 11:02 A.M. (EST) 14 December 1986. There were many anxious moments, including a series of storms over the South Pacific which forced a course deviation that took Voyager north of the Equator rather than the planned passage south of the Equator. Extreme turbulence was encountered when Dick flew blind into the edge of a nighttime thunderstorm over Africa, and a fuel shortage scare resulted from a faulty fuel transfer system. It was solved by Jeana, who rerouted some plumbing.

Voyager completed its 26,000-mile journey—nonstop and without refueling—at 11:06 A.M. (EST) 23 December at Edwards AFB, California, after nine days and four minutes in the air. A week later, Burt Rutan, Dick Rutan, and Jeana Yeager were awarded the Presidential Citizens Medal by President Reagan.

# Review questions

1. Why do you think private flying boomed and then busted in the immediate postwar period? What is the "Confederate Air Force"? How did air racing get started in the U.S. ?

2. What is the attraction for individuals to build their own aircraft? What are some of the pitfalls? Describe the purpose and role of the EAA.

3. Describe the FAA's position regarding Ultralights. Do you think it will change? Why?

4. How did William T. Piper, a successful oilman, at age 48 become involved with light aircraft? Why was the J-3 Cub so successful? List some of the successful aircraft which followed the Cub.

5. Describe some of the successful early aircraft produced by Beech Aircraft Corporation. Who took over the company upon Walter Beech's death in 1950?

6. Who was Dwane Wallace? How did he get started with Cessna Aircraft Company? What were some of the aircraft Cessna produced for the military during WWII? What were some of the postwar models?

7. Why do businesses use general aviation aircraft? What type of aircraft do they use? Describe some other uses of business aircraft. Who developed some of the early helicopters? What are civilian helicopters used for?

# 17

# Economic IFR

## Objectives

At the end of this chapter you should be able to:

- Discuss the development of the jet engine from the 1910 Coanda Jet.
- Explain why Boeing has held such a dominant position in jet aircraft development.
- Summarize the facts leading to the merger of McDonnell and Douglas.
- Highlight some of the problems and successes that Lockheed has experienced in recent years.
- Discuss some of the causes and effects of the airline deregulation of 1978, the air controllers' strike, the slot system, and flow control.
- Highlight the extraordinary career of William P. Lear and the development of the Learjet.

As the U.S. airline industry sought to become established on-course and pick its way through economically stormy skies in the uncertain 1980s, it was buffeted from all quadrants. The old automatic pilot of federal regulation had been disengaged and the industry was being hand-flown, IFR, into rapidly changing conditions.

Meanwhile, corporate airplanes proliferated, from light twins to Learjets, the latter having been so well conceived—and marketed—that company ownership of a Learjet had become synonymous with success, affluence, and progressive business practices.

## Jet aircraft engines

The appearance of the jet aircraft engine brought about the second great revolution in air transport. It was certain to come, although WWII hastened its arrival.

We cannot escape the fact that military spending has, from the outset, set the pace of aircraft development. The First World War advanced airframe design by as much as 20 years in the space of four years. During the early '20s, the U.S. Navy fostered development of the radial piston engine in America, which made possible the first practical airliners. Aircraft superchargers, controllable-pitch propellers, and the cylinder/valve designs featured on the Wasps and Whirlwinds were among the projects that came from the Air Service's research center at McCook Field between 1918 and 1926. The gas turbine or jet aircraft engine had a similar history.

The principle of jet propulsion had been understood at least since Isaac Newton postulated his laws of motion, and a jet airplane was

The Army Air service research center at McCook Field, Ohio, (now Wright-Patterson AFB) was experimenting with controllable and reversible-pitch propellers in 1922. This installation was on a DH-4.

displayed at the 1910 Paris Aircraft Show. But it was the prospect of war that at last forced development of the jet aircraft engine in the late '30s.

There are two major methods of classifying gas turbine engines: 1) by compressor type, and 2) by the way the power produced is used.

Compressor types fit into three categories:

- Centrifugal flow.
- Axial flow.
- Centrifugal-axial flow.

Power usage produces four categories:

- Turbojet.
- Turbofan.

- Turboprop.
- Turboshaft.

Secondary classifications include the path the air takes through the engine, the method of power extraction, and the number of spools in the engine.

The path the air takes through the engine refers mainly to the combustion section, and leads to such variations as:

- Straight-through flow.
- Reverse flow.
- Side-entry flow.

The method of power extraction refers to whether the engine has a single shaft for the

Aircraft supercharger development began at McCook Field in 1918. This 1931 installation was on a Curtiss P-6 fighter. Engine was a Curtiss D-12, a Prestone-cooled V-12 of 460 hp.

section where, mixed with fuel, it is ignited. The hot gasses are then expelled out the rear, flowing across the turbine blades, which, in turn, may drive accessories and/or turn a propeller, in addition to the compressor. If this energy is absorbed to turn a propeller, there isn't much left as jet thrust. Admittedly, this explanation is a tad simplified, but essentially, that is the way it works.

There are a lot of other considerations, including the desirability of controlling both the temperature and velocity of the exhausting gasses in the jet pipe to gain maximum efficiency. That is why the turbofan has evolved. Its turbine turns a ducted fan at the front of the engine that not only produces a lot of thrust of its own, but directs internal airflow around the engine to cool the exhaust, thus reducing exhaust velocity for greater efficiency and less noise. Bypass air is available in some engines for this purpose that do not employ the ducted fan, but the fan provides more thrust for the energy required to turn it than that energy will provide as jet exhaust thrust. Therefore, the turbofan, or fanjet, is more fuel-efficient than the pure turbojet.

## The 1910 Coanda Jet

The *Coanda Jet* was designed and built by Henri Coanda, a Rumanian, and although a biplane, it was a very clean machine, both wings being full-cantilever. The powerplant consist-

compressor, turbine, and load, or a free power (independent) turbine to drive the load. An engine may have one, two, or three independently rotating spools.

The centrifugal compressor works like the modern supercharger (or the pump that drains your flooded basement). It compresses air by spinning it off its circumference. The axial flow compressor is a large spool studded with vanes that pulls the air through in a straight line and compresses it.

In operation, the jet engine pulls air into its compressor and packs it into a combustion

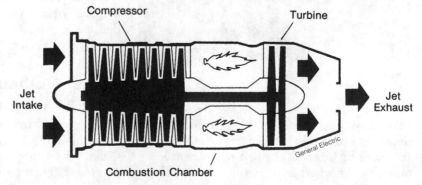

The Simple Turbojet . . . The Basic Engine of the Jet Age

How the gas turbine works.

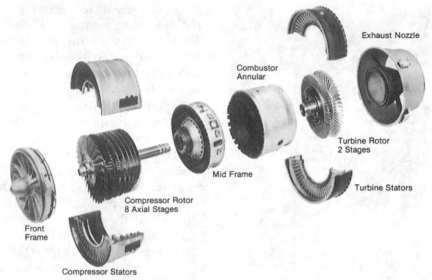

Basic parts of a turbojet aircraft engine, the CJ-610 which powers the Learjet Model 25, the Jet Commander Model 1121, and (as the military J-85) the Northrop T-38. General Electric

Pratt & Whitney turbojets

ed of a centrifugal compressor driven by a small gasoline engine. It had no propeller and depended on the velocity of its jet exhaust for propulsion. Coanda crashed this machine on takeoff, and whether or not it was capable of flight was never established. Coanda later worked on flying saucer designs in the United States.

## The Whittle engine

In England, 21-year-old Frank Whittle wrote an exam thesis on the possibility of gas turbine engines for airplanes in 1928. He took out his first patents on such an engine two years later, at about the time Hans von Ohain began similar research in Germany.

Whittle formed a company, Power Jets, Ltd., to develop his engine in 1936, but it was not until 1939, on the eve of WWII, that the British Government went knocking on Whittle's door, probably prompted by intelligence reports on the German's activity in that field.

## The von Ohain engine

The Germans were indeed busy. They had added a gas turbine engine division to Dr. Ernst Heinkel's airplane factory, and gave von Ohain the support he needed. Therefore, on 27 August 1939, near Rostock, the jet age was born—in secrecy—when the Heinkel He-178 jet airplane made its maiden flight.

## First U.S. jet engine

Almost two years later, on 25 May 1941, Britain's jet, the Gloster E-28/39, made its first flight from Cranwell, Lincolnshire, whereupon the chief of the USAAF, Gen. H.H. Arnold, managed to obtain a Whittle engine which he dispatched by air to General Electric in the United States with orders to study, reproduce, and improve upon it where possible. GE got the Whittle because: 1) They had been producing turbines for electric generating plants for 40 years, and because 2) GE's Dr. Sanford

Moss had been working on aircraft supercharger development at McCook and Wright Fields for 20 years.

GE's copy of the Whittle developed 1250 pounds of thrust, and a pair of them went into America's first jet airplane, the Bell P-59, which was first flown 1 October 1942.

Meanwhile, Secondo Campini in Italy reinvented the Coanda. His Campini-Caproni N-1 was fitted with a 900-hp piston engine driving a three-stage compressor, its single shaft turning a ducted fan in the plane's nose. The N-1 flew in August 1940, but its cruising speed of 140 mph was disappointing.

Since GE had American rights to the Whittle, Pratt & Whitney made a deal with Rolls-

P&W Aircraft

Pratt & Whitney fanjet, or turbofan

Royce, which was producing the Nene, an engine based on the Whittle, although of greater power. Concurrently, Andy Wilgoos at P&W began development of an axial flow type engine. The Whittle, it should be noted, was of the centrifugal compressor type.

At the end of WWII, a number of German Me-262 jet fighters fell into Allied hands, and their Jumo jet engines were available for study, bringing all U.S. enginemen abreast of the state of the art. Subsequent U.S. gas turbine engines depended upon American know-how for the direction and quality of their development.

# Boeing

It would appear that Boeing developed the first U.S. jet airliner on faith alone, because the first Model 707 was rolled out of the Seattle factory on 14 May 1954, but none were sold until 13 October 1955, when Pan Am ordered six 707-120s.

If that were the whole story, then Boeing did indeed take a large gamble. However, the 707 gave its airframe to the air force's KC-135 tanker, ordered in August 1954, and the KC-135 was a shoo-in because it was needed to refuel the B-52 in flight, and the B-52 had entered production in April 1953—about the time the first metal was cut for the first 707.

Gamble or not, Boeing was a year ahead of the next American-designed jet airliner to appear, the Douglas DC-8. Convair was close behind with their Model 880, the first of which entered service with Delta and TWA in January 1960. Lockheed did not penetrate this big-bucks market until the early '70s with their L-1011 TriStar.

Boeing clearly dominated the jet airline market, world-wide, for 20 years after the first

USAF

The KC-135 Air Force tanker and the Boeing 707 were developed simultaneously around the same basic airframe. The 707 prototype was completed in May 1954; the USAF ordered the KC-135 in October 1954, and Pan Am ordered the first 707 a year later.

707 was put in service on Pan Am's New York-London route on 26 October 1958.

Several factors contributed to Boeing's strong position. The 707 and its spinoff, the 720 (which began flying with United in July 1960), were offered in a number of sizes, configurations, and with a choice of engines that fitted those machines for a high percentage of both domestic and transoceanic routes. Well-engineered and relatively troublefree, these Boeings were built concurrently with B-52s and KC-135s and surely benefitted from the unusual amount of wind tunnel research (8000 hours for the B-52 wing alone) and in-flight testing accorded the military machines, including that of the earlier B-47 medium-range jet bomber. With plenty of money coming in from military contracts to keep the Boeing Seattle and Boeing Wichita plants busy, the Boeing Commercial Airplane Division was assured of all the support it needed.

Boeing did have a serious challenge from the Douglas DC-8, DC-9, and DC-10 during those years. Douglas, after all, had dominated the airline market from the time the DC-3 went into service in 1935.

# Douglas

The DC-3: There can never be another like it. No other single airplane can ever so completely represent air travel. At one time, 95 percent of all commercial air traffic was carried in DC-3s. Almost 11,000 were built (most of them as C-47s, C-49s, and C-53s for Army Air Forces during WWII), and their trial by fire generated countless reports that bordered on the unbelievable. One was dived to its terminal velocity; it shed its wingtips, but landed safely. Designed for 21 passengers, a C-47 once carried 74 refugees out of Burma. When a strafing Japanese fighter severely damaged one wing of a CNAC DC-3, a wing from a DC-2—markedly shorter—was substituted. It flew, although it was the only DC-2½ on record. As late as 1970, DC-3s (mostly refurbished C-47s) were still in service with almost 200 airlines around the globe, and one, retired by North Central Air Lines in 1968, had 52,000 hours on its airframe. In 11 million miles it had worn out 136 engines and 550 tires. It was once again refurbished and put back in service as a corporate airplane. It was registered as N21728,

Pan Am

The venerable Douglas DC-3, C-47, C-49, C-53, Gooney Bird, Spooky, Skytrain (officially), R4D, Dakota—she had many names, all spoken with affection. She had but one gait; she was noisy; her wingtips flapped, and her cockpit leaked, but she'd get you there.

The Douglas DC-4 was ordered by American, Eastern, and United in 1939, but by the time the prototype was developed, and its triple tail redesigned into a single unit, the U.S. was at war. More than a thousand were built during the war as C-54s and R5Ds (navy). After WWII, many entered airline service.

and it would not surprise us to learn that ol' 728 is still out there somewhere, still flying. The DC-4, DC-6, and DC-7 four-engine airliners that followed during the '40s and early '50s took much from the fabled DC-3.

These were the airplanes that built the Douglas Aircraft Company, a company started in 1920 by Donald Wills Douglas when he rented office space in the rear of a Santa Monica barbershop, possessing an order for one airplane. Douglas, the son of a Brooklyn bank cashier, had a B.S. degree in aeronautics from M.I.T., three years with Glenn Martin, and $600 in capital.

Douglas sold 50 torpedo planes to the navy during the next three years, and built the army's four World Cruisers for their 1924 round-the-world flight. By 1926, he had a payroll of 112 and an order for six M-2 mailplanes from Western Air Express.

Douglas delivered similar machines to National Air Transport and obtained a small but steady series of orders from the Army Air Corps for observation planes. Then, on 2 August 1932, Douglas decided to go for broke when he learned that TWA intended to buy "ten or more all-metal, trimotor transport airplanes." The Douglas DC-1, which flew on 1

The first Douglas DC-9s went to work for Delta in November 1965. The DC-9 deserved a larger share of the market than it got, because the airlines were rushing to order larger airplanes than most of them needed.

July 1933, was the result, and Douglas was in the airliner business.

Douglas was financially sound through the early '50s, but the transition to jet transports was painful. Boeing had beat Douglas into the market, and Boeing outsold DC-8s two to one. The short-haul Douglas DC-9, which began service with Delta in 1969, helped some, but again, while Douglas was selling 600 DC-9s through 1970, Boeing sold almost 900 727s, and had introduced the smaller 737 to further erode the DC-9 market.

## McDonnell

Douglas ended 1966 with a net loss of $27.6 million, and that attracted the attention of James S. McDonnell of the McDonnell Aircraft Corporation. McDonnell was fat with military and space contracts, could use a tax break the size of Douglas' deficit, and liked the idea of penetrating the airliner market with an old hand like Douglas.

Exactly how McDonnell and Douglas got together is not a matter of public record, but they did, and the shareholders of McDonnell and the shareholders of Douglas then voted to love, honor, and share one another's dividends, and the two companies were officially united on 28 April 1967 to become the McDonnell-Douglas Corporation.

It isn't possible to end such an account with, "and they lived happily ever after," because recurring cycles of boom and bust have plagued the aviation industry from the beginning.

## Lockheed

Some of the bust has been traceable to management errors, some to general economic conditions, and some to the fluctuating level of military spending. Braniff's problems in the early '80s, and Lockheed's a decade earlier, are examples of the first. In 1970, Lockheed enjoyed total sales in excess of $2 billion and had a backlog exceeding $5 billion, but less than two years later the federal government was forced to guarantee large cash loans to Lockheed to keep it afloat.

Lockheed's problems seem to have stemmed from the huge development costs of the L-1011 TriStar airliner, including a costly delay incurred by the bankruptcy of the L-1011's engine supplier, Rolls-Royce, compounded by the practice—not unknown to other aerospace companies—of underpricing military

McDonnell-Douglas Corporation

The first DC-10s went to United and American in July 1971 as 206 and 222-passenger versions; it was later approved for as many as 380 passengers. McDonnell-Douglas was too late into a dwindling market that it had to share with the Lockheed TriStar.

Allan (right) and Malcolm Loughhead in their 1918 F-1 Twin Hydroplane. The brothers changed their name to Lockheed, and in 1926, returned to plane building with the Northrop-designed Lockheed Vega.

Pilot Bob Cantwell and an early Lockheed Vega fitted with a Wright J-5 Whirlwind engine of 200 hp.

Walter Varney operated Lockheed Orions between San Francisco and Los Angeles in 1931. The Orions were among the first commercial airplanes to possess retractable landing gear. Varney, then into the second of his several airlines, was also to put up half of the $40,000 needed to buy the bankrupt Lockheed company in 1932.

projects and then renegotiating payment later as the "cost overruns" became obvious. With half of its business represented by military orders, and many of them simultaneously in renegotiation (the giant C-5A transport, originally priced at $28 million, ended up costing the air force $55 million each), Lockheed ran out of cash. The company blamed inflation and other factors, but whatever the causes, Lockheed's predicament had to be charged to bad decisions by management. That was underscored in 1976, when Lockheed's business practices were found to be less-than-honorable after former sales executive E.F. Hauser revealed payoffs to foreign government officials for doing business with Lockheed. That forced the resignations of several top Lockheed people, including board chairman Daniel J. Haughton, and substantially shook up the governments in Japan, Italy, and West Germany.

By 1978 Lockheed had been "regenerated"

(Lockheed's term); sales exceeded $3 billion, with a backlog of more than $4 billion, and Lockheed stock was up to 16¾ from 7¼ a year earlier.

Nevertheless, the L-1011 was clearly in trouble. Only 149 had been delivered by the end of 1977. Lockheed would announce the end of TriStar production in 1982, having lost $2.5 billion dollars on the program since 1968. The sad part is that the L-1011 TriStar is an excellent airplane, quieter and less expensive to operate than comparable machines—until Boeing brought out its new 757 and 767 in 1982.

Lockheed takes its name from the Lockheed brothers (originally, "Loughead"), Allan and Malcolm, a pair of automobile mechanics from Niles, California, who were in their late twenties when they entered the airplane manufacturing business in 1916 offering, of all things, a 10-place flying boat. They struggled through WWI with a two-plane order from the navy, then quietly went out of business in 1920 after their tiny, single-place sportplane found no buyers.

Allan sold real estate, and Malcolm worked on a hydraulic brake system for automobiles (later sold to Chrysler), while their youthful chief engineer, John K. Northrop, went to work for Donald Douglas, who was trying to build airplanes in Santa Monica.

The success of Malcolm's invention, and the close friendship that continued between Allan and Jack Northrop, brought the three of them together again, and, in December 1926, with additional financing from ceramics manufacturer Fred Keeler, and Northrop's drawings of the airplanes that would become known as the Vega and Air Express, the Lockheed Aircraft Company was formed. An early employee was Jerry Vultee.

The Lockheed airplanes of this period featured full cantilever wings and molded-shell fuselages. The unusual monocoque fuselage was made by lining the inside of a concrete mold with multiple strips of spruce plywood coated with casien glue. An inflated rubber

bag forced the shell against the mold until the glue set. Then the shell, made in two halves, was mated, and a series of spruce rings added inside for extra strength. This process resulted in a very strong yet lightweight structure possessing an exceptionally smooth outer surface. It made for an efficient and aerodynamically clean airplane.

A total of 196 wooden Lockheeds—Vegas, Orions, Altairs, etc.—were produced before the brothers sold out to a Detroit group in 1929. The new owners switched to metal aircraft, but were sunk by the depression and allowed the company to slide into receivership in 1932.

At that point, investment banker Robert E. Gross, who had previously backed Lloyd Stearman in Wichita, brought together some other optimists, and together they purchased Lockheed's assets for $40,000. This group included Walter Varney, Lloyd Stearman, Thomas F. Ryan III (of Mid-Continent Air Lines), broker E.C. Walker, and Mr. & Mrs. Cyril Chappellet. Engineer Hall Hibbard, who had worked for Stearman after earning a degree at M.I.T., was also brought in by Gross. Hibbard, in turn, brought in Clarence "Kelly" Johnson, and this

This static-test version of the TriStar, girded with 300 load frames which, when attached to hydraulic jacks, received the equivalent of 15 years of hard service in less than two years of torture testing—one reason that development costs are so high for such aircraft.

pair would be primarily responsible for a long line of highly successful Lockheeds, beginning with the Model 10 Electra in 1934 and the P-38 Lightning in 1937. Robert Gross was succeeded by his younger brother, Courtlandt Gross, as chief executive officer at Lockheed and held that post until Dan Haughton became board chairman in 1967. The TriStar program was initiated the following year.

Whether or not McDonnell-Douglas follows Lockheed out of the airliner market, Boeing confronted a tough market by 1983. Since the beginning of the jet age, only the 707 and 727 series had proven profitable, and the market was changing with deregulation of the air carriers. The 211-passenger 767 and the 186-passenger 757 should do well (market surveys indicated a 2500–3000 plane market for a 150–175 passenger airliner if the airlines could afford to buy them), but Boeing faced substantial competition from Airbus Industrie, a consortium organized and funded by the governments of Britain, France, and West Germany. Airbus Industries 200–300 passenger jets found more than 300 buyers in Europe during the '70s, and had penetrated the United States market with 26 machines delivered to Eastern Air Lines by January of 1983.

Boeing's main concern, however, was the confusion and uncertainties that marked the airline scene of the early '80s. Once it had been overregulation. Now, deregulation.

# FAA Act of 1958

The CAA was restructured and renamed in 1958. The Federal Aviation Act of that year gave American aviation's governing body agency status, while the separate Civil Aeronautics Board (CAB) continued to rule the airlines. But then Lyndon Johnson reduced the Federal Aviation Agency to an "administration" and stuffed it into his new Department of Transportation (DOT) on 1 April 1967.

Lockheed California Company

The extended-range TriStar L-10ll-100 was delivered to Saudi Arabian Airlines in June 1975. Hong Kong-based Cathay Pacific Airways also received dash-100s in 1975.

Wide-body jets might pack a lot of bodies in their wide cabins, but many air travelers are less enthusiastic about this dense-pack concept than are the operators.

The effects of that were felt more in Washington than out in the real world where airplanes fly, and the CAB's five-member board continued to hold almost as much power as that which was once concentrated in the office of Postmaster General Walter F. Brown. Then, with deregulation of the airlines in 1978, the

CAB was expected to slowly fade away, whatever residual duties and authority it had left being transferred to the Federal Aviation Administration no later than 1 January 1985. After that, the Federal Trade Commission could handle such things as unfair trade practices among the airlines.

## Deregulation

At the beginning of 1983, the airline situation in America bordered on the chaotic. A number of factors contributed: the lingering effects of a recession and high fuel costs, deregulation, and, in some cases, bad guesses on the part of management. Most of those would be lessened within a year except, perhaps, that of deregulation. The unique nature of the airline business strongly suggests that the public interest (and that of the airlines) is best served with sensible regulation of routes and rates.

The free-for-all that developed following deregulation attracted hundreds of potential airline operators, all of them small, and most of which had reason for optimism because the

LTU German Airlines had its TriStars specially fitted with a downstairs lounge (normally cargo space) to make transatlantic flying a bit more comfortable for 16 extra-fare passengers. Upstairs, 300 others are seated nine abreast, each with 34 inches of legroom.

Federal Aviation Administration (FAA) was still subsidizing local service airlines. Also, the FAA had the authority to guarantee loans to such air carriers if the FAA believed their organization to be sound and their proposed routes "essential."

As a result, there were more than 250 commuter airlines in operation in the United States by 1983, and more than 100 additional route applications pending.

Under the Airline Deregulation Act of 1978 the CAB was supposed to liquidate itself as soon as practicable, October 1983 being a target date, and whatever residual duties were left to it would then devolve to the FAA. When that happened there would, presumably, no longer be any restrictions on who could start an airline, or where, or the rates to be charged. Meanwhile, the CAB's only remaining function of significance was the authority to pass upon the "fitness" of a new commuter line, and that caused a lot of confusion. Airline management, big and small, found long-range planning next to impossible.

Lest the plight of the major airlines tugs too strongly at our heartstrings, we should note that they brought much of their trouble upon themselves. From the time that the big jets became available in the late '50s, they recognized that profits lay in the long haul routes, in getting up high and going long distances with as many seats per engine as possible. Landings and takeoffs are expensive, primarily because of the jet engine's voracious appetites for fuel at low altitudes. Domestically, the big air carriers wanted to fly only between about two dozen of the country's largest airports that accounted for as much as 80 percent of all airline boardings.

That left the smaller cities to the so-called "second level" or "regional" air carriers who flew smaller airliners—usually piston-engine craft or propjets in the 50-passenger class—that fed as much as 30 percent of their passengers to the big trunk lines at the super terminals.

That worked reasonably well during the '60s, but the regionals were not satisfied and also looked to greater efficiency in their operations (as opposed to public service). They, too, wanted to abandon stops that cost more to service than boardings justified, particularly as the CAB pushed to lower and/or eliminate subsidies.

That led to the CAB's "Use It or Lose It" order given to smaller cities, which meant that, if those communities could not provide a minimum number of boardings, the CAB would allow the air carriers to abandon those stops. And that opened the door to the "third level" or "commuter" airline, which could place in operation 15-to-30 passenger aircraft that could, with a little subsidy, profitably serve those limited-population centers.

The commuters, however, operating aircraft tailored to their needs, not only served the smaller communities the regionals did not want on their routes, but also, on their way to hub airports, stopped along the way to take hefty chunks of the regional carriers' business. And as the commuters proliferated, the regionals began to disappear, for the most part either expanding or merging into major systems.

Another reason that modern airplanes are costly in development—the wind tunnel at Lockheed's Georgia facility.

Lockheed engineers once envisioned a new type of thin-bladed propeller on a wide-body propjet of the future, which will be quieter and more fuel-efficient than jets. Should get about 15 seats abreast in that one.

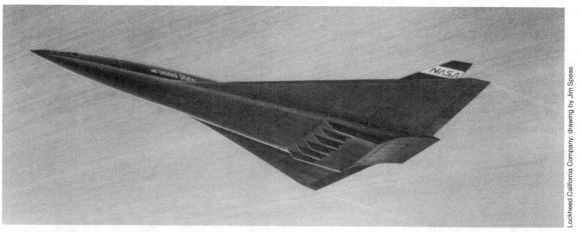

A Lockheed design concept contracted by NASA resulted in the predicted machine that President Reagan called the "Orient Express," a 4000-mph, 200-passenger airliner capable of flying from Los Angeles to Tokyo in two hours, 18 minutes. Turbojets would be used for landing and takeoff, while scramjets, fueled by liquid hydrogen, would boost the craft to hypersonic speeds.

The 40-seat Convair 240 entered production late in 1947 and was fitted with P&W R-2800 engines. The stretched 340 followed in 1951, then the 440 with more horsepower. Conversion of 340/440s to propjets began in the late '50s and produced the 540, 580, 600 and 640, depending upon engine installation; the 580, with Allisons, perhaps being the most numerous. Many remained in service into the early '80s.

A total of 103 Martin 404 pressurized, 40-passenger airliners were built, beginning in 1949, following an in-flight structural failure in the wing of the earlier Martin 202.

Therefore, as the airline industry entered the uncertain '80s, the domestic system consisted of the major airlines, flying between the big hub airports, and the commuters, flying from small towns and cities—from just about everywhere in the boonies—to eventually end up at the hub airports.

The future of this industry, even the immediate future, is difficult to predict as this is written, partly because of the several unusual factors (recession, controllers' strike, etc.) that have intruded into the airline picture since Teddy Kennedy pushed the Airline Deregulation Act through the Congress in 1978. Airline executives see everything from total collapse to a bright new day, although the optimists are almost exclusively commuter executives.

Departing from Baer Field at Fort Wayne, Indiana, Hub Airlines flew to Chicago and Cleveland in these 10-seat Beech Queen Airs.

One factor in this uncertainty is the outdated air traffic control system. Like Topsy, it just grew and now faces the fact that so much air traffic is funneled through less than 30 hub air terminals, and the very inconvenient fact that most air passengers want to fly at the same time. Even the most experienced and able air controllers can safely handle no more than 50 landings and takeoffs per hour per runway in good weather. The big jets cannot be spaced any closer than that. Crank into the system any of several common weather problems in the terminal vicinity, and aircraft movements are markedly slowed. That is why private airplanes are unwelcome at some major airports, especially during peak traffic

hours. That was also the reason for inauguration of the "slot" system at major airports following the air traffic controllers' illegal strike and subsequent firing in September 1981.

## Air controllers strike

Air controllers who were members of the Professional Air Traffic Controllers Organization (PATCO) decided, during the second week in August 1981, to strike. More than 12,000 walked off their jobs, demanding, among other things, $10,000 across-the-board pay increases, a shorter work-week, earlier retirement, and more respect from their superiors. They were averaging $33,000 per year (up to $50,000 after seven years on the job), about 25 hours per week, if overstressed could retire in five years at 40 percent of their pay—and were about to forfeit much of whatever respect they could claim.

The controllers struck in violation of federal law after rejecting Secretary of Transportation Drew Lewis's offer of a 34 percent pay increase over a three-year period. They were confident that the U.S. air transportation system could not function without them, and remained unmoved after President Reagan told them to return to work within 48 hours or be fired.

As unbelievable as it may sound as we review the facts, the PATCO controllers defied the president. He fired them all.

Commuter Air magazine

"That was a tasty morsel. Who's next?"

Secretary of Transportation Lewis asked FAA Administrator J. Lynn Helms to petition the Pentagon for 500 military air traffic controllers; they were added to the 2000 or so non-striking controllers and supervisory personnel, and this force, filled out with some furloughed airline pilots and recently retired controllers, manned the 23 Air Route Traffic Control Centers and the control towers at the hub airports, leaving towers in small cities unmanned or operating a limited number of hours each day.

At the end of a week, the system was functioning at about 65 percent of its normal capacity, and it was evident that the system had been padded by at least 3000 controllers when more than 12,000 had been on the payroll. It was also clear that many of the towers at small airports were not needed except, perhaps, for the training of neophite controllers.

Meanwhile, the FAA training center in Oklahoma City began sorting through a flood of applications, and accelerated its Air Traffic Control training program to replace as many of the discharged controllers as required. The FAA expected that, while it could fully staff, with new people, the nation's control towers and air route control centers by the spring of 1983, the system would operate at a slower pace for a couple of years after that because the newly trained controllers would attain efficiency only through experience.

By the spring of 1983, the slowdown was hardly apparent. The system was operating at somewhere between 90 and 98 percent of its pre-strike level (depending upon whose figures one accepted), and there had been no accidents traceable to an air controller's error, safety having been given priority over schedules and all else from the start.

During the first days immediately following the controller walkout, air traffic was curtailed as much as 50 percent, but some of that "loss" was actually beneficial to the major air carriers because it represented their cutback of profit-draining over-scheduling and abandonment of unprofitable routes. For years, the big

Beechcraft 99 Airliner was a 17-place propjet commuterliner. P&W PT-6A engines provided a top speed of 250 mph.

lines had chosen to fly half-empty airplanes on closely spaced schedules from the major terminals rather than risk the loss of a few passengers to a competing airline. That practice had been a convenience for the traveling public, but it greatly contributed to congestion at the hub airports during peak traffic hours.

It was private aviation that bore most of the post-strike restrictions, particularly, private pilots attempting to fly across country under instrument flight rules (IFR). Such a flight plan actually became an application for a reservation in the airspace, and was supposed to be submitted 12 hours in advance. Some were granted; some were not. A number of resourceful private pilots told the Flight Service Stations that they were air taxis in order to obtain clearances, but the FAA soon noticed the air taxi boom and uncovered the deceptions.

## Slot system

Each scheduled airline was assigned a given number of "slots" at the major air terminals.

For example, Braniff was given 12 slots per day at Oklahoma City's Will Rogers World Airport, meaning that Braniff could schedule 12 flights daily through that terminal. The slot system became unpopular due to the manner in which the CAB chose to administer it. It could have been used to protect the pioneering equities of the established carriers as deregulation tossed the entire system up for grabs, but instead, the CAB, headed by Marvin S. Cohen, took slots away from the major air carriers and gave them to new commuters. Eventually, after evidence surfaced of speculation with slots awarded to new commuters, the slots were more or less frozen, although some became available when a few of the newcomers, or an established line such as Braniff, folded. When Braniff ceased operations in May 1982, its slots were redistributed by lottery.

President Reagan's dismissal of the 12,000 PATCO controllers was applauded by a majority of the American people (according to a Newsweek magazine poll), certainly by most pilots, both private and commercial. Those of us accustomed to the bored, irreducible directions from air controllers were pleased to find ourselves suddenly dealing with professionals in the air route centers and towers who not only bent over backward to safely accommodate us, but were cheerful about it. That had its effect, because pilots are human, and just as suddenly began bending over backward in an effort to cooperate with those nice guys on the ground. The system may have been a tad slower, but it was also a lot more pleasant to use.

## Flow control

By mid-1983, the air traffic control system was operating about as normally as its equipment and the terminal facilities would allow, except FAA Administrator Helms decreed that the "flow control" of airliners be phased out at a measured pace. Flow control was first imposed in July 1968, when a weather inversion blanketed the busy Northeast with a stagnant ocean of smog that extended from Boston to Cape Hatteras, reducing visibility to 2½ miles all the way up to 10,000 feet!

All aircraft operating in that area were IFR, and that condition alone would have markedly slowed operations from the hub airports in that part of the country. But the air controllers added to the problem with a slowdown of their own. Unable to strike, they chose to space aircraft movements further apart as a "safety" measure. It was an effective tactic; airline traffic into the New York area was intolerably stacked up in holding patterns until FAA officials stepped in to hold on the ground, at their points of origin, all air traffic bound for the affected area. Those airliners waiting in Chicago, Miami, Los Angeles, etc., were then cleared for takeoff in dribbles as it became possible for them to land at their destinations.

That was flow control. And it was put in practice after the PATCO people went out on strike in August 1981, partly as a measure to save fuel, and partly because newly trained air controllers needed experience in stacking airliners temporarily when weather conditions forced delays. In February 1983, Helms said that flow control would be phased out slowly.

## Fare wars

Meanwhile, throughout the early '80s all the major airlines lost money, while most of the commuters possessed marginal balance sheets (the more successful commuters were calling themselves "regional" airlines by that time). Total airline profits plummeted from $1.3 billion in 1978, when deregulation began, to $199 million in 1979, and continued sharply downward to a loss of $550 million in 1982. The $99 coast-to-coast fare became common by late 1982, offered in desperation by major air carriers in need of instant cash. Everyone in the industry agreed that such fares were suicidal—no airline could stay in business forever flying passengers for 2½ cents per seat-mile while costs went as high as 10 cents per seat-mile—but the stronger lines could very well kill off some of the weaker ones that way, and thereby expect to later fill their own empty seats.

Investors seemed to agree. Pan Am, TWA (Trans World, after WWII; formerly, Transcontinental & Western Air), and United had no trouble marketing new stock issues early in 1983, and all airline stocks were up more than 60 percent during the fall and winter of 1982–83. That, of course, coincided with the overall advances in stock prices during that period as investors in general sent the Dow-Jones industrial averages to record highs, apparently because Wall Street was convinced that the recession had bottomed out and that good times where ahead.

The worldwide oil glut that developed during that period undoubtedly had its effect. Jet fuel was down to 95 cents per gallon early in 1983 and was expected to go lower. It had cost $1.02 a year earlier. Since fuel accounts for one-third of the airlines' operating costs, a 7 cents per gallon drop in the price of fuel meant an annual savings of $500 million. Also, in 1982, the biggest airlines trimmed costs by negotiating wage freezes or cuts, and thinned out their work forces. Since labor costs represent another third of the airlines' total expenses, that, too, was significant—although it was gained at the price of poorer union relations in some cases.

No one expected the industry to completely collapse, but the economic dogfights resulting from deregulation seemed certain to leave the survivors bidding for passengers on the basis of minimum air fares alone. The day of truly "no frills" air travel had arrived, echoing the Scrooge-like operating practices of the Ludington Lines in the 1930s.

## Survival of the richest

By mid-1986, it was not hard to predict the ultimate effects of deregulation on the U.S. airline industry. Two or three super carriers would have it all by the end of the decade. These would be United, American, and Delta with Northwest holding on to a financially shaky fourth position.

Far out? Not if you consider that 1) United bought Pan Am's lucrative Pacific routes—for $750 million—in April 1985 (Pan Am had previously sold its Manhattan headquarters and International Hotel chain); 2) TWA, then on the edge of bankruptcy which occurred later, hoped to buy its way to solvency by acquiring Ozark Air Lines for $225 million, and 3) Texas Air, which had already digested Continental and New York Air, had recently paid $600 million for Eastern Air Lines, and gobbled up Frontier Air Lines and People Express (People Express had given $305 million for Frontier just eight months earlier).

People Express epitomized the spirit and intent of airline deregulation—haul as many people as possible as cheaply as possible—and for a time it seemed to work very well. A 40 year-old entrepreneur by the name of Donald Burr started People Express with three airplanes, and in five years was operating 116 jets to more than 100 cities in North America, plus an Atlantic route. PE had become America's fifth-largest air carrier, with revenues exceeding $1 billion in 1985. Nonunion Peoples was operating for 5¼ cents per seat-mile, against an industry average of nearly 8 cents per seat-mile, which was a significant factor in People's low fares; but profits did not keep pace with revenues, the competition began meeting Burr's low fares at key terminals, and People Express became a money-loser in 1986. True, almost all other major air carriers were also losing money because of the cut-rate fares, but airlines like United and American, with deeper pockets, were much better prepared to ride out the rough weather. Industry observers expected People Express to merge or die, as it did when taken over by Texas Air.

## TEFRA

In 1982, the Tax Equity and Fiscal Responsibility Act (TEFRA) struck another blow at the already beleaguered private pilot by allowing the Reagan Administration to increase the federal tax on aviation fuel used for noncommercial purposes from 4 cents per gallon to 12 cents per gallon. A tax of 14 cents per gallon was slapped on noncommercial jet fuel as well. The rationale was that those who use the public airports and the airways system should be the ones who pay for them. It sounds fair, but it is not. The big airports, the air navigation aids, and the air traffic control system were primarily designed for the benefit of the scheduled air carriers. The private pilots could get along with a lot less. The general aviation fleet does not need runways two feet thick and 8000 feet long. Most of the electronic navaids are of no use to VFR pilots, who represent four out of 10 of the nation's licensed airmen.

But the system and all air regulations have, historically, favored the scheduled airlines, both in the letter of the law and in practice, and the reason given for that has always been that the government must favor that kind of air travel which serves the "greater good," and that presupposes that, since the scheduled

The ever-increasing cost of private flying resulted in a marked downturn in such activity by 1980. A steady decrease in the number of student pilot licenses continued through the 1980s.

air carriers transport more people inter-city than do private and business airplanes, the airlines serve the greater good.

## Bill Lear

William P. Lear, Sr., opened the bizjet market back in the mid-'60s, when he was almost the only person around who believed that such a market existed.

Bill Lear came from a tenement district on Chicago's south side. His parents had separated when Bill was six. He spent a lot of time in the streets, dropped out of school after the eighth grade, and quietly left home, such as it was, at age 16. That was in 1918. Bill went from job to job, and his lifelong affair with airplanes began when he worked as a flunky at Chicago's Grant Park Airport, where Matty Laird, the Stinsons, and other well-known pilots of that time were often seen. Bill moved on to other jobs, tinkered with wireless sets, was an apprentice automobile mechanic and, in 1922, opened a shop in Quincy, Illinois, to repair the recently developed home radio sets.

Bill miniaturized coils and worked out other improvements on those primitive sets that soon had him working for Motorola at an excellent salary.

By 1931, Lear had learned to fly, bought a WACO cabin biplane, and toured the U.S. demonstrating his new aircraft radio receiver. The Lear Radioaire worked well, but few pilots of that era could see much use for it.

Broke again in 1934, Lear returned to his workbench and designed a component for home radios that he called a "Magic Brain." RCA paid him a quarter-million dollars for it.

Bill's next project was the Lear Radio Compass for airplanes (called an automatic direction finder—ADF—today). A 35-watt transceiver followed, and then the Learmatic Omninavigator, the latter being identical in principle to present-day OMNIs, except that it was necessarily low frequency. Lear expanded into the electromechanical field during WWII and, during the late '40s, developed a three-axis autopilot so advanced that it brought him the Collier Trophy (civil aviation's highest award), presented by President Truman in 1950.

So it was that by 1959 Bill Lear headed a company that grossed $100 million per year. He was a rich man and could have retired to a less stressful life. He never considered it. "I'd rather wear out than rust out," he explained. Besides, Bill had a great new idea, the Learjet airplane.

But it was an idea that frightened his board of directors, and they wanted no part of it. Bill's vision of a six-place executive jet was, at the time, a bit startling. Who in the blue-eyed world would buy such an airplane? It would have to be priced at close to a million dollars, and U.S. corporations weren't exactly lining up to purchase the piston-engine twins then available for less than a tenth of that amount.

Bill Lear in his 1931 Monocoupe.

Learjet Model 23, the first of the Learjets, which first flew in September 1964. FAA certification followed in mid-1965.

But Bill, who at age 57 had lost none of his boldness, sold his share of Lear, Incorporated, and went into the jet airplane manufacturing business. He invested his own $10 million personal fortune, borrowed another $8 million from Wichita banks, built a factory on Wichita's Municipal Airport, and on 7 October 1963 saw his *Learjet* Model 23 make its first flight.

It was an elegant machine, based on Switzerland's P-16 fighter plane, so strongly built that it far exceeded the FAA's requirements for structural integrity. It was designed—with a great deal of input from Bill—by an engineering team headed by Dr. Hans Studer and Gordon Israel. Israel was an old-timer who had, during the '30s, designed airplanes for Curtiss and Stinson, as well as the famed racing planes flown by Ben O. Howard. Hans Studer, a veteran designer formerly with the German firm of Dornier, had been associated with the P-16 program. The first *Learjet* was delivered in October 1964, by which time Bill had firm orders for 72 more.

The market was there, all right, and Lear had a two-year lead on the rash of competitors he knew would be certain to follow.

Lear had given himself that lead by taking what most would have regarded as a gamble of enormous proportions. He had ordered the production tooling before building and testing the prototype airplane. That meant that the Learjet would have to be near-perfect as it came off the drawing board. Otherwise, some very expensive tooling would have to be junked. This unheard-of procedure did cut Lear's "start-up" costs, and offered the competition a very short Lear coattail to grab, but as Bill himself remarked at the time, "In a situation like this, you are either very right, or very wrong."

Bill was very right. However, the $18 million had been spent, so Lear went public with 50,000 shares of Learjet common priced at $10 per share. He kept 62 percent of that issue for himself and wife Moya (whom he had married in 1942).

The Learjet's impact on the gen-av scene is well known today. Less well known is that, for

Bill and Moya Lear with what's-his-name, a presidential candidate. Lear contributed to his campaign.

Another reason why airplanes are expensive; they are, by necessity, largely hand-built by skilled labor.

all of the brilliance and pure guts that Bill Lear displayed in bringing this series of airplanes into the market, Bill did not plan his sales and product support network well, and by the end of 1967 Learjet Industries was losing money at an alarming rate. And that is when Charles C. Gates, president of the Denver-based Gates Rubber Company, appeared on the scene.

## Gates Learjet

Unless Gates himself decides to tell it someday, we shall never know of the chain of events that brought Gates to Wichita with his checkbook in hand, just as the maneuvering that brought McDonnell and Douglas together must remain untold. Maybe Charles Gates merely picked up his phone, called Wichita, and asked, "Hey, Bill, you wanna sell?"

Anyway, Gates, a pilot since 1942 and a longtime user of corporate aircraft, paid a reported $16 million for controlling interest in Learjet Industries, restructured the company, paying particular attention to the establishment of a sound marketing and product support program, then coaxed Harry Combs to take charge of it all.

Combs has since been a key factor in Gates Learjet's success. When Combs—with some reluctance, it is said—assumed command of Gates Learjet in October 1971, he had been in aviation for more than 40 years, having soloed an open-cockpit biplane in 1928 when he was 15 years old. Combs had later built one of the largest fixed base flight operations in the world on Denver's Stapelton International Airport, and was semi-retired, a rich man, when old friend Charles Gates offered him a challenge that was irresistible to Combs' natural instincts.

Today, with well over 1000 Learjets in operation worldwide, the company has a large support and service facility on Tucson's International Airport in addition to the Wichita factory.

*Learjet* produced less than a dozen airplanes in 1986. Harry Combs had retired, and

The Learjet Model 55 "Longhorn," announced in 1977 and first delivered in late 1980. It featured winglets that turned the normal wingtip vortex into additional lift and thereby reduced induced drag as much as 20 percent in cruising flight.

Charles Gates negotiated the sale of his 64 percent of Gates Learjet stock late that year to the New York investment firm of M.J. Rosenthal & Associates. Eventually, in 1990, Learjet wound up in the hands of Canadian industrial giant, Bombardier.

Meanwhile, Bill Lear moved on to Reno, Nevada, where he spent several years and an estimated $10 million in an unsuccessful attempt to produce a practical steam-powered automobile. That didn't break Bill—at least, not for long. He next made somewhere between $13 and $15 million in Nevada real estate. Of course, that also was soon at risk. He was betting that poke on another revolutionary airplane—one made of carbon fiber plastic—when he died in 1977. Wife Moya, every bit as gutsy as Bill, attempted to carry on with the project, but encountered a succession of enervating problems (including lawsuits from her own children) that repeatedly halted development of the machine. As late as 1986, Moya insisted that she had not given up her lonely battle for the Learfan, while industry observers had written if off as a dying dream.

Bill Lear didn't win 'em all—and that is a most significant part of his story.

There are other Bill Lears out there, talented people with bold ideas and the courage to bet on them, and in our free society we will hear from them; we will certainly hear from them.

## Review questions

1. What is the relationship between the development of aircraft and engines for the military and civilian markets? How are gas turbine engines classified?

2. Who developed the first jet engines? How did GE develop their first jet engine?

3. Why was Boeing successful in selling their 707 to both the civilian and military markets? How did Douglas get started? What caused the company to fall on hard times? Why was McDonnell interested in the Douglas Aircraft Company?

4. Discuss some of Lockheed's problems starting in the mid-1970s. How was the company formed? What was their first successful aircraft? Identify several other aircraft built during the 1930s and 1940s.

5. What was the purpose of the FAA Act of 1958? Discuss some of the causes and effects of the Airline Deregulation Act of 1978. Why did the Professional Air Traffic Controllers Organization (PATCO) strike in 1981? Discuss some of the results of this illegal action. What is the Slot System? What is meant by "flow control"? What was the rationale for the Tax Equity and Fiscal Responsibility Act of 1982?

6. What were some of Bill Lear's earlier inventions? Why was the Learjet a big gamble? How successful has it been?

# 18

# America into space

## Objectives

At the end of this chapter you should be able to:

- Identify some of the early pioneers in rocketry and discuss their accomplishments.
- Describe the U.S. development of rocketry during the immediate postwar period.
- Describe the U.S. reaction to the Soviet launching of Sputnik I on October 4, 1957.
- Give the purpose of the Mercury and Gemini series of space probes.
- Discuss the development of the Apollo program leading to the landing on the moon.
- Give the purpose of the Space Shuttle program and the unmanned space probes of recent years.

Modern rocketry was fathered by an American, Robert H. Goddard. Goddard spent his life building a sound foundation for this new technology, then, like the Wright brothers, saw European experimenters take over initial development of his discoveries. Once again, the pupils surpassed the teacher, and when America at last began to recognize all that this new science portended, we appropriated the fruits of their labors to nourish an industry that should have grown up here in the first place.

At the end of WWII, American intelligence people scrambled around Germany tracking down German rocket experts. We didn't get them all—the Soviets were looking for them, too—but we found the ones at the top of the list, particularly Gen. Walter Dornberger and Wernher von Braun, along with several of their best technicians, and brought them to the United States. We also sought Maj. Gen. Wolfgang von Chamier-Glisczinski, but accepted the report that he had died in an American bombing raid on Peenemunde. When the Soviets orbited Sputnik I in 1957, we had reason to doubt that report.

In the United States, von Braun was placed in charge of the test firing of some captured German V-2 rockets (called the A-4 by the Germans) at White Sands Missile Test Center near Alamagordo, New Mexico. When our engineers asked von Braun about his early research and basic formulas, he seemed surprised. "Why, of course," he replied. "We started with the published papers of your Dr. Goddard!"

Dr. Robert Goddard was a rare person; he dedicated himself to a task that offered no tangible reward in his lifetime. Most people thought he was a nut.

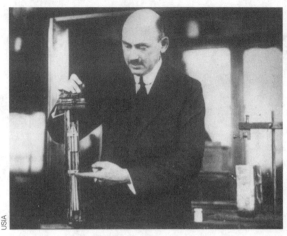

USIA

Dr. Robert Goddard, father of modern rocketry, began his work before WWI. He fired the world's first liquid-fueled rocket on 16 March 1926. Aided by Charles Lindbergh's intervention on his behalf, Goddard, with Guggenheim grants, made significant progress during the '30s.

General Dynamics

America's first intercontinental ballistic missile, the Atlas, first flew in June 1957, and became operational under the direction of the Strategic Air Command in September 1959. The Atlas had a range of 9000 miles and was built by General Dynamics.

Goddard was 17 years old when he decided that man would someday go to the moon. He always remembered the day—19 October 1899—and thereafter celebrated that date as the anniversary of his life's work.

After finishing high school in his hometown, Worcester, Massachusetts, Goddard attended Worcester Polytechnic Institute where he authored a paper suggesting the use of radioactive material as a fuel for deep space flight. The idea was ridiculed.

Goddard worked as a teacher while earning his master's degree, and then a PhD, after which he moved on to Princeton as a research fellow. But a year later he was told by his doctor that he was so seriously infected with tuberculosis that he had not long to live. He went to bed as ordered, but continued his computations.

A year later, in 1912, the disease was arrested and Goddard received patents on a multi-stage rocket system designed while bedridden.

During the next four years Goddard worked as an assistant professor at Clark University and spent much of his salary on experiments with small rockets; he authored a paper describing his experiments and what he had learned to date about rocket propulsion. He sent copies to several non-profit organizations, noting that he needed more money for additional research. That resulted in a $5000 grant from the Smithsonian Institution early in 1917, along with the suggestion that Goddard design a small battlefield rocket for the U.S. Army.

By the time Goddard's infantry rocket had been proven in army tests, WWI was over, and then the device was forgotten until, 25 years later, he reminded army authorities that it should prove useful against Hitler's panzers. It was. Produced as the 2.36-inch antitank weapon, it became known to American GIs as the "Bazooka."

Gemini command module, built by McDonnell Aircraft Corp. America's Gemini Program of two-man earth-orbit space missions began in March 1965. By the time Gemini 12 flew in November 1966, the Soviets' demonstrated space technology had been eclipsed in all areas of accomplishment by Americans.

But it was during the period between World Wars One and Two that Goddard accomplished his most significant work. On 16 March 1926 he tested the world's first liquid-propelled rocket. It was 10 feet in length, and had only a 2½-second burn that took it to an altitude of a mere 184 feet, but it represented Goddard's proof-of-concept vehicle, and as far as he was concerned it represented man's "first small step" into space.

Goddard tested two improved rockets during the next three years; then, on 17 July 1929, he tested a rocket that was far more successful than it at first appeared to be. It weighed 55 pounds, was 11½ feet in length, and was fueled with 14 pounds of gasoline and 11 pounds of LOX (liquid oxygen). It flew (from a converted windmill tower) a distance of 171 feet at about 90 feet of altitude. Most importantly, its gyro guidance system and on-board instrument package functioned perfectly. Unfortunately, the vehicle's thunderous and fiery flight, from the pasture of Aunt Effie Ward's farm near Auburn, Massachusetts, panicked a number of people and brought police, firemen, sheriff, and countless small boys with their dogs to investigate. As a result, a newspaper jibed that the professor's "moon rocket" had missed its target by approximately 239,000 miles, and the state fire marshal forbade any more nonsense of that kind.

The ridicule paid off that time, because the news wire services picked up the story and among those who read it was a man who saw past the crude humor. He was a man who, just two years earlier, had demonstrated how one could parlay courage, vision, and good planning into unmatched success. His name was Charles A. Lindbergh.

Lindbergh went to see Goddard and was clearly impressed, because shortly afterwards he phoned to say that he had talked with Daniel Guggenheim about Goddard's work, and Guggenheim had agreed to furnish $50,000 for rocket research over a two-year period. If Goddard were able to report reasonable progress at the end of that time, more money would be waiting.

Goddard and his wife Ester (a former Clark University honor student whom he had married in 1924 after she volunteered to type his papers for him) moved to New Mexico. There, in a barren valley some 15 miles northwest of Swell, Goddard continued his experiments, disturbing only those secretive four-footed inhabitants of the high desert.

By March 1935, a 75-pound Goddard rocket exceeded Mach 1 as it streaked beyond a mile in height and flew 9000 feet downrange. There were some failures, but Goddard learned something from each, and he maintained careful records. He fired rockets with a cluster of four engines, with gyro-controlled, gimbal-mounted tails, and with steering vanes positioned within the exhaust stream. In 1938 he made a series of demonstrations for the National Aeronautic Association, and although those representatives, as most others of the scientific world, were impressed, it is obvious that no one in America then knew quite what to do with Goddard's fire-breathing birds.

In Germany, however, there were men who did know—men who saw rockets as a form of extra-long-range artillery. They were members of the clandestine General Staff, and they especially liked the idea of rockets because such weapons could be made secretly, and outside conventional arms factories. The Treaty of Versailles forbade Germany to have an air force and severely limited the other military weapons it was allowed. The generals turned to Hermann Oberth, whose interest in rocketry was generally known and who, as it turned out, had been corresponding with Goddard on the subject. Gen. von Chamier-Glisczinski, a ballistics specialist, took charge of the Germans' first rocket research facility at Kummersdorf. Later, with Dornberger and the youthful von Braun aboard, a new facility was secretly opened at Peenemunde, on the Baltic Coast.

The Peenemunde complex became operational in 1937, and two years later, on the eve of WWII, a von Braun rocket attained an altitude of five miles. But Hitler then canceled the priority for rocket research in order to concentrate Germany's resources on the buildup of his panzers and aircraft designed for close support of the highly mobile Wehrmacht in the conquest of Europe. It was therefore not until four years later—3 October 1943—that the 5½-ton A-4 rocket (V-2) was deemed a success when it left the earth's atmosphere and flew a distance of 124 miles.

By that time, Hitler's drive into Russia had proven disastrous, Rommel had been defeated in North Africa, the Allies were moving north through Italy, the buildup of American airpower in Britain portended a massive assault on Festung Europa, and Hitler turned in desperation to the German rocket program. He was too late. There was no way that a suffi-

This how a Lockheed-built Agena Target Vehicle appeared to Gemini astronauts as they approached for docking in earth orbit. Space docking, extravehicular activity, and orbit manipulation were among new space skills acquired during Gemini flights.

cient number of A-4 rockets could be produced at that late date to alter the course of the war. Von Braun later said that the A-4 could have been ready at least a year earlier had not Hitler canceled Peenemunde's first priority, and the A-10 trans-Atlantic rocket, capable of striking New York City, would have been operational by 1946.

But wars are not decided by the "what ifs." Victory favors the side that makes the fewest mistakes.

# The first U.S. rockets

During the years immediately following WWII, the United States rocket program was limited to what could be learned from the firing of the captured A-4/V-2s (while Convair, as early as 1947, produced some slightly improved versions of this missile), and a low-priority effort was made at developing short-range artillery rockets such as the Corporal, along with an antiaircraft missile, the Nike-Ajax, both of which became operational in 1953. The air force meanwhile concentrated on flying bombs, unmanned miniature jet airplanes such as the Matador and Snark—with one notable exception.

In 1951, the Redstone Intercontinental Ballistics Missile program was born and nourished by Maj. Gen. Donald L. Putt and Brig. Gen. John W. Sessums, Jr. This pair of air force generals, arguing that the Soviets were already working feverishly in this field, faced a lot of high-level opposition but managed to slowly gain adherents. In 1953, Air Force Secretary Harold Talbot and Air Force Chief of Research and Development Trevor Gardner joined this minority crusade, and then others in the executive branch and in the Congress began to listen. Finally, in 1954, President Eisenhower gave America's ICBM program top priority. That sparked a crash program for development of a 6000-mile ballistics missile booster.

Born of that activity was the 100-ton, 80-foot Atlas, built by Convair, which first flew in June 1957 and became operational in September 1959. By March 1962, 119 Atlases had been fired, with the air force terming 80 completely successful. Four months earlier, an Atlas booster sent a chimpanzee named Enos twice around the Earth in a prelude to the Project Mercury manned orbital flights. On 20 February 1962 an Atlas-Mercury launch vehicle boosted Astronaut John H. Glenn, Jr., into America's first manned orbit of the Earth.

As Putt and Sessums had warned, the Soviets had, from the end of WWII, made an all-out effort to develop ICBMs. When they succeeded in orbiting the 184-pound Sputnik I on 4 October 1957, it became clear that they had gained a substantial lead in missile booster capability. Sputnik II, weighing 1121 pounds, was lofted into orbit on 3 November carrying a dog named Laika. The United States managed to put its first satellite into earth orbit on 31 January 1958 when a Jupiter C booster sent 31-pound Explorer I into space to discover the Van Allen Radiation Belt.

In October 1958, the National Aeronautics and Space Administration (NASA) was created from that venerable wellspring of aviation technology, the National Advisory Committee for Aeronautics (NACA). NASA became the official agency for all exploratory and scientific programs in space as well as in the air. Therefore, in 1961, when newly elected President Kennedy challenged the Soviets to a race for the moon, the United States had a proper organization to call its space shots, three years experience with its Explorer and Discover series, and a bold and youthful engineering force daily designing space hardware that had to be named as it was created.

By 1968 man had ridden thunderous rockets into space 24 times—the Americans 16 times, the Soviets eight times—but none had yet left Earth orbit to venture into deep space. America's Mercury shots, with Redstone and Atlas boosters, carried a single astronaut during the early '60s. Then came the Gemini series, with two astronauts aboard, thrust into orbit by the mighty Titan. It was, however, the Apollo series that took man to the moon, and at this writing, no Soviet manned spacecraft had been farther into space than you can drive your car in half a day.

The Lunar Landing Program had been suggested by NASA back in July 1960, and feasibility studies by several aerospace companies were handed to President Kennedy in mid-May, 1961. The president presented a plan to Congress ten days later, along with his dramatic commitment to put Americans on the moon by the end of the decade. Congress promised the money and the first engineering contracts were let in 1962. More than 20,000 companies were involved in the program, and the first unmanned Apollo was tested on 26 February 1966 (Apollo was the name given the complete vehicle; its Saturn V booster had three stages). Several more unmanned test flights were made, plus a manned orbital mission with three astronauts aboard—Walter

Schirra, Donn Eisele, and Walter Cunningham—before Apollos 8 and 10 flew to the moon and back prior to the actual moon landing by Apollo 11's lunar module 20 July 1969. Apollo 9 was the earth orbit mission that checked out the Lunar Excursion Module, the little space taxi that would actually land on the moon with two astronauts while the command module remained in moon orbit.

In the meantime, on 27 January 1967, three astronauts—Virgil Grissom, Edward White, and Roger Chaffee—died in an accident at Florida's Kennedy Space Center during a prelaunch test when the pure oxygen atmosphere in their Apollo command module was ignited by a short in the electrical system (three months later, Soviet Cosmonaut Komarov was killed on landing after an 18-orbit mission).

When man eventually travels into deep space to explore and perhaps colonize planets in another solar system (the closest sun besides our own is 4.5 light years away; it may or

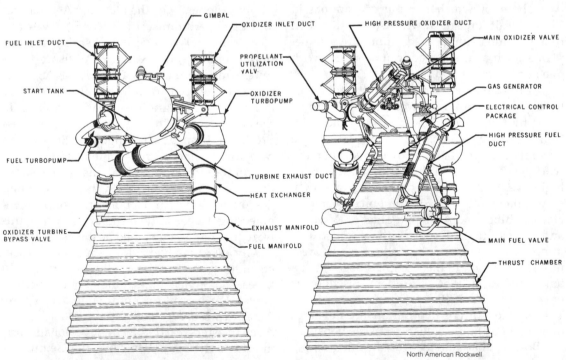

Rocketdyne J-2 rocket engine

North American Rockwell

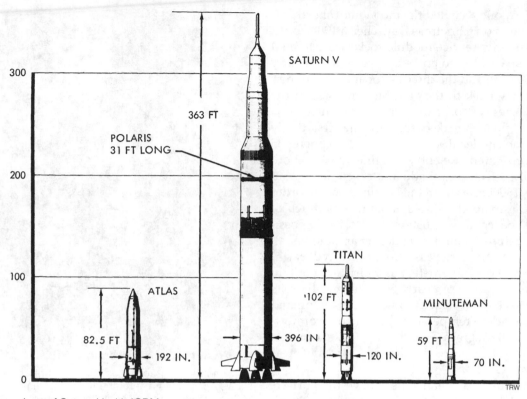

300

200

POLARIS
31 FT LONG

100

ATLAS

82.5 FT

192 IN.

0

SATURN V

363 FT

396 IN

TITAN

102 FT

120 IN.

MINUTEMAN

59 FT

70 IN.

TRW

Comparison of Saturn V with ICBMs.

may not have a planetary system), his children will undoubtedly be required to memorize the date of 21 December 1968 as that point in time when man first shed the bonds of earth's gravity to fly free into the cosmos. At 10:41 A.M. EST on that date, Air Force Colonel Frank Borman, Navy Captain James Lovell, and Air Force Major William Anders, in earth orbit in the predawn darkness 118 miles above Hawaii, ignited Apollo 8's third stage booster for a 302-second burn to thrust their craft into translunar injection at a speed of 24,196 mph. Translunar injection (TLI) results when just the right amount of thrust is applied, at the proper moment during earth orbit, to propel a spacecraft onto an intercepting course for the moon. It, of course, takes into account that the moon will be somewhere else by the time the spacecraft gets there (that is "deflection shooting" on a grand scale!).

Apollo 8 then coasted for the next 53 hours, gradually slowed by the earth's gravitational pull. Then it passed that point in space 214,000 miles from Earth where the pull of the moon's gravity became stronger than that of earth's. By then slowed to 2217 mph, its velocity began to increase as it was drawn toward the moon.

Passing close to the moon the next morning, Christmas Eve, and turned so that the spacecraft's rocket engines faced forward, a 240-second burn slowed Apollo 8 from 5758 mph to 3643 mph to balance its speed with the moon's gravitational pull, which gave an elliptical lunar orbit 194.5 miles at apogee and 69.6 miles at perigee. (Actually, apogee and perigee are correctly applied only to the orbits of objects circling the earth. In lunar orbit the high point is the apocynthion, and the low point the pericynthion.)

Apollo 8 circled the moon until shortly after noon on Christmas Day. Then a 198-second burn of its service module rockets accelerated the space-ship to an escape velocity of nearly 6000 mph and the three astronauts began their journey back to the "big blue marble" in the blackness of space that was their home.

Apollo streaked through the first thinly spread molecules of earth's atmosphere 35 hours later. Re-entry, beginning at about 400,000 feet, was made at a seven-degree angle, 1600 miles from the landing zone, in order to dissipate at an acceptable rate as much of the spacecraft's 24,630-mph velocity as possible before encountering denser air at lower altitudes. Nevertheless, Apollo 8 arced earthward like a giant meteor as air friction built up a temperature of nearly 5000 degrees F on its ablative heat shield. Inside the command module the temperature remained a comfortable 70 degrees F, although the astronauts were subjected to deceleration forces of near seven Gs.

Four and a half miles above the surface, Apollo's pair of 16-foot stabilizing parachutes opened, slowing the CM to 300 mph. A minute later the trio of orange-and-white main 'chutes were deployed, and at 10:51 A.M. EST on 27 December 1968, Apollo 8 splashed into the Pacific 1450 miles southwest of Hawaii and three miles from the carrier *Yorktown* that was standing by with helicopters ready to retrieve the CM and its crew. The spacecraft had completed a 537,000-mile journey in 147 hours.

Apollo 9 flew in March 1969 to check out the lunar excursion module (LEM), or "moon taxi." Apollo 10 took the LEM for a dry run to the moon in May, and then on Wednesday, 16 July 1969, Apollo 11 left Planet Earth to carry out the first moon landing. In command was civilian Astronaut Neil Armstrong, a former navy pilot. His crew were Air Force Lt. Col. Michael Collins, the Command Module pilot, and Air Force Col. Edwin Aldrin, Jr.

Four days later, on Sunday afternoon, 20 July, Armstrong and Aldrin separated from

This photo, taken from atop the assembly building, shows Apollo-Saturn at Kennedy Space Center as the 363-foot space vehicle and its launch umbilical tower move out of the assembly building for the launch pad on the crawler transporter.

the command module in the LEM and, at 3:08 P.M. EDT earth time, as Apollo 11 emerged from behind the moon's dark side, fired the LEM's braking rockets for half a minute to drop down into a moon orbit with a pericynthion of ten miles above the lunar surface.

Further use of the LEM's descent-stage rockets took the moon taxi out of orbit and to within 350 feet of the lunar surface by 4:15 P.M. Noting that the landing would be within a crater, Armstrong maneuvered the LEM to a more suitable spot within an area known to astronomers as Mare Tranquillitatis (Sea of Tranquility), and at 4:17 P.M. touched down gently.

The two astronauts rested and ate a leisurely supper. Then at 10:56 P.M. EDT 20 July 1969, Armstrong descended the LEM's

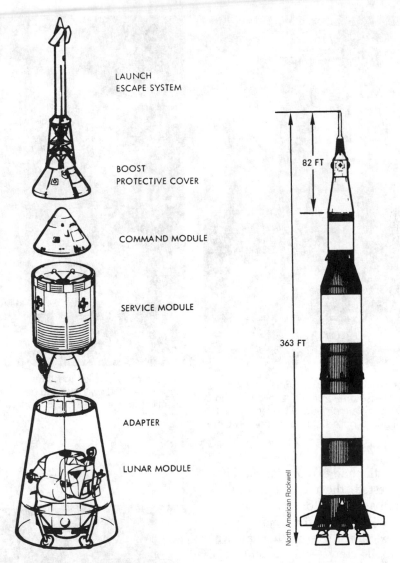

LAUNCH
ESCAPE SYSTEM

BOOST
PROTECTIVE COVER

COMMAND MODULE

SERVICE MODULE

ADAPTER

LUNAR MODULE

82 FT

363 FT

North American Rockwell

The Apollo spacecraft (left) represents the upper 82 feet of the Saturn V space vehicle.

ladder and set foot on the moon. "That's one small step for [a] man; one giant leap for mankind," he said to the millions of earthlings who watched the event via live television.

Aldrin joined Armstrong to plant the American flag, set up some experiments, and gather rock and dirt samples. Then they returned to the LEM for a few hours of sleep before blasting off to rendezvous with Mike Collins, orbiting above in the command module.

Apollo 11 returned to Earth at 12:50 P.M. EDT on 24 July. The three astronauts were held in quarantine for three weeks while doctors looked for signs of any exotic malady that may have been brought back from the moon, then they were freed to face hordes of news reporters—that part of the mission for which they were least prepared.

Subsequently, American astronauts would spend much more time on the lunar surface

The Apollo-Saturn vehicles weighed 6.2 million pounds when fueled. Here, an early Apollo mission is transported toward its launch pad, 9 November 1967. First manned flight, Apollo 7, began on 11 October 1968.

The control panel for the three-man Apollo command module had 250 switches and controllers, displayed 137 quantity measurements, and recorded 142 events.

for scientific studies and exploration, and if, as has been suggested, the moon one day becomes a sort of base camp for space safaris far beyond, those latter-day astronauts may find it amusing to examine the primitive hardware left there by Apollo crews—the descent stages of their LEMs, for example, and the electric car, Moon Rover.

The Mercury series space capsules of the early '60s, each of which carried a single astronaut, put America in space as the wood-and-cloth airplanes of 1910 put us into the air. Then Project Gemini, each capsule of that series carrying two astronauts into earth orbit, represented great advances in all areas of the U.S. space effort and in a remarkably short time. In 1965, Geminis 6 and 7 rendezvoused in orbit, flew in formation a few feet apart, and proved

A space shuttle orbiter test vehicle in Lockheed-California Company's "reaction frame," which contains more than 350 hydraulic jacks that exert loads on the orbiter of up to one million pounds to prove its structural integrity.

the concept of space-docking that followed with the Skylabs in the early '70s.

When President Nixon assumed office, he drastically cut funding for the space program, and except for a single docking mission in 1975, American astronauts did not leave earth again until April 1981, in the first of four tests of the new Space Shuttles.

## The space shuttles

The shuttles, officially known as Space Transportation Systems (STS), were conceived as space trucks—primarily to serve the Air Force, but also to serve commercial customers. The program was initially directed by air force Lt. Gen. James Abrahamson (who would later direct SDI), and the most interesting cargoes delivered into space by the shuttles were not announced to the public. In the early 1990s, the shuttles were to be used to construct a permanent American space station operated by the air force. Unfortunately, circumstances would dictate a revision in that schedule.

Between April 1981 and July 1982, shuttle flights 1 through 4, with two-man crews, completed the test phase of this program; by the spring of 1984, two shuttles were operational, the *Columbia* and *Challenger*. A third, *Discovery*, made its first flight that August, and *Atlantis* followed the next year (the test vehicle was the *Enterprise*).

In the meantime, a second launch and recovery complex was begun near Vandenberg AFB in California, which would have allowed the shuttles to place their payloads in polar orbits (those sent aloft from the Kennedy Space Center in Florida achieve equatorial orbits), but construction was halted on the Vandenberg shuttle port following the loss of the *Challenger* and its crew in January 1986, about which, more momentarily.

From the beginning, NASA took the position that for the shuttle program to be "economically viable," 24 flights per year, carrying significant commercial cargoes, were necessary.

The civilian customers were waiting, although the European Space Agency's unmanned Ariane rockets, which began flying in 1979 from a launch pad in French Guiana, were ready to accept a share of such business, primarily consisting of communications satellites.

NASA has taken the position that the manned shuttles are far more versatile than unmanned boosters, and some of that versatility was demonstrated on 8 April 1984 when George Nelson and James van Hoften, part of the five-man crew of STS 11, retrieved the satellite Solar Max from its orbit for maintenance and repair in space. The shuttles were also developed for the purpose of building a permanent American space station (see Proposed Future Projects).

In any event, the shuttles were deemed essential to the nation's security, and were the most cost-effective space vehicles for the several unique chores they would be called upon to perform. These huge, pressurized cargo gliders, serviced after each trip into space to fly again, actually have many emergency landing runways available when returning from a space mission, because the pilot has sufficient maneuverability to deviate as much as 1500

A Lockheed technician examines some of the silica tiles that shield the space shuttle from fiery temperatures when it returns from space to Earth's atmosphere. No two tiles are alike, and 24,000 are required for each of the shuttles.

miles from his planned landing approach. He will always prefer to land at the launch site, because otherwise the shuttle must be (expensively) transported piggyback on a Boeing 747 to its launch facility. Edwards AFB is currently the shuttle's first alternate landing field because of its 15,000-foot runway, and because a specially-built structure is located there to facilitate mounting the shuttles on the NASA 747 for cross-country ferry.

# The inevitable tragedy

On 28 January 1986 space shuttle *Challenger* exploded into a huge fireball 73.5 seconds after lift-off. The seven astronauts aboard probably died instantly. Their remains were later recovered in the wreckage of their control cabin 100 feet beneath the surface of the Atlantic 18 miles downrange from Kennedy Space Center. The seven were: Comdr. Francis R. Scobee, shuttle pilot Michael J. Smith, Judith Resnik, Ronald E. McNair, Ellison S. Onizuka, Sharon Christa McAuliffe, and Gregory Jarvis.*

The disaster struck on the 25th shuttle flight with the failure of a rubber O-ring employed as a seal between two sections of a solid-fuel booster. Two such boosters, manufactured by Morton Thiokol, were attached externally to the large main fuel tank to send each shuttle into orbit. A lengthy investigation revealed that NASA officials, although repeatedly warned about problems with the O-rings, nevertheless chose to continue shuttle launchings, in part due to pressure by a self-imposed goal of 24 launchings annually by 1988. It was evident that, following the departure of Gen-

---

* Neither Judy Resnik nor Christa McAuliffe was the first American woman in space; that distinction belongs to Sally Kristen Ride, who flew in shuttle 7 in June, 1983. First American woman to walk in space was Kathryn Sullivan who, during her October 1984, sojourn outside shuttle 13 to repair an antenna, remarked to helper astronaut Leetsma about the crew members inside, "I'll bet they ate our lunch." The first Soviet woman in space was Valentina Tereshkova, who flew in Vostok 6, June 1963.

eral Abrahamson, a leadership vacuum had developed at NASA; schedules and public relations projects were overriding more important considerations. The O-ring design flaw had been well documented prior to *Challenger*'s fatal flight, and with no fix in the works it was only a matter of time until *Challenger* or one of her sister space trucks would be lost. There is no law against incompetence. All we can do is bury our heroes and press on.

The *Challenger* tragedy set back America's space program at least two years. When *Challenger* was lost, NASA had a waiting list of 26 satellites scheduled for shuttle deployment in 1986 and 1987, while the air force said it would require at least 45 flights by 1992 in order to meet its defense obligations. In mid-1986, the air force had but one (out of nine launched since 1978) Keyhole spy satellite in polar orbit to watch the Soviets. Therefore, the air force began turning to unmanned launch vehicles for its immediate needs. A dozen old Titan IIs were ordered refurbished, along with some of the 40 Titan ICBMs deactivated by the installation of Minutemen and MX ICBMs.

Meanwhile, the West European consortium that operated the Arianes announced construction of a second launch facility in South America which would allow an increase to 10 launchings per year, while Japan and China developed their own unmanned rockets for satellite deployment, and in the United States at least two private companies—one of them headed by former astronaut Deke Slayton—hoped to get their unmanned boosters ready for commercial customers before the end of the decade. Such competition never materialized, however.

The shuttle program was back in operation by the autumn of 1988, after extensive overhaul of both hardware and management deficiencies. *Discovery* lifted off from the Kennedy Space Center on 29 September 1988 for a five-day mission, announcing America's return to space, with Frederick H. Hauck and four crewmembers on board. *Atlantis* followed with

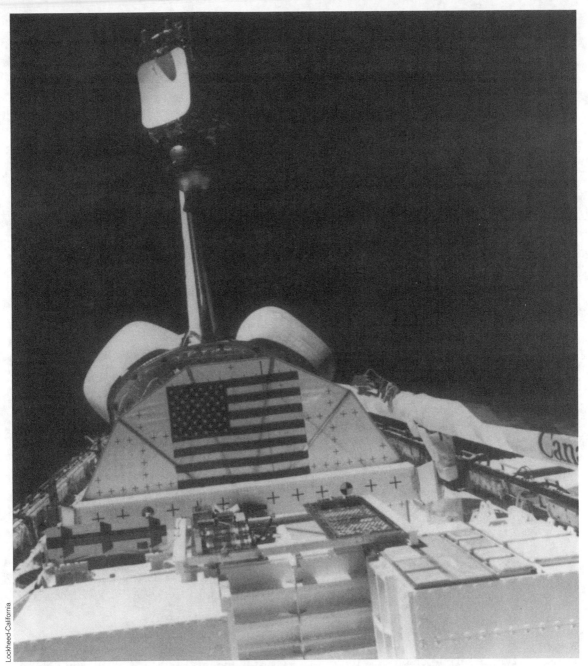

View of a space shuttle's cargo bay with doors open.

a brief four-day mission in December, and five flights were made in 1989, as *Columbia* rejoined the fleet. Six missions were logged in 1990 and 1991, and on 7 May 1992 the full compliment of four shuttles was once again in operation; *Endeavour*, the replacement for the lost *Challenger*,

Lockheed-built space telescope will be able to see objects 50 times fainter and almost 10 times farther away than the best earthbound telescopes.

Lockheed-California

roared into space for a ten-day shakedown cruise, carrying a seven-person crew under the command of Daniel C. Brandenstein.

This proved to be one of the most spectacular missions yet. On 10 May, *Endeavour* caught up with the disabled Intelstat 6 communications satellite, and on 13 May it was successfully captured for repairs. Three crewmembers, Comdr. Pierre Thout, Maj. Thomas Akers and engineer Richard Heib worked on the satellite for a record 8 hours and 29 minutes in the *Endeavour*'s cargo bay, attaching an 11.5-ton solid rocket booster that was used to fire the satellite into its proper or-

Astronauts Joseph Allen and Navy Commander Dale Gardner stow equipment in the cargo bay of the shuttle *Discovery* after snaring a communications satellite and bringing it aboard for repair.

Space shuttle *Columbia* lifts off from Cape Canaveral.

The newest member of the space shuttle fleet, *Endeavour*, lands on the Kennedy Space Center runway in Florida on 19 January 1993 to complete mission STS 54. The drag chute was added in mid-1992 to alleviate

Lockheed Missiles & Space Co., Joe Boyer, artist

Proposed 2001 space colony features artificial gravity living quarters and control center, three zero-gravity modules for scientific research, and three tetrahedral beam platforms connected by "shirt sleeve" air tubes. Each platform is positioned to allow 360-degree line-of-sight communications, while leaving open flight paths for shuttles.

NASA

Space shuttle *Columbia* returns to the Kennedy Space Center riding piggyback on a Boeing 747, following a landing at Edwards AFB, California.

bit the following day. Much valuable experience was gained for future rescue, repair and space station construction projects. *Endeavour* was launched again on 12 September 1992 for the 50th shuttle voyage, which it completed on 20 September with a landing on the Kennedy Space Center runway in Florida.

# Unmanned space vehicles

While the manned spacecraft may be of more immediate use to us, the unmanned probes into deep space serve a longer-range and more compelling function. These little instrument packages, roaming among the planets, help satisfy our compulsive need to know more about ourselves and our place in the universe. We launch them in the name of scientific investigation, but we seek greater truths than they are designed to discover. True, we send them to sample the atmosphere of Jupiter, mark the edge of the heliosphere, and chart the carrier waves of gravitational force, along with a hundred other measurements, but ultimately we hope to learn from these clues how our solar system was formed, and then the universe. Whether it was all an accident, a "Big Bang" in which the universe somehow created itself out of nothing (the theory currently fashionable among many scientists), or whether there is a Supreme Intelligence—and therefore, purpose—behind it all, is a question each of us must decide for ourselves, Charles Darwin and Carl Sagan notwithstanding.

Some of our space probes surprise us. Pioneer 10, built by TRW and launched by NASA on 3 March 1972—hopefully to make the first reconnaissance of Jupiter, if the 500-pound craft could survive passage through the asteroid belt beyond Mars—was one. If, by any chance, Pioneer 10 got that far, it might also confirm the outer limit of the heliosphere, the bubble of particles blown into space by the solar wind, and believed to be in the vicinity of Jupiter.

*Voyager I* took this photograph of Saturn on 18 October 1980 from a distance of 21.1 million miles from that planet. Dione, one of the inner moons, appears as a series of three dots just below the south pole. Among the previously unknown details is the gap within the darker innermost ring.

Pioneer 10 did indeed reach Jupiter—and then, accelerated by that great planet's gravitational field, raced beyond, passing the orbit of Uranus and, in June 1983 earth time, crossed Neptune's orbit headed out of our solar system into the realm of the stars. It had discovered the heliosphere to be far beyond its predicted boundary, and had sent back intriguing evidence of an unseen source of gravity—perhaps another planet beyond Pluto—as it left our solar system on its journey into infinity. It was traveling at 30,550 mph, three billion miles away, and scientists at the Ames Research Center in California hoped to receive its signals through 1986. Pioneer 10 was not expected to approach another sun for 10,000 years.

Twin probes, Voyager I and Voyager II, were launched in August and September of 1977 to make dual-perspective surveys of the gas-giants, Jupiter and Saturn, with their complex of moons. Voyager I, launched sixteen days after Voyager II, was given last minute reprogramming to allow it to approach Uranus and Neptune as well. Voyager I reached Jupiter on 5 March 1979, Voyager II arrived on 9 July, finding huge atmospheric storms, an unexpected ring similar to Saturn's rings, and, most surprising, active volcanoes on Io, the innermost of the four largest moons.

Saturn was approached by Voyager I on 13 November 1980, by Voyager II on 26 August 1981. The famous rings proved more complex than expected, winds in Saturn's atmosphere were three times as fast as Jupiter's and the large moon, Titan, was shrouded in clouds. Voyager I then tracked up and out of the solar

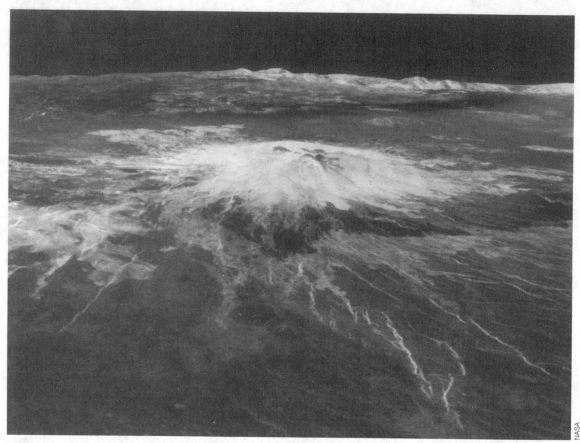

NASA

The *Magellan* spacecraft mapped most of the planet Venus's surface, including this spectacular computer-enhanced three-dimensional view of the region around Sapas Mons, a 9000-foot volcano with lava flows extending for hundreds of miles across the smooth plains (latitude .9 degrees north, longitude 188 degrees east).

system, while Voyager II flew on toward Uranus, which it reached on 24 January 1986. Uranus proved to have less turbulence in its atmosphere, being even colder, with a dark set of rings, and its moon, Miranda, showed a pocked and fissured face. Neptune, Voyager II's final goal, was approached on 25 August 1989. The great blue planet also proved to have rings, strangely clumped rather than thinly spread, and peak winds of 1250 mph were recorded in the atmosphere, instead of the frozen stillness expected. Triton, the largest moon, exhibited volcanism and a nitrogen-based atmosphere. After flying past Neptune, Voyager continued on out of the solar system;

Pluto's eccentric orbit would keep it inside Neptune's until 1999, so the spacecraft had no more worlds to conquer. If its radio continued to function, Voyager II was expected to send back data about the heliopause, the outer limits of the sun's magnetic influence.

Earlier, in 1962, Mariner II gave us the first reports on Venus's hostile environment. Three subsequent unmanned spacecraft went to Venus. Mariner IV flew by Mars for a preliminary look in 1965, and Mariner IX went to Mars in 1971, achieving the first-ever orbit on 13 November; more than 7000 pictures were beamed back to earth to fill in the long-awaited details. The soil of the Red Planet really is red, but there are no canals—and no visible Martians. Viking I and Viking II subsequently landed on Mars in 1976, functioning for several years with a wealth of scientific information.

Budget constraints in the early 1980s prevented NASA from undertaking ambitious planetary explorations, but on 4 May 1989, the Shuttle *Atlantis* carried Magellan into orbit, a mapping spacecraft bound for Venus. In September of 1990, Magellan began firing streams of data back to earth, gathered in 37-minute polar passes across the face of Venus. Using radar, rather than visual photography, the surface of Venus was revealed through the obscuring cloud layer. With resolution down to 360 feet in diameter and radar altimetry, Magellan covered about 84 percent of the planet surface, which proved to be rugged mountains up to 39,000 feet high, with 80 percent of the planet covered by volcanic features. The billions of bits of data continue to be analyzed and add to our store of knowledge, perhaps to help us understand our own earth.

To explore the larger universe, NASA launched the Hubble Space Telescope via space shuttle on 25 April 1990. Orbiting at 380 miles, beyond the earth's blurring atmosphere, HST promised to give us a clearer picture of far distant subjects than had heretofore been available. Unfortunately, the HST's 94-inch mirror proved to have been flawed with spherical aberrations during manufacture, and its performance, although spectacular, was somewhat below expectations. In addition, two of the HST's six stabilizing gyroscopes failed in 1991, further hindering its usefulness; repairs were scheduled for a shuttle mission in mid-1993. Even so, by 1992 observations from the HST had allowed scientists to estimate the age of the universe at least 15 billion years. Barring large amounts of unknown matter, data from HST now gives credence to the expanding universe theory, because there is not enough matter present to halt expansion.

The Galileo Probe, originally scheduled to be launched from the shuttle *Atlantis* in mid-1986, was delayed until 18 October 1989. Galileo is intended to thoroughly investigate Jupiter and its atmosphere, which it will reach in 1995 via a circuitous routing around Venus (February 1990) and earth (twice, in December 1990 and December 1992) to gain "free energy" for the trip. On its second pass around the earth, Galileo was programmed to observe the moon's north polar region as it flew past. Regrettably, in April of 1991 one of the spacecraft's main antennas failed to open; efforts to dislodge it continue.

In the heaviest lift ever taken into low earth orbit by space shuttle, a 35,000-pound Gamma Ray Observatory was launched on 7 April 1991. The mysterious gamma rays can only be studied in space, because the earth's atmosphere blocks their penetration. the GRC's four telescopes are equipped with detectors to determine the amount and source of distant gamma ray emissions. A spacewalk was required to extend a balky antenna before the GRC could be deployed from the shuttle cargo bay.

## Proposed future projects

Exciting adventures yet to come in the U.S. space program include Space Station *Freedom*, a scaled-back NASA plan for a modular manned station requiring 17 shuttle flights for construction. The station's framework measures 335 feet across, to which living and research modules are attached, each 27 feet long and 14.5 feet in diameter. If *Freedom* survives the budget cuts of a deficit-reduction program, the first elements are to be placed in orbit by early 1996, and the station should reach "tended" status during 1997, when it will be occupied for two-week durations. By the year 2000 it is to be occupied continuously by a four-person crew. Among *Freedom*'s features is an Assured Crew Return Vehicle, a re-entry "lifeboat" that will provide a means of escape in an emergency.

NASA's latest concept of Space Station *Freedom*, hopefully to become a permanently manned base for lunar and Mars explorations. A shuttle is nearing *Freedom* for resupply. Even this slimmed-down proposal was endangered by a bloated federal budget deficit in the '90s.

The Cassini project is an ambitious ($145 million) unmanned exploration of Saturn and its complex moon system, scheduled to be launched in December 1995 by Titan Centaur rocket. As part of Cassini's four-year tour, a parachute probe is to be landed on Saturn's moon, Titan, which possesses an atmosphere.

The Mars Balloon mission, a joint United States, France and Russian venture, is to be launched in October 1994, reaching Mars in September 1995. Deploying one or two balloons into the thin Martian atmosphere, the experiment will feature a unique blend of "suspended and distributed" payloads. During Martian nights the balloon is expected to cool and de-scend to the planet's surface. The upper gondola will remain clear of terrain, while a lower portion will drape across the surface, gathering scientific data. As the balloon warms after the next sunrise, it will lift off and drift to a new site for the next night's sampling. If an eventual manned mission to Mars is to be successful, as much information as possible must be accumulated about the conditions on the planet.

We have other means of searching the cosmos—a huge radiotelescope in New Mexico, for example, and the infrared Astronomical Satellite. The latter, launched in January 1983, is an infrared "telescope," placed in earth orbit to allow it to operate above the disturbing influences of earth's atmosphere. Within months, it found "something" orbiting the star Vega (all stars are suns). H.H. Aumann of the Jet Propulsion Laboratory, and Fred Gillett of Arizona's Kitt Peak Observatory, working at the telescope's tracking station at Chilton, England, made the discovery. The infrared data cannot reveal the size or composition of Vega's satellites, but it does give us firm evidence that another sun out there—this one 150 trillion miles away—has a satellite system of some kind and, perhaps, planets like those of our own sun.

## Extraterrestrials?

The question that always comes up when laypeople talk about space: Is there anyone else out there?

Well, consider: We live in the Milky Way Galaxy, which is an enormous pinwheel of suns (stars), perhaps as many as ten billion of them. There are millions of other galaxies similar to our own. We would have to possess a very narrow concept of life and the universe to conclude that, of all those billions of suns, only our own has a planetary system containing a habitable world.

There are many kinds of suns, ranging from the red giants to the white dwarfs. Ours is a yellow star, a very common type.

Draw your own conclusions.

## Review questions

1. How did the Germans get such a lead on us in rocket development after the pioneering efforts of Robert Goddard? Who was Werher Von Braun? How did Charles Lindbergh assist Robert Goddard? What were some of the practical developments of Goddard's research? Where did the German rocket research take place? Why was it given secondary priority until the end of the war?

2. How was the Redstone Intercontinental Ballistics Missile program started? What was the U. S. reaction to the Soviet launching of Sputnik I on 4 October 1957? When was the National Aeronautics and Space Administration (NASA) created? What was the purpose of the Mercury and Gemini series?

3. What was the objective of the Apollo program? Discuss the successes of Apollo 8 and 11. Why are space shuttles now used? What relation do they have to national security?

4. What is the purpose of the unmanned space probes into outer space? How was the universe formed? Why?

# 19

# Military aviation heads into the '90s

## Objectives

At the end of this chapter you should be able to:

- Summarize the major changes that have taken place in the former communist Eastern Bloc nations during the 1980s and early 1990s.

- Explain how these changes have affected military planning in the United States.

- Describe the purpose of the START agreements.

- Discuss some of the key military aircraft programs of the late 20th century.

- Explain the important role of the Lockheed F-117 Stealth Fighter in recent military engagements in Panama and the Persian Gulf War.

- Identify other aircraft and their role played in Operation Desert Storm.

## The world turned upside down

Little did the planners of America's military needs know that the 40-year Cold War with the Communist masters of the Eastern Bloc would end so suddenly, unexpectedly altering our defense posture in the late 1980s and early 1990s. The implacable enemy had ignored human needs and throttled freedom among its population for years. Finally, the pent-up pressure of peoples yearning to be free could be contained no longer. One by one, communist regimes from the Soviet Union to its satellite captives toppled from power.

It began in Poland, where the Solidarity labor movement was founded in 1980. Working slowly, Solidarity finally won the right to compete with the Communist Party in free elections in 1988, where it won 80 percent of the vote. Although the Polish Communists retained parliamentary power through a coalition with other parties, these splinter groups soon united with Solidarity and the Marxist stranglehold was no more. The rest of Eastern Europe's captive nations were watching.

In the Soviet Union, Mikhail Gorbachev's policies of *glasnost* ("openness") and *perestroika* ("restructuring") attempted to convince the USSR's people that their system was workable. Throughout the latter half of the 1980s, however, the tides of change ran against Gorbachev; by 1989 he had pulled Russian troops out of the Vietnam-style war in Afghanistan, and satellite puppet governments were warned not to expect help from Moscow if they were unable to control their population. Russia was having its own problems.

Gorbachev's faith in the Communist Party was not matched by an increasingly powerful opposition in the Soviet parliament, led by Russian President Boris Yeltsin. Yeltsin would be satisfied with nothing less than the abandonment of Communism, which he personally renounced in July 1990. After Yeltsin intervened in a failed coup attempt against Gorbachev, initiated on 19 August 1991 by rightists who wanted to return to pre-glasnost policies, the transfer of power was inevitable; Yeltsin's price for Gorbachev's rescue was democracy. On 29 August 1991 the unthinkable happened; the Soviet parliament voted to suspend all activities of the Communist Party.

By the autumn of 1991, the USSR was being referred to as the "former Soviet Union," and more formally as the CIS, or Commonwealth of Independent States. The Congress of People's Deputies voted to dissolve the Soviet Union in December, and the official breakup came on 25 December, when Gorbachev resigned. Russia was the largest remnant, joined by Ukraine, Byelorussia (Belarus), Georgia, Kazakhastan, and as many of the other former republics who wished to align with it.

The CIS confederation was sorely pressed to meet everyday needs of its citizens during the shift to a market economy. As subsidies and planned supply lines disappeared, prices of the goods available soared to five or ten times their former value. Tourism, trade, and joint ventures with the West were promoted to bring "hard currency" for the emerging governments. The old USSR had spent 17 percent of its GNP for military purposes, three times the U.S. figure. Now that money was sorely needed elsewhere.

Meanwhile, the hated Berlin Wall, erected across the divided city of Berlin in August 1961 to inhibit the often one-way passage of East German residents to the West, came crashing down on 9 November 1989 (actually, the gates were opened at midnight; removal took weeks). The borders of Hungary and Czechoslovakia had been opened to free travel in the spring of 1989 to placate restless citizens, giving East Germans an easy route to the West, so the East German Politburo eventually had no choice except to announce that the Wall was open. Nine weeks later, the government of President Erich Honecker, who had already resigned on 18 October, was overthrown in a bloodless revolution, an unthinkable event in a country that had seen defectors shot to death as they attempted to cross a sterilized death zone along the border of the divided nation.

Reunification of Germany, an understood goal at the end of WWII, had been stalled by the Soviets for decades while it operated a captive industrial plant in the German Democratic Republic. Finally it became a reality on 3 October 1990. The assimilation of less-affluent East Germans into a new single Germany brought considerable stress on the former Federal Republic of Germany, and as of this writing it remains to be seen if the dangers of German nationalism that allowed Hitler to rise to power can be avoided this time around.

Not long after the stirrings of Polish and East German freedom began, democracy movements were flourishing in Hungary, Czechoslovakia, Romania, Yugoslavia, Bulgaria, and the USSR's Baltic states, Estonia, Latvia, and Lithuania. Nicolae Ceausescu, the brutal dictator of Romania, was executed on 25 December 1989, in one of the few bloody revolutions accompanying the fall of Communism. Most government officials saw the inevitability of democracy, and former communists were quick to switch sides and stand for office as independent candidates in free elections. Only in Yugoslavia, where the Croatian and Serbian separatists resorted to violence as a means of settling their ethnic disputes, did the transition to free governments bring bloodshed. Albania, the last bastion of European Communism, embraced democracy in free elections held in March 1992.

# The rush to disarm

Against this upheaval of the country's former enemies, military preparedness in the United States took a freefall, not unlike that of 1946. The Strategic Air Command's round-the-clock alert, with missiles ready for launch and bombers continuously in the air, "stood down" by order of President George Bush on 17 September 1991, military talk for halted operation. This was the first time the United States had not had ICBMs on alert since the Cuban Missile Crisis of 1962. A drastic reduction in force began, with personnel numbers cut through encouraged early retirement, elimination of requirements, and a freeze on enlistments.

In accordance with the START (Strategic Arms Reduction Treaty) Agreements, signed by President Bush and then Soviet President Mikhail Gorbachev in July 1991, wholesale destruction of America's ICBM arsenal began in 1993. To achieve the required 30 percent reduction over seven years, the aging Minuteman II missiles were retired, their 90-foot-deep silos cleaned out, wired for explosives, and blasted into holes filled with rubble. These events were placed on a timetable scheduled to run through July 1995. To retain some semblance of strategic capability, Malmstrom AFB in Montana received upgraded Minuteman III missiles, and the former Minuteman base at Whiteman AFB, Missouri, was transformed into America's only B-2 Stealth Bomber base, home of the 409th Bomb Wing, activated on 1 April 1993. Thanks to escalating costs as the production run was pared back, the 20 B-2s in the Whiteman wing required an investment of almost $20 billion!

Many military leaders were uneasy at this sudden move to relax our defensive posture. After all, they argued, the very reason the Cold War sputtered to an end was the continual firm, unyielding threat of retaliation from the United States. Gorbachev was so concerned about the effect of Star Wars (SDI) on the balance of power that he was willing to make unheard-of concessions. Little did he know that SDI was only a remote possibility, still in the theoretical stage in the early '90s. The East Bloc masters could see that no clear-cut victory was possible in a nuclear age, so freedom eventually had to win out. While it was obvious that we no longer needed to target the USSR's secret military centers, the amount of scaling back was hotly debated. Defense advocates pointed to Red China's continued truculence, plus the threat posed by tin-horn dictators with grandiose ideas, both of which required a strong defense posture. In Russia, Yeltsin's position was far from secure as the old-line Communists exploited the people's unrest; there was a distinct possibility that right-wing members of his Russian Parliament, left over from the days of the Soviet Union, would seize power once again.

All of this upheaval affected military aviation severely. To complement the F-117 Stealth Fighter, Northrop's B-2 Stealth Bomber, as we noted above, was cut back to only a very few flying examples rather than the 132-airplane buy originally planned. The SR-71 Mach 3 strategic reconnaissance airplane was summarily taken out of service on 26 January 1990, at the peak of its mechanical maturity, primarily due to political pressure from the highest levels of the Pentagon. Sadly, the Blackbirds were retired with only a promise of improved spy satellites to take their place. However, there was speculation in some quarters that a hypersonic, super-secret "Aurora" aircraft mentioned in Chapter 15 was being tested as an SR-71 replacement. As peace broke out, this suspected project, as well as many other ongoing ones, was on shaky ground. Spending the "peace dividend" on social programs was the goal of a short-sighted, election-minded Congress.

# Key military aircraft programs of the late 20th century

The Advanced Tactical Fighter (ATF) flyoff, held in 1990, was won by a Lockheed's F-22 entry, over the competing Northrup design, the F-23. The YF-22 was built in two prototype aircraft that participated in the fly-off, resulting in the full-scale development aircraft, to be flown in mid-1995. The production F-22 will not be operational until 2002; the air force had plans to procure up to 648 F-22s. Thus, a re-placement for McDonnell-Douglas's F-15 Eagle, incorporating stealth technology and de-flected-thrust maneuvering, under study from the early 1980s, was to be delayed until the 21st century.

The F-22 is being developed by a team of Lockheed, Boeing, and General Dynamics

F-22 Photographic Team

Prototype of Lockheed/Boeing/General Dynamics F-22 Advanced Tactical Fighter aircraft (ATF), selected in April 1991 to replace the F-15 as USAF's first-line fighter. Incorporating stealth, supersonic cruise, long unrefueled range, and internal ordnance, it is expected to become operational in 2002.

*Key military aircraft programs of the late 20th century*    387

Bell Boeing

Bell/Boeing V-22 Osprey tilt-rotor aircraft combines helicopter and fixed-wing capability by swiveling the engines and rotors to the horizontal position after a vertical liftoff. A rear loading ramp is provided for cargo and troop carrier uses.

Bell Boeing

V-22 Osprey in airplane mode, enabling 300-knot cruise speed.

(now part of Lockheed), equipped with two F119-PW-100 engines provided by Pratt & Whitney, each having 35,000 pound thrust. Its stealth technology is enhanced by internal storage of all weapons, the clipped-diamond shape of the flight surfaces, a blended wing-body shape, and 35 percent composite materials used in the airframe. Advanced features like two-dimension vectored thrust up to 20 degrees from automatically movable exhaust nozzles, "supercruise" above Mach 1 without the use of afterburners, and large internal fuel capacity for long-range missions were to vastly improve the F-22's capability over the F-15. Top speed is well above Mach 2, so the F-22 is both fast and sneaky.

Despite some mishaps during its flight test program, Bell and Boeing (Vertol) teamed up to build the unique V-22 Osprey tilt-rotor VTOL transport, a hybrid combination of a helicopter and a 300-knot fixed-wing aircraft. It continued to advance toward operational status after a first flight on 19 March 1989. In late 1992, the U.S. Naval Air Systems Command ordered four V-22s to supplement the two remaining prototypes. Originally, the marines wanted 552 Ospreys for assault and support roles.

McDonnell-Douglas's C-17 Globemaster III transport, a four-engine widebody jet resembling a scaled-down C-5B Galaxy, was on fairly firm ground, because the air force planned to buy 120 of the C-17s to fill the gap between the C-130 and the C-5B, as a replacement for the aging Lockheed C-141 that first flew in 1962. The C-17's mission is overseas deployment of U.S. forces directly to small airports near battle zones, rather than offloading at major airports into C-130s, as is done with the mammoth C-5. Wingspan is 165 feet, overall length 174 feet, with an internal loading floor 88 feet long (including the rear ramp), 18 feet wide and up to 13½ feet high. The C-17's first flight occurred on 15 September 1991, and it was to become operational at Charleston AFB, South Carolina, in late 1993.

The McDonnell Douglas C-17 transport entered service in 1993, filling the gap between C-5 heavy lifter and C-130 assault transport. It can carry an 80-ton load 2400 miles into a 3000-foot airstrip and turn around on a 90-foot wide runway.

Initial problems with its "powered lift" system, which directs engine exhaust across the flaps to augment lift, required some modification to withstand the high temperatures, but the C-17's STOL (short takeoff and landing) capabilities were eventually fulfilled. Despite a maximum takeoff weight of 580,000 pounds, up to 172,000 pounds of which can be payload, the C-17 was designed to land as short as 3000 feet. Range is up to 4600 nautical miles, without aerial refueling.

The ubiquitous Lockheed C-130, first flown in the mid-1950s, continues as the mainstay freight hauler for the military in the 1990s; the 2000th C-130 was delivered in 1992. After a near collapse in the 1980s, Lockheed had built itself back into a strong company by 1993, when it was able to buy General Dynamics's Fort Worth, Texas, aircraft division for $1.5 billion in cash. Thus, the G-D F-16 became the Lockheed F-16.

The G and H versions of SAC's B-52 fleet remained in service as of April 1992, even though the last of the 744 B-52s built came off the line in October 1962. In August 1986, some of the BUFF's duties were turned over to the North American Rockwell B-1B, an aircraft that could never replace it, but only operate in different ways, with newer electronics, higher dash speeds, and more efficient engines. Initially, the B-1B was plagued by bird-strike, icing, and terrain-following crashes, as the swing-wing supersonic bomber was forced to become a low-level subsonic cruise-missile carrier, a role far different from the design mission envisioned in the 1970s.

Meanwhile, the Northrop B-2 Advanced Technology Bomber, the ultimate vindication of Jack Northrop's "flying wing" bombers of the late '40s, made its first flight on 17 July 1989. Following in the F-117 Stealth Fighter's operational path, the "low observables" B-2

Rockwell International Corporation

North American Rockwell B-1B swing-wing strategic bomber replaced some B-52s in 1986 as SAC's most advanced nuclear carrier. It first flew on 18 October 1984.

was designed to arrive on its target undetected, despite a 172-foot wingspan and a gross weight of 376,000 pounds. It was powered by four 19,000-pound-thrust General Electric F118 turbofan engines and was flown by a two or three-man crew.

The U.S. Navy's carrier-based aircraft became even more valuable as the Cold War

U.S. Air Force

One of the weirdest shapes ever to take wing, the Northrop B-2 Stealth bomber entered service in 1993 as SAC's precision strike tool, to be used against heavily defended targets while the B-1B and B-52 forces operate elsewhere. Low-observability technology renders the B-2 almost invisible on radar.

wound down. The American military needs of the moment were for rapid deployment of a highly mobile force, ready to move into "hot spots" where U.S. interests were threatened—situations made to order for the fleet's air arm. New aircraft, like the A-X replacement for the Grumman A-6 Intruder all-weather attack plane, were hard to get approved, however; the ATA proposal, which was to result in the A-12 attack aircraft from McDonnell-Douglas, was canceled in 1991 due to cost overruns. A-X proposals were under development by five teams in early 1993. Production of both the A-6 and the mature F-14 Tomcat from the Grumman Iron Works was to end in 1992, and no replacements were in sight. For now, the F-14A and the newer McDonnell-Douglas F/A-18 Hornet are the mainstay of the navy's tactical airplanes.

Unfortunately, peace between the Cold War giants did not change human nature. Despots remained in various places around the world, threatening U.S. interests as their activities increased. For this reason, American airpower was needed again and again to put down "brush fire" wars. Attempting to learn from the lessons of Vietnam, the emphasis was placed on rapid response, surgically clean strikes, and early disentanglement. While political ends might have been served at times by our incursions into other areas of the world, the reality of honoring public sentiment against foreign wars demanded that "the deed was best done quickly."

During the 1980s and early 1990s, events proved time and time again that air superiority was vital to the success of U.S. military endeavors. The 25 October 1983 invasion of Grenada was staged to remove the threat of a military-size airport under construction by Soviet-backed Cuban workers, who just happened to be heavily armed. Rather than risk the establishment of another Marxist government in the Carribean, President Reagan landed rangers and marines on the island and restored the noncommunist government.

## Stealth Fighter proves its worth in Panamanian invasion

Long a thorn in the flesh of U.S. interests in the Canal Zone, Panamanian dictator Manuel Noriega was captured during an invasion of his country, Operation Just Cause, mounted on 20 December 1989. Accused of acting as a forwarding agent for Central and South American drug cartels supplying the U.S. market, Noriega finally surrendered on 3 January 1990 and was whisked away to Florida to stand trial for his crimes. The Panamanian operation was surgical, the buzzword used to describe a military action against a specific target that is conducted with minimal disturbance to the surrounding area. Once again, airpower, most particularly the Lockheed F-117 Stealth Fighter, made it possible.

If there is to be an airplane of the decade, the F-117A is the plane of the '90s. As with the SR-71 in the 1970s, the F-117A was developed and placed into service in great secrecy. Only after the Panamanian invasion were its true capabilities unveiled. First flown in June 1981, operational F-117As were being delivered in October 1983, but their existence was not revealed for five years. In the interim, various "Stealth" rumors came out, resulting in some notably inaccurate model aircraft in hobby stores. Eventually, enough sightings were reported to convince the air force to show the airplane publicly on 21 April 1990. By that time, the Lockheed-USAF F-117A team had received the 1989 Collier Trophy for the greatest achievement in aeronautics in America. In May 1992, the Collier Trophy was presented to the team that produced the B-2 Stealth Bomber.

The F-117's mission is clandestine operation, achieved through low observability. While the SR-71 successfully operated as a bold "catch-me-if-you-can" airplane, with no losses even though it was fired on more than 100 times, its operation at Mach 3 above 80,000 feet precluded accurate delivery of ordnance. The F-117A, on the other hand, flew subsoni-

Lockheed Corporation

Lockheed F-117 Stealth fighter was first used operationally in the invasion of Panama to capture military dictator Manuel Noriega. A pinpoint night attack from its Nevada base to a specific spot in Central America proved its ability to arrive undetected.

cally with two GE 404 turbofan engines providing 10,800 pounds of thrust each. It was designed to be flown "down in the weeds," usually during hours of darkness, and could seek out the tiniest target without detection, allowing its internal ordnance load to be delivered with no warning. The cost? About $42.6 million apiece. But, like the F-117 T-shirt pizza-delivery caption said, "Delivered on time, or the next one is free."

Even when displayed during broad daylight, the Stealth Fighter is difficult to discern. Its highly swept wing blends into a fuselage composed of flat, angular planes, giving a different profile from each angle. Radar beams are reflected away, rather than directly back to the antenna, presenting all the radar signature of a sparrow. Engine exhaust is ejected through narrow slits, dispersed in the slipstream to minimize infrared emissions. Because of the airplane's odd design, it could be flown only by computers; no human pilot could keep up with its unstable flight characteristics. The pi-

lot's control movements merely command responses from the computer system, which automatically inhibits dangerous flight regimes. Thus, the black aircraft, sneaking up on its objective in the dead of night, became known as the "Wobbly Goblin."

Only 59 F-117As were built through the 1980s, an exclusive force flown by elite pilots. When the Panamanian invasion of late 1989 was ordered by President Bush, six F-117s were flown south from the secret Tonapah, Nevada, AFB, requiring at least four aerial refuelings for the round trip, solely to deliver 2000-pound bombs within 500 feet of crack Panamanian Defense Forces infantry barracks at Rio Hato, 60 miles southwest of Panama City. The intent of the early morning raid was to confuse and stun without casualties to the troops or damage to the structures. The bombs exploded in the nearby field as planned and had the desired diversionary effect. Meanwhile, A-7 Corsair II attack jets and AC-130 gunships provided ground support for the invading U.S. troops throughout Panama, along with AH-64 Apache attack helicopters.

## War in the desert

Of larger concern than a Central American drug dealer and money launderer was the bully of Baghdad, Saddam Hussein, ruler of Iraq. In the summer of 1990, Saddam declared neighboring Kuwait, an oil-rich sheikdom on the Persian Gulf, to be a historic part of Iraq, and like Hitler in the 1930s, he simply marched in on 2 August and took it. Repeatedly ordered to remove his pillaging occupation force over several weeks by U.N. resolution, Saddam showed no sign of compliance. A coalition of Arab and Western nations, led by the United States, built up an imposing force in neighboring Saudi Arabia, under the code name Desert Shield. By mid-September, 200,000 troops were massed against Iraq, 140,000 of them American. Saddam had sadly underestimated the willingness of the United States to protect its oil supplies and free Kuwait, but he refused to capitulate.

After the passing of the final U.N. deadline on 16 January 1991, all hell broke loose. The first air strikes began at 2:51 A.M., 17 January, and continued in unrelenting massive blows. Tomahawk cruise missiles from navy surface ships in the Gulf were the first to hit Iraq, followed closely by precision strikes by F-117A Stealth Fighters armed with 2000-pound bombs; the 36 F-117s based in Saudi

F-117A flew 1 percent of the missions in Operation Desert Storm, but accounted for nearly one-half of the strategic targets destroyed in Iraq. It operated clandestinely at night, and conventional defenses were powerless against it.

Arabia hit radar sites and communications centers all over Iraq, as well as headquarters buildings in Baghdad. Putting laser-guided bombs into specific doorways of the target buildings was the F-117's goal; it was the only aircraft assigned targets in the Baghdad area. Although it flew only a bit over 1 percent of the war's 110,000 missions, the Stealth accounted for 47 percent of the strategic targets destroyed in Iraq. As Col. Alton Whitley, Commander of the Stealth's 37th Tactical Fighter Wing, put it on 18 January 1991, "(It was) a leisurely drive through Baghdad . . . the Stealth owned the skies."

To say the air bombardment of Iraq was relentless would be the mother of all understatements, to paraphrase one of Saddam's famous boasts. In the first seven hours, 750 sorties were flown, a figure doubled by the end of the first 24 hours. Every conceivable combat aircraft was in the skies over the desert, taking its turn at pounding Iraqi targets; following the lead F-117s were F-15Es, F-111s, F-16s, F-4G Wild Weasels, A-10 Warthogs, B-52Gs, A-6E Intruders, F/A-18 Hornets, A-7E Corsair IIs, and AV-8B Harriers. The Kuwaiti forces flew A-4KU Skyhawks, the British flew Tornados and Jaguars, and the French flew Jaguars as well. Top cover was provided by F-15Cs, F-14s, and F/A-18s, while EF-111 and EA-6B electronic-countermeasure aircraft jammed Iraqi defenses. Aerial refueling was the task of KC-10, KC-135, and KA-6 tankers, and overall command and control was performed by E-3A and E-2C airborne warning and control system (AWACS) aircraft. C-5 Galaxies brought in heavy loads of cargo, while C-130s ferried supplies to the field, landing on roads if the need arose.

The air bombardment saved a lot of ground soldiers, and when Iraq began to launch mobile Scud missiles on 17 January in desperate attacks against Israeli and Saudi civilian targets, U.S. Patriot defense missiles were brought in four days later, intercepting most of them in mid-air. When the ground invasion finally began on 24 February, after 5½ weeks of bombardment, Saddam Hussein's forces were demoralized and devastated, to the point of surrendering en masse to which-ever Western unit would receive them. One pocket of Iraqi soldiers even attempted to give itself up to a combat journalist. The vaunted Iraqi tank forces were destroyed by A-10s and F-111Fs using laser and infrared targeting systems, and AH-64 Apache attack helicopters suppressed any hostile fire.

The U.N. forces simply rolled into Kuwait City behind fleeing Iraqi forces, and the southern third of Iraq was secured to stabilize the Kuwaiti border. On 24 February, with the ground operation only 100 hours old, President Bush declared a cease-fire, with all its objectives met. Operation Desert Storm ended officially on 6 April 1991. Iraq signed an agreement to abide by all U.N. resolutions to enforce the peace. In all, 532,000 U.S. personnel participated in Desert Storm, with 266 giving their lives in the effort. Iraq's losses, thanks to Saddam's intransigence, totalled 40,000 to 100,000 deaths, depending on whose estimate is accepted. Stopping short of total conquest, which would have been extremely unpopular with Arab members of the coalition, also avoided the civilian bloodbath that would have accompanied the taking of Baghdad. Saddam was thus left alive, hopefully wiser for his experience, although few observers expect peace as long as he remains in power.

The goal of Desert Storm's central command was to eliminate half of the enemy's equipment before the ground war began, concentrating on destroying its war-making ability rather than personnel. The figure achieved was actually 60 percent. On 10 April 1992, in the Pentagon's final assessment of Desert Storm, Defense Secretary Dick Cheney said victory was "attributable in large measure" to air power. The Middle East remains one of the world's perennial hot spots, but the lessons of Desert Storm might keep it from boiling over for a while.

# Review questions

1. How did *glasnost* and *perestroika* eventually lead to the breakup of the former Soviet Union? What were some of the effects of this breakup? How did the breakup affect military planning in the United States?

2. What is the START agreement? SDI? Give several examples of how the end of the Cold War has affected military aviation.

3. Discuss some of the key military aircraft programs of the late 20th century, including Lockheed's F-22, McDonnell-Douglas's C-17 Globemaster, and Northrop's B-2 Advanced Technology Bomber. How has the navy's role changed since the end of the Cold War?

Describe some of the navy's front-line aircraft for the remainder of the century.

4. How has the F-117 Stealth Fighter performed in recent military engagements in Panama and the Persian Gulf? Distinguish between Desert Shield and Desert Storm. Explain the role played by the following aircraft employed in Desert Storm: F-117s, F-15s, F-16s, A-10 Warthogs, B-52s, F/A-18 Hornets, and AV-8B Harriers.

5. What is the mission of the following aircraft: KC-10 and KC-135, E-3A and E-2C (AWACS), C-5 and C-130s? Describe the importance of the air bombardment before the ground assault during Desert Storm. What was the role of the Patriot missiles?

# 20

# The airlines soldier on

## Objectives

At the end of this chapter you should be able to:

- Explain how the structure of the airline industry has changed since deregulation.
- Compare and contrast the following major carriers before and after deregulation: American, United, Delta, Braniff, Eastern, Pan Am, Continental, USAir, TWA, Northwest, and Southwest.
- Describe the growing trend of foreign airline investment in domestic air carriers.
- Discuss the factors that led to the decision to develop the Boeing 747.
- Explain how Airbus Industrie got established in the world aircraft market.
- Identify some of the fuel-efficient commercial aircraft that are now in service with the world's carriers.
- Highlight several new commercial aircraft that are in various stages of development for the late 1990s and beyond.

## Mass transit in the skies

As deregulation began to be accepted as the normal way of doing business in the airline industry, volatile market moves were undertaken in the late 1980s and early 1990s. Decisions to serve, or stop serving, a community could be made anytime, for any reason. Rate wars could be touched off whenever a crucial lease payment was due. Unimpeded by CAB restrictions, the players shuffled through mergers, takeovers and bankruptcies, exchanged routes to raise cash, and traded gates and landing slots at prime airports as if they were real estate.

These were perilous times; few start-up airlines entered this high-roller game during the late 1980s and many old established names fell by the wayside. Total operating costs had to average somewhere in the neighborhood of 9.5¢ per seat-mile to compete in the dereg era, and debt service, often the aftermath of a leveraged buyout takeover, kept many carriers from meeting that target. During the three years from 1990 through 1992, the U.S. airline industry reported losses of $8 billion! Had it not been for relatively low interest rates during this period, the situation would have been much worse.

Much of the red ink was due to overcapacity; too many airplanes flying with too many empty seats, because an expected increase in passenger traffic in the late 1980s never materialized. The big three airlines added 445 aircraft from 1988 through 1992, while the smaller airlines shrank their fleets by 149. Excess capacity leads to rate wars, ruinous for all concerned. In

1992, for instance, passenger traffic grew by 6.5 percent, but U.S. airlines posted an operating loss of $1.9 billion, largely due to low fares.

Despite the uncertainties, airframe builders continued to introduce new equipment, promptly snapped up by "launch customers" seeking cutting-edge prestige and early-buy bargain prices. However, these orders more often than not were contingent on financial health. As the world economy cooled, some of the optimistic ardor cooled and these "paper orders" or options evaporated, resulting in major layoffs at Boeing and McDonnell-Douglas. Boeing released 14,249 workers in 1992, and in January 1993 it announced it would cut 27,000 more workers by mid-1994.

## Braniff, Eastern, Pan Am—all gone

Braniff International Airways was the first major airline to succumb, shutting down on 12 May 1982; it actually went belly-up not just once but three times, after two attempts at resurrection. Midway Airlines, a bright star of the brave new era of deregulation, bankrupted and shut down in 1991 after a merger with Northwest Airlines failed to materialize. Another dereg luminary, People Express, also disappeared; it was folded into Continental, contributing its large hub at Newark to the Continental system as it did so. Once-proud Eastern and Pan Am likewise foundered on the financial shoals of 1991. Eastern Airlines, in Chapter 11 bankruptcy since 1989, shut down for good in January 1991, while Pan Am made it to December.

Pan Am struggled especially hard to survive under deregulation, but it had too many strikes against it. Juan Trippe had retired without a plan of succession, and his death in 1978 poignantly came in the same year as deregulation. The shedding of excess assets bought time, but it was already running out when a bomb was slipped into Pan Am Flight 103's forward baggage hold by Arab terrorists as the Boeing 747 was departing from London on 21 December 1988. Exploding as it climbed through 31,000 feet, the big jet fell into the small village of Lockerbie, Scotland, killing all 259 persons on board plus 11 on the ground. The frustration of Flight 103's loss added mostly mental, rather than fiscal, pain to the already-ailing carrier, but it was another nail in the coffin.

Chapter 11 bankruptcy was followed by a final shutdown, after 64 years, on 11 December 1991. Among the airplanes stranded at Pan Am's overhaul base at New York's Kennedy airport was a sky-weary Boeing 747 Clipper, N747PA, the first production jumbo jet built by Boeing. Across the nose was its christened name: Clipper Juan T. Trippe.

## The big three

By the early 1990s, some 60 percent of the airline business was concentrated in the "big three": American, Delta and United. In terms of passengers carried during 1991, American boarded nearly 76 million, Delta just over 74 million and United roughly 62 million. Each busily acquired routes, gates and equipment from weaker airlines through the 1980s and early '90s. Under its outspoken chairman, Robert Crandall, American conserved cash and pared routes to avoid losses, wisely withdrawing from costly rate wars after they proved fruitless. Giant United, long the biggest U.S. carrier, ordered a large fleet of new-technology airlines in preparation for the booming 1990s, then backed off when the recession deepened. In March 1993, United announced it would stop taking Boeing deliveries at end of the summer, resuming only with deliveries of the new Boeing 777 in May 1995. Unfortunately for the Puget Sound economy, United was continuing to accept the 50 European Airbus airplanes it had on order, with an option for 50 more.

## Delta, the wonder airline

Delta, the wonder airline, started in a Mississippi delta cotton field as a crop-dusting outfit in 1928, soon diversifying into passenger carrying with Travel Air 6000s, six-passenger monoplanes powered by a single Wright J-5 engine. By 1991, Delta was an international airline earning annual revenues of more then $9 billion. Chairman Ronald Allen sidestepped the standard move to Boeing 747-400 jumbos when Delta acquired Pan Am's North Atlantic routes in 1991, preferring to operate big tri-jets instead, the venerable Lockheed L-10l1s and new McDonnell-Douglas MD-11s. On the long Atlantic hops, Delta saved even more money by flying its twin-engine equipment on ETOPS (extended twin-engine operations) approvals that had been granted to Pan Am for its A310 Airbuses, some of which were now flying in Delta livery. Boeing 767-300 extended-range widebodies were Delta's more normal ETOPS equipment over the Atlantic, however.

For the Big Pond, the Pacific Ocean, Delta relied on its tri-jet jumbos. Delta was the first airline to fly the MD-11, an automated, high-efficiency growth version of the DC-10. Delta's international expansion grew to reach Moscow, Paris, Hong Kong, Taipei, and Tokyo. The acquisition of Eastern Airline assets, following the bankruptcy of the Great Silver Fleet under the guiding hand of its chairman, Frank Lorenzo, also helped Delta grow from a regional carrier to one of the major players, with more than 9000 pilots on its payroll.

Hard times eventually caught up with Delta in 1992, when it lost $526.8 million, and in mid-1993 it laid off 600 pilots, the first permanent employees to be let go in 36 years. Delta was merely responding to the same malaise that was affecting the rest of the airline industry during the early 1990s; a tide of red ink from rate wars and sluggish business growth.

Even with the high-tech Boeing 757 and 767 and the long-haul MD-11, Delta's fleet mix in the early '90s retained such standbys as the Boeing 727-200, of which it owned 150 examples, and the DC-9. The venerable Boeing three-holer was a likely candidate for nacelle hush kits, enabling its Pratt & Whitney JT8D-9 turbofans to meet Stage 3 noise requirements, and a two-person cockpit modification, eliminating the flight-engineer position. However, 16 older 727s were retired in 1993.

The DC-9, on the other hand, carried only 65 passengers and was not considered worth installing new engines to meet Stage 3 noise and pollution standards. In service since 1965, the last Delta DC-9 lifted off from Dallas-Ft. Worth on 1 January 1993 on its final flight to Atlanta, closing out nearly 28 years of faithful service. To replace the little DC-9, Delta chose the airplane's direct descendant, the stretched MD-88, which carried 155 passengers on two JT8D turbofans.

# The plight of the also-rans

The remaining 40 percent of the 1990s airline market was split between still-viable but financially shaky carriers and those staving off disaster day by day. In this second tier, USAir carried 55.5 million passengers in 1991; Northwest, 41 million; and Continental, 37 million. TWA and America West followed with 20.5 million and 16.8 million, respectively. America West was another dereg start-up, beginning its operations in the southwestern United States before expanding to the northeast and internationally. America West was forced to seek Chapter 11 protection in 1991 as the Gulf War boosted fuel prices and dampened travel.

Northwest Airlines, which flew its first passenger in 1927, gradually grew to become the fourth largest American carrier and the most dominant U.S. airline in the Pacific. It was the first U.S. airline to fly the European fly-by-wire A320 airbus and the extended-upper-deck Boeing 747-400, both in 1989, and it had bought Republic airlines in 1986 to expand its domestic routes. However, its growing debt had swelled to $3.65 billion, primarily because of a 1989 leveraged buyout led by its new chairman, Alfred Checchi. Servicing this debt made it difficult to meet optimistic growth and fleet-upgrade objectives, and in

December 1992 the carrier was forced to delay major purchases of more than $6 billion in new airplanes ordered five years earlier, primarily A320 and A340 Airbuses and Boeing 757s. With 6000 pilots (one 747-400 alone requires 12 crews) and 360 aircraft, Northwest was far from finished, however.

The other major player in the second tier was USAir, an amalgam of Allegheny and Mohawk airlines that subsequently purchased Piedmont Airlines and, later, Pacific Southwest Airlines. USAir managed to turn a profit in 1991, a neat trick in an era of hemorrhaging bank accounts and fare wars to raise spot cash. Concentrating on domestic hub-and-spoke operations, USAir was continuing to struggle through the dereg mine field.

## TWA—bankrupt

No-longer-mighty TWA, once Howard Hughes's personal prized possession, had suffered under the flensing knives wielded by its chairman, financier Carl Ichan. After acquiring his controlling interest in 1985 with an investment of $440 million, he gradually increased his holdings until he took the airline's stock out of the public market in 1988, when he had 90 percent of the company. Ichan then used TWA money to buy Texaco and USX (steel) stocks, leaving the airline $469 million in debt and unable to turn a profit, eventually seeking a "prepackaged" Chapter 11 bankruptcy in 1992.

Finally forced to divest his controlling interest in what was left of TWA on 8 January 1993, Ichan had already presided over the stripping away of such TWA assets as its London routes, Chicago slots, half of its PARS computerized reservation system, and much of its fleet. Ozark Airlines was absorbed by TWA in 1987, primarily for its valuable St. Louis gates. By the early 1990s, TWA was down to 167 airplanes flying to 84 destinations, a far cry from its heyday. Its fleet was also aging faster than any of the other major airlines.

Chairman Ichan's stock acquisitions to take TWA private became his personal petard, however. As his ownership percentage rose past 80 percent, a requirement was triggered that made his other companies responsible for any TWA pension fund shortfalls, under Federal Pension Benefit Guaranty Corporation rules. Upon inspection, the airline's pension fund was found to be $1 billion in arrears, and Ichan was forced to give up his ownership in December 1992 to preserve the rest of his fortune. Whether his departure came in time for the airline to survive remains to be seen. The reborn TWA hoped to be out of Chapter 11 by early 1993.

## Continental—bankrupt twice

By the early 1990s, the reborn Continental Airlines was the sole surviving repository of buyout-artist Frank Lorenzo's Texas Air dynasty. Continental's chairman took that great carrier into Chapter 11 bankruptcy for the second time in late 1990. A previous bout with his recalcitrant machinists union in 1983 had resulted in a non-union reorganization under Chapter 11, from which Continental emerged in 1986. The 1990 bankruptcy was prompted by the carrier's inability to weather high fuel prices and a fall-off in traffic, both from the Gulf War. However, unlike its stablemate, Eastern Airlines, Continental continued to fly into the 1990s under Chapter 11 protection and emerged from bankruptcy in mid-1993.

Lorenzo's acquisitions of Eastern, People Express, Frontier and New York Air hadn't fared so well; all were gone. Lorenzo had even attempted a buyout of TWA in 1986 before the airline's unions, in desperation, encouraged the offers of Carl Ichan. Lorenzo was forced to resign in August 1990, barred by the courts from pursuing airline adventures for seven years; he bought his way out of that restriction 2½ years later by paying $7.5 million to Continental's creditors.

# Southwest—a niche to fly in

The beginnings of most U.S. airlines were found in a profitable niche, such as a route between two cities that wasn't being filled by other sources, or a steady-demand market like the New York-to-Washington shuttle. Southwest Airlines, boarding 25 million passengers in 1991 under the fun-to-watch management of Herb Kelleher, has brought convenience and no-frills budget fares to aviation since 1971, initially flying unregulated intrastate routes within Texas between Dallas, Houston and San Antonio. When dereg arrived, Kelleher's open management methods fit like a glove. Noted for riding along on one of his Boeing 737s, passing out Southwest's trademark packets of peanuts ("no meals, no first class, no seat assignments") to amazed passengers, chairman Kelleher liked to involve himself with the line employees, and they were encouraged to swap roles when extra

hands were needed to hasten a ten-minute turnaround, so pilots (paid by the trip, not by the hour) might be cleaning up the cabin, ramp workers could be found selling tickets, and counter personnel unloading baggage carts.

Kelleher had obstacles to overcome in getting his airline started, as well as keeping it aloft. Although the corporation was started in 1967, no flights lifted off until three-and-one-half years later, in 1971, due to court battles over the legality of his competition against CAB-regulated carriers. However, Southwest did get off the ground (with only four airplanes) and it enjoyed steady growth through the '70s, Southwest's $20 fares got the competition's attention; company president Lamar Muse, former president of several airlines, knew how to make waves. After encountering another lawsuit, this one by the DFW Regional Airport Board seeking to force the convenience airline to move from its Love Field base, Southwest was given a

Southwest Airlines

The Southwest Hustle is typified by these flight attendants in weekend "fun uniforms," racing to get airplanes into the air on time. Southwest Airline's schedule performance is legendary.

To commemorate its 20th anniversary in 1991, Southwest Airlines painted one of its Boeing 737s in Lone Star flag colors. The unconventional airline also has three "Killer Whale" 737s to promote Sea World destinations.

boost by the (Congressman Jim) Wright Amendment to the Air Transportation Act of 1979. By forbidding airline flights from Love Field to destinations beyond Texas and its bordering states, this law encouraged all the Dallas-serving airlines to move their operations to the newer DFW (Dallas-Fort Worth International) airport, a huge complex about the size of most counties, lying west of town, that opened in 1974. Southwest opted to live with the Wright restrictions and stay. Since 1975, its American stock exchange symbol has been "LUV".

You have to understand Dallas to understand why Southwest wanted to punt its baby Boeings over the noise restrictions at land-locked Love Field. As with Houston's William F. Hobby Airport, another close-in link for Southwest, Love is located conveniently close to everything in downtown Dallas. Old Love had been the destination of choice since 1927, when it was first used for commercial flights. Braniff was born there, operating out of Love right into the 747 era. So, public (if not governmental) support was high to keep Southwest flying out of Love (it also employs 17,000 people in and around Love), and after two trips to the U.S. Supreme Court its right to do so was upheld. Riding any distance from Love involves hopscotching, as one must stop at an intermediate destination within the Wright limits and change to another of Southwest's 100-odd 737s to continue.

By 1985, Southwest was profitable enough to buy out Muse Air, a rival started up by its original president. It had grown to 109 planes by 1991, entering markets, far beyond its original Texas borders, from Detroit to Los Angeles. By staying just the right size, however, Southwest could avoid the illness of larger carriers.

## Exporting our flag carriers

The issue of foreign investment in U.S. airlines remained a thorny subject in the 1990s. Under U.S. law, no more than 49 percent of a U.S. airline may be owned by a foreign entity, and no more than 25 percent of its voting stock may be foreign-owned. Financially strapped carriers were often eager to accept funding from any source. Thus in early 1993 Northwest Airlines and KLM Royal Dutch airlines, its 49 percent partner, agreed to operate as a single carrier, giving KLM open access to the Northwest route system in return for Northwest entry to two Dutch cities. The U.S. Department of Transportation required that the plan be resubmitted for review after five years, however.

In late 1992, USAir and British Airways negotiated a plan to gain British investment of $750 million dollars in exchange for 44 percent ownership and access to all U.S. markets without reciprocal European rights. This latter deal was nixed by U.S. lame ducks Andrew Card, Secretary of Transportation, and President George Bush, after the other major U.S. carriers complained loudly of foreign alliances, citing unfair subsidies by government-owned airlines and an imbalance of access exchange in favor of the foreign carriers. Not to be rebuffed, privately-owned British Airways forged a new agreement to give $300 million for 19.9 percent ownership, and tried again with the new Clinton Administration and its D.O.T. secretary, Fredrico Peña. Cannily, Peña approved the code-sharing aspect of the plan for only one year, allowing USAir to gain its funds while limiting the 36-city route system exchange.

Through it all, deregulation spelled cutthroat rate wars and a here-today, gone-tomorrow attitude toward markets by the airlines. The tradeoff has been one of stability versus cost. Consumers benefited from below-cost $99 coast-to-coast fares, but lost when forced to pay pumped-up prices for last-minute trips over remote routes. The hub-and-spoke concept spawned by dereg meant one sometimes started a westbound trip by flying east, to reach a hub where a plane was boarding passengers to go west. Also, there was no assurance, under dereg, that the airline you rode into Morgantown last month would still be flying there today.

## A new generation of airliners

On 30 December 1969, the Boeing Company achieved certification of an airplane that revolutionized airline travel forever. Just as the original 707 brought vibration-free, over-weather flying to piston-engine passengers, the giant 747 was to bring low-cost travel to the masses.

But, as described in John Newhouse's excellent book *The Sporty Game*, the development of the Boeing 747 was very nearly the company's undoing.

As with most great projects, the Boeing Jumbo Jet was the result of concepts and desires pushed through to fruition by one or two ambitious, capable individuals. Committees are great for handling the pesky details, but they aren't very good at imagination. The great Kelly Johnson, chief of Lockheed's Skunk Works section that solved many thorny design problems, is reported to have said, "There will be no more great airplanes, because they are being designed by committees. There will be good airplanes, but not great ones." In the case of the Boeing 747, it was William Allen of Boeing and Juan Trippe of Pan Am who got together in 1965 and worked out plans for a monster airliner, one with nearly twice the passenger capacity of anything that had gone before.

Trippe agreed to buy 25 of the huge airplanes; Allen agreed to build them if he could sell another 25 before August 1966. The undertaking was enormous, even for Boeing, which had handled big jobs like the B-52 and 707 previously. The final assembly building alone, to be built a few miles north of Boeing's Renton, Washington, base at Everett, would become the biggest enclosed space on earth, covering some 300 million cubic feet, roughly 100 acres under roof. The design grew and grew as it took shape, ballooning from 550,000 pounds of takeoff weight to 710,000 pounds. The engines, three times as large as any built previously, had to be developed along with the airplane. Pratt and Whitney was up to the task, but it wasn't easy. Getting the JT-9Ds up to the required 43,500 pounds of thrust delayed the project almost to the breaking point; in 1969, new engineless 747s were sitting on the Boeing ramp with concrete weights to keep the nosewheels on the ground.

Orders for the developing 747 came trickling in during the 1960s, mostly because no airline could afford to let its competitors fly

The massive, powerful Boeing 747-400, latest of the superjets, has become a fixture of prestige among the world's airlines—but it nearly sent the company under before it started selling.

such a prestigious aircraft unchallenged. An economic downturn from 1969 to 1972 dried up Boeing's order pad; not a single 747 was sold in those years, a time when Boeing was in greatest need of the cash and credit such orders would bring.

Pan Am, with Juan Trippe no longer at the helm, made the first revenue flight of the jumbo jet in January 1970, and the world of aviation would never be the same. Orders began to flow in a steady stream after the first two years of teething troubles, but it was a near brush for Boeing.

A landing 747 has a grace unlike any other airliner. Because of its bulk, it looms into view long before smaller aircraft, making it seem to float in the air as slowly as the Goodyear blimp. The 18-wheel multi-bogey main landing gear, designed to save pavement by spreading weight, has both body and wing trucks, the former steerable to help negotiate taxiways. The humpback profile of the airplane resulted from an early decision to maximize freight-carrying capability; a tilt-up nose for the 747F (freighter) and 747C (convertible) versions allowed direct insertion of cargo containers. Doing so required a cockpit that was removed from the main deck, with a generous afterbody for streamlining, and, at Juan Trippe's insistence, an upper deck first-class lounge was added in the area behind the cockpit. In the latest winglet-equipped 747-400 variant, an extended upper deck brought total seating up to 660 in all-tourist configuration (550 on main deck, 110 on upper deck, 65 more than - 200B).

The 747's cavernous interior brought a new term to commercial aviation: "widebody". The cabin was nine seats across, but with two aisles no passenger was more than a pair of seats from a walkway, just as in the earlier Boeing jet-

liners. The tri- jet Douglas DC-10 and Lockheed L-1011, under development at the same time as the big Boeing, shared the definition as well, although their cross section was not quite as large as the 747's.

After its tumultuous beginning, the 747 became a great success story, plying the skies worldwide in the colors of just about every airline in the free world, and some that weren't. As the program matured, subassemblies were farmed out to other Boeing divisions and suppliers; the cockpit was built in Boeing's Wichita, Kansas plant, the wings in Auburn, Washington. Vought, Northrup, and Rockwell

The Boeing Company

Cockpit of the Boeing 747-400, a marvel of computerization and display technology. All control, navigation, and management information is displayed on five giant CRT readouts, relegating conventional instruments to backup. The cockpit crew of this giant consists of only two persons.

built fuselage components, in Texas, California, and Oklahoma, respectively. Many more parts come from overseas subcontractors, the result of trade offset arrangements; that it all fits together on the assembly line is nothing short of a miracle. At $140 million per copy, the 747-400 makes the ultimate statement in civil aviation, and it is not likely to be supplanted in the near term. It was a great gamble for Boeing, but it paid off handsomely. By the end of 1992, some 1147 of the superjets had been sold.

Boeing had not been idle on other projects during the years of the 747 program, of course. The three-engine 727 short-haul airliner began as a 100-seat regional carrier, eventually stretching into lengthened versions that matched the 707's length. Both the 727 and the "baby Boeing" 737 used the fuselage cross section of the 707 series, giving short-range customers similar amenities to those experienced on the longer trips. The twin-engine 737, certificated in July 1967 to compete with Douglas' DC-9, was basically built out of Boeing's parts bin; the cockpit was from the 707, as was the fuselage tube and the empennage (only the 727 among Boeing's jets used a T-tail), and the underwing engines were reliable old JT8D turbofans from the 727. In 1987 the 737 passed the 727 in sales, having grown from a 100-seat short-range jet to a 160-passenger medium carrier. But there were more advances to come.

## Doing more for less

In the early 1980s, after years of flying evolutionary developments of the Boeing 727, 737 and 747, and the McDonnell-Douglas DC-8, DC-9 and DC-10, the airlines were ripe for newer, more efficient designs, not just rehashed versions of the old ones. If the two dominant American airliner makers would not supply them, foreign sources, notably the Airbus Industrie consortium from Europe, would oblige. After all, the U.S. commuter airliner industry had been neglected during the 1970s, defaulting to firms such as British Aerospace, Embraer of Brazil, Dornier of Germany, and ATR of Italy.

The world's heavy iron still flowed predominantly from Boeing's Everett, Washington, works, but Big B's market share was being eaten into by Airbus competition. To stay in the lead, Boeing introduced two new airliners, the 757 and 767, certificated in October of 1984 after a development that may have cost as much as $3 billion. Both were giant twin-engine airplanes with underwing powerplants supplied by GE/Snecma, Pratt & Whitney or Rolls-Royce, as the customer chose. Flown by two-person crews (no flight engineer unless the purchaser wanted one), they could carry 190 persons in the narrow-body 757 version or 230 in the wide-body 767. The new twins fit neatly between the 115–145 seat 737 and the smallest 420-seat 747. The 757 quickly supplanted aging 727s with its greater efficiency, and the roomy 767 proved an economical means of handling long legs like transatlantic runs.

With the increasing reliability of modern jet engines, the FAA had approved extended twin-engine operations (ETOPS) over routes that did not meet the FAR 121.161(a) requirement for continuous availability of a landing site within one hour of single-engine cruise. Historically the province of three-engine DC-10 and L-1011s, as well as four-engine Boeing and Douglas airliners, the new 120-minute ETOPS exemptions allowed the 767 to fly to Europe without deviating over an uneconomic northern route to stay near land.

First approved in February 1985 for TWA's Boeing 767-200, the basic criteria for ETOPS was a documented inflight shutdown rate of less than .05 per 1000 hours of operation, or less than one shutdown in 20,000 hours. As mature turbine powerplants were experiencing shutdown rates as low as .02 per 1000 hours, the risk assumed by flying over routes that would require two or even three hours of single-engine cruise to reach a diversionary

The big-twin Boeing 767 carried large loads across the Atlantic profitably by using the ETOPS alternate airport exclusion for long overwater hops.

airport was quite small. Within eight years, ETOPS had become so commonplace that 400-seat twin-engine airliners, such as the Airbus A330 and Boeing 777, were being developed for the North Atlantic run.

The little 737, on the other hand, became the most-built jetliner in 1987, surpassing the 727's previous record of 1832. More than 3000 737s have been sold to date, and the 300-series, introduced in 1981, began a new cycle of success. The 737-300, -400, and -500 are all equipped with new-technology GE/Snecma CFM-56 turbofans and "glass cockpits" with EFIS (electronic flight instrumentation) re-

placing the old mechanical flight directors and engine gauges; EFIS had been introduced earlier on the 757 and 767. The unchallenged heavyhauler, the 747, was given an upgrade to 747-400 status in 1989 with an extension to the upper deck, an area that could be used for crew bunks on long-range trips spanning a third of the globe, or for extra passenger seats on high-density routes.

## McDonnell-Douglas

By improving its basic airframes, McDonnell-Douglas was able to remain a presence in the airliner business during the 1980s and '90s. The former DC series acquired MD prefixes in later iterations, thus a stretched DC-9-80 became known as an MD-80, subsequently growing into the MD-81, MD-82, MD-83, MD-87, and MD-88, each differing chiefly in gross weight and wing size. An MD-90 version with further updating was rolled out on 13 February 1993. Glass cockpits became the norm, along with flight management systems that choreographed flights for maximum efficiency.

The giant DC-10 was prime for an upgrade; new generation engines promised better seat-mile fuel costs, a two-person cockpit was desired by airlines eager to eliminate their flight engineers, and an all-glass cockpit stuffed with computers was the way of future. Thus, in 1989 the last DC-10 came off the production line at Long Beach, California, and on 10 January 1990 the maiden flight of the first MD-11 took place.

Powered by a choice of GE/Snecma, P&W or Rolls engines, the new airliner grossed 602,500 pounds for takeoff and carried as many as 405 passengers, 45 more than the DC-10. The wingspan was increased only four feet, to 169 feet, with double winglets used to "fool" the wing into thinking its span was even longer during cruise flight. The panel carried six 8-inch CRT displays, replacing all the mechanical gauges of the DC-10, and with the aid of flight management computers, it was simpler to fly, even with two pilots. To its credit, McDonnell-Douglas decided to offer the option of manual cable controls when the autopilot was not engaged, rather than the full fly-by-wire systems popularized by the Airbus A320.

## International airplanes

More and more, airliners were being built in component form, with only the final assembly taking place at the parent companies' plant. As soon as a paper proposal began circulating, investment partnerships were sought, to share the risk of building and certifying such a complex product. In the case of the MD-11, the wings were built in Canada, Italy's Aeritalia built the winglets, the tailcone came from Mitsubishi, and control surfaces were manufactured by such sources as Embraer and CASA.

Boeing, seeking to close the gap between the 767 and 747, has developed the 777, an even-larger twin-engine airliner capable of carrying 305 to 440 passengers. Powered by huge GE, P&W or R-R fanjet engines in the 84,000- to 90,000-pound thrust class, with fan diameters approaching ten feet, the 777 will offer efficiency and long range in a larger size. One of the 777's unique options will be folding wingtips, reducing the 200-foot span to less than 160 feet for simplified docking at crowded gates. Target date for the 777's rollout is March 1994, with first flight in mid-1994, leading to certification in May 1995.

Even larger airliners are under consideration, carrying 600, 800, or even 1000 passengers. Boeing will not likely be willing to bet the company on a single huge project; there are too many corporate memories of its near escape with the 747. The company was discussing the concept with several prospective partners in the early 1990s, even partners within its Airbus competitor such as Deutche Aerospace and British Aerospace, as well as Aerospatiale in France and CASA of Spain. Such cooperation is the only way the proposed Boeing Superjet will be built, because its development could cost as much as $10 billion. These gargantuan airliners are dependent on restricted international routes, where only a small number of flights are allowed into a country. If a move is made to "open skies", allowing anyone to fly anywhere with reciprocal rights, few larger airplanes would be needed.

In a similar vein, the proposed McDonnell-Douglas MD-12, originally to be a stretched trijet some 34 feet longer than the MD-11, has grown into a four-engine double-deck behemoth carrying 430 to 500 passengers. The MD-12 project, like Boeing's Superjet, is too costly for the parent company to undertake; initially,

The Boeing 777 scheduled to enter service in 1995, a 300- to 400-passenger twin for higher load factors on less fuel.

How big can an airliner get? Only the market will decide. Boeing was discussing plans for 600- to 1000-passenger behemoths with risk-sharing partners in the mid-'90s. Decisions to build will await economic upturns.

McDonnell-Douglas openly courted Taiwanese investors to share the risk, wooing cities nationwide to help build the MD-12 assembly plant. The Republic of China investors backed off in 1992; pending economic recovery in the airline industry, certification could not take place until at least mid-1998, at the earliest.

# Review questions

1. What were the factors that led to increased competition in the airline industry during the 1980s? Why was there so much excess capacity during the early 1990s? How has this affected the airframe manufacturers? What were some of the reasons for the failure of Braniff, Eastern, and Pan Am? How has the competitive position of the "Big Three" changed since deregulation?

2. Describe some of the financial and marketing problems faced by TWA and Northwest. How have Continental and USAir changed since deregulation? What are some of the factors that have led to the success of Southwest?

3. What is the limitation and reason for foreign airline investment in U.S. carriers? Why was the development of the B-747 such a tremendous risk for Boeing? What has been the result since its certification in 1969? Why was the B-737 developed and how successful has it been?

4. How did Airbus Industrie get started and how successful has it been? What models did Boeing and McDonnell-Douglas develop to compete with Airbus models? Why did the FAA permit twin-engine aircraft operations over the Atlantic?

5. Why have the world's major airframe manufacturers sought cooperation in the development of future aircraft?

# 21

# General aviation— what went wrong?

## Objectives

At the end of this chapter you should be able to:

- Discuss the reasons for the decline in general aviation aircraft sales since 1978.
- Identify several reasons why businesses continue to use corporate aircraft.
- Describe some of the changes that have taken place in light aircraft manufacturing including ownership and types of aircraft produced.
- Recognize the growing interest in specialty-aircraft manufacturers and kitplanes.
- Identify some of the new developments in helicopter technology that are revolutionizing that segment of the industry.

At the end of the 1970s, it seemed as if the general aviation industry could do nothing wrong. Airplanes were selling in record numbers, innovations poured forth from manufacturers intent on capturing another percentage of market share, and no end of students kept showing up to learn to fly in response to the advertisements sponsored by the Big Three (Beech, Cessna and Piper), each of whom sold training aircraft and audio visual teaching aids.

## The industry declines

Five years later, it had all turned around, and instead of cycling back to prosperity in short order, as it had so many times before, a full fifteen years after the peak the depression was as bad as ever. From 17,000 units built in 1978, the U.S. general aviation manufacturers had plunged to less than 1000 airplanes in 1988. In 1992, civil general aviation deliveries totalled only 899 units. Meanwhile, the dollar value of U.S. general aviation shipments was maintained at a billion-dollar level only with the aid of inflation and the fact that most of the production was high-ticket turbine-powered aircraft.

Much finger-pointing accompanied the industry's decline. No single factor was responsible, it seems; instead, a concurrent assault by multiple threats combined to destroy much of what had been the world's envy, the U.S. lightplane industry. There were three major liabilities dragging the sales chart down (numbers of new airplanes sold being the chief barometer of concern).

# GAMA
# SHIPMENTS AND BILLINGS

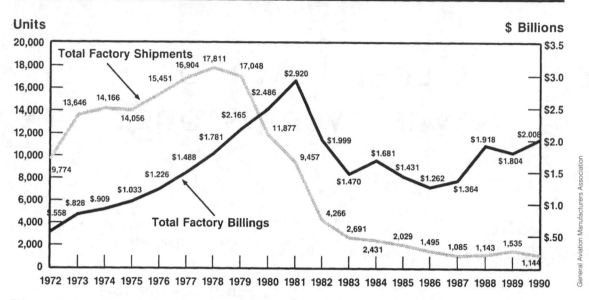

**Units** | **$ Billions**

This graph shows the severity and persistence of the depression gripping general aviation manufacturing during the '80s. After peaking in 1979 at 17,811 airplanes produced, 1990 saw a dismal 1144 units shipped. Only strong business aircraft sales kept the dollar value of the few airplanes sold at a relatively high level.

First, an industry largely supported by venture capital and discretionary income has a hard time withstanding double-digit inflation and interest rates, the "misery index" presided over during the presidency of Jimmy Carter, 1977 to 1980. The cost of borrowing money simply eliminated many buyers, who couldn't make the payments, along with most marginal manufacturers, who were unable to hold on until things got better. The price of a new airplane escalated obscenely; fewer units with the same basic overhead means prices have to rise almost vertically. The buyers decided to sit this period out.

Second, the 1970s had seen a exponential growth in the supply of personal injury attorneys in the United States. In 1970, we got along with only 175 lawyers per 100,000 persons in the total population. By 1980 that figure had

reached 250 per 100,000 and in 1990 we were up to some 310 per 100,000. The number of product liability lawsuits climbed in response to this increase in legal horsepower, each of which had to be defended at great expense, and juries were increasingly disposed to award multi-million dollar judgments for what would have been viewed as "tough luck" situations in years past. For many companies, product liability insurance to shield themselves against being forced into receivership became costly or impossible to obtain.

It's all too easy to blame "those lawyers" for plundering an industry, but one has to remember that no lawyer can file a case alone, or award a judgment on his own. The problem stemmed from a societal change, wherein we were no longer willing to accept personal responsibility for our own actions. A new generation had grown up being told that "for every-thing that goes wrong, somebody must be held accountable", and they so firmly believed this that they were willing to hire a readily-avail-able lawyer to address any grievance. When seated on juries, this same generation listened to a parade of "expert witnesses" promote their side of the case and turned a sympathetic ear toward any sad circumstance. If a "rich" company was involved with the alleged faulty product, however remotely, it would be found guilty. After all, it, or its insurance company, could afford it. Or could they? Insurance pre-miums, as it turns out, are paid by real people, ultimately the customer buying the company's product, driving the price up to unsupportable levels.

Aviation was particularly ripe for the plucking, and was ill-prepared to withstand it. People killed or injured in aircraft accidents have a higher-than-average earning potential, requiring hefty judgments to compensate for their loss. The spectacular portrayal of an in-nocent victim being carried to his death, help-lessly trapped in an infernal machine while plunging from a great height, played well to a jury. The very success of the general aviation industry during the 1970s created "deep pockets" to be looted in court. The small fam-ily-owned businesses of the 1950s were now publicly held companies, controlled and man-aged by non-aviation conglomerates with seemingly inexhaustible resources. Finally, airplanes are built to last forever; there being no statute of repose in product liability law, a 50-year-old Piper *Cub*, even when extensively modified or poorly maintained, carried the potential of an expensive defense at the least, or a multi-million dollar judgment at the worst, for the owners of Piper aircraft assets, even though they had nothing to do with the J-3's design or production.

Third and finally, there was a clear over-supply of aircraft built up in the 1970s. Al-though a fourth or third of production was exported, the U.S. market was being glutted with new airplanes. Since a 1964 Cessna 182 with new avionics could do most of the job of a 1984 model, there seemed little incentive for buying a new airplane at five times the price. The answer, of course, would have been to de-velop new markets, but the economics of the 1970s kept this from happening.

As the 1980s evolved, production was ex-tremely low, fixed costs, including the product liability insurance bill for previous produc-tion, had to be absorbed into fewer and fewer units, leading to price increases far outpacing the consumer price index. Opting for the abun-dant supply of used planes was the logical choice until the inventory was mined out. As the new airplane delivered few marketable ad-vantages, the buyers stayed away in droves, further depressing production, and further in-creasing the percentage of fixed costs.

The smaller companies, such as Mooney, were better equipped to survive the crunch, but the Big Three were missed because of their withdrawn support for the industry's founda-tion. Student starts, a traditional barometer of future growth derived from the number of persons applying for student pilot licenses, dropped through the 1980s; 179,912 persons held a student license in 1981, while only 120,203 chose to learn to fly in 1991. Although the number of total pilot licenses held de-creased only 9.4 percent in these years, the 33 percent drop in student starts augured ill for any future growth.

Active aircraft numbers went down as well, from 213,226 in 1981 to 198,475 in 1991. Low production numbers failed to offset losses from accidents and exports of good, clean used American aircraft, which became popular as the dollar weakened on the foreign exchange market. Even the remaining aircraft saw less flight activity. Estimated annual flight hours flown by general aviation dropped by 26 per-cent in the 1980s, from 40.7 million in 1981 to 30.1 million in 1991.

Despite the statistical gloom, general avia-tion retained its hard core of devotees, and its inherent appeal was undimmed. The advantages of general aviation travel was only heightened by airline deregulation; the airlines concentrated on serving a few major hub airports in diametric opposition to industry dispersal away from large industrial centers to small cities where costs were less. In addition, there is an inborn yearn to escape from ground level and join the birds, and the appeal of fun-av was still there. If the paranoid security fences at small airports (required by stiff new federal air regulation) didn't keep them at bay, people would still wander out to the airport to look at airplanes and perhaps learn to fly.

## Business flying gets the service

After waiting for business to bounce back in the mid-1980s, general aviation firms either disappeared or trimmed their sails drastically. As the industry's slump lengthened, the old balance of flight training, personal flying, air taxi charter and corporate aviation shifted toward business flying. More and more fixed-base operators (FBOs) turned their friendly, unsophisticated airport businesses into slick, shiny lounges for the bizjet trade. Million dollar palaces for the convenience of corporate executives and their pilots, these modern FBOs feature spotless lobbies, conference rooms, snoozing and exercise facilities, flight planning tables and a big-screen television set that is always on. Geared to pumping 500 gallons of jet fuel, business terminals often discourage visits by small piston powered aircraft, which are directed to park well away from the front door.

For the traditional private flyer, who owns or rents a small airplane for enjoyment or personal transportation, the 1980s and 1990s were a time to deal with bigger and better (but less friendly) airports, increasing government requirements, and higher costs. The freedom to hop into a private aircraft and fly anywhere in the country without restriction was threatened

Gulfstream Aerospace's Gulfstream IV, the epitome of business aircraft, carries as many as 21 persons in stand-up, shirtsleeve comfort. A working office aloft, it carries corporate executives across continents and oceans at more than 500 mph, for $18 million per copy.

Cessna, once the builder of half the world's light airplanes, abandoned piston-engine aircraft production in 1986, concentrating on profitable turbine-powered models. The Caravan utility turboprop was introduced in 1985, becoming popular with cargo and bush-flying operators. Powered by a 675-shp Pratt & Whitney of Canada PT-6A engine, it can carry 14 persons at 210 mph (U.S. regulations limit single-engine aircraft to 10 seats).

and diluted, as the manufacturers no longer saw such pilots as the source of next year's sales and seldom bothered to protest government encroachment.

## The manufacturers retrench, finetune their lines

Cessna Aircraft Company was acquired by a military plane and submarine builder, General Dynamics Corporation, in September 1985. That year it built 878 aircraft; in 1977 it had produced 8839! After decades of building half of the world's annual output of light airplanes, Cessna shut down piston engine production com-

pletely in 1986, to concentrate on the Citation jet and Caravan utility turboprop lines. This abandonment of light aircraft would have been completely out of character for the old Cessna company, but it made perfect business sense in the 1980s and 1990s, allowing Cessna to turn a profit building readily-marketed aircraft.

General Dynamics evidently found the field of general aviation to be too far removed from its military core business, so Cessna was sold to Textron in 1992. This caused much speculation in general aviation circles about a return to lightplane production, because Textron also owned Lycoming engines, which had been used in Cessna's 152, 172, 172RG,

Cessna Citation V carries on the original Citation's straight-wing layout, combining simple systems and easy flying habits with a 489-mph cruise speed. It requires only 3160 feet of runway, thanks to stall speeds as low as 94 mph in landing configuration.

T182 and 182RG models, and it would be logical to create a market for them. However, Textron also owned Bell Helicopter, and there was about as much chance for Cessna to switch over to helicopter production as to start building Lycoming-powered lightplanes again. The company's present management was satisfied to be building Caravan single-engine turboprops, operated primarily under contract to Federal Express over small-parcel freight routes. Cessna was also content with its line of six business jets, ranging from the 10,400-lb CitationJet, powered by tiny FJ44 fanjets from Williams Research, to the 31,000-lb Citation X, which flies at Mach .9 on a pair of huge Allison GMA 3007C engines. More than 2000 Citations had been sold since September 1972, when the first one was delivered; the 2000th airplane, a Citation VII, was rolled out on 30 March 1993.

Piper, on the other hand, bravely maintained some measure of lightplane production through the drought of the '80s, from trainers to turboprops. In 1987, the veteran planemaker marked its 50th Anniversary, although it almost missed the party. A series of ownership changes had left it ill-equipped for the managerial decisions of hard times. In 1970, control passed from the Piper family to Bangor Punta Corp., itself acquired by Lear Seigler in 1984. Lear Seigler was taken over by investment bankers Forstmann Little Inc. in the mid-1980s, and with shutdown imminent, private entrepreneur and aviation buff Stuart Millar bought Piper in May 1987, with the idea of returning it to owner-management. Piper tried "going naked" (dropping product liability insurance) to decrease its attraction for lawsuits. Prices were slashed and enthusiasm ran high, but the company slipped into Chapter 11 bankruptcy

The Citation X, tenth model of Cessna's business jet line, flies at Mach .9 (nine-tenths the speed of sound), slightly faster than other top-line business jets. Up to 12 persons can be carried, with an ocean-spanning range of 3800 miles. Base price was $12.5 million; first flight in late 1993 is to be followed by deliveries in 1995.

in 1991, unable to build airplanes cheaply enough to fill the large backlog of orders taken at bargain prices. It was purchased in April 1992 by another entrepreneur, A. Stone Douglas. A trickle of airplanes continued to flow from the production lines under the protection of the court.

Beech survived by withdrawing from the learn-to-fly and family airplane market, retreating to its traditional role as a supplier of business airplanes for upscale buyers. With over 90 percent of the executive turbo-prop market firmly in the hands of the various King Airs, ranging from the seven-passenger King Air C90B to a 10-place Super King Air 350, only limited plant space was devoted to piston aircraft production.

However, Beech still realized that customers are grown as much as found, and it offered the newly-mobile bus-inessman a Bonanza F33A four-place retract-able (basically unchanged from 1970), a six-seat Bonanza A36 or turbocharged B36TC and a twin-engine Baron 58. These finely-crafted (and expensive) piston-powered products served to introduce future King Air buyers to Beechcraft quality.

Beech acquired the rights to Mitsubishi's Diamond business jet in 1986, giving it a fast entry into the bizjet field, just above the largest King Air. This was actually Beech's third attempt at jets; the company had entered into marketing agreements for the French Morane-Saulnier MS760 in 1955 (about the time it was

Piper Malibu Mirage, introduced in 1988, offered a pressurized cabin for six persons, cruising at 259 mph at 25,000 feet behind a 350-hp Lycoming TIO-540-AE2A engine.

Beechcraft's Super King Air 350, the largest and most-capable of the King Air turboprop family that began in 1965. It carries up to 11, has a top speed of 361 mph and flies up to 35,000 feet. It was introduced in 1990 at a price of $3,753,000.

Mooney Aircraft Corporation

Popular Mooney MSE (a development of the M-20J, or 201) offers efficient four-place cruising at 194 mph, sold for $143,945 in 1993.

flying a prototype jet trainer for the USAF), and the British-made Hawker BH-125 in the 1970s, neither of which ventures had been overly profitable. This time Beech was in a position to take over the production of its jet, which it redesigned and built as the BeechJet 400A.

The rest of the U.S. general aviation industry held on through the 1990s by staying small (a lack of assets being the best defense against lawsuits) or merging and diversifying. Mooney had been owned by the French firm Eurualair since 1984, and was still building fast singles in

Questair

The Questair Spirit all-aluminum kit aircraft, powered by a 210-hp Continental IO-360 engine. Once completed by an amateur builder, it outperforms certificated factory-built airplanes, thanks to its small size and relatively large engine. The Spirit cruises at 228 mph and carries two persons in comfort under the bubble canopy.

*The manufacturers retrench, finetune their lines*

the Kerrville, Texas, plant it occupied in 1953. Learjet had been sold to Canadian industrialist Bombardier, remaining in Wichita, Kansas, across the municipal airport from Cessna. Lear wisely backed off from plans to expand into a Tucson, Arizona, plant, and forged ahead with new products like Delta-fins to tame slow speed handling. The stretched Model 55 grew into the Model 60, certificated in late 1992.

Speciality-aircraft builders endured by exploiting their particular niche, such as manufacturers of fabric-covered tailwheel airplanes (Husky, Maule, Taylorcraft, American Champion), amphibian flying boats (Lake), custom-made wood and steel-tube nostalgia aircraft (Bellanca, Waco Classic) and family/rental ships (Commander's 114B and the American General Tiger, a rebirth of the Grumman AA-5B).

## Interest grows in kits

In the absence of low-cost factory-built airplanes, many individuals purchased kitplanes, ready-to-assemble aircraft that could be licensed under the FAA's "Experimental" cat-egory without meeting production criteria. Although limited to non-commercial uses, such amateur-built aircraft satisfied an unmet need for innovative low-cost wings, and the sales of Kitfox, Avid Flyer, Glasair and Lancair kits exceeded factory-built airplane production in many years. Ultralights evolved into true small aircraft during the 1980s, acquiring cockpit enclosures, full three-axis controls, wing struts instead of wires and, most of all, reliable two-stroke engines, primarily the Rotax series from Austria. As proven by the increasing sophistication of homebuilt and ultralight aircraft, people will always find a way to fly, despite all obstacles.

Helicopters did not escape the recession of the 1980s, but several new developments were seen despite the moribund sales figures. Light, powerful turbine powerplants had revolutionized rotary-wing aviation through the 1970s, and instrument flying capability added utility

Owner Benny Davis spent years constructing his Eagle homebuilt biplane, including 1500 hours finishing the full-feather paint job. Experimental aircraft builders enjoy flying unique aircraft not available at any price from a factory.

in the 1980s. Still, the aircraft's unique abilities were its strength, and rather than simply copying executive airplanes in flying the airways from airport to airport, helicopters did their best work when finding their own uses. Emergency medical transportation, applying lessons learned in Vietnam, became popular in the 1980s, and few large hospitals were without a helipad with a million-dollar EMT chopper on standby, ready to bring high-profit trauma victims to the emergency room. Police surveillance, traffic spotting, and news gathering were other valuable uses.

## Special niche for helicopters

For the 1990s, the most significant advance in rotary-wing aircraft was the introducion of McDonnell-Douglas Helicopter's NOTAR anti-torque system. Historically, all single-rotor helicopters have used a side-thrusting tail rotor to balance the torque reaction of the engine's output to the main rotor. First appearing in 1987,

Typical of the streamlined ultralights of the '80s, the Challenger by Quad City Aircraft flies at 63 mph on a 28-hp Rotax 277 two-cycle engine. Ultralight pilots no longer sit outside in the breeze, and wire-braced wings have given way to struts.

Largest U.S. helicopter in production, the $16 million Boeing 234 is a civil version of the military CH-47. With up to 44 passenger seats, it flies 650 miles at 165 mph, powered by two Lycoming AL5512 turbines delivering 2975 hp each. Its first flight was 19 August 1980.

McDonnell-Douglas Helicopter's revolutionary NOTAR (no tail rotor) antitorque system, as used on the MD-520N single-turbine utility helicopter.

McDonnell-Douglas' patented NOTAR system employed the main rotor's downwash circulating around a circular cross section tailboom. When modulated by a jet of air from a fan inside the tailboom, exiting from a slot near the tip of the boom, this downwash circulation can be used for anti-torque control. Because the tail rotor produces much of a helicopter's perceived noise, the NOTAR system proved much quieter, the hazard of a person walking into a spinning tail rotor was eliminated, and there was no longer a danger of control loss from striking wires or brush with the tail rotor.

McDonnell-Douglas, formerly Hughes Helicopters, got into the civilian helicopter business in the early 1960s with a tiny 2-place piston-engine whirlybird called the 269A, a lighter, cheaper aircraft than the Bell 47 and Hiller UH-12A that had dominated the market until then. By winning a U.S. Army bid for a light turbine-powered observation helicopter in the mid-1960s, the famed OH-6 "Loach" of Vietnam, Hughes was able to offer the egg-shaped machine as the fast, nimble 5-place Model 500 in civil use. Hughes became a subsidiary of McDonnell-Douglas on 6 January

MD Explorer twin-turbine helicopter, carrying up to 8 persons with two Pratt & Whitney of Canada 206A engines of 629-shp, flies at 170 mph.

Bell JetRanger III is the safest single-engine aircraft, fixed or rotary wing. Powered by a single Allison 250-C20J turbine, it flies at up to 140 mph, seats 5, can hover in ground effect at 12,800 feet.

Bell Helicopter Textron

Bell's medium-twin Model 230 helicopter features retractable or skid landing gear, can carry up to 10 passengers in a comfortable executive cabin. It is powered by two Allison 250-C30 engines. With an 18-inch fuselage stretch and a four-blade rotor system, it will become the Model 430 in 1995.

1984. In addition to the AH-64 Apache attack helicopter for the army, the 5-place MD 520N and 8-seat MD Explorer twin, both equipped with the NOTAR system, were in production in 1993.

Bell Helicopter Textron forged ahead with new executive ships to replace the dwindling military and offshore oil markets. Its JetRanger model 206 compiled the best overall safety record of any single-engine aircraft, combining the reliability of turbine power with the ability to escape from weather traps by landing on any level spot. The JetRanger begat the stretched LongRanger in 1975, and was modified with twin engines in 1993 as the Twin-

Ranger. Meanwhile, Bell's larger utility ships, descendants of mid-1960's UH-1 "Huey" Vietnam troop carriers, were still in production in the '90s as the 212 and 412 twins, with two- and four-blade rotors.

Early on, Bell realized its Hueys were too large and slow for executive work, and, in any event, the market was evolving toward twin-engine powerplants turning a single rotor through a combining gear box. So, Bell brought out its Model 222 specifically for the corporate market in 1980, powered by a pair of new LTS-101 turbines from another Textron-owned company, Lycoming Engines. The engine's early service problems kept the 222

Sikorsky Model S-76 was the manufacturer's first helicopter designed solely for a civilian market. Its sleek shape and outstanding performance made it a popular corporate shuttle. Shown is the S-76B, powered with two P&W PT6A-36 turbines, giving it 167-mph speed.

from fulfilling its potential, despite the aircraft's comfortable cabin, retractable gear for 150 mph speed and good looks. The 222 was replaced by a Model 230 twin in 1993, powered by Allison 250-C30G engines, larger versions of the C20 used in the JetRanger and LongRanger. Already on the drawing board is an 18-inch stretched version of the 230 with a four-blade rotor system, to be known as the 430.

Meanwhile, a healthy support business emerged in the 1990s, composed of firms refurbishing, overhauling and maintaining the fleet of general aviation airplanes, many of which were no longer supported by a manufacturer. The average age of U.S. general aviation aircraft was more than 20 years, and an increasing ef-

fort was required to keep them in the air. With upgraded avionics (radios) in the instrument panel, 20- and 30-year-old airplanes could deliver good, economical service. General Aviation ended the 20th Century as a mere shadow of its robust self in the '70s, but it was far from dead.

## Review questions

1. What are some of the reasons for the sharp decline in general aviation aircraft sales since 1978? Why has the industry been so vulnerable to products liability claims? What is a statute of repose and how might it affect products liability? How has the availability of used aircraft affected the production

Typifying the increasing sophistication of general aviation aircraft, a Collins Pro Line 4 avionics package installed in a Lear Model 60 corporate jet displays all flight and systems information on four CRT displays in front of the pilots. Weather radar information is on the pilot's right-hand display, while a route map is shown on the copilot's left-hand CRT.

and pricing of new aircraft? Student starts have been a traditional barometer of future industry growth. What has this barometer shown in recent years and why?

2. Give several reasons why businesses seek the benefit of their own transportation. How has this affected the FBO business?

3. How have the light-aircraft manufacturers changed since the late 1970s with regard to ownership and type aircraft manufactured? Describe the approach Piper took when it was taken over by Stuart Millar in 1987. Was it successful? Why was Beech's acquisition of Mitsubishi's Diamond business jet successful when earlier attempts into the business jet field had failed?

4. Why has there been so much interest in specialty aircraft and kitplanes in recent years?

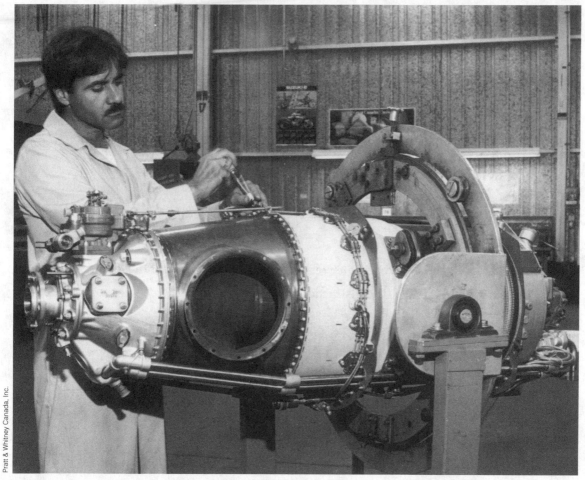

Technician making final adjustments to a Pratt & Whitney PT6A-60 series turboprop engine, typical of advanced components found in business aircraft service centers. Maintaining corporate aircraft requires many such highly trained individuals.

Describe some of the recent developments in helicopter technology. Why will helicopters remain important in certain lines of work?

Give several examples. Why has the general aviation support business remained strong into the 1990s?

# A

# Objective questions

## Introduction

**I. Multiple Choice**—Choose the best answer and place it in the blank at the left.

_____ 1. This individual holds the distinction of being the first to fly.
    a. Eitienne Montgolfier
    b. Pilatre de Rozier
    c. Ferdinand von Zeppelin
    d. Octave Chanute

_____ 2. This Englishman designed the first true aircraft as we know it today with wings, fuselage, and tail section. Several of his gliders were successfully test flown.
    a. Samuel P. Langley
    b. Charles Manley
    c. George Cayley
    d. Glenn H. Curtiss

_____ 3. Between 1891 and 1896 this German glider pilot made a number of fights in his biplane, some reaching 750 feet in length. His work was studied closely by the Wrights.
    a. Ferdinand von Zeppelin
    b. Otto Lilienthal
    c. Octave Chanute
    d. Alexander Mozhaisky

_____ 4. Secretary of the Smithsonian Institution and a noted scientist, this individual developed an aerodrome that crashed on takeoff after two unsuccessful launchings from a houseboat on the Potomac River.
    a. Alexander Graham Bell
    b. Thomas Walker
    c. George Cayley
    d. Samuel P. Langley

_____ 5. Wing warping (bending the tip of the wings as the buzzards bend theirs in flight) was the first step in the development of:

a. wing camber ratio.

b. ailerons.

c. wing aspect ratio.

d. rudder pedals.

6. The Wright brothers completed their epic flight on:

a. October 7, 1903.

b. December 8, 1903.

c. December 17, 1903.

d. January 5, 1904.

7. The Aerial Experimental Association was formed by:

a. Alexander Graham Bell.

b. Samuel P. Langley.

c. Wilber Wright.

d. Griffith Brewer.

8. The Wright brothers broke the problem of flight into three principal parts. All of the following are included except:

a. power.

b. balance and control in the air.

c. durability of materials.

d. wing shape and resulting lift.

9. To counter "well digging" (adverse yaw), the Wrights developed a:

a. better wing-warping system.

b. longer right wing to offset weight of the pilot.

c. movable rudder.

d. vertical stabilizer.

10. The most successful product of the AEA was:

a. Red Wing.

b. Golden Flyer.

c. June Bug.

d. Demoiselle.

11. A name that is synonymous with the development of dirigibles is:

a. Louis Bechereau.

b. Henri Farman.

c. Ferdinand von Zeppelin.

d. Robert Esnault-Pelterie.

12. Sir George Cayley's paper, published in 1810, that laid the foundation for the study of aerodynamics was titled:

a. *Progress in Flying Machines*.

b. *On Aerial Navigation*.

c. *Aeronautical Science*.

d. *Aerodrome Design*.

**II. True/False**—Circle "T" if the statement is true; circle "F" if it is false.

T    F    1. Sir George Cayley published a paper titled *On Aerial Navigation* in 1810.

T    F    2. Known as Germany's birdman, Otto Lilienthal completed his hang glider experiments from an artificial hill near Berlin.

T    F    3. Stephen M. Balzer piloted Professor Langley's aerodrome on its two unsuccessful flights.

T    F    4. The first of the Wright brothers' flights on 17 December 1903, lasted 12 seconds and covered a distance of 120 feet.

T    F    5. The Wright brothers received considerable press coverage after their historic flight and consequently were immediately recognized as the first to achieve powered flight.

T    F    6. The U.S. Army was quick to recognize the potential of the Wright brothers' machine and shortly after the historic flight they placed a substantial order.

T    F    7. Professor Langley's Aerodrome was modified by Glenn Curtiss in 1914 and then successfully flown.

T    F    8. Dr. Albert P. Zahm of the Smithsonian Institution confirmed that Glenn Curtiss had not made any major changes to Professor Langley's aerodrome.

T    F    9. The Wright brothers were amazed to find that many of Otto Lilienthal's calculations were absolutely correct, which aided them immeasurably.

T    F   10. The Wrights' "horizontal elevator" controlled their Flyer's pitch.

T    F   11. The Wright Flyer remained in Great Britain's Science Museum until 1948.

T    F   12. On 5 June 1783, the Montgolfier brothers successfully launched a hydrogen balloon in Annonay, France.

# Chapter 1

**I. Multiple Choice**—Choose the best answer and place it in the blank at the left.

_____ 1. In August 1909, the first great air meet was held near:
a. Rheims, France.
b. Los Angeles, California.
c. Boston, Massachusetts.
d. Martiques, France.

_____ 2. The Bennett Cup race at Belmont Park in October 1910 was won by:
a. Glenn Curtiss.
b. Alberto Santos-Dumont.
c. Ralph Johnstone.
d. Jacques de Lesseps.

_____ 3. One of the most daring of the early showmen in the pre-World War I era was:
a. Claude Graham-White.
b. Lincoln Beachey.
c. Roy Knabenshue.
d. Louis Bleriot.

_____ 4. The control system that incorporated foot-operated pedals for rudder control and a wheel that activated both elevators and ailerons was developed by:

        a. Glenn Curtiss.
        b. Orville Wright.
        c. Louis Bechereau.
        d. Louis Bleriot.

_____ 5. Calbraith P. Rodgers:
        a. performed the first inside loop in a Curtiss biplane.
        b. established the speed record at the 1909 Rheims meet.
        c. was the first to fly coast-to-coast across the United States.
        d. was killed while performing at San Francisco's Panama Pacific Exposition.

_____ 6. Clyde Cessna built the first airplane after ordering which of the following aircraft?
        a. Bleriot Monoplane
        b. Curtiss Pusher
        c. Farman Biplane
        d. Wright Flyer

_____ 7. This individual built aircraft for the U.S. Army Signal Corps and employed several early aviation pioneers, including Donald W. Douglas.
        a. Clement Keys
        b. Matty Laird
        c. Elmer Partridge
        d. Glenn Martin

_____ 8. One of the earliest women pilots, this individual was the fourth pilot to master the inside loop.
        a. Lillie Max
        b. Matilde Moisant
        c. Katherine Stinson
        d. Helene Dutrieux

_____ 9. Built primarily as a training aircraft for the U.S. Army Signal Corps during WWI, this aircraft was the most popular in terms of number produced.
        a. Bleriot XI
        b. Curtiss Jenny
        c. Wright Model B
        d. Laird Swallow

_____ 10. Many of the early U.S. aircraft manufacturers were:
        a. controlled by the government during the war years.
        b. purchased by auto and banking interests.
        c. under contract to produce British aircraft during WWI.
        d. successful in developing the first fighter aircraft.

**II. True/False**—Circle "T" if the statement is true; circle "F" if it is false.

T    F    1. Wilber Wright won the first Gordon Bennett cup race with a speed of 47 mph.
T    F    2. John Moisant won the Bennett Cup race at Belmont Park but was disqualified on a technicality.

| | | |
|---|---|---|
| T | F | 3. An altitude record of 4165 feet was established in January 1910 at an air meet held near Los Angeles. |
| T | F | 4. Louis Bleriot was the first to fly across the English Channel in a heavier-than-air aircraft on July 25, 1909. |
| T | F | 5. Katherine Stinson was one of the first pilots to perform a loop-the-loop in her air show appearances. |
| T | F | 6. Matty Laird, Buck Weaver, Clyde Cessna, and others established their aircraft manufacturing facilities in Wichita, Kansas. |
| T | F | 7. The Curtiss Aeroplane and Motor Company was sold to a company controlled by Clement Keys. |
| T | F | 8. The Wright Aeronautical Corporation and the Curtiss Aeroplane and Motor Company were taken over by banking and auto interests prior to WWI. |
| T | F | 9. Robert Esnault-Pelterie flew his "Demoiselle" in 1906 to become the first European to fly a powered aircraft. |
| T | F | 10. Glenn Curtiss was the winner of the first Gordon Bennett Trophy. |
| T | F | 11. Lincoln Beachey was killed while performing at San Francisco's Panama Pacific Exposition. |
| T | F | 12. Donald W. Douglas began his aviation career with the Wright Aeronautical Corporation. |

# Chapter 2

**I. Multiple Choice**—Choose the best answer and place it in the blank at the left.

_____ 1. In March 1916, the First Aero Squadron received orders to report to:
  a. Texas.
  b. France.
  c. New Mexico.
  d. England.

_____ 2. Naval aviation was born in November 1910 when _____ made the first takeoff from a platform on the bow of the cruiser *Birmingham*.
  a. Harold E. Geiger
  b. Eugene Ely
  c. Benjamin Foulois
  d. Glenn Curtiss

_____ 3. The synchronized machine gun mounted in front of the pilot was first developed by:
  a. A. V. Roe & Co.
  b. Handley Page.
  c. Rumpler.
  d. Moraine-Saulnier.

_____ 4. At the beginning of the war, most military strategists looked upon the aircraft as a(n):
  a. observation post.
  b. tactical fighter.
  c. long-range bomber.
  d. novelty that had little military significance.

_____ 5. Germany's ace of aces, "The Red Baron," with 80 confirmed victories, was:
   a. Max Immelman.
   b. Kurt Wintgens.
   c. Manfred von Richthofen.
   d. Ritter von Tutschek.

_____ 6. Considered by many as the best Allied fighter aircraft of the war, this aircraft had a distinctive humped engine cowling.
   a. Nieuport 17
   b. Curtiss JN-2
   c. Vickers Gunship
   d. Sopwith Camel

_____ 7. This British aircraft was manufactured in the United States under contract, but very few reached the front lines by the war's end.
   a. de Havilland DH-4
   b. Bristol F-2B
   c. Vickers Gunbus
   d. Handley Page 0/400

_____ 8. This superior German fighter aircraft was developed toward the end of the war and presented a match for any of the Allied aircraft.
   a. Fokker E-1 Eindecker
   b. Albatros D-III
   c. Pfalz D-III
   d. Fokker D-VII

_____ 9. Head of the Royal Flying Corps and one of the earliest air war strategists, this individual had a strong influence on America's Billy Mitchell.
   a. Mason Patrick
   b. Hugh Trenchard
   c. Edward Deeds
   d. Elliot White Springs

_____ 10. America's leading ace during World War I was:
   a. Major Raoul Lufberry.
   b. Captain Eddie Rickenbacker.
   c. Lt. Frank Luke.
   d. Lt. Joseph F. Wehner.

_____ 11. This individual scored 17 victories as a member of the Lafayette Escadrille.
   a. Major Raoul Lufberry
   b. Major Edward Mannock
   c. Lt. Georges Guynemer
   d. Lt. Charles Nungesser

_____ 12. The United States decided not to build fighter aircraft during WWI because:
   a. we did not want to compete with our allies.
   b. of the difficulties in delivering aircraft to Europe.

c. we were too far behind the Allies in aircraft development.

d. we preferred to concentrate on long-range bombers.

_____ 13. The German _____ of 1915 was fitted with a machine gun that was synchronized by an interrupter gear to fire between the rotating propeller blades.

      a. Moraine-Saulnier Bullet

      b. Fokker Eindecker

      c. Fokker Dridecker

      d. Pfalz D-III

_____ 14. The leading Allied ace during WWI was:

      a. Captain Eddie Rickenbacker.

      b. Captain René Fonck.

      c. Major Edward Mannock.

      d. Major Francesco Baracca.

_____ 15. Parachutes were generally worn only by:

      a. fighter pilots.

      b. dirigible crew members.

      c. balloon observers.

      d. bomber crew members.

**II. True/False**—Circle "T" if the statement is true; circle "F" if it is false.

T    F    1. The First Aero Squadron was led by Capt. Benjamin Foulois.

T    F    2. If WWI had continued into 1919, the Allies would have controlled the air because of numerical superiority.

T    F    3. A popular aircraft used for training many U.S. pilots was the Curtiss JN-2 Jenny.

T    F    4. British, French, and German aircraft development during WWI was greatly advanced over our aircraft development.

T    F    5. The Lafayette Escadrille was one of the most famous squadrons of French fighter pilots during WWI.

T    F    6. The Germans used their zeppelins as long-range (strategic) bombers during the early years of the war.

T    F    7. Early aircraft production in the U.S. was controlled by automobile manufacturers.

T    F    8. The water-cooled Liberty engine was developed by the Wright Aeronautical Company.

T    F    9. General William "Billy" Mitchell was Commander of the Army Air Services during WWI.

T    F   10. The SPAD was a rugged aircraft developed by the British Sopwith Company.

T    F   11. Observation balloons were used by both sides during WWI.

T    F   12. Significant technical developments took place during WWI that resulted in improved aircraft performance, greater engine power output, greater speeds, stronger airframes, and larger payloads.

T    F   13. Frank Luke was known as the balloon buster from Arizona because of his dogged pursuit of German *drachens* (observation balloons).

T    F   14. The U.S. Air Service was actually part of the Army Signal Corps until May 1918.

T    F   15. The United States had fallen behind the Europeans in aircraft development by the start of WWI.

T    F    16. The first sustained strategic bombing in history was the zeppelin strikes against England during WWI.

T    F    17. The U.S. First Aero Squadron was assigned to General Pershing's command in March 1916 to serve in France.

T    F    18. The U.S. Air Service evolved out of the Aviation Section of the Signal Corps.

T    F    19. Major Billy Bishop, with 72 aerial victories during WWI, went on to help found the Canadian Air Force.

T    F    20. The German *drachens* were fighter squadrons designed to strafe Allied trenches before major assaults.

## III. Matching (Individuals):

_____ 1. First pilot to use a synchronized machine gun on his Moraine-Saulnier Bullet monoplane.

_____ 2. France's top scoring ace during WWI.

_____ 3. Scored 17 victories as a member of the Lafayette Escadrille before transferring to the U.S. Air Service.

_____ 4. The balloon buster from Arizona who was awarded the Congressional Medal of Honor posthumously.

_____ 5. Head of the Royal Flying Corps.

_____ 6. Commander of the Army Air Services.

_____ 7. Proposed that the Air Service be a separate and equal department of the U.S. military.

_____ 8. Commanding officer of the U.S. First Aero Squadron.

_____ 9. Germany's leading ace.

_____ 10. America's leading ace.

a. Hugh Trenchard
b. Manfred von Richthofen
c. Eddie Rickenbacker
d. Frank Luke
e. Raoul Lufberry
f. René Fonck
g. Benjamin Foulois
h. Roland Garros
i. Mason Patrick
j. Billy Mitchell

## IV. Matching (Aircraft):

_____ 1. Used by the British early in the war primarily as an observation plane.

_____ 2. Early German fighter that became the scourge of the skies during 1915 with its synchronized machine guns.

_____ 3. Flown by von Richthofen's Jadgstaffel 11 during the Spring of 1917 and the aircraft in which he scored the greatest number of victories.

_____ 4. One of Great Britain's best fighter aircraft during WWI.

_____ 5. British heavy bomber designed to carry 1000 pounds of bombs to Berlin.

_____ 6. British aircraft manufactured in the U.S. under contract.

a. de Havilland DH-4
b. Albatros D-III
c. JN-4
d. SE-5
e. SPAD
f. Fokker Eindecker
g. BE2
h. Handley Page V/1500

_____ 7. A French fighter that was flown by many
American pilots.

_____ 8. Used to train U.S. pilots.

# Chapter 3

**I. Multiple Choice**—Choose the best answer and place it in the blank at the left.

_____ 1. During the 1920s, U.S. military aircraft were primarily designed for:
a. long-range bombing missions.
b. defensive purposes.
c. tactical ground support.
d. none of these.

_____ 2. During the 1920s, military appropriations for the Air Service:
a. expanded significantly.
b. increased in the immediate post war period then leveled off.
c. were adequate.
d. were not a high priority.

_____ 3. The Treaty of Versailles:
a. stripped Germany of all overseas territories.
b. required that Germany pay billions of dollars in reparations.
c. forbid Germany from having any military aircraft.
d. all of these.
e. only b and c.

_____ 4. The first men to fly the Atlantic nonstop from Newfoundland to Ireland and claim the $50,000 prize offered by a British newspaper were:
a. Tower and Read.
b. Alcock and Brown.
c. Smith and Arnold.
d. Nelson and Harding.

_____ 5. Lt. Commander _____ and his five-man crew, aboard the NC-4, successfully flew across the Atlantic from Long Island to England in May 1919.
a. Douglas Taylor
b. Charles Menoher
c. Albert C. Read
d. Lowell H. Smith

_____ 6. The World Cruisers, specially built for the army's epic flight around the world, were developed by:
a. Curtiss.
b. Martin.
c. Douglas.
d. Boeing.

_____ 7. Which of the following World Cruisers completed the epic flight around the world?
a. *Seattle* and *Boston*

b. *Boston* and *Chicago*
c. *Chicago* and *New Orleans*
d. *New Orleans* and *Seattle*

_____ 8. General Mitchell's secret report to the War Department in October 1924:
a. predicted a naval air attack by the Japanese on Pearl Harbor.
b. suggested that the U.S. Pacific Fleet stop the flow of war materials to Japan.
c. provided the basis for a substantial buildup of military air power in the late 1920s.
d. predicted the German attack on Poland in 1939.

_____ 9. Which of the following statements is not true?
a. General Charles Menoher, an infantry commander with no aviation background, replaced Gen. Mason Patrick as Chief of the Air Service.
b. The R-34, commanded by Maj. G. H. Scott, completed the first aerial round trip across the Atlantic.
c. Captain St. Clair Street completed a round trip flight from New York to Nome, Alaska, in June 1920.
d. The World Cruisers *Chicago* and *New Orleans* completed their epic flight in a total of 97 days or roughly three months.

_____ 10. An outspoken proponent of military aviation, this individual attempted to demonstrate the importance of aviation by sending his army pilots on numerous record-breaking flights.
a. Glen L. Martin
b. Mason M. Patrick
c. William E. Mitchell
d. James Doolittle

**II. True/False**—Circle "T" if the statement is true; circle "F" if it is false.

T  F  1. It can be said that the peace treaty signed with Germany at the close of WWI led to the Nazi takeover of Germany.

T  F  2. Adolf Hitler was elected chancellor of Germany by an overwhelming majority.

T  F  3. Commander John Tower successfully flew the NC-4 from Rockaway Beach, Long Island, to Plymouth, England, in May 1919.

T  F  4. The German dirigible R-34, commanded by Hugo Eckener, was the first airship to cross the Atlantic both ways.

T  F  5. The U.S. Navy acquired one of its first dirigibles from the Germans under a post-war reparations agreement.

T  F  6. The U.S. and Germany signed a separate peace treaty in 1921.

T  F  7. The NC number originally stood for "Navy-Curtiss."

T  F  8. Many of the epic flights by General Mitchell's army pilots served to gain significant congressional support.

T  F  9. Although several World Cruisers were slightly damaged, all completed the flight around the world.

T  F  10. Gen. Billy Mitchell's secret report to the War Department in October 1924 resulted in a significant buildup in military air power during the late 1920s.

T  F  11. RAF Capt. John Alcock and Lt. Arthur Whitten-Brown completed the first transatlantic nonstop flight from Newfoundland to Ireland on June 14, 1919.

T    F    12. The first round trip aerial crossing of the Atlantic was completed by the British dirigible R-34 in July 1919.

# Chapter 4

**I. Multiple Choice**—Choose the best answer and place it in the blank at the left.

_____ 1. A strong proponent of navy aviation who became Director of Naval Aviation in March 1921 was:
      a. Josephus Daniels.
      b. William S. Benson.
      c. William A. Moffett.
      d. Bruce G. Leighton.

_____ 2. Bombers developed by which of the following companies were used by the Army Air Service to sink the *Ostfriesland* in July 1921.
      a. Curtiss
      b. Douglas
      c. Martin
      d. Wright

_____ 3. The Wright *Whirlwind* engine was first developed by:
      a. George J. Mead.
      b. Charles L. Lawrance.
      c. Bruce G. Leighton.
      d. Frederick B. Rentschler.

_____ 4. The navy was particularly interested in Lawrance's engine because it:
      a. was water-cooled and easier to maintain.
      b. had more horsepower for less weight.
      c. was air-cooled and developed 400 hp.
      d. had a water-cooled rotary radial engine.

_____ 5. The navy's first aircraft carrier was named the USS:
      a. *Maryland*.
      b. *Shenandoah*.
      c. *Langley*.
      d. *Los Angeles*.

_____ 6. The evolution of large multi-engine flying boats used by the navy developed slowly for all of the following reasons, except:
      a. lack of reliable engines of sufficient power.
      b. smaller float planes catapulted from ships were more effective in covering greater distances.
      c. Admiral Moffett had great faith in large rigid dirigibles.
      d. none of these.

_____ 7. Which of the following statements is not true concerning Billy Mitchell?
      a. He was reduced in rank to colonel and transferred to Fort Sam Houston, Texas.
      b. Major General Mason Patrick quietly supported his position.

c. He lost public support when he criticized the War Department.

d. He demanded that the President appoint a panel of representative Americans to investigate the War and Navy Departments.

_____ 8. The Morrow Board:

a. found Mitchell guilty of treasonable acts.

b. investigated the best means of developing and applying aircraft in national defense.

c. represented a cross section of nonpartial business and military leaders.

d. supported Mitchell's charges.

_____ 9. Which of the following statements regarding the use of airplanes by the military during the 1920s is not correct?

a. The navy feared that Congress might support an independent air force.

b. The navy placed more emphasis in developing dirigibles partly due to the lack of reliable engines for large aircraft.

c. Congress strongly supported the development of military airplanes.

d. None of these.

_____ 10. General Mitchell's bombers sunk this German battleship on July 21, 1921, in a demonstration of air power.

a. *Von Zeppelin*

b. *Graf Spee*

c. *Ostfriesland*

d. *Sharnhorst*

_____ 11. Which of the following statements concerning Billy Mitchell is not correct?

a. He condemned the War Department for not replacing obsolete aircraft, which he called "flying coffins."

b. He predicted that the "next war may start in the air."

c. He accused President Coolidge of "dereliction of duty" in responding to the Air Services' needs.

d. He was charged with "conduct prejudicial to good order and military discipline."

_____ 12. The Lawrance J-1 engine evolved into the famous:

a. Curtiss D-12.

b. Wright J-4 Whirlwind.

c. Liberty engine.

d. Hispano-Suiza V-8.

**II. True/False**—Circle "T" if the statement is true; circle "F" if it is false.

T   F     1. In his crusade for an independent air force, General Mitchell claimed that the airplane had made the navy's surface ships obsolete.

T   F     2. Adm. William S. Benson was a strong proponent of naval air power.

T   F     3. The sinking of the German battleship *Ostfriesland* had proved Mitchell's point to the top navy brass.

T   F     4. Lawrance's J-1 engine evolved into the Wright J-4 *Whirlwind*.

T   F     5. The navy first used airplane catapults mounted on the stern of battleships and cruisers.

| | | |
|---|---|---|
| T | F | 6. Adm. William A. Moffet discouraged the development of dirigibles but was over-ridden by the CNO. |
| T | F | 7. The first turntable airplane catapult was fitted to the stern of the USS *Jupiter* in 1922. |
| T | F | 8. The navy's ZR-3 *Los Angeles* was ordered from the zeppelin works at Friedrichshafen, Germany. |
| T | F | 9. Maj. Gen. Mason Patrick was vehemently opposed to Billy Mitchell's crusade for a strong independent air force. |
| T | F | 10. The navy dirigible *Shenandoah* had a long and productive career before it was decommissioned in 1929. |
| T | F | 11. The Lampert-Perkins Committee made recommendations largely favorable to Mitchell's position. |
| T | F | 12. Mitchell was charged with "conduct prejudicial to good order and military discipline" but was found not guilty. |
| T | F | 13. The Martin MB-2 bomber was used by the Army Air Service in 1922 to sink the German battleship *Ostfriesland*. |
| T | F | 14. The dirigible *Los Angeles* was decommissioned in 1933 and eventually scrapped. |
| T | F | 15. The U.S. Navy acquired one of its first dirigibles from the Germans under a post-war reparations agreement, which they subsequently named *Shenandoah*. |
| T | F | 16. General Mitchell predicted the war with Japan as early as 1924. |
| T | F | 17. On balance, it can be said that the navy had rather good success with their dirigibles during the 1920s. |
| T | F | 18. The navy was greatly impressed by Mitchell's bombers sinking the *Ostfriesland* and immediately took steps to expand its air arm. |

# Chapter 5

**I. Multiple Choice**—Choose the best answer and place it in the blank at the left.

_____ 1. Air mail service was inaugurated on 15 May 1918 when _____ attempted to fly the first leg between Washington, D.C., and New York City.
  a. Reuben H. Fleet
  b. Albert Burleson
  c. James H. Knight
  d. George L. Boyle

_____ 2. Between 12 August 1918, and the end of 1925 the mail was flown by:
  a. Army pilots.
  b. Navy pilots.
  c. Post Office pilots.
  d. private contractors.

_____ 3. The Air Mail Act of 1925 (Kelly Bill):
  a. turned over the carriage of air mail to private contractors.
  b. eliminated all subsidies for air mail carriage.
  c. turned over the carriage of air mail to the Post Office Department.
  d. set limits on the amount of mail that could be transported by air.

_____ 4. One of the problems of early air mail service was:
    a. lack of support from the postmasters general and Congress.
    b. no market for new civil aircraft.
    c. how to justify the unusually high profits.
    d. pilot training.

_____ 5. The primary purpose of the cross-country flight staged by the Post Office Department in February 1921 was:
    a. to influence the army to give up air mail service.
    b. to influence the public and Congress for financial assistance.
    c. to eliminate carriage of the mail by rail.
    d. to obtain better-equipped aircraft.

_____ 6. This Post Office pilot flew three legs of a cross-country flight in February 1921 and became a national hero.
    a. Frank Yeager
    b. Homer Berry
    c. Ernest Allison
    d. Jack Knight

_____ 7. The airway system was lighted from coast to coast by:
    a. 12 August 1918.
    b. 22 February 1921.
    c. 1 July 1924.
    d. 2 February 1925.

_____ 8. The most prevalent air mail aircraft of the early 1920s was the:
    a. Laird Swallow.
    b. Cessna Model A.
    c. de Havilland DH-4.
    d. Curtiss JN-4.

_____ 9. Which of the following statements concerning the early years of air mail service is not true?
    a. Flashing beacons marked the airway system from coast to coast.
    b. Very few new aircraft were available.
    c. Instrument flying was very primitive by today's standards.
    d. The accident and fatality rates were rather good, everything considered.

**II. True/False**—Circle "T" if the statement is true; circle "F" if it is false.

T    F    1. The first air mail service was established between Washington, D.C., and Boston.
T    F    2. Curtiss Jennies were first used to fly the mail.
T    F    3. Early air mail service was very profitable for the Post Office Department.
T    F    4. By the end of 1921 de Havilland DH-4s became the standard air mail airplane.
T    F    5. By the summer of 1919 air mail service had been established between New York and Chicago.
T    F    6. During the time the Post Office operated the air mail service, very few pilots were killed primarily because parachutes were used from 1919.

T   F    7. President Warren Harding first took the position that air mail was a waste of money.

T   F    8. Jack Knight's epic flight was between North Platt, Nebraska, and Chicago.

T   F    9. The first cross-country air mail flight took seven pilots a total of 108 flying hours.

T   F   10. The Post Office Department primarily used war surplus aircraft for air mail service.

T   F   11. By the fall of 1920, the Post Office offered regular transcontinental service between San Francisco and New York.

T   F   12. Air mail service in the United States was inaugurated on 15 May 1918, between Washington, D.C., and New York.

T   F   13. In August 1918 civilian pilots took over the mail route between New York and Washington.

# Chapter 6

**I. Multiple Choice**—Choose the best answer and place it in the blank at the left.

_____ 1. Which of the following aircraft was not generally used by the barnstormers for their aerial shows?
    a. Standard
    b. Curtiss Jenny
    c. Thomas Morse Scout
    d. de Havilland DH-4

_____ 2. All but one of the following barnstormers started their own airplane manufacturing company. Which one did not?
    a. Buck Weaver
    b. Matty Laird
    c. Lloyd Stearman
    d. Wiley Post

_____ 3. The Air Commerce Act of 1926:
    a. transferred the carriage of air mail to private contractors.
    b. provided for the first aviation regulations and required federal licenses for all civil pilots and aircraft.
    c. gave the Postmaster General authority to consolidate air mail routes.
    d. established the Federal Aviation Administration.

_____ 4. Described in the June 1920 issue of *Aviation* as the "first commercial airplane capable of carrying a pilot and two passengers with fuel enough for 225 miles at full speed," this was the:
    a. Laird Swallow.
    b. Travel Air.
    c. Cessna Model A.
    d. Stearman C-1.

_____ 5. Wichita, Kansas, became the home of general aviation largely because of this individual.
    a. Charlie Meyers
    b. Jake Moellendick

c. Clyde Pangborn
    d. Roscoe Turner

_____ 6. Clyde Cessna's 1912 *Silver Wings* was a home-built copy of the:
    a. Curtiss Jenny.
    b. Thomas Morse Scout.
    c. Bleriot.
    d. Standard.

_____ 7. In 1924, Beech, Cessna, and Stearman formed the:
    a. WACO Aircraft Company.
    b. Swallow Airplane Company.
    c. Travel Air Manufacturing Company.
    d. Advance Airplane Company.

_____ 8. Stearman Aircraft Company eventually became a part of:
    a. Boeing Airplane Company.
    b. Cessna Aircraft Corporation.
    c. Douglas Aircraft Corporation.
    d. Lockheed Aircraft Corporation.

_____ 9. Cessna Aircraft Corporation's first aircraft was the:
    a. Standard.
    b. Model 6.
    c. Model A.
    d. Scout.

_____ 10. This aircraft was advertised as a sister ship to Lindbergh's famous airplane:
    a. Stinson Detroiter.
    b. Ryan Brougham.
    c. Great Lakes Sport Trainer.
    d. Meyers Midget.

_____ 11. Cessna's first aircraft, a home-built copy of the French Bleriot, was the:
    a. Model A.
    b. Travel Air.
    c. Model 120.
    d. Silver Wings.

_____ 12. The Laird Swallow:
    a. was the first commercial airplane capable of carrying a pilot and two passengers with enough fuel for 225 miles.
    b. won the Ford Reliability Tour race in 1925 and 1926.
    c. first appeared as an army trainer in 1919.
    d. was a popular aerobatic aircraft during the 1920s.

_____ 13. One of the direct results of the Morrow Board was the:
    a. restriction of aerobatics to military pilots.
    b. transfer of air mail carriage from the Post Office to civilian carriers.
    c. Air Commerce Act of 1926.
    d. growth in the number of aircraft manufacturers.

_____ 14. Which of the following statements is correct concerning some of the early barnstormers?
 a. Clyde Cessna served in the infantry during WWI.
 b. Lloyd Stearman learned to fly while serving in the navy.
 c. Walter Beech was a mechanic in the army and never actually learned to fly.
 d. Buck Weaver received his flying lessons from Clyde Cessna after WWI.

_____ 15. With pilots Art Goebel and Bill Davis at the controls, this aircraft won the 1927 Pineapple Derby flight between California and Hawaii.
 a. Cessna DC-6A
 b. WACO 10
 c. Travel Air 5000
 d. Laird Swallow

**II. True/False**—Circle "T" if the statement is true; circle "F" if it is false.

T  F  1. Many of the barnstormers in the early 1920s flew Curtiss Jennies.
T  F  2. Walter Beech, Clyde Cessna, and Charles Lindbergh got their start in aviation on the barnstorming circuit.
T  F  3. During the early 1920s, there were no aviation regulations, no federal pilot licenses, and no airworthiness certificates for airplanes.
T  F  4. The Air Commerce Act of 1926 was the result of recommendations from the Morrow Board.
T  F  5. Many of the barnstormers used wing walkers who performed gymnastics in flight as a means of attracting crowds.
T  F  6. Clyde Cessna preferred biplanes over monoplanes during his early years in aircraft manufacturing.
T  F  7. Charles Lindbergh's Ryan monoplane was called the _Dallas Spirit_.
T  F  8. Winners of the 1927 Pineapple Derby were Art Goebel and Lt. Bill Davis, flying a _Travel Air_ 5000.
T  F  9. By the late 1920s, WACO had become one of the most popular civilian aircraft.
T  F  10. The first _Travel Air_ was a monoplane powered by a 120-hp Anzani engine.
T  F  11. Barnstorming started to decline in popularity during the mid- to late-1920s.
T  F  12. Clyde Cessna and Walter Beech learned to fly during WWI.
T  F  13. Businessmen-pilots of the 1920s used their airplanes more for advertising than for business travel.
T  F  14. The Great Lakes biplane was a favorite of aerobatic pilots into the 1960s.
T  F  15. WACO sold almost half of the new civil aircraft built in the U.S. in 1927.
T  F  16. Most aviation historians would agree that the barnstormers contributed to the growth and development of aviation.

# Chapter 7

**I. Multiple Choice**—Choose the best answer and place it in the blank at the left.

_____ 1. The Postmaster General during the Hoover Administration was:
 a. Walter Varney.
 b. Elmer Partridge.
 c. Walter Folger Brown.
 d. J. Paul Riddle.

_____ 2. CAM-1 was awarded to:
   a. Colonial Air Transport.
   b. National Air Transport.
   c. Boeing Air Transport.
   d. Pacific Air Transport.

_____ 3. Under the Kelly Bill, the Post Office Department:
   a. exercised very little control over the air carriers.
   b. encouraged the air carriers to add passenger service.
   c. made adequate profits through 1929.
   d. matched the subsidies given to the railroads.

_____ 4. CAM-9 between Chicago and Minneapolis-St. Paul was started by Charles Dickinson and formed the foundation for:
   a. United Airlines.
   b. American Air Lines.
   c. Northwest Orient Air Lines.
   d. Trans World Airlines.

_____ 5. Embry-Riddle, Southern Air Transport, Colonial Airways, and Universal Aviation formed the foundation for today's:
   a. United Airlines.
   b. Delta Airlines.
   c. Northwest Airlines.
   d. American Airlines.

_____ 6. Boeing Air Transport, Pratt and Whitney, Hamilton Propellers, Stearman, Northrup, and Sikorsky all came under which of the following holding companies?
   a. AVCO
   b. North American Aviation
   c. United Aircraft and Transport
   d. Transcontinental Air Transport

_____ 7. The North American Aviation holding company was formed by:
   a. William B. Boeing.
   b. Frederick Rentschler.
   c. Clement Keys.
   d. Sherman Fairchild.

_____ 8. Southern Air Transport became a part of:
   a. AVCO.
   b. United Aircraft and Transport Corporation.
   c. North American Aviation.
   d. National Air Transport.

_____ 9. American Airways was organized under:
   a. AVCO.
   b. United Aircraft and Transport Corporation.
   c. North American Aviation.
   d. Universal Aviation Corporation.

_____ 10. Eastern Air Transport, the forerunners of Eastern Airlines, was acquired by:
a. AVCO.
b. United Aircraft and Transport Corporation.
c. North American Aviation.
d. Universal Aviation Corporation.

_____ 11. Charles Lindbergh's aircraft, *The Spirit of St. Louis*, was built by the:
a. Stearman Aircraft Co.
b. Ryan Co.
c. Curtis Aircraft Co.
d. Fairchild Aviation Corp.

_____ 12. Varney Air Lines, Pacific Air Transport, Boeing Air Transport, and National Air Transport formed the foundation for today's:
a. American Air Lines.
b. Continental Airlines.
c. Trans World Airlines.
d. United Airlines.

_____ 13. The North American Aviation holding company was formed by:
a. William B. Boeing.
b. Frederick Rentschler.
c. Clement Keys.
d. Sherman Fairchild.

_____ 14. Pratt and Whitney was formed by:
a. Henry Ford.
b. William Stout.
c. Charles Lawrance.
d. Fred Rentschler.

_____ 15. The Curtiss-Wright Aeronautical Corporation was owned by:
a. AVCO.
b. Ford Motor Co.
c. North American Aviation.
d. United Aircraft and Transport Corp.

_____ 16. The Stout Metal Plane Company was purchased by:
a. Stinson Aircraft Co.
b. Curtiss Aeroplane and Motor Co.
c. Ford Motor Co.
d. United Aircraft and Transportation Corp.

_____ 17. The Ford *TriMotor* (Tin Goose) was:
a. inspired by the Fokker *TriMotor*.
b. powered by Wright J-4 Whirlwind engines.
c. first flown on 11 June 1926.
d. all of the above.

_____ 18. The decade of the 1920s ended with control of virtually all elements of aviation by:

a. United Aircraft and Transport Corp.; North American Aviation; and AVCO.
b. Ford Motor Co.; Boeing Airplane Co.; and AVCO.
c. Transcontinental Air Transport; United Aircraft and Transport Corp.; and Curtiss-Wright Aeronautical Corp.
d. North American Aviation; National Air Transport; and AVCO.

## II. True/False—Circle "T" if the statement is true; circle "F" if it is false.

T  F  1. Charles Lindbergh completed his epic flight in May 1927.
T  F  2. Lindbergh's specially built Ryan monoplane was powered by Pratt and Whitney's 400-hp Wasp engine.
T  F  3. Most of the early contract air mail carriers were not particularly interested in carrying passengers.
T  F  4. Charles Lindbergh was an air mail pilot flying for the Robertson brothers on CAM-2 between St. Louis and Chicago.
T  F  5. David L. Behneke, a pilot for Northwest Airways, was one of the founders of the Air Line Pilots Association
T  F  6. Henry Ford was the successful bidder on two early CAM routes.
T  F  7. Harry Chandler founded and edited *Aerial Age*, one of the earliest U.S. aviation magazines.
T  F  8. The Ford TriMotor was affectionately dubbed the "Tin Goose".
T  F  9. Pacific Aero Products Company formed the beginning of Douglas Aircraft Corporation.
T  F  10. The Boeing Model 40A biplane was used to fly the air mail route between Chicago and San Francisco.
T  F  11. During 1933, General Motors actually gained control of North American Aviation.
T  F  12. Transcontinental Air Transport merged with Western Air Express to form the beginnings of today's TWA.
T  F  13. National Air Transport was a combination air and rail service across the United States.
T  F  14. Pratt and Whitney's first engine was the air-cooled 400-hp Wasp.
T  F  15. William Boeing designed the merger of Curtiss Aeroplane and Motor with Wright Aeronautical Corporation.
T  F  16. AVCO began its route expansion by acquiring Embry-Riddle's CAM-24 route operating between Chicago and Cincinnati.
T  F  17. The Curtiss-Wright Aeronautical Corporation was acquired by United Aircraft and Transport Corporation.
T  F  18. Boeing Air Transport, Pratt and Whitney, Stearman, Northrup, and Sikorsky all came under the corporate umbrella of North American Aviation.
T  F  19. The early contract air mail operators were not particularly interested in carrying passengers.
T  F  20. The first Braniff Air Lines was acquired by AVCO.

## III. Matching:

_____  1. Postmaster General during the Hoover
            Administration

a. Harris Hanshue
b. William Stout

_____ 2. Formed Pacific Air Transport
_____ 3. Formed Western Air Express
_____ 4. Started Pacific Aero Products Company in 1915
_____ 5. Left Wright Aeronautical to form Pratt and Whitney
_____ 6. Formed North American Aviation
_____ 7. Aircraft manufacturer whose company was bought by Ford Motor Company
_____ 8. Flew a Ford TriMotor over the North Pole
_____ 9. Developed a successful monoplane called the Detroiter
_____ 10. Former Chief of the U.S. Air Service

c. Frederick Rentschler
d. Mason Patrick
e. Edward Stinson
f. Walter Folger Brown
g. Clement M. Keys
h. Richard Byrd
i. Vern C. Gorst
j. William E. Boeing

# Chapter 8

**I. Multiple Choice**—Choose the best answer and place it in the blank at the left.

_____ 1. The Air Mail Act of 1930 (McNary-Watres) included all of the following provisions except:

    a. operators were paid for flying the mail according to space available for mail in their airplanes.

    b. the Postmaster General could extend or consolidate routes according to his judgment.

    c. it designated three transcontinental routes that would be opened for competitive bidding.

    d. routes would be awarded to the lowest bidder who had offered a daily schedule of at least 250 miles over a period of six months.

_____ 2. The Air Mail Act of 1930 (McNary-Watres):

    a. gave the operators an incentive to acquire large multi-engine aircraft.

    b. discouraged passenger service.

    c. encouraged smaller, newly established operators.

    d. eliminated subsidies.

_____ 3. Which of the following did not occur during the "Spoils Conferences"?

    a. The merger of TAT and Western Air Express.

    b. American Airways acquired the southern route after purchasing SAFEway and Delta Air Service.

    c. United Aircraft and Transport Corporation acquired National Air Transport.

    d. Qualified bidders must have flown at night for six months over a route of not less than 250 miles.

_____ 4. Delta Air Service:

    a. was acquired by TAT.

    b. was merged into SAFEway.

    c. shared the southern route with American Airways.

    d. was acquired by American Airways.

_____ 5. The three transcontinental routes included all but one of the following carriers. Which one?
  a. United
  b. TWA
  c. American
  d. Delta

_____ 6. This carrier actually submitted the low bid for the air mail contract between New York and Washington, D.C., but the route was given to Eastern Air Transport.
  a. Reed Airline
  b. Century Air Line
  c. Ludington Line
  d. Central Air Line

_____ 7. Ludington Lines operated:
  a. Douglas M-2s.
  b. Northrup Alphas.
  c. Stinson TriMotors.
  d. Ford TriMotors.

_____ 8. E. L. Cord, founder of Century Air Line and Century Pacific Line, claimed that the major carriers:
  a. were grossly overpaid for flying the mail.
  b. were poorly managed.
  c. were favored by the Post Office Department.
  d. all of these.

_____ 9. This act gave the Postmaster General authority to consolidate routes and change the method of payment for carrying mail.
  a. Air Mail Act (Kelly) of 1925
  b. Air Mail Act (McNary-Watres) of 1930
  c. Air Mail Act (Black-McKellar) of 1934
  d. Air Commerce Act (Bingham-Parker-Merritt) of 1926

_____ 10. The McNary-Watres Act:
  a. discouraged carrying passengers.
  b. offered the air mail contractors outright subsidies.
  c. encouraged the use of single-engine aircraft as a cost-saving measure.
  d. required the successful bidder to have operated a daily schedule of at least 500 miles over a period of one year.

_____ 11. When Postmaster Brown was engineering the transcontinental southern route, AVCO's American Airways took over SAFEway by:
  a. direct purchase.
  b. acquiring Delta, which had merged with SAFEway.
  c. forcing TWA to sell their SAFEway stock.
  d. merger, with SAFEway retaining its authority to fly as an AVCO commuter.

_____ 12. Under the "Spoils Conferences":
  a. air mail rates were increased significantly.

b. TAT was forced to merge with Western Air Express.

c. passenger service was encouraged.

d. routes would be awarded to the lowest responsible bidder.

_____ 13. Many smaller companies like Reed Airline and Century Air Line:

a. competed very effectively against the major carriers.

b. received higher air mail subsidies than the major carriers.

c. were forced out of business by the major carriers.

d. actually carried more passengers than the major carriers.

_____ 14. The first Delta Air Service:

a. began as a crop-dusting business in Louisiana.

b. was purchased by American Airways.

c. flew between Birmingham and Dallas.

d. all of the above.

_____ 15. Ludington Line:

a. underbid Eastern Air Transport on the air mail route between New York and Washington.

b. was acquired by American Airways.

c. flew less costly Ford TriMotor aircraft.

d. all of the above.

**II. True/False**—Circle "T" if the statement is true; circle "F" if it is false.

T   F   1. Postmaster Brown was the primary author of the Air Mail Act of 1930.

T   F   2. The McNary-Watres Act gave the postmaster almost absolute control over the airlines.

T   F   3. Postmaster Brown favored competition and smaller operators with limited resources.

T   F   4. The "Spoils Conferences" favored smaller independent operators.

T   F   5. The president and directors of Western Air Express were generally in favor of the merger with Transcontinental Air Transport.

T   F   6. Both Delta Air Service and SAFEway were excluded from bidding on the southern route because they had not flown at night for six months over a route of not less than 250 miles.

T   F   7. Delta Air Service began as a crop-dusting business in Louisiana in the early 1920s.

T   F   8. Small carriers such as Reed Airline and Century Air Lines were favored by the Post Office Department.

T   F   9. Ludington Line flew passengers profitably, which was unusual for most carriers during the early 1930s.

T   F   10. Fulton Lewis's publisher refused to print his story regarding the scandalous air mail bidding practices.

T   F   11. By the early 1930, all segments of aviation were dominated by three powerful holding companies.

T   F   12. Ludington Lines' air mail bid for the New York to Washington, D.C., route was actually 64 cents lower than Eastern Air Transport's, but the latter carrier was the successful bidder.

T   F   13. Under the Air Mail Act (McNary-Watres) of 1930, routes would be awarded to the lowest bidder that had operated an airline on a daily schedule of at least 250 miles over a period of one year.

T   F   14. Officials at Western Air Express were generally pleased with the merger with TAT.

T   F   15. Both Delta and SAFEway were excluded from bidding on the transcontinental southern route because of Postmaster Brown's night-flying requirement.

T   F   16. David "Tex" Behneke was the founder and general manager of Western Air Express.

T   F   17. United Aircraft and Transport Corporation acquired National Air Transport during the Spoils Conference.

T   F   18. E. L. Cord maintained that most other airlines were poorly managed and, with proper cost controls, could profitably operate with far less money from the Post Office Department.

# Chapter 9

**I. Multiple Choice**—Choose the best answer and place it in the blank at the left.

_____ 1. Walter Folger Brown testified before Senator Black's committee that he:
    a. favored small independent carriers.
    b. was determined to develop an outstanding air carrier network in the United States.
    c. discouraged carriers from developing passenger service.
    d. did not force any major carriers to accept route extensions.

_____ 2. One of the results of Senator Black's committee was:
    a. Postmaster Brown was charged with violation of proper code of conduct while in office.
    b. the cancellation of all air mail contracts.
    c. substantial fines levied on all major air carriers who were overpaid for carrying the mail.
    d. the transfer of all air mail contracts held by Eastern Air Transport to Ludington Line.

_____ 3. Under the Air Mail Act of 1934 (Black-McKellar Bill), the Bureau of Air Commerce:
    a. approved air mail contracts, routes, and schedules.
    b. established air mail rates.
    c. provided subsidies to the air carriers.
    d. regulated the airway system and the licensing of pilots and aircraft.

_____ 4. Which of the following was not a provision of the Black-McKellar Act?
    a. It subjected the air carriers to control by the Post Office Department, Interstate Commerce Commission, and the Bureau of Air Commerce.
    b. All airlines were required to separate themselves from manufacturing firms.
    c. It transferred authority for establishing air mail routes and schedules from the Post Office Department to the Interstate Commerce Commission.
    d. It required that all routes were to be rebid each year.

_____ 5. Certificates of Public Convenience and Necessity were issued by the:
   a. Air Carrier Economic Regulation Division of the CAA.
   b. Post Office Department.
   c. Bureau of Air Commerce.
   d. Interstate Commerce Commission.

_____ 6. The Civil Aeronautics Board (CAB) was created in 1940 to:
   a. license pilots and aircraft.
   b. operate the airway system.
   c. regulate the airlines and investigate air accidents.
   d. only regulate the airlines.

_____ 7. Pan American Airways began scheduled service on 28 October 1927, between Key West, Florida, and:
   a. Cuba.
   b. Haiti.
   c. Puerto Rico.
   d. Dominican Republic.

_____ 8. Which of the following was not a problem faced by Juan Trippe in expanding Pan Am's routes into the Caribbean, Central America, and South America?
   a. Colombian government
   b. Cuban government
   c. W. R. Grace & Company
   d. New York, Rio & Buenos Aires Line (NYRBA)

_____ 9. The arrival of the _____ gave Pan Am the range to cross the Atlantic nonstop.
   a. Sikorsky S-38
   b. Sikorsky S-42
   c. Martin M-130
   d. Boeing B-314

_____ 10. Which of the following carriers did not seek international routes in the postwar period?
   a. American
   b. Braniff
   c. TWA
   d. United

_____ 11. AMEX was purchased by:
   a. American.
   b. Northwest.
   c. Pan Am.
   d. United.

_____ 12. Which of the following companies was not entirely controlled by Pan Am?
   a. West Indian Aerial Express
   b. Compania Mexicana de Aviacion
   c. Panagra
   d. Panair do Brasil

_____ 13. Pan Am's chief competitor in the Pacific after WWII was:
  a. American.
  b. National.
  c. Northwest.
  d. TWA.

_____ 14. On 1 June 1945, the CAB ruled that three U.S. air carriers should fly the Atlantic to European terminals. Which of the following was not included?
  a. American
  b. Braniff
  c. Pan Am
  d. TWA

_____ 15. One of the charges Senator Hugo Black made during his investigation of airlines in the 1930s was that:
  a. airlines collected money for mail not carried.
  b. the Postmaster General forced many smaller independent air carriers out of business and required the major lines to accept route extensions.
  c. Pan Am illegally obtained exclusive landing rights in South America.
  d. Transcontinental Air Transport illegally paid Charles Lindbergh huge sums to act on their behalf.

_____ 16. After WWII, Pan Am had two competitors on the transatlantic route. They were:
  a. American and Braniff.
  b. Braniff and Northwest.
  c. Northwest and TWA.
  d. American and TWA.

_____ 17. Which of the following statements is correct concerning the immediate post-WWII period?
  a. Panagra extended their routes in the United States.
  b. The CAB allowed Braniff to go to South America.
  c. Pan American was awarded the great circle route.
  d. The CAB favored expansion of the trunk carriers into smaller cities, while at the same time discouraging the growth of feeders.

_____ 18. Which American airline was the first to order jets?
  a. Pan Am
  b. Eastern
  c. United
  d. TWA

_____ 19. Which of the following statements concerning Pan Am's service during the 1930s is correct?
  a. The DC-3 was used on flights to Brazil and Argentina.
  b. NYRBA was a formidable competitor throughout the 1930s.
  c. Having conquered the Caribbean and South America, Pan Am started service across the Atlantic in 1935.
  d. The Boeing B-314 went into transatlantic service for Pan Am in 1939.

_____ 20. The State Department:
     a. appointed Pan Am the "chosen instrument" to carry the American flag on over-seas air routes.
     b. forced the merger between W. R. Grace & Company and Pan Am to form Panagra.
     c. disapproved Pan Am's request to fly across the mid Pacific.
     d. assisted Pan Am in the purchase of the Consolidated Commodore flying boats.

_____ 21. Douglas' first pressurized aircraft, which began service in 1946, was the:
     a. DC-4.
     b. DC-5.
     c. DC-6.
     d. DC-7.

_____ 22. Which of the following is not considered one of the family of "jumbo" jets?
     a. B-727
     b. B-747
     c. DC-10
     d. L-1011

**II. True/False**—Circle "T" if the statement is true; circle "F" if it is false.

T   F   1. The Special Committee on Investigation of the Air Mail and Ocean Mail Contracts was chaired by Senator Pat McCarran.

T   F   2. Postmaster Brown testified that Ludington was merely "skimming cream from a short, high-density route."

T   F   3. Eastern Air Transport's costs per mile were higher than Ludington's because it served a much wider airway network with many low-density routes.

T   F   4. The Black Committee established that Postmaster Brown had been a dictator.

T   F   5. The accident rate experienced by the army during the period in which it flew the mail was so low that the president considered leaving the mail with the army on a permanent basis.

T   F   6. Many of the air carriers changed their names after the Black Committee hearings so that they could submit air mail bids.

T   F   7. In the first few years following passage of the Black-McKellar Act, the major air carriers enjoyed very high profits.

T   F   8. The arrival of the Douglas DC-3 enabled the carriers to earn profits on passenger traffic alone.

T   F   9. About 8000 individuals were employed by the air carriers in 1935.

T   F   10. The Civil Aeronautics Board (CAB) was created in 1940.

T   F   11. Pan Am's first route was between Miami, Florida, and Havana, Cuba.

T   F   12. NYRBA flew Consolidated Commodore flying boats, which were superior to Pan Am's Sikorsky S-38s.

T   F   13. Pan Am began scheduled service across the mid-Pacific in November 1935.

T   F   14. The U.S. State Department decided to continue the "chosen instrument" policy in the immediate postwar period.

T   F   15. The CAB was organized to operate the airway system, while the CAA was responsible for regulating the economic aspects of the carriers, including pricing and route awards.

| | | |
|---|---|---|
| T | Ϝ | 16. Under the Black-McKellar Act all airlines were required to separate themselves from manufacturing affiliates. |
| T | F | 17. Pan Am began jet operations over the Atlantic with the Boeing 707 in October 1958. |
| T | F | 18. The Lockheed *Constellation* was primarily flown on short-haul routes by the feeder carriers during the immediate postwar period. |
| T | F | 19. The Douglas DC-6 was the last of the large commercial prop aircraft to be flown by the major carriers. |
| T | F | 20. Juan Trippe built Pan Am with influence, money, and ability. |

# Chapter 10

**I. Multiple Choice**—Choose the best answer and place it in the blank at the left.

_____ 1. America's reaction to the aggressive actions by Japan, Germany, and Italy during the mid-1930s was:
   a. outrage.
   b. neutrality.
   c. a massive military buildup.
   d. a declaration of war.

_____ 2. The Curtiss *Sparrowhawks* were used with the navy dirigibles as:
   a. torpedo bombers.
   b. dive bombers.
   c. scout-fighter planes.
   d. long-range bombers.

_____ 3. Which of the following navy dirigibles was not lost in an accident?
   a. *Shenandoah*
   b. *Akron*
   c. *Macon*
   d. *Los Angeles*

_____ 4. The famous Douglas DC-3 saw service during the war as the army:
   a. R4D.
   b. O-46A.
   c. C-47.
   d. P-12C.

_____ 5. The first military precision flying team was the:
   a. Red Devils.
   b. Blue Angels.
   c. Fighting Hawks.
   d. Thunderbolts.

_____ 6. Built in 1922, the navy's first aircraft carrier was the:
   a. *Saratoga*.
   b. *Lexington*.
   c. *Langley*.
   d. *Ranger*.

_____ 7. A new era in U.S. fighter airplane design began in 1934 when Don Berlin designed the:
  a. Curtiss P-36.
  b. Republic P-47.
  c. Lockheed P-38.
  d. Curtiss P-40.

_____ 8. The _____ first appeared in 1940 and became the principal U.S. fighter in Europe. America's top aces in the European Theater flew this aircraft.
  a. Curtiss P-40
  b. Republic P-47
  c. Lockheed P-38
  d. Curtiss P-36

_____ 9. The _____ first flew in 1935 and evolved into the famous B-17 series of WWII.
  a. Boeing 247
  b. Boeing 299
  c. Douglas O-4A
  d. Boeing P-12C

_____ 10. The United States Army Air Forces (USAAF) was created on:
  a. March 11, 1941.
  b. June 20, 1941.
  c. December 7, 1941.
  d. March 9, 1942.

_____ 11. This individual was a strong proponent of dirigibles for the U.S. Navy.
  a. Benjamin Foulois
  b. Fred Rentschler
  c. William Moffett
  d. Henry Arnold

_____ 12. This all-metal, low-wing, twin-engine craft carried 10 passengers and entered service with United Airlines in 1933.
  a. Travel Air 6000B
  b. Curtiss T-32 Condor
  c. Stinson Model A
  d. Boeing 247

_____ 13. During the late 1930s:
  a. the navy was relatively better funded than the army.
  b. consideration was given to funding a strategic bombing force.
  c. the air corps gained equal status with ground forces.
  d. none of the above.

_____ 14. At the start of WWII, these two aircraft provided the front-line fighters for the army and navy.
  a. P-38 Lightning and Chance Vought Corsair
  b. Republic P-47 Thunderbolt and Brewster Buffalo
  c. Curtiss P-40 and F4F Wildcat
  d. Douglas O-46A and Curtiss Helldiver

**II. True/False**—Circle "T" if the statement is true; circle "F" if it is false.

T   F   1. As Assistant Secretary of the navy from 1913 to 1921, future President Roosevelt was a strong advocate of military aviation.

T   F   2. The U.S. Navy had reasonably good success with its dirigibles during the 1930s, and many naval personnel felt that the airship program should have continued.

T   F   3. Admiral Moffet was killed when the *Akron* crashed in a storm off the New Jersey coast.

T   F   4. The first modern airliner, the Boeing 247, was produced in 1933 for United Air Lines—an all-metal, low-wing, twin-engine aircraft with seating for 10 passengers.

T   F   5. The navy's first aircraft carrier was the *Yorktown*.

T   F   6. Naval aviation was relatively better funded during the 1930s than army aviation.

T   F   7. Henry "Hap" Arnold was appointed Chief of the Army Air Corps in 1938.

T   F   8. The Lockheed XP-38 was officially described as a defensive interceptor in order to get it past General Craig and Congress.

T   F   9. The Curtiss P-40 was simply a P-36 with a more powerful engine.

T   F   10. America's reaction to the aggressions of Japan and Germany during the late 1930s was basically one of neutrality.

T   F   11. The United States was quick in responding to aggressions of Japan and Germany during the late 1930s.

T   F   12. The McNary-Watres Act encouraged contractors to use multi-engine aircraft by increasing the rate of payment for air mail carried on larger aircraft.

T   F   13. President Roosevelt was generally in favor of the way the airway system had been mapped out during the Spoils Conference.

T   F   14. President Roosevelt decreed that no airline company represented at the Spoils Conference should be allowed to carry mail in the future.

T   F   15. Curtiss OC-2 Falcons were used as scout-fighters aboard Navy dirigibles.

T   F   16. During the late 1930s, the Army General Staff strongly favored a modern air force.

# Chapter 11

**I. Multiple Choice**—Choose the best answer and place it in the blank at the left.

_____ 1. The U.S. military's primary failure at Pearl Harbor was:
    a. inadequate number of aircraft.
    b. lack of reconnaissance.
    c. poor training.
    d. the inability to supply our forces.

_____ 2. This Japanese fighter aircraft was used in the attack on Pearl Harbor and throughout the war in the Pacific.
    a. Nakajima *Hayate*
    b. Kawasaki *Hien*
    c. Mitsubishi *Zero*
    d. Kawanishi *Shiden*

_____ 3. This was the first sea battle in which neither side ever sighted the other from a surface ship; the entire battle was fought with air power.
  a. Bismarck Sea
  b. Coral Sea
  c. Midway
  d. Leyte Gulf

_____ 4. The battle of _____ was an incredible victory for the U.S. Navy and a severe blow to Japan, from which it never recovered.
  a. Bismarck Sea
  b. Coral Sea
  c. Midway
  d. Santa Cruz

_____ 5. Japan entered WWII with the primary objective of:
  a. allying with Germany to obtain world domination.
  b. securing natural resources and fighting a defensive war.
  c. neutralizing the U.S. Navy in Hawaii and then attacking the U.S. mainland.
  d. controlling the Pacific Ocean.

_____ 6. One of the first amphibious assaults took place on 7 August 1942, in the southern Solomon island chain. It would take until February 1943 to secure this island.
  a. New Guinea
  b. Okinawa
  c. Iwo Jima
  d. Guadalcanal

_____ 7. The U.S. Pacific Fleet Commander during WWII was:
  a. Frank J. Fletcher.
  b. Chester W. Nimitz.
  c. Raymond A. Spruance.
  d. Ernest J. King.

_____ 8. Japanese fleet commander and military strategist in the Pacific during WWII was:
  a. Chuichi Nagumo.
  b. Yahachi Tanabe.
  c. Isoruku Yamamoto.
  d. Chiang Kai-Shek.

_____ 9. Which of the following statements concerning the Japanese in the Pacific is not correct?
  a. Japan could probably never have won the war after the devastating losses at Midway.
  b. U.S. forces met very little resistance from the Japanese during the Aleutian campaign.
  c. Admiral Yamamoto's aircraft was intercepted on a flight over the Pacific by a P-38 and shot down.
  d. Japanese supply ships were very successful in supplying troops at Guadalcanal, which prolonged the fight for over one year.

_____ 10. At the battle of Midway, Lt. Cmdr. McClusky's dive bombers commenced the attack on Nagumo's carriers virtually unmolested by Zeros because:

a. the SBDs (McClusky's) came under the protection of cloud cover.

b. the Zeros had been called down to take on the American torpedo planes.

c. McClusky cleverly attacked from the south instead of the east where the U.S. fleet was located.

d. too many Japanese aircraft had been lost on bombing raids over Midway Island.

_____ 11. Four Japanese aircraft carriers, *Akagi*, *Kaga*, *Hiryu*, and *Soryu*, were sunk by American planes during the battle of:

a. Coral Sea.

b. Guadalcanal.

c. Leyte Gulf.

d. Midway.

_____ 12. One of the most significant dive bombers flown by the navy during the war in the Pacific was the Douglas-built:

a. F4F Wildcat.

b. SBD Dauntless.

c. TBF Avenger.

d. B-25 Mitchell.

_____ 13. Which of the following statements is not correct?

a. The surprise attack on Pearl Harbor virtually eliminated any feeling of isolationism in the United States.

b. General MacArthur immediately issued orders for B-17 strikes against Formosa upon hearing the attack on Pearl Harbor.

c. The Japanese invasion of the Philippines began on 22 December 1941.

d. No supplies reached the Philippines after the war started.

_____ 14. The Japanese Operation I-go:

a. was an attempt to regain control of the air over New Guinea and the Solomons.

b. referred to the planned invasion of the Philippines.

c. attempted to supply besieged Japanese troops on Guadalcanal.

d. secured several bases in the Aleutian islands.

**II. True/False**—Circle "T" if the statement is true; circle "F" if it is false.

T   F   1. The attack on Pearl Harbor took place on 7 December 1941.

T   F   2. Most military analysts of the time expected that any possible Japanese attack would be made first against the Philippines.

T   F   3. U.S. bases in the Philippines were attacked by Japanese air forces shortly after the attack on Pearl Harbor.

T   F   4. General Jonathan Wainwright's forces repelled the Japanese invasion of the Philippines and took many prisoners, which was a severe blow to the Japanese early in the war.

T   F   5. The Battle of Coral Sea was probably a slight tactical victory for the Japanese but a major strategic victory for the U.S. because it forced the enemy to abandon its planned invasion of Port Moresby.

T   F   6. The U.S. aircraft carriers that participated in the battle of Midway were the *Enterprise*, the *Yorktown*, and the *Hornet*.

| | | |
|---|---|---|
| T | F | 7. The most severe damage to the Japanese fleet during the battle of Midway was done by Douglas SBD Dauntless dive bombers. |
| T | F | 8. The USAAF Fifth Air Force was commanded by Gen. Douglas MacArthur. |
| T | F | 9. The military's primary failure at Pearl Harbor was the lack of fighter aircraft to meet the Japanese onslaught. |
| T | F | 10. Most military strategists during the late 1930s felt that Japan would attack British or Dutch possessions in the Far East and would carefully avoid the United States. |
| T | F | 11. The chief goal of American deployment to the Pacific during most of 1942 was securing Hawaii and the Panama Canal, as well as building a base in Australia and securing the chain of islands leading to it. |
| T | F | 12. Commander of the U.S. Pacific Fleet during WWII was Adm. Ernest J. King. |
| T | F | 13. The U.S. Navy's front line fighter during the early war years was the Grumman F-4F Wildcat. |
| T | F | 14. U.S. Navy cryptographers in the Office of Naval Intelligence broke the Japanese diplomatic code prior to Pearl Harbor. |
| T | F | 15. Japanese special attack corps "kamikazes" (divine wind) were used extensively throughout the war in the Pacific, including the attack on Pearl Harbor. |
| T | F | 16. The chief Japanese planner for the attack on Pearl Harbor was Adm. Akira Sakamoto. |
| T | F | 17. Victory for the Americans at the Battle of Midway was largely attributable to the attacks by TBD Devastator Torpedo planes from the U.S. carriers. |
| T | F | 18. The U.S. aircraft carrier *Yorktown* was sunk by a Japanese submarine after the Battle of Midway. |
| T | F | 19. Operation I-go was an all-out attempt by the Japanese to regain control of the air over New Guinea and the Solomon islands. |
| T | F | 20. Admiral Yamamoto was killed during a routine flight back to Japan when his aircraft developed engine trouble. |
| T | F | 21. The U.S. naval forces in the Pacific were dealt a crushing blow with the loss of three heavy aircraft carriers at Pearl Harbor. |
| T | F | 22. Most P-40s and B-17s based in the Philippine Islands were destroyed within several days after the first assault by Japanese naval air forces. |

# Chapter 12

**I. Multiple Choice**—Choose the best answer and place it in the blank at the left.

_____ 1. The invasion of North Africa was referred to as Operation:
    a. D-Day.
    b. Overlord.
    c. Torch.
    d. Tunisia.

_____ 2. The German general known as the "Desert Fox," who faced Allied forces in the North African campaign, was:
    a. Carl Spaatz.
    b. Albert Kesselring.

c. Jergen von Arnim.

d. Erwin Rommel.

_____ 3. Colonel Jimmy Doolittle led a flight of 12 B-25 Mitchell bombers off the deck of the carrier _____ in April 1942.

a. *Hornet*

b. *Wasp*

c. *Ranger*

d. *Yorktown*

_____ 4. This aircraft was probably the best German fighter during the war. Its 1760-hp BMW engine gave it a speed of close to 400 mph at 17,000 feet.

a. Junkers JU-87

b. Messerschmitt Bf-109F

c. Focke-Wulf 190

d. Junkers JU-52

_____ 5. Which of the following U.S. aircraft was the predominant fighter used during the North African campaign?

a. Lockheed P-38J

b. Curtiss P-40F

c. Republic P-47

d. North American P-51

_____ 6. The Italian campaign:

a. ended in September 1943.

b. resulted in heavy losses of Allied aircraft.

c. was decided during the first two months of combat.

d. lasted until shortly before the war in Europe ended.

_____ 7. The primary aim of the combined British and American bomber offensive decided at the Casablanca Conference was the:

a. destruction of German cities to break the morale of the people.

b. elimination of the Luftwaffe and Germany's sources of oil.

c. breaking down of all communications and rail lines.

d. cutoff of all supply lines and demoralization of German ground troops.

_____ 8. _____ with 108-gallon drop tanks were used to escort B-17s on bombing runs over Germany during the last year of the war.

a. P-38 Lightnings

b. P-47 Thunderbolts

b. P-51 Mustangs

d. A-26 Invaders

_____ 9. The war in Europe ended on:

a. 25 July 1944.

b. 8 September 1944.

c. 25 April 1945.

d. 7 May 1945.

_____ 10. General von Rundstedt, commander-in-chief of the German armed forces in Western Europe, attributed Germany's defeat to three factors. Which of the following was not one of those factors?
>    a. superiority of Allied air forces
>    b. lack of fuel
>    c. demoralization of troops due to bombing
>    d. destruction of all rail lines

_____ 11. The primary goal of the invasion of North Africa by Allied troops was to:
>    a. defeat Field Marshal Rommel's Afrika Corps.
>    b. eliminate the threat to Britain's oil supply from the Middle East.
>    c. open up the Mediterranean Sea to Allied shipping.
>    d. all of the above.

_____ 12. Operation Torch referred to the:
>    a. invasion of North Africa by the Allies.
>    b. evacuation of North Africa by the Germans.
>    c. night bombing of Japanese cities.
>    d. return of MacArthur to the Philippines.

_____ 13. Which of the following statements is not correct concerning the North African campaign?
>    a. The Junkers JU-87 dive bomber was not as effective in supporting troop movements as it was in Europe.
>    b. A major early priority in the campaign was the defeat of the Luftwaffe.
>    c. The surrender of 270,000 German and Italian troops took place in May 1943.
>    d. The "Palm Sunday Massacre" referred to the American defeat at Kasserine Pass.

_____ 14. The Germans' winter line, 90 miles south of Rome, was broken primarily as a result of:
>    a. Allied landings at Anzio.
>    b. air power.
>    c. naval bombardment.
>    d. transfer of German troops to the Russian front.

_____ 15. Operation Overlord, the cross-channel invasion:
>    a. involved 11,000 Allied aircraft and 4,000 ships.
>    b. took place on 6 June 1944.
>    c. placed 50,000 Allied soldiers on the beaches in France during the first day.
>    d. all of the above.

_____ 16. The V-1 vengeance weapon was powered by a:
>    a. ramjet engine.
>    b. rocket engine.
>    c. pulse-jet engine.
>    d. none of the above.

_____ 17. Which of the following statements is not correct?
>    a. For all intents and purposes, Germany was defeated by the summer of 1944.
>    b. V-2s were first fired against London and Paris in September 1944.

     c. Allied armies swept across France largely because of superior Allied air power.

     d. By the spring of 1945, gasoline production in Germany had dropped to 50 percent of normal capacity.

_____ 18. This superior fighter aircraft, flown with wing tanks, escorted bombers on long-range missions into Germany.

     a. Republic P-47 Thunderbolt

     b. North American P-51 Mustang

     c. Grumman TBF Avenger

     d. Douglas SBD Dauntless

**II. True/False**—Circle "T" if the statement is true; circle "F" if it is false.

T    F    1. The Lend-Lease Act swept away any pretense of neutrality on the part of America.

T    F    2. General Eisenhower put General Doolittle in command of the 12th Air Force during the North African campaign.

T    F    3. Over 270,000 German and Italian troops escaped from North Africa in Junkers JU-52 transport aircraft.

T    F    4. The Republic P-47 Thunderbolts were referred to by Luftwaffe pilots as "forked-tail devils."

T    F    5. General Ira Eaker replaced Air Chief Marshall Tedder as air commander in the Mediterranean Theater of Operations.

T    F    6. The B-17 Flying Fortress was flown by the 8th Air Force on long-range bombing missions from England to Germany.

T    F    7. By late March 1944, Allied air power was dominant over the European skies.

T    F    8. More than 11,000 Allied airplanes were used during the D-Day invasion.

T    F    9. In July 1944, 20,000 German soldiers, attempting to outflank General Patton's U.S. 3rd Army, surrendered directly to the air force.

T    F   10. The V-2 rocket was first used against the Allies during the Normandy invasion.

T    F   11. The Junkers JU-87 Stuka primarily served as a long-range bomber.

T    F   12. The "Palm Sunday Massacre" arose out of the attempt by the Germans to supply their troops in North Africa.

T    F   13. Operation Overlord, the cross-channel invasion of occupied France, took place on 6 July 1943.

T    F   14. The Italian campaign lasted for 19 months before the Germans surrendered on 2 May 1945.

T    F   15. The Germans invaded the Soviet Union in June 1941 after the Battle of Britain.

T    F   16. In 1941, America, along with the British and Dutch, embargoed oil shipments to Japan and imposed other trade sanctions.

T    F   17. The Tokyo raid by Colonel Doolittle's B-25s in April 1942 inflicted heavy damage to the Japanese war machine early in the war.

T    F   18. The Italian campaign proved to be "Europe's soft underbelly," as President Roosevelt described it earlier.

T    F   19. The Allies faced very little Luftwaffe opposition during Operation Overlord.

### III. Matching (Individuals):

_____ 1. Led the B-25 raid over Tokyo in April 1942
_____ 2. Supreme Allied commander
_____ 3. Reichmarschall of the Luftwaffe
_____ 4. The Desert Fox
_____ 5. German commander in Italy
_____ 6. Head of the U.S. 8th Air Force
_____ 7. British Air Chief Marshal
_____ 8. U.S. air commander in the Mediterranean
_____ 9. Head of the U.S. 3rd Army
_____ 10. Head of the USAAF

a. Herman Goering
b. Carl Spaatz
c. Ira Eaker
d. Albert Kesselring
e. Dwight D. Eisenhower
f. Charles Portal
g. George Patton, Jr.
h. James Doolittle
i. Henry Arnold
j. Erwin Rommel

### IV. Matching (Aircraft):

_____ 1. German dive bomber
_____ 2. Flying Fortress heavy bomber
_____ 3. U.S. fighter used in North Africa
_____ 4. German fighter aircraft
_____ 5. German transport aircraft
_____ 6. Rugged U.S. fighter called the Jug
_____ 7. U.S. fighter flown with tip tanks to escort bombers
_____ 8. Germans referred to this U.S. fighter as a forked-tail devil
_____ 9. Italian fighter aircraft
_____ 10. U.S. bomber known as the Liberator

a. Focke-Wulf 190
b. Junkers JU-52
c. Boeing B-17
d. Macchi C 202
e. Republic P-47 Thunderbolt
f. North American P-51 Mustang
g. Junkers JU-87 Stuka
h. Lockheed P-38 Lightning
j. Curtiss P-40 Warhawk
i. Consolidated B-24

# Chapter 13

**I. Multiple Choice**—Choose the best answer and place it in the blank at the left.

_____ 1. The major problem during the Aleutian campaign was the:
    a. difficulty in supplying our troops.
    b. weather conditions.
    c. large concentration of Japanese troops.
    d. Japanese navy.

_____ 2. The Flying Tigers were organized and commanded by:
    a. Claire L. Chennault.
    b. Lewis Brereton.
    c. Albert Baumler.
    d. David Campbell.

_____ 3. The Air Transport Command (ATC) serving in the Far East and referred to as the "Assam Trucking Company":
    a. played a limited role in supplying the Flying Tigers.
    b. was under the command of Colonel David Hill.

c. supplied Chiang Kai-Shek's forces.

d. formed the major supply line between Australia and China.

_____ 4. The retaking of the Philippines:

    a. was primarily a psychological victory.

    b. virtually ended the war in the Pacific.

    c. had little strategic importance.

    d. provided a major base of operations for U.S. forces.

_____ 5. The Imperial Japanese Navy was decisively defeated in this battle, which took place during October 1944.

    a. Bismarck Sea

    b. Lingayen Gulf

    c. Leyte Gulf

    d. Tokyo Bay

_____ 6. The name of the B-29 that dropped the first atomic bomb was:

    a. *Lady-be-Good.*

    b. *My Fair Lady.*

    c. *Miss Fortune.*

    d. *Enola Gay.*

_____ 7. Which of the following statements is not true?

    a. During the Okinawan campaign, kamikazes sank 35 U.S. ships and damaged 288.

    b. General Curtis LeMay recommended against the invasion of Japan.

    c. Had the war not ended as it did, another 7000 to 9000 kamikazes were waiting for the expected invasion of Japan.

    d. The price paid for Iwo Jima was probably too high, considering the fact that we recently acquired bases in the Marianas for our B-29s.

_____ 8. This fighter flown by marine squadrons throughout the Pacific theater had a speed of 424 mph at 23,000 feet.

    a. Northrop P-51 Black Widow

    b. Grumman F-6F Hellcat

    c. Chance Vought F4U Corsair

    d. Curtiss P-40 Warhawk

_____ 9. On 6 August 1945, the first A-bomb was dropped from a B-29 on which of the following Japanese cities?

    a. Hiroshima

    b. Nagasaki

    c. Tokyo

    d. Toyama

_____ 10. The American Volunteer Group (AVG) that fought the Japanese in Burma and China was called the:

    a. American Warhawks.

    b. Flying Tigers.

    c. Hellcats.

    d. Air Cobras.

_____ 11. The American Volunteer Group (AVG) that fought with the Chinese:
  a. was headed by Col. David "Tex" Hill.
  b. entered combat before the attack on Pearl Harbor.
  c. became the USAAF's 23rd FG on 4 July 1942.
  d. suffered heavy losses during its first year of combat.

_____ 12. Which of the following statements concerning the B-29 strikes on Japan during 1945 is not true?
  a. In the spring, they were used for low-altitude incendiary bombing of major cities during night raids.
  b. By the summer, General LeMay began announcing in advance where he would strike next in order to cut civilian casualties.
  c. B-29 losses dropped to near zero during July and August.
  d. Kamikaze aircraft were used against the B-29 formations during the early fall in a last desperate effort by the Japanese.

_____ 13. The Japanese attacked Dutch Harbor in the Aleutian Islands:
  a. in preparation for a major assault on Alaska.
  b. as a diversionary thrust immediately preceding the Battle of Midway.
  c. to establish a major seaport for their naval vessels.
  d. because it was part of the former Japanese empire prior to 1905.

_____ 14. Retaking the Philippine Islands:
  a. was primarily for psychological purposes because we had sufficient bases in the Pacific.
  b. provided a major base of operations both for ships and land-based aircraft.
  c. was needed for air strikes against the Japanese in China.
  d. none of the above.

_____ 15. On 2 September 1945, formal surrender documents were signed:
  a. aboard the carrier _Enterprise_.
  b. at the Imperial Palace in Tokyo.
  c. aboard the battleship _Missouri_.
  d. at the White House in Washington, D.C.

**II. True/False**—Circle "T" if the statement is true; circle "F" if it is false.

T    F    1. The Aleutian Islands had to be controlled to prevent a possible strike by the Japanese on the North American continent.

T    F    2. The Flying Tigers primarily flew Northrop P-61 Black Widow night fighter aircraft.

T    F    3. The American Volunteer Group (Flying Tigers) were fighting the Japanese in China six months before the attack on Pearl Harbor.

T    F    4. The China National Aviation Corporation (CNAC) was established and partly owned by Pan Am.

T    F    5. Kamikaze attacks accounted for at least half of all damage to U.S. Navy ships during the war.

T    F    6. The primary purpose of taking Iwo Jima was the fact that we needed a fueling base for our fleet.

T F 7. In the spring of 1945, B-29s were loaded with incendiary bombs and used on low-level fire bombing raids over Tokyo and other Japanese cities.

T F 8. Kamikazes came out in force during the Okinawan campaign, causing a high loss of ships and lives.

T F 9. After Okinawa was taken, General LeMay began announcing in advance where his B-29s would strike next in order to reduce civilian casualties.

T F 10. Japan surrendered on 2 September 1945, aboard the battleship *Missouri* in Tokyo Bay.

T F 11. The Japanese occupation of the Aleutian Islands in 1942 led to their attempting an amphibious assault on Point Barrow, Alaska, in 1943.

T F 12. The *Enola Gay* dropped a second atomic bomb on Yokahama on 9 August 1945.

T F 13. The American Volunteer Group flew under the flag of China, and their airplanes carried Chinese insignias.

T F 14. The major Japanese base at Rabaul was cut off from supply after its air units were destroyed.

T F 15. Bases in the Mariana Islands enabled the B-29s to strike the Japanese home islands.

T F 16. In March 1945, B-29s were loaded with incendiary bombs for low-level raids on Tokyo at night.

T F 17. The Okinawan campaign was the last and least violent for the U.S. Navy because Japan was virtually beaten by that time.

T F 18. Thousands of kamikazes and a well-equipped army was prepared to resist the invasion of Japan.

# Chapter 14

**I. Multiple Choice**—Choose the best answer and place it in the blank at the left.

_____ 1. The USAF's first operational jet fighter was the:
  a. Bell X-1A.
  b. Lockheed F-94 Starfire.
  c. North American F-86 Sabre.
  d. Lockheed F-80 Shooting Star.

_____ 2. The wartime Air Transport Command (ATC) became the:
  a. Air Transport Service Command (ATSC).
  b. Military Air Transport Service (MATS).
  c. Strategic Air Command (SAC).
  d. Tactical Air Command (TAC).

_____ 3. The Boeing B-52 Stratofortress:
  a. preceded the Convair B-36.
  b. is still being flown today.
  c. was first flown in 1941.
  d. is powered by four prop-jet engines.

_____ 4. When North Korean troops crossed the 38th parallel in June 1950:
  a. the South Korean army, backed by U.S. occupation forces, were prepared for the invasion.

b. General MacArthur was put in command of troops from 15 nations.

c. President Truman ordered the 5th Air Force to commence attacking North Korean cities.

d. U.N. forces started a counteroffensive with an amphibious landing at Inchon.

_____ 5. In January 1953, President Eisenhower warned the Communists that if negotiations did not progress:

a. hostilities may no longer be confined to the Korean peninsula.

b. we would drop the A-bomb as we did on Japan.

c. their next defensive position would be the outskirts of Moscow.

d. North Korea would be asked to leave the United Nations.

_____ 6. With the combination of veteran WWII pilots and the arrival of this aircraft, the kill ratio jumped to 10-to-1 in the skies over Korea.

a. North American F-51 Mustang

b. Douglas A-26 Invader

c. Grumman F-7F Tigercat

d. North American F-86 Sabre

_____ 7. In 1951, General MacArthur called for all of the following, except:

a. a naval blockade of the China coast.

b. an amphibious assault at selected points along the Chinese coastline by U.S. Marines.

c. an invasion of China by Chiang Kai-Shek's Nationalist Chinese forces.

d. air attacks on China's war industries.

_____ 8. The Korean War led to a:

a. strengthening of the NATO Alliance.

b. lessening of tensions between Western and Eastern block nations.

c. buildup of Japanese military forces, which were now our allies.

d. cutback in U.S. jet aircraft development and procurement.

_____ 9. Helicopters were primarily used during the Korean War for:

a. construction work.

b. troop support.

c. medical evacuation.

d. low-level bombing.

_____ 10. Which of the following is a direct result of the Korean War?

a. Better relations with the USSR during the late 1950s

b. Strengthening of the NATO Alliance

c. U.S. withdrawal from the United Nations in 1955

d. The Vietnam conflict during the 1960s

_____ 11. The Berlin Airlift:

a. was referred to as Operation Overlord.

b. lasted for 13 months.

c. was exclusively an American operation.

d. was successful primarily because of U.S. fighter aircraft support.

12. The Korean War included four major offensives and counteroffensives. Which of the following is not one of these offenses?
   a. the North Korean drive to the southern end of the country by September 1950
   b. Communist China entering the war
   c. U.N. forces crossing the Chinese border
   d. U.N. amphibious landing at Inchon, just south of Seoul

13. On June 14, 1948, the Russians stopped all surface transportation into the western sectors of Berlin for all of the following reasons, except:
   a. the migration of East Germans.
   b. they wanted to make Berlin a free city devoid of foreign influence.
   c. heightened Cold War tensions with the Allied powers.
   d. because of its location, they felt that it should be part of East Germany.

14. The dream of Billy Mitchell came true on 18 September 1947, with the:
   a. development of an intercontinental ballistic missile.
   b. creation of a separate air force.
   c. establishment of a U.S. Air Force Academy.
   d. formation of the North Atlantic Treaty Organization (NATO).

15. North American F-51 Mustangs were flown in Korea:
   a. on a very limited basis because of the use of jets.
   b. in support of ground operations.
   c. primarily in air-to-air combat.
   d. only during the first year of the war.

16. The primary mission of the newly created U.S. Air Force was assigned to:
   a. SAC.
   b. ATC.
   c. TAC.
   d. MATS.

17. The combination of experienced American pilots and this aircraft increased the kill ratio to 10-to-1 in the skies over Korea.
   a. F-82 Twin Mustang
   b. F-80 Shooting Star
   c. T-6 Texan
   d. F-86 Sabre

**II. True/False**—Circle "T" if the statement is true; circle "F" if it is false.

T  F  1. The C-47 (civilian DC-3) provided the backbone for the Berlin Airlift.
T  F  2. Gen. George Kenney, the first commander of the Strategic Air Command (SAC), was a strong proponent of the B-52 and B-36.
T  F  3. The B-52 was the backbone of the Strategic Air Command (SAC) for more than 30 years.
T  F  4. The first B-52 prototype made its maiden flight in April 1952.
T  F  5. President Truman termed the U.N. response to the North Korean invasion a "total war."

T   F   6. Helicopters were used during the Korean war primarily for evacuation of wounded troops.
T   F   7. P-51 *Mustangs* were primarily used for air-to-air combat during the Korean War.
T   F   8. U.N. field commanders had great latitude in developing and implementing battle plans during the Korean War because of the multiplicity of authority.
T   F   9. The Vultee (Stinson) L-5s and Cessna L-19s were primarily used as tactical support fighters.
T   F   10. The Soviet MiG-15 was the standard fighter for the Soviet-bloc air forces during the 1950s.
T   F   11. The Bell X-1A, piloted by Joseph Walker, reached a speed of Mach 1 on 17 October 1947.
T   F   12. The Korean conflict was strictly an American operation although it was under the auspices of the United Nations.
T   F   13. The Chinese entered the Korean War at the outset on 25 June 1950, by sending 300,000 troops in support of the Korean invasion.
T   F   14. Many of the U.S. pilots in Korea had seen action during WWII.
T   F   15. General MacArthur was asked by President Truman to resign his command in April 1951 because he opposed the U.N. (and U.S.) policy in Korea.
T   F   16. The acronym MATS stands for Military Air Tactical Support.
T   F   17. General George Kenney was appointed the first commander of the Strategic Air Command (SAC) in March 1946.
T   F   18. American warplanes dominated the air and provided close air support for ground troops in Korea that was a decisive factor.
T   F   19. President Eisenhower threatened that unless hostilities ceased, America intended to move more decisively without inhibition in our use of weapons.
T   F   20. The Korean War strengthened the NATO alliance.

# Chapter 15

**I. Multiple Choice**—Choose the best answer and place it in the blank at the left.

_____ 1. The theory of flexible response postulated that:
    a. we must meet force with maximum counterforce.
    b. the amount of force used should always be commensurate with the threat.
    c. we should do nothing unless the threat jeopardized national security.
    d. the amount of force used should enable us to win and eliminate the threat as soon as possible.

_____ 2. The Geneva Accords:
    a. established conditions for a cease-fire in Indochina.
    b. provided for the independence of Laos and Cambodia, as well as Vietnam.
    c. called for free elections throughout Vietnam.
    d. all of these.

_____ 3. The Southeast Asia Treaty Organization (SEATO):
    a. tried to re-establish French rule in Indochina.

b. was set up to ensure free elections in Vietnam.

c. pledged aid to any Southeast Asian country that asked for help if attacked.

d. supported the North Vietnamese.

_____ 4. The Gulf of Tonkin resolution:

a. greatly curtailed presidential action.

b. warned North Vietnam that shipping in the Gulf of Tonkin would be attacked by U.S. forces.

c. committed military aid to all countries bordering the Gulf of Tonkin.

d. gave the President virtually a blank check to do what was necessary.

_____ 5. The army's AH-1G Huey *Cobras* were primarily used for:

a. medical evacuation.

b. ground attack support.

c. delivering supplies.

d. observation purposes.

_____ 6. Which of the following statements is not true?

a. In November 1968, President Johnson halted all bombing of North Vietnam.

b. President Nixon secretly authorized B-52 strikes against enemy sanctuaries in Cambodia.

c. Secretary McNamara planned to equip the air force and navy with a single fighter airplane that could also serve as a strategic bomber.

d. Gen. Creighton Abrams recommended that we increase troop strength to two million men.

_____ 7. The Convair F-111:

a. was originally designed to serve both the air force and navy.

b. has experienced an outstanding performance record.

c. was strongly favored by the navy during its early stage of development but not by the air force.

d. was originally designed as a light defensive tactical fighter for the air force.

_____ 8. Which of the following statements is true?

a. With the growth of ICBMs, manned bombers have been relegated to a minor role as a nuclear retaliatory strike force.

b. U.S. nuclear defense forces relative to the Soviets was strengthened during the 1970s.

c. The manned bomber is more vulnerable to enemy defenses.

d. None of these.

_____ 9. This aircraft has been the backbone of the Strategic Air Command for more than 30 years.

a. B-57

b. XB-70

c. B-47

d. B-52

_____ 10. Used by the navy as an anti-submarine warfare (ASW) aircraft, more than 400 of these planes are in service.
        a. F-14 Tomcat
        b. Lockheed TR-1
        c. P-3 Orion
        d. A-6A Intruder

_____ 11. Flown by a number of NATO countries, this versatile lightweight fighter can perform various missions.
        a. Fairchild A-10
        b. General Dynamics F-16
        c. Convair F-106A
        d. Lockheed F-104

_____ 12. It was under the SEATO agreement that:
        a. France reoccupied Vietnam after WWII.
        b. President Eisenhower sent the first military advisors to South Vietnam.
        c. the partitioning of Vietnam at the 17th parallel took place.
        d. the first free elections were held in Vietnam.

_____ 13. Which of the following aircraft did not see action in Vietnam?
        a. F-105 Thunderchief
        b. F-4C Phantom
        c. F-15 Eagle
        d. F-100 Super Sabre

_____ 14. Which of the following statements is not true?
        a. By May 1972, 200 B-52s were committed to the war in Southeast Asia.
        b. The Huey Cobras were mostly employed in an attack role and were especially effective in close air support situations.
        c. By late 1968 the U.S. had a half million men in South Vietnam, and American combat deaths were approaching 33,000.
        d. The air offensive against North Vietnam began in March 1965 with strikes against important strategic targets.

_____ 15. The CH-21 Shawnee (Flying Banana):
        a. served in Korea and saw limited service in South Vietnam.
        b. was the first helicopter to fly in large numbers in South Vietnam.
        c. was employed in an attack role similar to the Huey Cobra.
        d. both a and b are correct.

_____ 16. The Fairchild A-10 was primarily designed for:
        a. ground support.
        b. electronic surveillance.
        c. air-to-air combat.
        d. anti-submarine warfare.

**II. True/False**—Circle "T" if the statement is true; circle "F" if it is false.

T    F    1. The USAF and navy air strike forces could have eliminated North Vietnam's ability to make war or feed its people.

| | | |
|---|---|---|
| T | F | 2. The French attempted to recolonize Indochina after WWII. |
| T | F | 3. The Geneva Accords provided for the independence of Vietnam and called for free elections. |
| T | F | 4. The CIA warned against free elections in Vietnam because the Viet Minh had terrorist agents throughout South Vietnam. |
| T | F | 5. President Truman tried to defuse the deteriorating situation between North and South Vietnam by withdrawing some of our military advisors. |
| T | F | 6. On 2 August 1964, North Vietnamese torpedo boats attacked the U.S. Navy destroyer *Maddox* in the Gulf of Tonkin. |
| T | F | 7. The Vietnamese conflict was unquestionably a civil war. |
| T | F | 8. The first major U.S. offensive in Vietnam involved air power. |
| T | F | 9. The Vietnam War was unusual in that there were no front lines; the enemy could be anywhere. |
| T | F | 10. Helicopters were used as an attack vehicle during the Vietnam War. |
| T | F | 11. President Nixon was elected on a platform that committed us to winning the war. |
| T | F | 12. President Nixon secretly authorized B-52 strikes against enemy sanctuaries in neutral Cambodia. |
| T | F | 13. The Russians had more aircraft carriers than the U.S. Navy, but the Allies had approximately an equal force if we include the British fleet. |
| T | F | 14. The Grumman A-6 Intruder is a navy attack bomber flown off aircraft carriers. |
| T | F | 15. The SEATO pact pledged aid to any Southeast Asian country that asked for it if attacked. |
| T | F | 16. On 2 August 1964, North Vietnamese torpedo boats attacked the U.S. Navy destroyer *Maddox* cruising in international waters in the Gulf of Tonkin. |
| T | F | 17. The Gulf of Tonkin resolution was passed by a close vote in both houses of Congress. |
| T | F | 18. Rolling Thunder referred to the major air offensive against the Hanoi/Haiphong area in December 1972. |
| T | F | 19. Throughout the 1970s, U.S. defense forces eroded in comparison to those of the Soviet Union. |
| T | F | 20. The Pershing is a short-range tactical missile with a low trajectory. |

**III. Matching—** Match the aircraft named below with the description.

_____ 1. A liquid-fueled ICBM
_____ 2. An anti-submarine warfare (ASW) aircraft
_____ 3. A lightweight air combat fighter flown by the USAF
_____ 4. A submarine-based missile
_____ 5. A MAC aircraft used as an emergency hospital aircraft
_____ 6. Largest of the transport aircraft flown by MAC
_____ 7. A high-altitude spy plane
_____ 8. A carrier-based fighter aircraft
_____ 9. A SAC bomber
_____ 10. An Army helicopter

a. General Dynamics F-16
b. Boeing B-52
c. Douglas C-9
d. U-2
e. Polaris A3
f. McDonnell F-4
g. Titan II
h. AH-1G Huey Cobra
i. Lockheed C-5A
j. P-3 Orion

# Chapter 16

**I. Multiple Choice**—Choose the best answer and place it in the blank at the left.

_____ 1. In 1931, Jimmy Doolittle won the Thompson Trophy Race in a:
   a. Travel Air Model R.
   b. Laird DW 300.
   c. Gee Bee R-1.
   d. Stearman PT-17.

_____ 2. The National Air Races are held at:
   a. Las Vegas, Nevada.
   b. Phoenix, Arizona.
   c. Roswell, New Mexico.
   d. Reno, Nevada.

_____ 3. This nonprofit organization has more than 130,000 members in 600 local chapters and promotes sport aviation. Many members build their own aircraft.
   a. AOPA
   b. EAA
   c. GAMA
   d. NBAA

_____ 4. The FAA has decreed that ultralights must not:
   a. exceed 254 pounds in weight.
   b. operate in controlled airspace.
   c. fly over populated areas.
   d. all of these.

_____ 5. Piper's most successful aircraft has been the:
   a. J-3 Cub.
   b. Tri-Pacer.
   c. Cherokee.
   d. Tomahawk.

_____ 6. Which of the following Beech aircraft had been in continuous production from 1947–1982?
   a. Twin Beech Model 18
   b. King Air B-99
   c. Bonanza Model 35
   d. Baron Model 55

_____ 7. Cessna's first postwar models were the _____ series.
   a. 120/140
   b. 170/172
   c. 180/182
   d. 190/195

_____ 8. One of the most popular civilian training and business aircraft has been the:
   a. Cessna 190.
   b. Piper Cheyenne.

    c. Cessna 172.
    d. Beech Baron.

_____ 9. The general aviation manufacturers have looked upon which of the following markets as offering the greatest potential?
    a. pleasure
    b. agriculture
    c. training
    d. business

_____ 10. The first successful helicopter in the United States was developed by:
    a. Juan de la Cierva.
    b. Igor Sikorsky.
    c. Dwane Wallace.
    d. Paul Poberezny.

_____ 11. During the 1980s, Beech and Cessna primarily relied upon:
    a. single-engine business and pleasure customers.
    b. the flight training market.
    c. corporate customers.
    d. military customers.

_____ 12. Which of the following factors was not a reason for the growth in the use of business aircraft since deregulation?
    a. concentration of airline service
    b. decline in the number of regional airlines
    c. flexibility and reliability of business aircraft
    d. decentralization of industry

_____ 13. The _____, piloted by Dick Rutan and Jeana Yeager, completed a 26,000-mile nonstop flight around the world in 1986.
    a. *Starship*
    b. *Voyager*
    c. *Long-EZ*
    d. *Ultralight*

_____ 14. The S-64 Skycrane was introduced by:
    a. Lockheed.
    b. Hughes.
    c. Sikorsky.
    d. Bell.

_____ 15. The first successful helicopter in the United States was designed by:
    a. Martin.
    b. Bell.
    c. Hughes.
    d. Sikorsky.

_____ 16. The general aviation community felt that private flying after WWII would:
   a. primarily be restricted to business use.
   b. greatly expand.
   c. be cut back significantly.
   d. grow modestly.

_____ 17. Which of the following statements is not true?
   a. Cessna's first twin-engine airplane, the T-50, was introduced in 1939.
   b. The Raytheon Corporation purchased Cessna in 1980.
   c. Production of single-engine Cessnas was suspended in 1986.
   d. The Cessna 150 first appeared in 1959.

_____ 18. Helicopters:
   a. are primarily designed for military purposes.
   b. experienced their greatest technological advances during the 1960s.
   c. demonstrated their potential during WWII.
   d. have declined in popularity in recent years because of increased competition with fixed-wing aircraft.

**II. True/False**—Circle "T" if the statement is true; circle "F" if it is false.

T   F   1. The G.I. Bill and the exposure to military aviation expanded private flying for the first few years after the war.

T   F   2. Prewar general aviation aircraft and ex-military aircraft were flown by private fliers after the war.

T   F   3. Air racing during the 1920s was dominated by the military.

T   F   4. The EAA's annual fly-in and convention is held in Reno, Nevada.

T   F   5. Ultralights can operate only during the hours of darkness with an FAA-approved lighting system.

T   F   6. Primary flight training during WWII at many colleges and universities was given in Piper Tri-Pacers.

T   F   7. William T. Piper, Sr. got his start in aviation working for Walter Beech at Travel Air Manufacturing Company.

T   F   8. Beech Aircraft Corporation's first successful aircraft was the Model 17 Staggerwing.

T   F   9. Cessna's UC-78 multi-engine transition trainer used by the USAAF during WWII was referred to as the "Bamboo Bomber."

T   F   10. Business aviation is declining as a result of the tremendous growth in airline service since deregulation.

T   F   11. The Germans used helicopters quite extensively during WWII.

T   F   12. The autogyro was developed by Juan de la Cierva in 1923.

T   F   13. Business aircraft can include everything from a Cessna 172 to a Boeing 737.

T   F   14. Beech Aircraft Corporation was acquired in 1980 by General Dynamics.

T   F   15. Ultralight aircraft are prohibited from operating in controlled airspace.

T   F   16. William Piper acquired the Travel Air Manufacturing Company in 1931.

T   F   17. Helicopters have a very limited number of uses in the civilian market.

T   F   18. Piper's successful Tri-Pacer, Colt, and Comanche models arrived during the 1950s.

T   F   19. In some cases, the use of business aircraft can actually be less expensive than flying on scheduled airlines.

T    F    20. Women pilots represent about 15 percent of the total active pilots in the United States.

# Chapter 17

**I. Multiple Choice**—Choose the best answer and place it in the blank at the left.

_____ 1. The first jet aircraft was a 1910 biplane powered by a centrifugal compressor driven by a small gasoline engine. It was developed by:
  a. Papst Von O'Hain.
  b. Henri Coanda.
  c. Frank Whittle.
  d. Ernst Heinkel.

_____ 2. The Boeing 707 has the same airframe as the air force's:
  a. A-26.
  b. B-52.
  c. C-5A.
  d. KC-135.

_____ 3. The wide-bodied DC-10 was designed to compete with which of the following aircraft?
  a. Boeing B-737
  b. Convair 240
  c. Martin 404
  d. Lockheed L-1011

_____ 4. Which of the following was not a problem with Lockheed during the 1970s?
  a. development costs of the L-1011 TriStar airliner
  b. lack of new military contracts
  c. bankruptcy of the L-1011's engine supplier
  d. poor cash flow position

_____ 5. One of the earliest Lockheed aircraft was the:
  a. Electra.
  b. P-38 Lightning.
  c. TriStar.
  d. Vega.

_____ 6. Which of the following was not an effect of deregulation?
  a. phase-out of the CAB
  b. concentration of service to large hubs by the major carriers
  c. growth in the number of commuter carriers
  d. air traffic controllers' strike

_____ 7. Flow control means:
  a. not clearing aircraft to takeoff unless they can land at their destination.
  b. assigning landing slots at selected airports.
  c. keeping the flow of landing aircraft in homogeneous groupings to avoid a slow-down due to varying speeds.
  d. assigning quotas to the 23 Air Route Traffic Control Centers.

8. The Learjet Model 23:
   a. was conceived by Charles C. Gates.
   b. was based on Switzerland's P-16 fighter plane.
   c. was not in great demand by corporate buyers for the first several years after production started.
   d. had competition from several other aircraft as soon as it became available.

9. The Boeing 707 was:
   a. developed by obtaining money for research and development from the airlines.
   b. America's first commercial jet.
   c. part of a joint venture with Douglas.
   d. not a successful venture for the first five years.

10. Which American airline was the first to order jets?
    a. Pan Am
    b. Eastern
    c. United
    d. TWA

11. This short-range commercial jet went into service in November 1965.
    a. Boeing 707
    b. Douglas DC-8
    c. Douglas DC-9
    d. Vickers VC-10

12. The FAA Act of 1958:
    a. was largely in response to the arrival of jet aircraft in the U.S. airline fleet.
    b. placed the FAA under the control of DOT.
    c. created the Civil Aeronautics Board.
    d. created the National Transportation Safety Board.

13. This German jet was developed during WWII.
    a. Meteor I
    b. Messerschmitt 262
    c. MiG 15
    d. Junkers JU-87

14. Eastern Airlines, Continental, New York Air, People Express, and Frontier were acquired by:
    a. United.
    b. American.
    c. Northwest.
    d. Texas Air.

15. Which of the following statements concerning jet power is not true?
    a. The British flew their first jet in May 1941.
    b. The Germans flew their first jet in August 1939.
    c. America's first jet was flown in October 1942.
    d. Italy's first jet was flown in August 1943.

_____ 16. Jet power:
    a. would probably have not been developed except for WWII.
    b. has been understood at least since Leonardo da Vinci postulated his laws of motion.
    c. was first developed with the experiments of Secundo Campini in Italy.
    d. includes four categories: turbojet, turbofan, turboprop, and turboshaft.

_____ 17. During the late 1930s, this aircraft dominated the airline market and is considered by many the granddaddy of commercial aviation.
    a. Ford TriMotor
    b. Douglas DC-3
    c. Boeing Stratoliner
    d. Lockheed Electra

_____ 18. Since deregulation in the airline industry:
    a. commuters (regionals) have moved into many long-haul routes in competition with the majors.
    b. the major carriers have dropped many smaller cities from their schedules.
    c. the air traffic control system has become less congested.
    d. the FAA has increased subsidies to the major carriers.

**II. True/False**—Circle "T" if the statement is true; circle "F" if it is false.

T    F    1. The principle of jet propulsion had been understood at least since Isaac Newton.

T    F    2. The jet engine pulls air into its compressor and packs it into a combustion chamber where, mixed with fuel, it is ignited.

T    F    3. The Germans developed the Me 109F jet fighter during WWII.

T    F    4. United Airlines became the first airline to order jet aircraft when they purchased six 707-120s on 13 October 1955.

T    F    5. Boeing 707s outsold Douglas DC-8s two to one.

T    F    6. Lockheed lost about $2.5 billion on the L-1011 TriStar production.

T    F    7. One of Boeing's chief competitors, particularly in the international market, comes from Airbus Industrie.

T    F    8. The Federal Aviation Administration was created in 1958 by the Federal Aviation Act.

T    F    9. The air traffic control system was not affected as greatly as PATCO had anticipated when it went on strike.

T    F    10. The slot system became very popular because it was the only equitable way of assigning landing rights.

T    F    11. Fare wars were very prevalent in the early 1980s.

T    F    12. The Tax Equity and Fiscal Responsibility Act (TEFRA) of 1982 was welcomed by the general aviation community.

T    F    13. Production of the Lockheed L-1011 TriStar ended in 1982.

T    F    14. The fact that regional air carriers operating smaller aircraft can better serve low-density airports was one of the arguments in favor of deregulation.

T    F    15. Boeing was contracted by NASA to develop an SST, designated "the Orient Express," by the 21st century.

T    F    16. In 1985 Pan Am sold its Pacific routes to Continental for $750 million.

T    F    17. People Express was the fifth largest U.S. air carrier by 1985.

T   F   18. The Learjet Model 23 was based on a Swiss fighter plane design.

T   F   19. President Reagan's dismissal of the 12,000 PATCO controllers was opposed by many members of Congress and the public at large.

T   F   20. Boeing clearly dominated the jet airline market worldwide for 20 years after the first 707 was put into service.

T   F   21. The Learjet is primarily used by the scheduled carriers for short-haul flights.

# Chapter 18

**I. Multiple Choice**—Choose the best answer and place it in the blank at the left.

_____ 1. The father of modern rocketry is:
    a. Virgil Grissom.
    b. Wernher von Braun.
    c. Richard Gordon.
    d. Robert Goddard.

_____ 2. Which of the following individuals was not an early German rocket scientist?
    a. Herman Oberth
    b. Walter Dornberger
    c. Wernher von Braun
    d. Paul Weitz

_____ 3. German rocket research during WWII:
    a. was very limited compared to Goddard's work.
    b. was given high priority in 1941 but curtailed greatly by Hitler in 1944.
    c. took place in Berlin under the control of the German military command.
    d. led to the development of American ICBMs.

_____ 4. America's first series of space missions was called:
    a. Mercury.
    b. Titan.
    c. Gemini.
    d. Saturn.

_____ 5. The first suborbital flight by a U.S. astronaut was made on 12 April 1961, by:
    a. Thomas Stafford.
    b. John Glenn.
    c. Alan Shepard.
    d. Virgil Grissom.

_____ 6. The purpose of Apollo 8 was to:
    a. perfect the space-docking procedure.
    b. land on the moon.
    c. circle the moon.
    d. leave supplies on the moon.

_____ 7. The first astronaut to step foot on the moon was:
    a. Frank Borman.
    b. Neil Armstrong.

c. Michael Collins.

d. Alan Shepard.

_____ 8. The first moon landing mission was Apollo:

     a. 8.

     b. 9.

     c. 10.

     d. 11.

_____ 9. America's first satellite was:

     a. *Vanguard I.*

     b. *Explorer I.*

     c. *Voyager I.*

     d. *Pioneer II.*

_____ 10. The Soviet Union's first woman cosmonaut was:

     a. Chamier Glisczinski.

     b. Alexei Leonov.

     c. Valentina Tereshkova.

     d. Judith Resnik.

_____ 11. On 28 January 1986, this space shuttle exploded 74 seconds after liftoff, killing the seven astronauts aboard.

     a. *Columbia*

     b. *Challenger*

     c. *Enterprise*

     d. *America*

_____ 12. The Gemini series was designed to do all of the following except:

     a. extend orbital missions.

     b. develop techniques of orbital maneuvering.

     c. photograph the moon for future landing sites.

     d. docking of two space vehicles.

_____ 13. The first lunar landing took place on:

     a. 27 December 1968.

     b. 27 January 1967.

     c. 20 July 1969.

     d. 25 December 1969.

_____ 14. Which of the following astronauts was killed during a prelaunch test in January 1967?

     a. Michael Smith

     b. Virgil Grissom

     c. Carl Sagan

     d. Michael Collins

_____ 15. Which of the following statements is not true?

     a. The German A-10 transatlantic rocket could have been operational by 1946.

     b. It was not until 1954 that President Eisenhower gave American's ICBM program top priority.

c. The Soviet Union succeeded in orbiting *Sputnik I* on 4 October 1957.

d. The National Aeronautics and Space Administration (NASA) was created in 1948.

_____ 16. The Lunar Landing Program:

a. was part of the goals in the formation of NASA.

b. culminated with the Gemini series of launches.

c. was opposed by Congress when President Kennedy presented the plan in 1961.

d. involved more than 20,000 companies.

_____ 17. Space-docking was accomplished during this series.

a. Mercury

b. Columbia

c. Apollo

d. Gemini

_____ 18. With every advance in the history of aviation have come the inevitable tragedies. Which of the following flights was not a tragedy?

a. Otto Lilienthal's hang glider flight on 9 August 1896.

b. Max Immelmann's flight in his Fokker Eindecker on 18 June 1916.

c. Charles Yeager's flight in the Bell X-1A on 14 October 1947.

d. Edward White's space launch on 27 January 1967.

**II. True/False**—Circle "T" if the statement is true; circle "F" if it is false.

T F 1. The German rocket research facility during WWII was located at Warnemunde, on the Baltic Coast.

T F 2. Robert Goddard's research led to the WWII antitank weapon called the "Bazooka."

T F 3. Robert Goddard was helped by Charles Lindbergh in getting a grant so that he could continue his rocket research in New Mexico.

T F 4. German V-2 rockets were brought to the United States after WWII, establishing the foundation for our ICBM program.

T F 5. In 1954, President Eisenhower gave America's ICBM program top priority.

T F 6. The Soviet *Sputnik I* was launched in April 1961.

T F 7. The National Aeronautics and Space Administration (NASA) was first established as part of the U.S. Air Force research efforts.

T F 8. The Gemini series was primarily designed to perfect space docking.

T F 9. The Apollo 11 moon landing took place on 20 July 1969.

T F 10. Three astronauts were killed during the Gemini series.

T F 11. The space shuttle was developed as a reusable vehicle.

T F 12. The unmanned space probes are primarily for military purposes.

T F 13. The space age really began on 4 October 1957, when the Russians launched *Sputnik I*.

T F 14. The German A-10 transatlantic rocket would have been operational by 1946.

T F 15. The Army Redstone Intercontinental Ballistics Missile program was started in 1951.

T F 16. The Lunar Landing Program was suggested by NASA in July 1960.

T F 17. On 27 January 1967, three astronauts—Alan Shepard, James Lovell, and William Anders—died during a prelaunch test at the Kennedy Space Center.

T F 18. The purpose of Apollo 8 was to test the Lunar Excursion Module (LEM) on the surface of the moon.

T   F   19. The latter Mercury series of space launches carried two astronauts.
T   F   20. The space program was drastically cut during the late 1970s.

**III. Matching**—Match the individual in the list below with these descriptions.

| | | |
|---|---|---|
| _____ | 1. Commander of Apollo 8 mission | a. Neil Armstrong |
| _____ | 2. American pioneer in rocketry | b. Trevor Gardner |
| _____ | 3. German rocket scientist who developed the V-1 and V-2 rockets | c. John Glenn |
| | | d. Robert Goddard |
| _____ | 4. The first astronaut to set foot on the moon | e. Herman Oberth |
| _____ | 5. Pre-WWII German rocket scientist | f. Virgil Grissom |
| _____ | 6. First astronaut to orbit the earth | g. Frank Borman |
| _____ | 7. Command module pilot during the Apollo 11 flight | h. Michael Collins |
| | | i. Alan Shepard |
| _____ | 8. First astronaut killed during a prelaunch test | j. Wernher von Braun |
| _____ | 9. Air Force Chief of Research and Development who favored rocket development | |
| _____ | 10. America's first astronaut | |

# Chapter 19

**I. Multiple Choice**—Choose the best answer and place it in the blank at the left.

_____ 1. The Communist hold on the Eastern Bloc of nations began to crack with the:
   a. establishment of the Commonwealth of Independent States (CIS).
   b. reunification of Germany.
   c. solidarity labor movement in Poland.
   d. opening of Hungarian and Czechoslovakian borders to East Germans.

_____ 2. One of the largest of the former Soviet Republics is:
   a. Armenia.
   b. the Ukraine.
   c. Moldavia.
   d. Tadzhikistan.

_____ 3. The former Soviet Union spent approximately _____ percent of its GNP for military purposes.
   a. 17
   b. 25
   c. 31
   d. 36

_____ 4. The democracy movement developed faster in:
   a. Czechoslovakia.
   b. Romania.
   c. Albania.
   d. Yugoslavia.

_____ 5. The START agreement provides for the reduction in:
   a. military personnel.
   b. ICBMs.
   c. submarines.
   d. strategic bombers.

_____ 6. The B-2 Stealth Bomber program has been:
   a. increased commensurate with the decrease in ICBMs.
   b. put on hold because of military uncertainties.
   c. cut back severely from the original plan.
   d. eliminated.

_____ 7. The F-22 is being developed by:
   a. Grumman.
   b. McDonnell-Douglas.
   c. Hughes.
   d. Lockheed.

_____ 8. Which of the following statements concerning the F-22 Advanced Tactical Fighter is not true?
   a. It will not become operational until the turn of the century.
   b. It will incorporate Stealth technology.
   c. Its top speed will approach Mach 1.5.
   d. Large internal fuel capacity for long-range missions will greatly improve its capability over the F-15.

_____ 9. The primary mission of the C-17 Globemaster III transport is:
   a. similar to the C-5B Galaxy.
   b. overseas deployment of U.S. forces directly to small airports near battle zones.
   c. offloading at major airports into C-130s.
   d. to serve as a gunship as well as a cargo transport aircraft.

_____ 10. The F-117 Stealth Fighter:
   a. is designed to fly at Mach 3 above 80,000 feet.
   b. generally is flown during hours of darkness.
   c. was not flown during the Panamanian invasion because of problems with the de-icing system.
   d. has not been particularly effective in avoiding radar detection at low altitude and slower speeds.

_____ 11. The KC-10 is used for:
   a. airborne warning.
   b. hauling cargo.
   c. anti-tank attack.
   d. aerial refueling.

_____ 12. Patriot missiles were used during Desert Storm:
   a. to intercept Scud missiles.
   b. by navy surface ships in the Gulf against targets in Iraq.
   c. for air-to-air combat.

d. by allied tank crews in their first assault against Iraqi positions.

_____ 13. A-10 Warthogs are primarily used:
   a. to provide top cover against attacking aircraft.
   b. against tanks.
   c. to bomb personnel with fragmentary bombs.
   d. against mobile Scud launchers.

_____ 14. Total conquest of Iraq during Desert Storm:
   a. was part of the U.N. mandate, but President Bush chose not to carry it out.
   b. was not possible given the number of allied troops involved.
   c. would have been extremely unpopular with Arab members of the coalition.
   d. was strongly favored by Iran and Syria.

_____ 15. The F-117A flew one percent of the missions in Operation Desert Storm but accounted for nearly _____ of the strategic targets destroyed in Iraq.
   a. one-quarter
   b. one-half
   c. two-thirds
   d. three-quarters

**II. True/False:**—Circle "T" if the statement is true; circle "F" if it is false.

T    F    1. *Glasnost* and *perestroika* attempted to convince the Soviet people that the Communist system was workable.

T    F    2. Boris Yeltsin felt satisfied working within the Communist system.

T    F    3. On 29 August 1991, the Soviet parliament voted to suspend all activities of the Communist Party.

T    F    4. The former Soviet Union spent approximately 27 percent of its GNP for military purposes.

T    F    5. Reunification of Germany had been encouraged by the Soviet Union as early as 1961.

T    F    6. Albania, the last bastion of European communism, embraced democracy in free elections held in March of 1991.

T    F    7. SAC's round-the-clock alert was halted in September 1991.

T    F    8. Whiteman AFB, Missouri, is the only B-2 Stealth Bomber base.

T    F    9. Most military leaders are in favor of relaxing our defensive posture with the breakup of the former Soviet Union.

T    F    10. Bell and Boeing (Vertol) were teamed up to build the unique V-22 *Osprey* tilt-rotor VTOL transport.

T    F    11. The F-22 Advanced Tactical Fighter will include Stealth technology and deflected-thrust maneuvering.

T    F    12. The mission of the C-17 Globemaster III transport is overseas deployment of U.S. forces directly to small airports near battle zones.

T    F    13. The range of the C-17 Globemaster III transport with a full payload is 7000 miles without aerial refueling.

T    F    14. SAC's B-52 fleet remained in service for more than 30 years.

T    F    15. The B-1B has been a very successful replacement for the B-52.

T    F    16. The F-14A and F/A-18 are the mainstay of the navy's tactical airplanes.

T  F  17. In recent years the emphasis on U.S. air power has been placed on rapid response, surgical air strikes, and early disengagement.

T  F  18. The Lockheed-USAF F-117A design team won the 1989 Collier Trophy for achievement in aeronautics.

T  F  19. The continual air bombardment during Desert Storm eliminated most of the Scud missile launchers.

T  F  20. The air bombardment during Desert Storm greatly demoralized Iraqi troops.

**III. Matching**—Match the aircraft listed below with these descriptions.

| | |
|---|---|
| _____ 1. Stealth bomber | a. C-17 |
| _____ 2. Strategic reconnaissance aircraft | b. A-10 |
| _____ 3. Tilt-rotor VTOL transport | c. SR-71 |
| _____ 4. Stealth fighter | d. F-14A |
| _____ 5. Cargo transport | e. AC-130 |
| _____ 6. Navy fighter-bomber | f. F-22 |
| _____ 7. Ground support gunship | g. B-2 |
| _____ 8. Attack helicopter | h. EA-6B |
| _____ 9. Anti-tank aircraft | i. AH-64 |
| _____ 10. Electronic countermeasures aircraft | j. V-22 Osprey |

# Chapter 20

**I. Multiple Choice**—Choose the best answer and place it in the blank at the left.

_____ 1. Severe financial losses in the airline industry during the early 1990s resulted from:
    a. less traffic than forecasted, causing excess capacity.
    b. high interest rates.
    c. an increase in the number of new carriers.
    d. all of the above.

_____ 2. All of the following major air carriers went bankrupt in 1991, except:
    a. Eastern.
    b. Midway.
    c. Braniff.
    d. Pan Am.

_____ 3. More than half of the industry's passenger enplanements are carried by the "Big Three." They are:
    a. American, Delta, and USAir.
    b. America West, Continental, and United.
    c. Delta, TWA, and Northwest.
    d. United, Delta, and American.

_____ 4. Republic Airlines was acquired by _____ Airlines in 1986.
    a. American
    b. Delta
    c. Northwest
    d. Southwest

_____ 5. Continental Airlines was forced into bankruptcy for the second time in 1990 primarily as a result of:
   a. union labor's demand for higher wages.
   b. high fuel prices and fall-off in traffic caused by the Persian Gulf War.
   c. high interest rates on flight equipment debt.
   d. illegal stock manipulations by top management.

_____ 6. Southwest Airlines got started in 1971:
   a. initially by flying unregulated intrastate routes within Texas.
   b. by being one of the first carriers to operate out of the new Dallas-Fort Worth (DFW) International Airport.
   c. as a commuter carrier feeding traffic to Braniff Airlines at Love Field.
   d. flying B-727s between Dallas and Chicago.

_____ 7. Under U.S. law, no more than _____ percent of a U.S. airline may be owned by a foreign entity.
   a. 25.0%
   b. 33.3%
   c. 49.0%
   d. 66.7%

_____ 8. This individual literally put Boeing's assets on the line when he took the risk of developing the 747 jumbo jet.
   a. Kelly Johnson
   b. Herbert Kelleher
   c. William Allen
   d. Lamar Muse

_____ 9. The fuel-efficient B-757 was designed to replace aging:
   a. B-707s.
   b. B-727s.
   c. B-737s.
   d. B-747s.

_____ 10. Boeing's _____ now represents the largest number of aircraft sold to the world's airlines.
   a. B-707
   b. B-727
   c. B-737
   d. B-747

_____ 11. Powered by fanjet engines in the 84,000-to-90,000-pound thrust range, this aircraft, featuring folding wingtips, will accommodate 300 to 400 passengers.
   a. A-320
   b. B-777
   c. MD-11
   d. DO-228

_____ 12. Future superjets carrying up to 1000 passengers:

    a. are likely to be cost-prohibitive for one company to entertain alone.

    b. are being considered by Airbus Industrie along with additional partners from the Middle East.

    c. are being planned as a joint venture of Boeing and McDonnell-Douglas.

    d. a and c are correct.

**II. True/False:** Circle "T" if the statement is true; circle "F" if it is false.

T   F    1. Excess capacity in the airline industry leads to price increases.

T   F    2. Midway was the first major airline to go bankrupt following deregulation.

T   F    3. People Express was acquired by USAir.

T   F    4. Among the many problems faced by Pan Am was the difficulty in building traffic following a terrorist attack on one of its Boeing 747 aircraft in December 1988.

T   F    5. Delta is one of the few air carriers that has never furloughed any pilots.

T   F    6. Northwest Airlines was the first U.S. airline to fly the "fly-by-wire" A-320 and the Boeing 747-400.

T   F    7. USAir acquired Piedmont Airlines and Pacific Southwest Airlines.

T   F    8. TWA has one of the oldest airline fleets.

T   F    9. Texas Air acquired Continental, Eastern, People Express, Frontier, and New York Air.

T   F   10. Southwest Airlines chose to fly out of Houston's Intercontinental Airport instead of Hobby because of better connecting service.

T   F   11. Under U.S. law, no more than 49 percent of a U.S. airline's voting stock can be foreign-owned.

T   F   12. TWA was the first airline to order the B-747.

T   F   13. Boeing decided not to introduce EFIS in the 757 and 767 models.

T   F   14. The B-777 is a medium-range jet carrying up to 150 passengers.

T   F   15. Future superjets carrying up to 1000 passengers can only be considered economically through a joint venture.

**III. Matching**—Match the airline in the list below that was acquired by the carrier.

_____ 1. TWA           a. People Express

_____ 2. USAir         b. Republic

_____ 3. Northwest    c. Pan Am's North Atlantic routes

_____ 4. Continental   d. Muse Air

_____ 5. Delta         e. Pacific Southwest

_____ 6. Southwest    f. Ozark

# Chapter 21

**I. Multiple Choice**—Choose the best answer and place it in the blank at the left.

_____ 1. General aviation manufacturers produced a record 17,000 aircraft in:

    a. 1972.

    b. 1978.

    c. 1982.

    d. 1986.

_____ 2. All of the following are major factors that have contributed to the decline of new general aviation aircraft sales, except:
        a. high interest rates during the early 1980s.
        b. product liability claims.
        c. competition from foreign manufacturers.
        d. the availability of used aircraft.

_____ 3. During the 1980s, student starts:
        a. increased slightly.
        b. remained about the same.
        c. decreased slightly.
        d. decreased significantly.

_____ 4. Businesses have continued to seek the benefits of their own air transportation for all of the following reasons, except:
        a. concentration of airline service at major hubs.
        b. generally less expensive than airline travel.
        c. decentralization of industry to smaller cities.
        d. flexibility.

_____ 5. Cessna Aircraft Company is now owned by:
        a. United Technologies.
        b. General Dynamics.
        c. Textron.
        d. Raytheon.

_____ 6. Cessna and Beech have concentrated on producing _____ aircraft since the mid-1980s.
        a. single-engine piston
        b. multi-engine piston
        c. turbine
        d. military

_____ 7. Piper Aircraft:
        a. continued to produce a wide range of aircraft from trainers to turboprops throughout the 1980s.
        b. has experienced a number of changes in ownership since the 1970s.
        c. dropped its product liability insurance coverage.
        d. all of the above.

_____ 8. Which of the following statements is not true?
        a. Federal Express operates a number of Cessna Caravan single-engine turboprops.
        b. More than 2000 Cessna Citations have been sold since 1972.
        c. Beech acquired the rights to Mitsubishi's Diamond business jet in 1986.
        d. Mooney was purchased by the Canadian company Bombardier in 1984.

_____ 9. The revolutionary NOTAR anti-torque system:
        a. eliminates the need for a side-thrusting tail rotor.
        b. reduces the noise level.
        c. helps reduce accidents.
        d. all of the above.

_____ 10. Hughes Helicopter became a subsidiary of _____ in 1984.
   a. Boeing Vertol
   b. Bell-Textron
   c. McDonnell-Douglas
   d. Sikorsky

_____ 11. The use of helicopters:
   a. is quite limited.
   b. between metropolitan airports has grown significantly.
   c. will eventually replace short-haul commuter aircraft.
   d. none of the above.

_____ 12. Bell's new twin-engine helicopters such as the Model 222 have been specifically designed for the _____ market.
   a. military
   b. corporate
   c. pleasure
   d. off-shore oil drilling

**II. True/False:** Circle "T" if the statement is true; circle "F" if it is false.

T   F   1. A statute of repose covers the time between an accident and the time in which a claim must be filed.

T   F   2. The availability of used aircraft at considerably lower prices affected new aircraft sales during the 1980s.

T   F   3. The number of active general aviation aircraft only increased slightly during the 1980s.

T   F   4. The cost of product liability insurance increased aircraft prices faster than the consumer price index during the 1980s.

T   F   5. Increased FAA requirements and regulations have probably had little effect on the number of pilots flying for personal reasons.

T   F   6. Cessna stopped producing piston aircraft in 1986.

T   F   7. Piper dropped its product liability insurance coverage in the mid-1980s.

T   F   8. The Beechjet 400A was redesigned from the Mitsubishi Diamond, which Beech purchased in 1986.

T   F   9. The Beech Bonanza model was dropped during the mid-1980s as the company concentrated on multi-engine turbine aircraft.

T   F   10. Mooney Aircraft was purchased by the French firm Eurualair in 1984.

T   F   11. Sales of kitplanes have exceeded factory-built airplane production in some years during the 1980s.

T   F   12. Helicopter sales increased throughout the 1980s.

T   F   13. The use of helicopters for emergency medical transportation has decreased in many metropolitan areas because of poor accident experience and lack of landing facilities.

T   F   14. The Bell JetRanger Model 206 has compiled an excellent safety record.

T   F   15. The average age of the U.S. general aviation aircraft fleet is more than 20 years.

# B

# Answers to objective questions

## Introduction

### I. Multiple Choice

| | |
|------|--------|
| 1. b | 7. a |
| 2. c | 8. c |
| 3. b | 9. c |
| 4. d | 10. c |
| 5. b | 11. c |
| 6. c | 12. b |

### II. True/False

| | |
|------|--------|
| 1. T | 7. T |
| 2. T | 8. T |
| 3. F | 9. F |
| 4. T | 10. T |
| 5. F | 11. T |
| 6. F | 12. F |

## Chapter 1

### I. Multiple Choice

| | |
|------|--------|
| 1. a | 6. a |
| 2. d | 7. d |
| 3. b | 8. c |
| 4. c | 9. b |
| 5. c | 10. b |

### II. True/False

| | |
|------|--------|
| 1. F | 2. T |

| | |
|------|--------|
| 3. T | 8. T |
| 4. T | 9. F |
| 5. T | 10. T |
| 6. T | 11. T |
| 7. T | 12. F |

## Chapter 2

### I. Multiple Choice

| | |
|------|--------|
| 1. c | 9. b |
| 2. b | 10. b |
| 3. d | 11. a |
| 4. a | 12. c |
| 5. c | 13. b |
| 6. d | 14. b |
| 7. a | 15. c |
| 8. d | |

### II. True/False

| | |
|-------|--------|
| 1. T | 11. T |
| 2. T | 12. T |
| 3. T | 13. T |
| 4. T | 14. T |
| 5. F | 15. T |
| 6. T | 16. T |
| 7. T | 17. F |
| 8. F | 18. T |
| 9. F | 19. T |
| 10. F | 20. F |

### III. Matching (Individuals)

| | |
|------|--------|
| 1. h | 6. i |
| 2. f | 7. j |
| 3. e | 8. g |
| 4. d | 9. b |
| 5. a | 10. c |

### IV. Matching (Aircraft)

| | |
|------|--------|
| 1. g | 5. h |
| 2. f | 6. a |
| 3. b | 7. e |
| 4. d | 8. c |

## Chapter 3

### I. Multiple Choice

| | |
|------|--------|
| 1. b | 6. c |
| 2. d | 7. c |
| 3. d | 8. a |
| 4. b | 9. d |
| 5. c | 10. c |

### II. True/False

| | |
|------|--------|
| 1. T | 7. T |
| 2. F | 8. F |
| 3. F | 9. F |
| 4. F | 10. F |
| 5. T | 11. T |
| 6. T | 12. T |

# Chapter 4

## I. Multiple Choice

| | |
|---|---|
| 1. c | 7. c |
| 2. c | 8. b |
| 3. b | 9. c |
| 4. b | 10. c |
| 5. c | 11. c |
| 6. b | 12. b |

## II. True/False

| | |
|---|---|
| 1. T | 10. F |
| 2. F | 11. T |
| 3. F | 12. F |
| 4. T | 13. T |
| 5. T | 14. T |
| 6. F | 15. F |
| 7. F | 16. T |
| 8. T | 17. F |
| 9. F | 18. F |

# Chapter 5

## I. Multiple Choice

| | |
|---|---|
| 1. d | 6. d |
| 2. c | 7. c |
| 3. a | 8. c |
| 4. b | 9. d |
| 5. b | |

## II. True/False

| | |
|---|---|
| 1. F | 8. T |
| 2. T | 9. F |
| 3. F | 10. T |
| 4. T | 11. T |
| 5. F | 12. T |
| 6. F | 13. T |
| 7. T | |

# Chapter 6

## I. Multiple Choice

| | |
|---|---|
| 1. d | 9. c |
| 2. d | 10. b |
| 3. b | 11. d |
| 4. a | 12. a |
| 5. b | 13. c |
| 6. c | 14. b |
| 7. c | 15. c |
| 8. a | |

## II. True/False

| | |
|---|---|
| 1. T | 9. T |
| 2. T | 10. F |
| 3. T | 11. T |
| 4. T | 12. F |
| 5. T | 13. T |
| 6. F | 14. T |
| 7. F | 15. T |
| 8. T | 16. T |

# Chapter 7

## I. Multiple Choice

| | |
|---|---|
| 1. c | 10. c |
| 2. a | 11. b |
| 3. b | 12. d |
| 4. c | 13. c |
| 5. d | 14. d |
| 6. c | 15. c |
| 7. c | 16. c |
| 8. a | 17. d |
| 9. a | 18. a |

## II. True/False

| | |
|---|---|
| 1. T | 11. T |
| 2. F | 12. T |
| 3. T | 13. F |
| 4. T | 14. T |
| 5. T | 15. F |
| 6. T | 16. T |
| 7. F | 17. F |
| 8. T | 18. F |
| 9. F | 19. T |
| 10. T | 20. T |

## III. Matching

| | |
|---|---|
| 1. f | 6. g |
| 2. i | 7. b |
| 3. a | 8. h |
| 4. j | 9. e |
| 5. c | 10. d |

# Chapter 8

## I. Multiple Choice

| | |
|---|---|
| 1. c | 9. b |
| 2. a | 10. b |
| 3. c | 11. a |
| 4. d | 12. b |
| 5. d | 13. a |
| 6. c | 14. d |
| 7. c | 15. a |
| 8. d | |

## II. True/False

| | |
|---|---|
| 1. T | 10. T |
| 2. T | 11. T |
| 3. F | 12. T |
| 4. F | 13. F |
| 5. F | 14. F |
| 6. T | 15. T |
| 7. T | 16. F |
| 8. F | 17. F |
| 9. T | 18. T |

# Chapter 9

## I. Multiple Choice

| | |
|---|---|
| 1. b | 12. c |
| 2. b | 13. c |
| 3. d | 14. b |
| 4. c | 15. b |
| 5. a | 16. d |
| 6. c | 17. b |
| 7. a | 18. a |
| 8. b | 19. d |
| 9. d | 20. a |
| 10. d | 21. c |
| 11. a | 22. a |

| 1. F | 11. F |
|------|-------|
| 2. T | 12. T |
| 3. T | 13. T |
| 4. T | 14. F |
| 5. F | 15. F |
| 6. T | 16. T |
| 7. F | 17. T |
| 8. T | 18. F |
| 9. T | 19. F |
| 10. T | 20. T |

# Chapter 10

## I. Multiple Choice

| 1. b | 8. b |
|------|------|
| 2. c | 9. b |
| 3. d | 10. b |
| 4. c | 11. c |
| 5. a | 12. d |
| 6. c | 13. a |
| 7. a | 14. c |

## II. True/False

| 1. F | 9. b |
|------|------|
| 2. F | 10. T |
| 3. T | 11. F |
| 4. T | 12. T |
| 5. F | 13. F |
| 6. T | 14. T |
| 7. T | 15. F |
| 8. T | 16. F |

# Chapter 11

## I. Multiple Choice

| 1. b | 8. c |
|------|------|
| 2. c | 9. d |
| 3. b | 10. b |
| 4. c | 11. d |
| 5. b | 12. b |
| 6. d | 13. b |
| 7. b | 14. a |

## II. True/False

| 1. T | 12. F |
|------|-------|
| 2. T | 13. T |
| 3. T | 14. T |
| 4. F | 15. F |
| 5. T | 16. F |
| 6. T | 17. F |
| 7. T | 18. T |
| 8. F | 19. T |
| 9. F | 20. F |
| 10. T | 21. F |
| 11. T | 22. T |

# Chapter 12

## I. Multiple Choice

| 1. c | 10. c |
|------|-------|
| 2. d | 11. d |
| 3. a | 12. a |
| 4. c | 13. d |
| 5. b | 14. b |
| 6. d | 15. d |
| 7. b | 16. c |
| 8. c | 17. d |
| 9. d | 18. b |

## II. True/False

| 1. T | 11. F |
|------|-------|
| 2. F | 12. T |
| 3. F | 13. F |
| 4. F | 14. T |
| 5. T | 15. T |
| 6. T | 16. T |
| 7. T | 17. F |
| 8. T | 18. F |
| 9. T | 19. T |
| 10. F | |

## III. Matching (Individuals)

| 1. h | 6. b |
|------|------|
| 2. e | 7. f |
| 3. a | 8. c |
| 4. j | 9. g |
| 5. d | 10. i |

## IV. Matching (Aircraft)

| 1. g | 6. e |
|------|------|
| 2. c | 7. f |
| 3. j | 8. h |
| 4. a | 9. d |
| 5. b | 10. i |

# Chapter 13

## I. Multiple Choice

| 1. b | 9. a |
|------|------|
| 2. a | 10. b |
| 3. c | 11. c |
| 4. d | 12. d |
| 5. c | 13. b |
| 6. d | 14. b |
| 7. d | 15. c |
| 8. c | |

## II. True/False

| 1. T | 10. T |
|------|-------|
| 2. F | 11. F |
| 3. F | 12. F |
| 4. T | 13. T |
| 5. T | 14. T |
| 6. F | 15. T |
| 7. T | 16. T |
| 8. T | 17. F |
| 9. T | 18. T |

# Chapter 14

## I. Multiple Choice

| 1. d | 10. b |
|------|-------|
| 2. b | 11. b |
| 3. b | 12. c |
| 4. b | 13. b |
| 5. a | 14. b |
| 6. d | 15. b |
| 7. b | 16. a |
| 8. a | 17. d |
| 9. c | |

**II. True/False**

| | |
|---|---|
| 1. T | 11. F |
| 2. F | 12. T |
| 3. T | 13. F |
| 4. T | 14. T |
| 5. F | 15. T |
| 6. T | 16. F |
| 7. F | 17. T |
| 8. F | 18. T |
| 9. F | 19. T |
| 10. T | 20. T |

## Chapter 15

**I. Multiple Choice**

| | |
|---|---|
| 1. b | 9. d |
| 2. d | 10. c |
| 3. c | 11. b |
| 4. d | 12. b |
| 5. b | 13. c |
| 6. d | 14. d |
| 7. a | 15. d |
| 8. c | 16. a |

**II. True/False**

| | |
|---|---|
| 1. T | 11. F |
| 2. T | 12. T |
| 3. T | 13. F |
| 4. T | 14. T |
| 5. F | 15. T |
| 6. T | 16. T |
| 7. F | 17. F |
| 8. T | 18. F |
| 9. T | 19. T |
| 10. T | 20. T |

**III. Matching**

| | |
|---|---|
| 1. g | 6. i |
| 2. j | 7. d |
| 3. a | 8. f |
| 4. e | 9. b |
| 5. c | 10. h |

## Chapter 16

**I. Multiple Choice**

| | |
|---|---|
| 1. c | 10. b |
| 2. d | 11. c |
| 3. b | 12. b |
| 4. d | 13. b |
| 5. a | 14. c |
| 6. c | 15. d |
| 7. a | 16. b |
| 8. c | 17. b |
| 9. d | 18. b |

**II. True/False**

| | |
|---|---|
| 1. T | 11. F |
| 2. T | 12. T |
| 3. T | 13. T |
| 4. F | 14. F |
| 5. F | 15. T |
| 6. F | 16. F |
| 7. F | 17. F |
| 8. T | 18. T |
| 9. T | 19. T |
| 10. F | 20. F |

## Chapter 17

**I. Multiple Choice**

| | |
|---|---|
| 1. b | 10. a |
| 2. d | 11. c |
| 3. d | 12. a |
| 4. b | 13. b |
| 5. d | 14. d |
| 6. d | 15. d |
| 7. a | 16. d |
| 8. b | 17. b |
| 9. b | 18. b |

**II. True/False**

| | |
|---|---|
| 1. T | 12. F |
| 2. T | 13. T |
| 3. F | 14. T |
| 4. F | 15. T |
| 5. T | 16. F |
| 6. T | 17. T |
| 7. T | 18. T |
| 8. F | 19. F |
| 9. T | 20. T |
| 10. F | 21. F |
| 11. T | |

## Chapter 18

**I. Multiple Choice**

| | |
|---|---|
| 1. d | 10. c |
| 2. d | 11. b |
| 3. d | 12. c |
| 4. a | 13. c |
| 5. c | 14. b |
| 6. c | 15. d |
| 7. b | 16. d |
| 8. d | 17. d |
| 9. b | 18. c |

**II. True/False**

| | |
|---|---|
| 1. F | 11. T |
| 2. T | 12. F |
| 3. T | 13. T |
| 4. T | 14. T |
| 5. T | 15. T |
| 6. F | 16. T |
| 7. F | 17. F |
| 8. T | 18. F |
| 9. T | 19. F |
| 10. T | 20. T |

**III. Matching**

| | |
|---|---|
| 1. g | 6. c |
| 2. d | 7. h |
| 3. j | 8. f |
| 4. a | 9. b |
| 5. e | 10. i |

# Chapter 19

## I. Multiple Choice

| | |
|---|---|
| 1. c | 9. b |
| 2. b | 10. b |
| 3. a | 11. d |
| 4. a | 12. a |
| 5. b | 13. b |
| 6. c | 14. c |
| 7. d | 15. b |
| 8. c | |

## II. True/False

| | |
|---|---|
| 1. T | 11. T |
| 2. F | 12. T |
| 3. T | 13. F |
| 4. F | 14. T |
| 5. F | 15. F |
| 6. T | 16. T |
| 7. T | 17. T |
| 8. T | 18. T |
| 9. F | 19. F |
| 10. T | 20. T |

## III. Matching

| | |
|---|---|
| 1. g | 6. d |
| 2. c | 7. e |
| 3. j | 8. i |
| 4. f | 9. b |
| 5. a | 10. h |

# Chapter 20

## I. Multiple Choice

| | |
|---|---|
| 1. a | 7. c |
| 2. c | 8. c |
| 3. d | 9. b |
| 4. c | 10. c |
| 5. b | 11. b |
| 6. a | 12. a |

## II. True/False

| | |
|---|---|
| 1. F | 9. T |
| 2. F | 10. F |
| 3. F | 11. F |
| 4. T | 12. F |
| 5. F | 13. F |
| 6. T | 14. F |
| 7. T | 15. T |
| 8. T | |

## III. Matching

| | |
|---|---|
| 1. f | 4. a |
| 2. e | 5. c |
| 3. b | 6. d |

# Chapter 21

## I. Multiple Choice

| | |
|---|---|
| 1. b | 7. d |
| 2. c | 8. d |
| 3. d | 9. d |
| 4. b | 10. c |
| 5. c | 11. d |
| 6. c | 12. b |

## II. True/False

| | |
|---|---|
| 1. F | 9. F |
| 2. T | 10. T |
| 3. F | 11. T |
| 4. T | 12. F |
| 5. F | 13. F |
| 6. T | 14. T |
| 7. T | 15. T |
| 8. T | |

# Index